Islamic Historiography

How did Muslims of the classical Islamic period understand their past? What value did they attach to history? How did they write history? How did historiography fare relative to other kinds of Arabic literature? These and other questions are answered in Chase F. Robinson's *Islamic Historiography*, an introduction to the principal genres, issues, and problems of Islamic historical writing in Arabic, and the first such _____ rical writing in the Islam_____ e eighth and ninth centu_____ he sixteenth century, thi_____ omplex and forbidding_____ l in Islamic history or A_____

Chase F. R_____ University of Oxford. Hi_____ n Conquest: The Transf___

THEMES IN ISLAMIC HISTORY comprises a range of titles exploring different aspects of Islamic history, society and culture by leading scholars in the field. Books are thematic in approach, offering a comprehensive and accessible overview of the subject. Generally, surveys treat Islamic history from its origins to the demise of the Ottoman empire, although some offer a more developed analysis of a particular period, or project into the present, depending on the subject-matter. All the books are written to interpret and illuminate the past, as gateways to a deeper understanding of Islamic civilization and its peoples.

Editorial adviser:
Patricia Crone, Institute for Advanced Study, Princeton

Already published:
Jonathan P. Berkey *The Formation of Islam: Religion and the Near East, 600–1800*
0 521 58214 8 hardback
0 521 58813 8 paperback

To Mayumi

Islamic Historiography

CHASE F. ROBINSON
University of Oxford

CAMBRIDGE
UNIVERSITY PRESS

PUBLISHED BY THE PRESS SYNDICATE OF THE UNIVERSITY OF CAMBRIDGE
The Pitt Building, Trumpington Street, Cambridge, United Kingdom

CAMBRIDGE UNIVERSITY PRESS
The Edinburgh Building, Cambridge CB2 2RU, UK
40 West 20th Street, New York, NY 10011–4211, USA
477 Williamstown Road, Port Melbourne, VIC 3207, Australia
Ruiz de Alarcón 13, 28014 Madrid, Spain
Dock House, The Waterfront, Cape Town 8001, South Africa

http://www.cambridge.org

First published 2003
Reprinted 2004

Printed in China by Everbest Printing Co.

Typeface Jaghbub 10/12 pt. *System* QuarkXPress [PC]

A catalogue record for this book is available from the British Library

National Library of Australia Cataloguing in Publication data
Robinson, Chase F.
Islamic historiography.
Bibliography.
Includes index.
ISBN 0 521 62081 3.
ISBN 0 521 62936 5 (pbk.).
1. Civilization, Islamic – Historiography. 2. Islamic
Empire – Historiography. I. Title.
907.2053

ISBN 0 521 62081 3 hardback
ISBN 0 521 62936 5 paperback

Contents

Plates

Maps

Acknowledgments

Although the idea of this book emerged from my reading and teaching only slowly (and sometimes very reluctantly), the nerve to carry it through was produced in the course of a brief conversation with a former teacher, Kevin Reinhart, who reminded me one afternoon in Harvard Square that Islamicists are responsible not only to fellow Islamicists, but to their colleagues and students. Needless to say, former teachers are entitled to take credit for their students' achievements, but should never be held accountable for their shortcomings. Much of the researching and writing took place during a fruitful year (1999–2000) spent at the Institute for Advanced Study in Princeton, an opportunity for which I have the pleasure of thanking its staff in general and P. Crone in particular. That year of leave was supported by the Board of the Faculty of Oriental Studies of Oxford University, to whom I am, as always, indebted. Much of the rest of the writing took place in Meredith, New Hampshire, which was only made possible by my parents' characteristic generosity of time and energy. I am also grateful to the British Academy for the award of a research grant that defrayed some costs.

Of those who helped in various ways (such as reading drafts, answering and raising questions and supplying material), I have the following to offer special thanks: H. Bone, P. Crone, F.M. Donner, R. Foote, G.J. van Gelder, J. Gelvin, M. Gordon, J. Howard-Johnston, H. Jamieson, N. Jamil, J. Johns, E. Landau-Tasseron, A. Marsham, J.S. Meisami, C. Melchert, D.S. Richards, J.S. Robinson, E. Rowson and C. Wakefield.

Abbreviations

AHR	*American Historical Review*
BEO	*Bulletin d'études orientales*
BSOAS	*Bulletin of the School of Oriental and African Studies*
DI	*Der Islam*
EI	*The Encyclopaedia of Islam*
EI^2	*The Encyclopaedia of Islam*, New Edition
GAL	C. Brockelmann, *Geschichte der arabischen Litteratur*
GAS	F. Sezgin, *Geschichte des arabischen Schrifttums*, vol. 1.
IC	*Islamic Culture*
IQ	*Islamic Quarterly*
IS	*Islamic Studies*
IJMES	*International Journal of Middle East Studies*
JA	*Journal Asiatique*
JAL	*Journal of Arabic Literature*
JAOS	*Journal of the American Oriental Society*
JESHO	*Journal of the Economic and Social History of the Orient*
JNES	*Journal of Near Eastern Studies*
JRAS	*Journal of the Royal Asiatic Society*
JSAI	*Jerusalem Studies in Arabic and Islam*
JSS	*Journal of Semitic Studies*
MW	*The Muslim World*
MSR	*Mamlūk Studies Review*
REI	*Revue des études islamiques*
SI	*Studia Islamica*
WI	*Die Welt des Islams*
ZDMG	*Zeitschrift der deutschen Morgenländischen Gesellschaft*

Glossary

akhbārī: one who writes, collects and/or transmits *akhbār*; historian; see *khabar*.
amīr: emir – commander or governor.
autograph: a manuscript copied out by its author, rather than by a copyist.
dhayl: lit. 'tail'; continuation (cf. *mudhayyal*) of an earlier work.
fiqh: religious understanding in general, and jurisprudence in particular.
*fuqahā*ʾ (s. *faqīh*): people who possess *fiqh*; jurists.
futūḥ (s. *fatḥ*): conquests; usually said of the great Islamic conquests of the seventh and early eighth centuries.
ḥadīth: a report of the words or deeds of a religious authority, this almost invariably being the Prophet Muḥammad, which consists of a *matn* and an *isnād* (see below); it is usually adduced for the purposes of generating or understanding the law; cf. *khabar*.
Hijaz: the region of western Arabia where Mecca and Medina are located.
hijra (adj.: *hijrī*): Muḥammad's flight from Mecca to Medina in 622, which marked the beginning of the Islamic calendar.
Ibāḍīs: see Khārijism.
ikhtiṣār: lit. 'summarizing'; see *mukhtaṣar*.
ᶜilm: knowledge, especially religious knowledge; cf. *ᶜulamā*ʾ.
isnād: the *ḥadīth*'s chain of transmitters that prefaces the *matn*.
Jāhiliyya: the name given by Muslims to describe the pre-Islamic period in the Hijaz.
khabar (pl. *akhbār*): an account of the past that has primarily historical, rather than legal, significance.
khalīfa (pl. *khulafā*ʾ): caliph.
Khārijism: schismatic revolutionary movement of early Islam, of which only the quietist Ibāḍīs now survive.
mabᶜath: lit. 'sending', but when used in connection with the Prophet, God's sending of Muḥammad.
madrasa: the institution of advanced learning that emerged during the tenth and eleventh centuries.
maghāzī: the Prophet's raids against Hijazi tribesmen and settlements; Prophetic biography; cf. *sīra*.

maqtal: lit. 'murder' or 'killing', conventionally used as the first part of a book title, e.g. *Maqtal Ḥusayn*, *The Killing of Ḥusayn*.
matn: the text of a *ḥadīth* that follows the *isnād*.
muʾarrikh (pl. *muʾarrikhūn*): one who assigns dates, and so a chronographer; historian; see *taʾrīkh*.
mudhayyal: continuation; cf. *dhayl*.
muḥaddith (pl. *muḥaddithūn*): a transmitter of *ḥadīth*; traditionist.
mukhtaṣar: (usually) an abridged or epitomised version of another work.
sharḥ: commentary.
sharīʿa: Islamic law as constituted by the Qurʾān and *sunna*.
ṣila: lit. 'connection'; usually a continuation of a book; cf. *dhayl*.
sīra (pl. *siyar*); paradigmatic behavior or conduct; biography.
sunna: the paradigmatic way of an authoritative figure, this usually being the Prophet Muḥammad.
ṭabaqa (pl. *ṭabaqāt*): a class, category or generation of men.
tarjama: a biographical entry in a prosopography.
taʾrīkh (or the variant *tārīkh*); date; dating; cf. *taʾrīkh ʿalā al-sinīn*: 'history organized by annual entries' and *taʾrīkh ʿalā al-khulafāʾ*: 'history organized by caliphal reigns'; chronography; history.
traditionalism: a conserving attitude towards the past (see chapter 5).
traditionism: the study of the traditions of the Prophet (see chapter 5).
ʿulamāʾ (s. *ʿālim*): Muslims who have acquired religious knowledge, especially of the law; the religious élite.

Chronology I: The historians of the formative period*

	Caliphs	*Historians*
600		
	'Four Rightly Guided Caliphs' (rg. 632–661)	
	Abū Bakr (632–634)	
	ʿUmar (634–644)	
	ʿUthmān (644–656)	
650		
	ʿAlī (656–661)	
	The Umayyads (661–750)	
	Muʿāwiya b. Abī Sufyān (661–680)	
	ʿAbd al-Malik b. Marwān (685-705)	
700		
		ʿUrwa b. al-Zubayr (Medina; 712)
	Hishām b. ʿAbd al-Malik (724–743)	al-Zuhrī (Medina; 742)
750		
	The Abbasids (750–1258)	
	al-Saffāḥ (749–754)	Ibn Isḥāq (Medina/Iraq; 761)
	al-Manṣūr (754–775)	Abū Mikhnaf (Iraq; 774)
		Sayf b. ʿUmar (Iraq; 796)
	Hārūn al-Rashīd (786–809)	
800		
	al-Maʾmūn (813–833)	al-Haytham b. ʿAdī (Iraq; 822)
		al-Wāqidī (Medina/Iraq; 823)
		al-Madāʾinī (Iraq; 830–850)
		Ibn Hishām (Iraq; 835)
		Ibn Saʿd (Iraq; 845)
		Khalīfa b. Khayyāṭ (Iraq; 854)
850		
	al-Mutawakkil (847–861)	ʿUmar b. Shabba (Iraq; 878)
		al-Dīnawarī (Iraq; 891)
		al-Balādhurī (Iraq; 892)
900		
	al-Muqtadir (908–932)	al-Yaʿqūbī (Iraq; *ca.* 900)
		al-Ṭabarī (Iraq; 923)

* The following includes only those historians who appear in the text most frequently. All the caliphs' dates are regnal, and the historians' are either approximate or conventional death dates.

Chronology II: The historians of the classical period

	Spain, N. Africa, Egypt, Syria	*Iraq, Iran, and the East*
950		al-Masʿūdī (955)
		Thābit b. Sinān al-Ṣābiʾ (976)
1000		
	al-Musabbiḥī (1030)	Ibn Miskawayh (1030)
		al-ʿUtbī (1036)
1050		Hilāl b. al-Muḥassin al-Ṣābiʾ (1055)
	Ibn Ḥazm (1063)	al-Khaṭīb al-Baghdādī (1071)
	Ibn ʿAbd al-Barr (1071)	Abū Isḥāq al-Shīrāzī (1083)
1100		
	al-Qāḍī ʿIyāḍ (1149)	
1150	Ibn al-Qalānisī (1160)	
	Ibn ʿAsākir (1176)	
		Ibn al-ʿImrānī (1184)
1200		Ibn al-Jawzī (1201)
	ʿImād al-Dīn al-Iṣfahānī (1201)	
	Ibn al-Athīr (1233)	
	Bahāʾ al-Dīn b. Shaddād (1235)	
	al-Kalāʿī (1237)	
1250		
	Sibṭ Ibn al-Jawzī (1256)	
	Ibn al-ʿAdīm (1262)	
	Abū Shāma (1267)	Ibn al-Sāʿī (1276)
	Ibn Khallikān (1282)	Ibn al-Fuwaṭī (1323)
	Ibn ʿAbd al-Ẓāhir (1292)	
1300		
	Baybars al-Manṣūrī (1325)	
	Abū al-Fidāʾ (1331)	
	al-Nuwayrī (1332)	
	al-Mizzī (1341)	
	al-Dhahabī (1348)	
1350		
	Ibn al-Dawādārī (1335)	
	al-Ṣafadī (1363)	
	Ibn Kathīr (1373)	
1400		
	Ibn al-Furāt (1405)	
	Ibn Khaldūn (1406)	
	al-Maqrīzī (1442)	
	Ibn Ḥajar al-ʿAsqalānī (1449)	
1450		
	al-ʿAynī (1451)	
	al-Sakhāwī (1497)	
1500		
	al-Suyūṭī (1505)	

Preface

As it is currently used, the English word ‘history’, in this respect like the Arabic word *taʾrīkh*, has a two-fold meaning. It usually means the past, be it prehistoric, ancient, medieval, modern or even contemporary, such as is recorded in a diary. But ‘history’ can also describe our thinking, teaching and writing about the past – that is, a discipline or branch of learning – and it is in this sense that British university students read history and American students major in history. ‘History’ thus overlaps with ‘historiography’, an inelegant term that is extremely useful because it means only one thing: *writing about the past*. And since historiography means nothing more than writing about the past, the title of this book suggests that it is about how and why Muslims wrote history. This is true, but it is also imprecise, since I actually describe how Muslims wrote history in *Arabic* during the *formative and classical periods of Islam*. Why only Arabic, and why only the formative and classical periods – whatever that may mean? A few words of explanation are in order.

According to one recent estimate, there are well over one billion Muslims living today, the great majority in Asia and Africa, but over 32 million in Europe and five million in North America. They speak a variety of languages and belong to a variety of ethnic groups. Much of the growth of Islam is a relatively recent phenomenon, but throughout nearly all of Islamic history, Muslims have encouraged (and only very rarely compelled) conversion, and this by setting inspirational examples, offering fiscal or commercial incentives, building cities and otherwise transforming patterns of settlement and social life. The result is that for nearly all of Islamic history Arabs have been in the numerical minority. Now it is true that Islam was born amongst the Arabs of early seventh-century Arabia, that nearly all positions of authority in the early state (the caliphate) were monopolized by Arabs, and, according to nearly all who defined it, that the position of the caliph was to be held by a kinsman of Muḥammad himself, that is, a member of the Arab tribe of the Quraysh. But after about AD 900 Islamic history has relatively little to do with Arabs – indeed, even less to do with Arab tribes and kinship – and much more to do with Persians, Turks and many other non-Arab ethnic groups. Although Muḥammad’s native town of Mecca would always remain at the centre of the ritual world, at least for those Muslims who regularly prayed towards it or made the pilgrimage there, already by the end of the seventh century Muslims had abandoned it as the centre of their political world, which they made first in Syria and then in Iraq. The Near East has long held strategic significance for those engaged in East–West trade, but Arabia proper is now politically significant principally because of the chance discovery of oil.

If ethnic Arabs were edged off the centre stage of Islamic history at a relatively early date, their written language always retained its prestige amongst Muslims of nearly all stripes. Far more than Latin matters to Christians and even Hebrew to Jews, Arabic matters to Muslims: the responsibility to command some of the language, even if just a passing acquaintance with its alphabet or a few memorized lines of the Qurʾān, is commonly felt by non-Arab Muslims, wherever they may live. In part, this can be explained by attitudes towards scripture, or, more precisely, by attitudes concerning scripture and authority: whereas Christians of the Reformation made translating the Latin Bible into vernacular languages part of their programme of wresting authority away from an established clergy, the Arabic of the Qurʾān was generally held to be inviolate by all Muslims, reformist or otherwise. When Ibn Tūmart (d. 1130) preached a puritanical Islam amongst the Berbers of North Africa, he made a point of teaching them Arabic so that they could read the Qurʾān in God's own language. This said, attitudes towards scripture alone cannot explain the near monopoly enjoyed by Arabic on virtually all fields of higher learning in North Africa and the Middle East that took hold during the seventh and eighth centuries, and, in any case, attitudes towards scripture were influenced by broad trends.

The conquests of the mid-seventh century, when Muslim armies pushed the Byzantines out of North Africa, Egypt, Syria and Palestine, and put an end to the 400-year-old rule of the Sasanians in Iraq and Iran, resulted in an Islamic state that was ruled, at least initially, by and for Arab Muslims, some of whom had been townsmen, but many of whom saw themselves as pastoralists. Still, as one Chinese aphorism has it, 'it is possible to create an empire on horseback, but it is impossible to rule from that position'. Muslims, too, understood that empire building meant settling, building cities, putting in place an administration and bureaucracy, and generating a cultural matrix in which Arabs and non-Arabs alike could participate. During the first centuries of Islamic rule, Arab and non-Arab, Muslim and non-Muslim – indeed, virtually anyone with any intellectual ambitions to speak of – accordingly adopted Arabic as the language of high culture. This process of Arabicization, which should be distinguished from that of Islamicization (that is, conversion to Islam), took some time, and its course naturally varied from region to region; but in one form or another, it was nearly irresistible. Arabic almost entirely replaced Aramaic as the *lingua franca* of the Fertile Crescent, while in Iran, and in other regions where early Islamic administration was thinner and local culture more robust, its impact was still strong: Persian would survive, but only in Arabic dress, written in an Arabic alphabet and teeming with Arabic loan words. So even though the political unity of the Middle East that resulted from the great Islamic conquests of the mid-seventh century was relatively short lived (about 200 years), the cultural and intellectual patterns that Arab-Muslim imperialists had created by settling and patronising learned culture in Arabic would endure. Even today, Arabic survives outside the Arab Middle East as a written language of theological and legal expression, much like Latin in some Catholic institutions of learning. History has probably not seen a more successful instance of linguistic imperialism than the spread of Arabic, propelled as it was by the expansion of the Islamic state.[1]

The emergence and spread of Arabic in the Middle East count not merely as one of the signal achievements of early Islamic rule, but as an exceptionally creative moment in human history, one which would produce a volume and variety of literature that rival any other linguistic tradition. Early Islamic scholarship was initially concentrated in centres of post-conquest Arab settlement and administration, particularly the Iraqi cities of Basra, Kufa and, somewhat later, Baghdad itself, which was founded soon after the Abbasid branch of the Quraysh overthrew the Umayyad branch in 750 (the 'Abbasid Revolution'). It was in cities such as these that Arabic was transformed from a largely oral medium into a language and literature of great possibilities: grammar was worked out, thereby making Arabic literary culture universally accessible, and disciplines of learning and genres of literature emerged, particularly under the patronage of eighth- and ninth-century caliphs. That the metropolitan centre of the empire was to generate so much learning is natural enough: it was where patrons and resources were concentrated, attracting in equal measure the ambitious and talented from Iraq and beyond. But it is also natural that the provinces should eventually produce some learning too, and this they did, particularly during the ninth and tenth centuries, when Iraq fell into political and economic decline. By this time, the *formative period* of Islam had come to an end. Arab settlement in many of these regions had originally been relatively thin: in numbers, Arab settlers in the far Islamic west (present-day Spain) and east (Turkmenistan, Uzbekistan, Afghanistan) were always dwarfed by non-Arab indigenous populations, but after years of assimilation and cultural transformation, provincial cities now began to produce scholars in large numbers, particularly under the patronage of newly independent dynasties.

The Baghdad-centred caliphate of the earliest Abbasids was to some degree unifocal, but already in the days of Hārūn al-Rashīd (rg. 786–809) the seeds for these provincial dynasties were being sown. The result was a polyfocal Islamic world, in which dynasties, great and small, long and short-lived, Turkish, Kurdish, Persian or otherwise, would take root in areas stretching from the western Mediterranean to central Asia. With the notable exceptions of the Umayyads of Spain, independent since the Abbasid Revolution in 750, and the Fatimids, a Shī^{c}ite dynasty that would rule Egypt from 969 to 1171, virtually all of these dynasties owed their legitimacy either to the now-enfeebled Abbasid caliph himself, or to the law (the *sharī^{c}a*) that he had come to symbolize. In either case, these dynasties had

[1] For the aphorism, I draw upon A. Khazanov, 'Muhammad and Jenghiz Khan compared: the religious factor in world empire building', *Comparative Studies in History and Society* 35 (1993), p. 469.

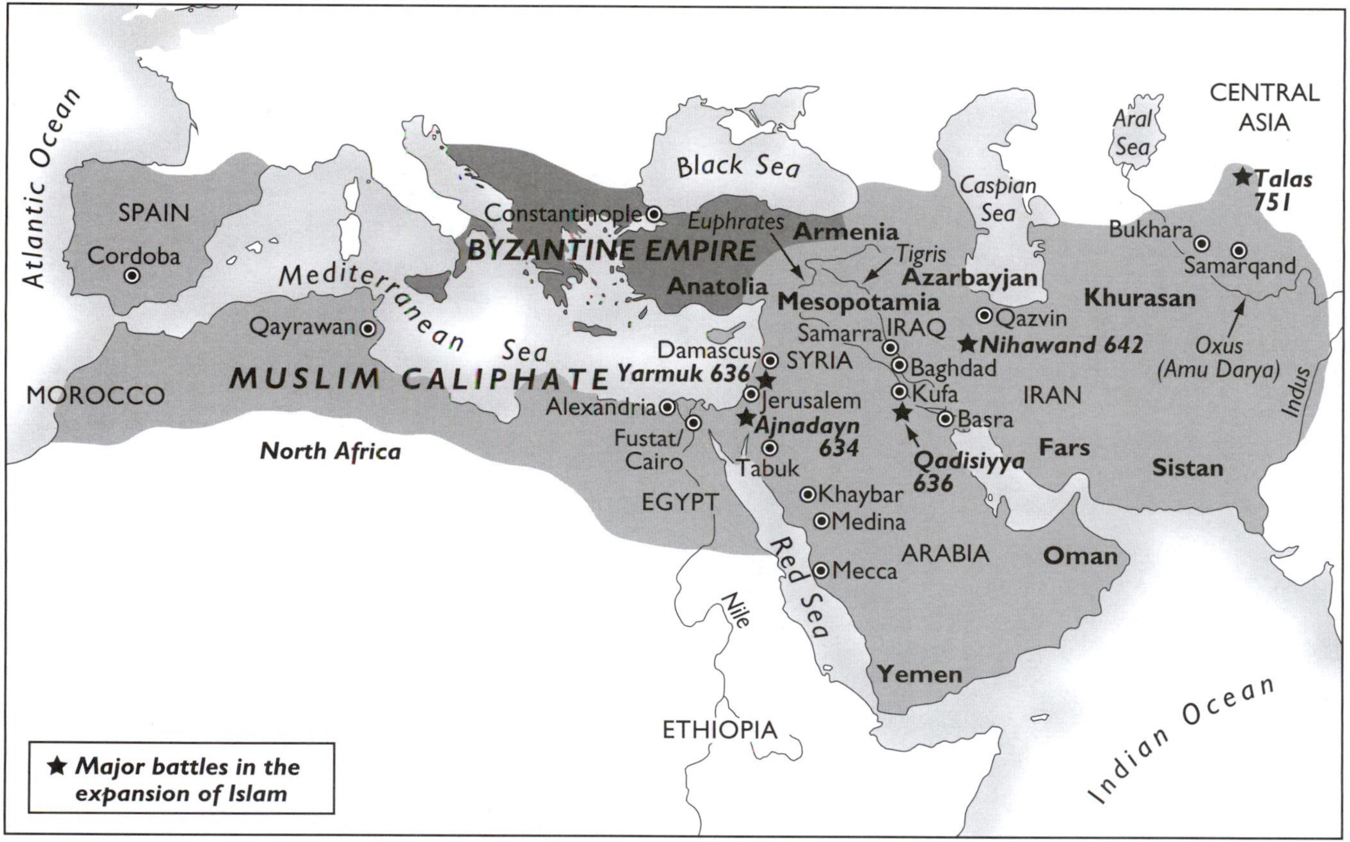

Map 1 The early Islamic Middle East

a stake in patronizing the cultural patterns first mooted in Iraq, which, as far as learning was concerned, meant patronizing Arabic, Arabic letters or an Arabicized language (such as New Persian). Even those exceptional dynasties (including, but not limited to the Fatimids) that had Shīᶜite sympathies would follow suit. Such historical affinity as exists between Shiᶜism and Iran only dates from shortly after the discovery of the New World, which is recent history in Near Eastern terms. At this point, we have entered the early sixteenth century, which produced not only the first dynasty to make Shiᶜism the faith of an Iranian state (the Safavids), but also the Ottoman conquest of Cairo, which put an end to the long-lived Mamluk dynasty of Egypt (rg. 1250–1517). Arabic learning would survive both the Safavids and the Ottomans, and in some respects it would even flourish. But for the purposes of this book, these events mark the end of what I have called the *classical period*, and only exceptionally shall I have anything to say about the tradition after 1500.

Being the prestige language of scholarship, Arabic was the language of historiography, exclusively so for early Muslims, and increasingly so even for Christians living under Islamic rule. This pattern holds until the late tenth and eleventh centuries, when dynasts in the eastern Islamic world began to reinvigorate Persian as a written language, first its poetry and then its prose; Persian-speaking historians such as Ibn Funduq al-Bayhaqī were writing in Arabic as late as the middle of the twelfth century, but the fashion was now changing, and the East would eventually produce a vibrant tradition of Persian historiography. Much later, the Ottoman Turks would also patronise Turkish historiography, and other Islamic languages would produce traditions of their own. No doubt some of my critics will fasten onto this point, insisting that this book should have been entitled something like *Islamic Historiography in Arabic* (the preceding paragraphs should make it clear why *Arabic Historiography* is out of the running). But *Islamic Historiography in Arabic* is both indecorous and pleonastic. Like it or not, the fact is that much of what was written in Arabic in this period was written by non-Arabs (perhaps the greatest of all historians of the first three centuries, Abū Jaᶜfar al-Ṭabarī, was Persian) who, as learned Muslims, expressed themselves according to the linguistic norms of the day. This meant writing in Arabic. Islamic historiography would become polyglot, but it had always been a collective endeavour. And by the time that Muslims began to write their history in Persian or Turkish, the tradition had begun to follow a number of discernible patterns, some of which were set already by the middle of the ninth century, others emerging in the twelfth and thirteenth. To understand Persian historiography one needs not only Persian, but also some grounding in the Arabic tradition from which it emerged; and an understanding of Persian historiography only complements what the Arabic tradition can teach us about Islamic historiography. The same survey that demonstrates the great vitality of local history writing in Persian also speaks of the 'remarkable continuity' of that tradition from Arabic into Persian. Similarly Turkish: there may be nothing in Arabic that can match Babur's glorious autobiography in Chagatai Turkish, but by this time (the early sixteenth century), earlier objections to autobiographical writing

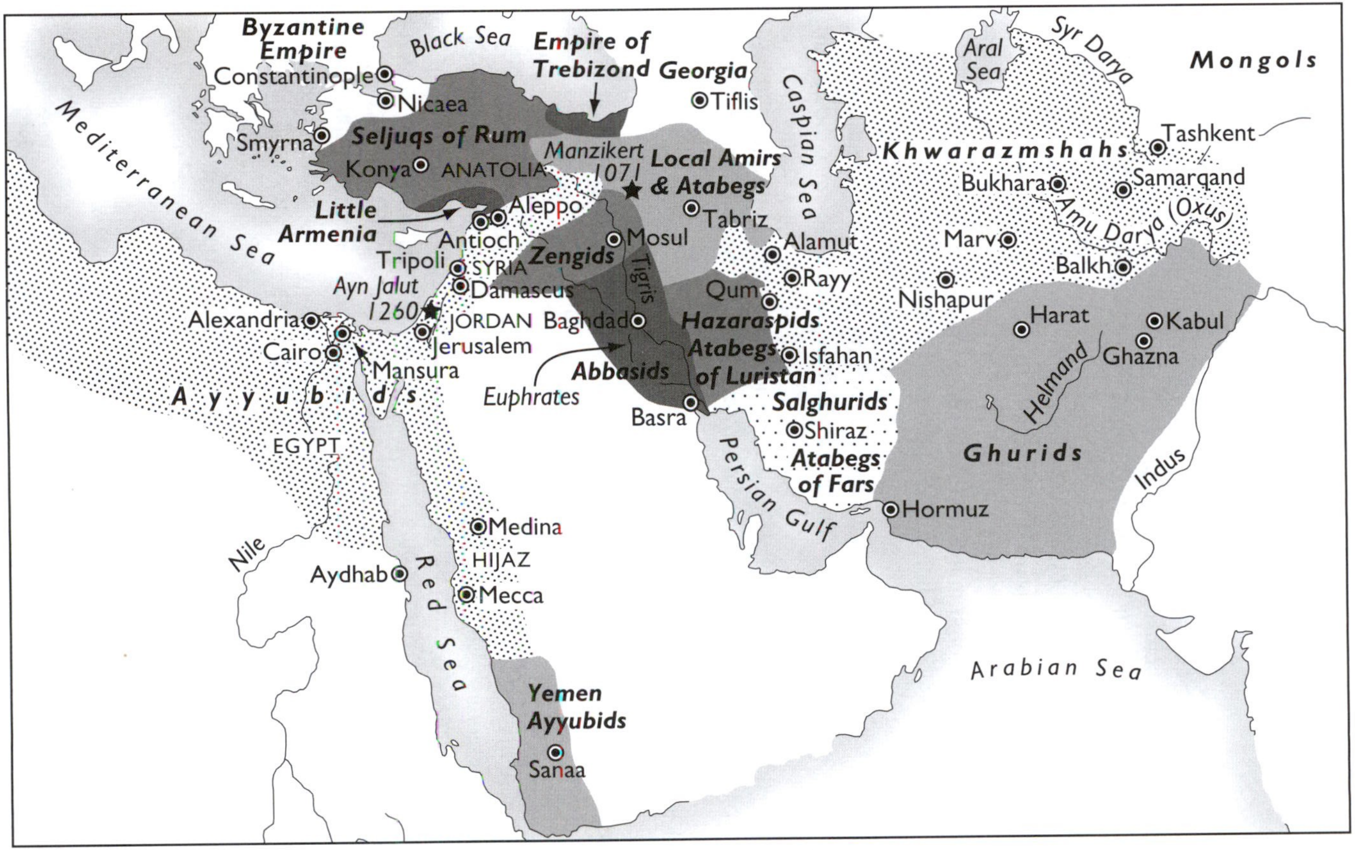

Map 2 The Islamic commonwealth of states in the middle of the thirteenth century

had been overcome in Arabic. Like the Persian historiographic tradition, the Turkish is rooted in the Arabo-Islamic tradition.[2]

* * *

This book assumes that the reader is curious enough about Islamic history and historiography to bother reading about it, but that he or she possesses no training in Islamic history, much less the Arabic language. In fact, I would regard it as a ringing success even if only a few of its readers were inspired to take up either of the two, and it is in part for those who wish to learn more that I bother with transliterating Arabic terms into their standard forms. Those who learn Arabic will come to know how to pronounce ẓ, ṭ, ṣ, etc. For Arabophile and Arabophobe alike, a few simple points of grammar and vocabulary must be made at the outset, however. First, the Arabic definite article (there is no indefinite article) is *al*, which is prefixed upon the qualified noun: so *kitāb* (a book) and *al-kitāb* (the book). Second, when feminine nouns are put in the construct state, their *a* ending becomes *at*: so the *sīra* (biography) of Muḥammad and the *sīrat Muḥammad* ('the *sīra* [life] of Muḥammad') refer to the same work. Third, 'Ibn' (or 'ibn') means 'son', and will frequently appear in abbreviated form ('b.') in genealogies, as will 'Abū' (father; in the genitive, 'Abī'): so '[c]Alī b. Abī Ṭālib', which is the full name of Muḥammad's cousin and son-in-law [c]Alī, literally means '[c]Alī, the son of the father of Ṭālib' (bt. abbreviates bint, 'daughter'). Fourth, the adjective ending 'ī' (fem. 'iyya') denotes a relationship of one kind or another, e.g. 'al-Ṭabarī' (geographic, 'the person from Ṭabaristān'), 'Ḥanbalī' (academic, 'the person who follows the legal thinking of Aḥmad b. Ḥanbal'), and 'al-Qurashī' (tribal, 'the person from the tribe of the Quraysh').

To simplify and clarify things for non-Arabists and non-Islamicists, I have drawn some illustrations from pre-existing translations, and included a brief glossary, maps, a chronology, death dates, and some suggestions for further reading. For similar reasons, I have made only infrequent mention of Islamic dating, which is based on a lunar rather than solar cycle, and which began in 622 of the Common Era (C.E.). This *hijrī* dating, which takes its name from Muḥammad's emigration (the Hijra or Hegira) from Mecca to Medina, more frequently appears here in the publication details of Arabic texts, where it is marked by 'H' (books published in Iran are generally dated according to a modified *hijrī* calendar, which need not concern us). On occasion I cite more than one Arabic edition, but in this regard, as in many others, I make no attempt to be comprehensive. The reader should also

[2] For the Persian local tradition, see A.K.S. Lambton, 'Persian local histories: the tradition behind them and the assumptions of their authors', in *Yād-Nāma in memoria di Alessandro Bausani* (Rome, 1991), i, pp. 227–238; for the Persian rhetorical tradition's debts to Arabic, K.A. Luther, 'Islamic rhetoric and the Persian historians, 1100–1300 A.D.', in J.A. Bellamy, ed., *Studies in Near Eastern Culture and History in Memory of Ernest T. Abdel-Massih* (Ann Arbor, 1990), p. 93; for a translation of Babur's autobiography, his *The Baburnama: Memoirs of Babur, Prince and Emperor*, trans. W.M. Thackston (Washington, D.C., 1996); for a study, S. Dale, 'Steppe humanism: the autobiographical writings of Zahir al-Din Muhammad Babur, 1483–1530', *IJMES* 22 (1990), pp. 37–58.

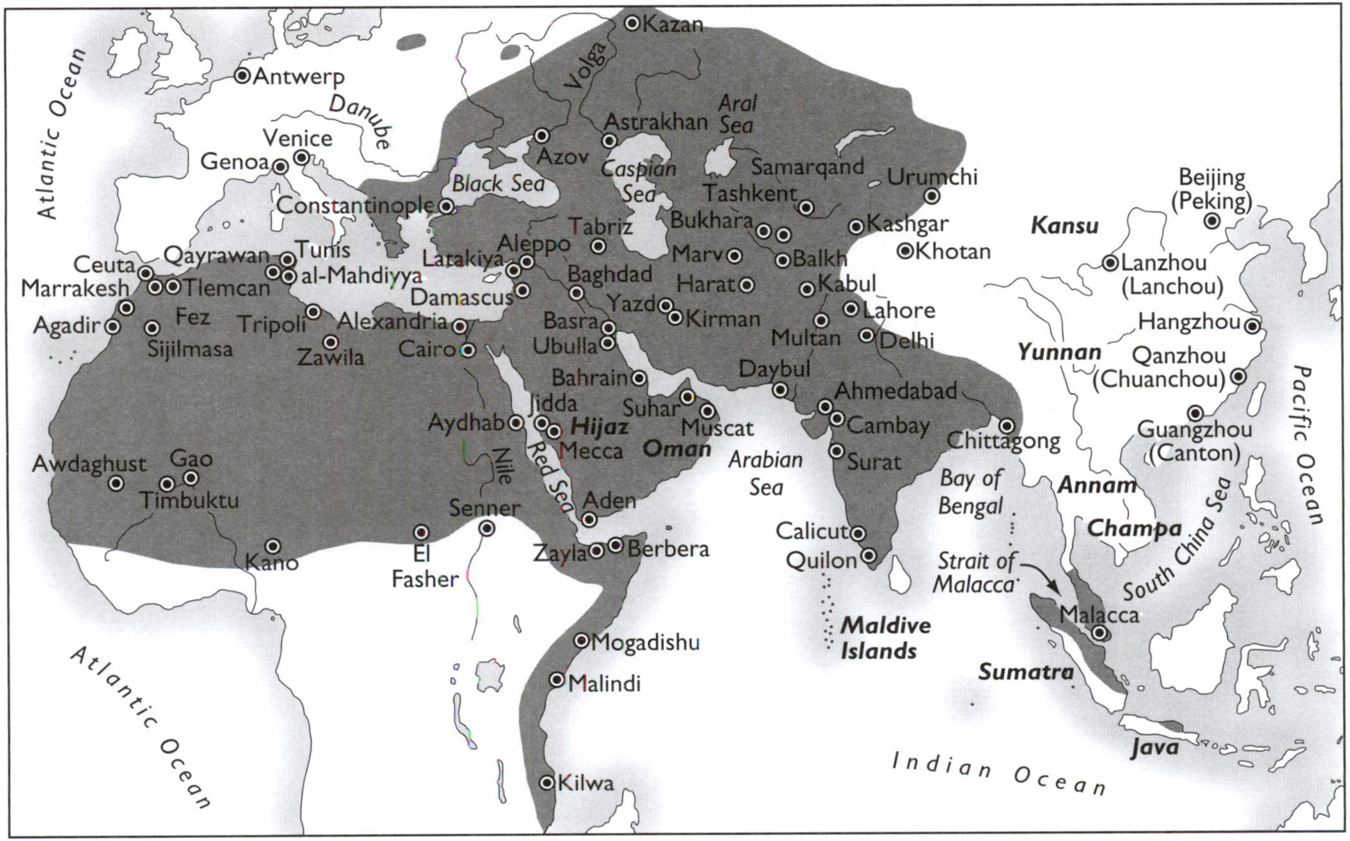

Map 3 The Islamic world in 1500

know that most of the authors and books mentioned here can be tracked down in the new edition of the *The Encyclopaedia of Islam* (Leiden, 1954–), which has now reached the letter Y, and in J.S. Meisami and P. Starkey, eds., *Encyclopedia of Arabic Literature* (London and New York, 1998), which is complete; both provide even more bibliography. For those equipped with greater ambition and rudimentary German, the standard reference works are C. Brockelmann, *Geschichte der arabischen Litteratur* (Weimar, Leipzig and Leiden, 1898–1949) and F. Sezgin, *Geschichte des arabischen Schrifttums*, vol. 1 (Leiden, 1967); the former covers all the ground covered here, the latter, the first four centuries of Islam. Those with Arabic will almost certainly also know of ᶜU. Kaḥḥāla, *Muᶜjam al-muʾallifīn* (Damascus, 1957–1961, with multiple Beirut reprints).

As an introduction to what obstinately remains a forbidding field, this book is intended to complement some pre-existing literature, particularly F. Rosenthal, *A History of Muslim Historiography*, second ed. (Leiden, 1968), T. Khalidi, *Arabic Historical Thought in the Classical Period* (Cambridge, 1994), and J.S. Meisami, *Persian Historiography to the End of the Twelfth Century* (Edinburgh, 1999), all of which must be read by anyone whose interest in the topic has survived the present book. From these it differs in what it asks of the reader, and, even more important, in approach. As a social historian who works primarily (but not exclusively) on the basis of texts, I have put what some may feel is undue emphasis on the social function and production of the historiographic tradition. In other words, I have said nearly as much about how and why Muslim historians wrote as I have said about what they wrote. I leave it to the reader to determine if this emphasis is undue, or, as I believe, overdue. Suffice it to say here, my intention has not so much been to survey (as does Rosenthal) or interpret (as does Khalidi) the classical tradition, as much as to make it comprehensible. I set about doing this in two ways. First, I have tried to describe the production of historiography within the sociology of learning broadly conceived, which means touching on everything from the historians' conceptual debts to Islamic law to how they earned their living and organised their notes. Second, I have proposed a three-part typology of historiography – chronography, biography and prosopography – that is intended to impose some order on a huge and unruly body of books.

What do these terms mean?

1. By *chronography*, I mean those genres that describe events as they occur in time, organizing them according to annual entries (in which case it is annalistic) or caliphal reigns. Universal histories, which begin with Creation, and cover the non-Islamic world generally insofar as it relates to Islamic history, are conventionally chronographic, local history less frequently so, since it often takes one prosopographical form or another.
2. The Islamic tradition produced biographical narrative of various sorts, but by *biography* I mean only single-subject works that relate the life of a person, the coverage usually being representative rather than comprehensive. As we shall see, in Arabic it is conventionally called *sīra* ('way of acting'), which clearly expresses the paradigmatic force of biographical writing. If the prestige form

of chronography was universal history, the prestige subject of biography was Prophetic biography, but there were others, even in the earliest period.

3. By *prosopography*, I mean writing about social groups, rather than the collective study of social groups, as the term is commonly understood by modern historians (the Greek *prosōpon* means 'face' or 'person'). Whereas biography is about exemplary or otherwise distinctive individuals whose lives – however exceptional or heroic – take meaning from their times, prosopography compiles and organises those items of biographical data that *mark an individual's belonging to a group*, the individual entry generally being called a *tarjama*. (We shall see that the growth of the *tarjama* would blur the distinction between prosopography and biography.) Many of these works, which have parallels in western and non-western traditions (e.g., the Chinese), are conventionally called 'biographical dictionaries'.[3]

Much more about these definitions will be said in chapter 4. Here it is enough to note that the categories are meant primarily to be heuristic, rather than pragmatic: this is not a *Handbuch* intended for practitioners, and I limit myself to some general comments about the utility of the sources for writing Islamic history. For excellent discussions along those lines, the reader might consult C. Cahen, *Introduction à l'histoire du monde musulman médiéval: VIIe–XVe siècle (méthodologie et éléments de bibliographie)* (Paris, 1983) (a revision of J. Sauvaget and C. Cahen, *Introduction à l'histoire de l'Orient musulman* [Paris, 1961], which has been translated into English as *Introduction to the History of the Muslim East: A Bibliographical Guide* [Berkeley, 1965]), R.S. Humphreys, *Islamic History: A Framework for Inquiry* (rev. ed., Princeton, 1991), and T. Nagel, *Die islamische Welt bis 1500* (Munich, 1998). All three are exemplary in several ways.

It is a historiographic truism that the survival of historical sources is a matter of history itself, and the same thing can be said of the ideas and categories that historians invent to make some sense of their sources. The historical context of this book and series is the growth of the academic study of Islam and Islamic history, their intention being to open a door into Islamic studies for the uninitiated and, it is my own special hope, to ventilate some of its mustier corners as well. To serve a broad audience – students, scholars, and the odd Islamicist, too – I have tried to strike a balance between simplifying, generalizing and comparing on the one hand, and exemplifying on the other; the syntax of this sentence is deliberately unbalanced. Here and throughout I take consolation in an aphorism credited to H.H. Munro: 'A little inaccuracy sometimes saves tons of explanation'.

[3] I am not the first to use the term 'prosopography' in this sense; see M.J.L. Young, 'Arabic biographical writing' in M.J.L. Young et al., eds., *Religion, Learning and Science in the ʿAbbasid Period* (Cambridge History of Arabic Literature; Cambridge, 1990), p. 170.

PART I

Origins and categories

CHAPTER 1

Origins

In the 377th year after the Prophet Muḥammad's emigration from Mecca to Medina, a year which began on 2 May 987 and ended on 20 April 988, a Baghdadi book-lover named Ibn al-Nadīm was putting the finishing touches on a book of his own. We know this because he mentions the date in the preface to this book, and so do at least two indefatigable writers who were equally the product of classical Islamic bibliophilia, Yāqūt (d. 1229) and al-Ṣafadī (d. 1363). In fact, aside from the book itself, much of our knowledge of Ibn al-Nadīm comes from compilers such as Yāqūt and al-Ṣafadī, both non-Arab outsiders whose learning brought them celebrity in Islamic lands, and both, too, writers of massive books on learned men (and some women), often thousands of them. Yāqūt's work, which is concerned exclusively with men of learning, has recently been edited in seven thick volumes. Al-Ṣafadī's work tackles past celebrities more generally, which there means not only men of learning, but men of politics and culture, too; the editors began their work as long ago as 1931, and 71 years later the project, having exceeded 30 volumes, is only now coming to a close. In addition to this work, al-Ṣafadī wrote a single-volume biographical dictionary devoted entirely to blind scholars, a topic which will seem less strange once we understand the crucial role of audition – *hearing* books – in Islamic learning, and a three-volume work on the celebrities of his own day. This, he tells us in the introduction, begins in 'year 696 [1297], which is the year of my birth'. Other historians of this and later periods, such as Ibn Ḥajar al-ᶜAsqalānī (d. 1449), would begin their works in the same immodest fashion.[1]

Ibn al-Nadīm, one learns in Yāqūt, al-Ṣafadī and elsewhere, was a Shīᶜite Muslim who worked, as his father had, as a bookseller in Baghdad, then as now the first city of Iraq. He seems to have lived on the eastern side of the Tigris river, in a

[1] The most recent edition of Yāqūt's *Irshād al-arīb ilā maᶜrifat al-adīb* is Beirut, 1993, but I shall cite the first (and less complete) edition of London and Leiden, 1907–1913; the editing of al-Ṣafadī's *al-Wāfī bi'l-wafayāt* began in Leipzig, 1931; for the birth date, see his *Aᶜyān al-ᶜaṣr wa-aᶜwān al-naṣr* (Frankfurt, 1990), i, p. 3; on al-Ṣafadī in general, D.P. Little, 'Al-Ṣafadī as biographer of his contemporaries', in D.P. Little, ed., *Essays in Islamic Civilization Presented to Niyazi Berkes* (Leiden, 1976), pp. 190–210; his work on the blind is the *Nakt al-himyān fī nukat al-ᶜumyān* (Cairo, 1911), on which F. Malti-Douglas, 'Dreams, the blind, and the semiotics of the biographical notice', *SI* 51 (1980), pp. 137–162; Ibn Ḥajar's work is the *Inbāᵓ al-ghumr bi-abnāᵓ al-ᶜumr* (Hyderabad, 1967–1976).

predominantly Christian quarter of the city, and to have taken his sobriquet ('son of the boon-companion', *nadīm*; he is also called 'al-Nadīm' *tout court*) from his position as courtier to at least one patron, perhaps the Abbasid ruler, or perhaps a member of the Buyid family, an Iranian dynasty that had taken *de facto* control of the Abbasid caliphate in 945. Our author would have been around 20 or 25 at the time, still young enough to adapt to the political and cultural changes set into motion by the Buyid usurpation of Abbasid authority. As a book dealer, Ibn al-Nadīm contributed to the flourishing trade of books in tenth-century Baghdad, still the capital of the caliphate as it had been since 762, and still, too, one of the world's greatest and most literate cities: the *sūq al-warrāqīn* (book dealers' market) lay in the eastern – and more prosperous – side of his city, and at one point it boasted something like 100 bookshops. It was there that books were bought, sold and traded, where commissions for new books were taken, and, some 900 years before the printing press became widespread, where books were painstakingly or carelessly copied out by scribes, both on order and on speculation. So Ibn al-Nadīm knew the book market, and in his capacity as boon-companion – that is, adviser/raconteur/drinking mate to his wealthy patrons – he also had access to court culture and all that it favoured: magic, divination, alchemy, ribaldry, clowning around and buffoonery, alongside philosophy, music, mathematics and astronomy, all of which feature in his book. Again, the combination may seem strange to us, but it was a perfectly ordinary feature of courtly culture of the time, be it amongst Muslim or non-Muslim rulers.[2]

One imagines that Baghdad had other booksellers who doubled as courtiers, men who knew market forces and court tastes. What distinguishes Ibn al-Nadīm from his contemporaries is that he recorded his vast knowledge in a book, leaving what would turn out to be our best source for Islamic learning in the early middle ages. The title of this book is *al-Fihrist*, which is usually translated as the 'Index' or 'Catalogue', and to paraphrase his very brief introduction, it offers nothing less than a comprehensive survey of Arabic books and learning, together with bio-bibliographic information about their authors. It is thus a book about books and the people who wrote them, at once the product of a hard-headed bookseller (he specifies the exact length of some books, since unscrupulous copyists occasionally sold incomplete volumes to unwary customers), and the educated man's guide to 'the attainment of success' (as an alternative title has it) that books were thought to provide.

[2] The standard edition of the work is now R. Tajaddud's *al-Fihrist* (Tehran, 1971), which has been reprinted (without proper credit to the editor) in Beirut; for a translation with a useful index, B. Dodge, *The Fihrist of al-Nadīm* (New York, 1970); on Ibn al-Nadīm, the conference articles collected in *Ibn an-Nadim und die mittelalterliche arabische Literatur* (Wiesbaden, 1996); on the institution of the *nadīm*, A. Chejne, 'The boon-companion in early ʿAbbāsid times', *JAOS* 85 (1965), pp. 327–335; for a detailed description of Baghdad, J. Lassner, *The Topography of Baghdad in the Early Middle Ages: Texts and Studies* (Detroit, 1970).

Ibn al-Nadīm divided his *Fihrist* into ten chapters, each divided into a number of sub-sections:

1. On the conventions of writing (e.g. scripts and penmanship), some non-Islamic scriptures, and the Qurʾān, including what Islamic learning calls 'the Qurʾānic sciences' (e.g., works on interpreting and reciting the text);
2. On grammarians of the Arabic language;
3. 'Chapter 3 of *al-Fihrist*, which gives accounts of the *akhbārī*s, genealogists and those concerned with events' (the meaning of *akhbārī*s is made clear below);
4. On poetry and poets of the pre-Islamic, Umayyad (661–750), and Abbasid period (750–);
5. On Muslim theologians, ascetics and mystics;
6. On jurists;
7. On philosophers (that is, those translating and working within traditions of classical antiquity), including mathematics, astronomy and medicine;
8. On entertainers of various sorts (such as storytellers, performers, magicians) and related *miscellanea*;
9. On non-Islamic sectarians and accounts concerning the Far East;
10. On alchemists.

There are at least two things that should be said about the contents of *al-Fihrist*. The first, which I shall discuss below, concerns the categories with which Ibn al-Nadīm has chosen to describe Baghdad's written culture. Ibn al-Nadīm's third chapter brings together authors of works of what we would conventionally call genealogy, hagiography (saints' lives), legend, annalistic history, geography, prosopography, antiquarianism, natural history, administration, biography and a very great deal more besides. What does it mean that he puts them all together in a single chapter? Why does historiography, unlike law and philosophy, fail to secure a chapter of its own? Neither of these questions should be taken to suggest that all western critics agree on how to classify narrative and on what constitutes historiography, nor that Muslims of the medieval period went about it in a single or wrong way. Narrative, be it fact or fiction, poetry or prose, Arabic or English, is a continuum upon which we, as historians and critics, readers and writers, collectively create and impose our own categories. We need conventional categories to talk with each other about literature, but we should not fool ourselves into thinking that these categories are intrinsic to it: the use of these categories is historically conditioned, and in some measure even political. This is as true of narrative that purports to describe the past (a work of history) as it is of narrative that conjures up a past (a novel).[3]

The common understanding of history today, as a variety of non-fiction that is distinguished from 'literature', even an autonomous branch of learning, is relatively

[3] More will be said about literary categories below; for now see L. Patterson, *Negotiating the Past: The Historical Understanding of Medieval Literature* (Madison, 1987), esp. pp. 41f.

new and altogether narrower than the traditions from which it emerged. It would have confused most pre-modern writers, be they Muslim or non-Muslim. (The English word *history* comes via Latin from the Greek *historia*, and generally meant 'inquiry'; it earlier described a variety of genres, including geography, folklore and ethnography, in addition to what we would commonly understand to be history.) Because we regard history as a useful and important thing, in some measure because we have rooted our national identities in it, we give it a variety of institutional forms, such as museums, local historical societies, dedicated sections in bookshops and libraries, and university departments. We also privilege some forms of history over others, again for cultural and political reasons. Now history was certainly important to Muslims of the classical period, and it hardly needs pointing out that this book of history is only worth writing because pre-modern Muslims wrote so many books of history, filling their libraries with volume after volume. But most learned Muslims of that period accorded the historian far less authority than we do, and envisioned his activity not so much as a discipline independent from other disciplines, but as a kind of narrative practice. Medieval Muslim historians, unlike modern western ones, only rarely insisted that they were doing something special. What distinguished a Muslim historian, who was usually called an *akhbārī* ('one concerned with [past] events'; 'historian') or *muʾarrikh* ('chronologer'; 'historian') was not that he belonged to a history department, paid dues to some analogue of the American Historical Association, nor even that he saw himself primarily as an *akhbārī* or *muʾarrikh*. Almost to a man, Muslim historians made their living doing something other than history, especially tutoring, teaching (particularly the law, and, starting in the middle of our period, in institutions of learning), and writing – everything from copying out books to drafting letters for a patron. In fact, we shall see that for much of the classical period Muslim historians kept their heads low, choosing to follow the cultural and academic patterns set by those who *did* enjoy enormous social authority – the jurists – out of whose ranks they frequently came, especially during the ninth and tenth centuries. What made an author a historian was that he chose to arrange accounts of events past (*akhbār*) in one or more distinctive ways that, unlike those of other purveyors of written narrative, were explicitly or implicitly chronological. A great French Arabist once asked if al-Masʿūdī (d. 956), author of a hugely ambitious cultural history of the world, was a historian or a littérateur. The answer is that he was both.[4]

This brings us to the second thing that should be said about the contents of Ibn al-Nadīm's book, which is in no way incompatible with the first: they reflect tenth-century Baghdad's voracious appetite for knowledge, including the historical narrative that figures so prominently in his third chapter. Historiography did not

[4] On the etymology of *taʾrīkh*, see F. Rosenthal, *A History of Muslim Historiography* (Leiden, 2nd rev. ed., 1968), pp. 11ff.; very infrequently one finds *khabarī* instead of *akhbārī*, such as in Ibn ʿAbd al-Munʿim al-Ḥimyarī, *al-Rawḍ al-miʿṭār fī khabar al-aqṭār* (Beirut, 1975), p. 133; the French historian is C. Pellat, 'Was al-Masʿūdī an historian or an *adīb*?' *Journal of the Pakistan Historical Society* 9 (1961), pp. 231–234.

secure so prestigious a place in the medieval world of Islamic learning as other branches of learning, especially the law, but it was still produced in great quantity. Of the *Fihrist*'s ten chapters, the third occupies nearly 20 per cent of the book as a whole, and lists nearly 100 authors, many prolific by the standards of this or any other time, and over 1000 titles (we shall see that these 'titles' are actually something of a problem). All this added up, and it had been adding up for more than 200 years. At his death, the historian al-Wāqidī (d. 823) is said to have left behind no fewer than 600 trunks of books, each to be hoisted by a pair of men (he had employed two scribes to copy books for him, both working, we are told, day and night); we can only imagine how many of these were works of history. The great essayist al-Jāḥiẓ (d. 868), paralytic in his old age, was famously crushed to death by his books; the story is probably concocted, but it remains telling. One tenth-century courtier declined a post on account of the difficulty of moving his library, which is said to have included 400 camel loads of books – and these were just the theology titles. One of the manuscripts of the history written by al-Ṭabarī (d. 923) calls the work an 'abridgment' (*mukhtaṣar*), and according to some reports, the fuller version was ten times the length of the extant work – a hypothetical 77,870 pages in length! This number stretches credulity, for sure, but there can be no doubt that by this time very lengthy books were commonplace. Indeed, the market for books and learning was as insatiable as it was sophisticated: one late tenth-century library in Cairo seems to have housed hundreds of thousands of books, including multiple copies of what had by then become standard histories. Nothing in the contemporaneous Christian world, East or West, compared with this bibliomania, nor had Greece or Rome produced anything on its scale. Perhaps outside of China, one must wait for the printing press to find a comparable phenomenon.[5]

In fact, the rise of historical writing in Islam corresponds almost exactly to the period of the T'ang dynasty (618–907) in China, but there is at least one crucial difference between Chinese and Islamic literary culture. T'ang bibliomania was the product of centuries of momentum and growth: historiography may be said to have started already with Confucius (d. 479 B.C.) and paper had been available for some 500 years. Its Abbasid analogue exploded in the space of four or five generations. The Prophet Muḥammad died in 632, an enormously charismatic, shrewd and gifted man – and one who is also said to have been illiterate. It seems that literacy amongst the Muslim élite began to catch on with the generation of his grandson, and then it very quickly accelerated: the standard reference work (controversially) credits a great-grandson (ᶜAlī b. al-Ḥusayn, d. 715) with seven titles, and ᶜAlī's grandson, the deeply learned Jaᶜfar al-Ṣādiq (d. 765), with 32. This

[5] For al-Wāqidī, see Ibn al-Nadīm, *Fihrist*, p. 111 (Dodge, *Fihrist,* p. 214); the tenth-century courtier is al-Ṣāḥib b. ᶜAbbād, for which see A. Mez, *The Renaissance of Islam,* trans. S.K. Bakhsh and D.S. Margoliouth (Patna, 1937), p. 174; on al-Ṭabarī, F. Rosenthal, *General Introduction, and From the Creation to the Flood* (Albany, 1989; al-Ṭabarī translation, vol. i); for libraries and the proliferation of books in general, J. Pedersen, *The Arabic Book*, trans. G. French (Princeton, 1984), especially chapter 9, and below.

chapter tries to shed some light on how historiography figures in the explosive growth of written culture, which was triggered by the rise of Islam.[6]

Orality, tradition and history

Jaᶜfar al-Ṣādiq reflected the cultural ideals of early Abbasid Kufa, the prosperous southern Iraqi city in which he lived and taught. So too did Muḥammad, who was born in the Arabian town of Mecca in about 570, and to whom God had sent serial revelations that were collected after his death to form the Qurᵓān. Unlike late eighth-century Kufa, in Muḥammad's world little room was made for writing, at least beyond the occasional contract or treaty. Even less was made for books. This was because its social organisation – families, clans, tribes and confederations of tribes, all held together by kinship, whether real or fictitious – did not require it, while its low level of economic development, which was determined by thin populations of herders and settled folk in small and scattered oasis towns, did not encourage it. In its very lean culture of writing, the town of Mecca contrasted sharply not only with Abbasid Kufa of Jaᶜfar's time, but with that of the contemporaneous settled south, where written culture (including written dating systems) was relatively sophisticated. The modest level of literacy in the Hijaz is reflected in the technology of writing itself. As experienced by Muḥammad, the Qurᵓān was a series of communications orally transmitted by God through the angel Gabriel, and when first written out, it was inscribed on pieces of leather and animal bones. The Qurᵓān itself makes some mention of books and other writing media, but these are generally associated with monotheism – the revolutionary idea that Muḥammad fought so hard to spread – rather than paganism, which was the prestige form of religiosity.[7]

There is nothing exceptional about the very modest level of Arabian literacy and literature in the seventh century. Arab and non-Arab pastoralists and semi-pastoralists of earlier and subsequent periods have generally produced little writing, relying instead on the more pliant medium of orality. Amongst pre-Islamic Arabs, orality's highest register was apparently occupied by poetry, particularly the ode. As one early tenth-century historian (al-Yaᶜqūbī) put it, pre-Islamic Arabs 'had

[6] The standard reference work is Sezgin's *GAS*, pp. 526ff.; on contemporaneous Chinese historiography, D. Twitchett, *The Writing of Official History under the T'ang* (Cambridge, 1992), and, for older essays that remain useful, E.G. Pulleyblank and W.G. Beasley, eds., *Historians of China and Japan* (Oxford, 1961), and E.G. Pulleyblank, 'The historiographical tradition', in R. Dawson, ed., *The Legacy of China* (Oxford, 1964), pp. 143ff.

[7] On the Hijaz and Arabian pastoralism in general, see F.M. Donner, *The Early Islamic Conquests* (Princeton, 1981), pp. 11ff.; on South Arabia, A.F.L. Beeston, *Epigraphic South Arabian Calendars and Dating* (London, 1956); on the modest use of written documents, G. Schoeler, 'Schreiben und Veröffentlichen: Zu Verwendung und Funktion der Schrift in den ersten islamischen Jahrhunderten', *DI* 69 (1992), pp. 2ff., which is partially translated as 'Writing and publishing: on the use and function of writing in the first centuries of Islam', *Arabica* 44 (1997), pp. 423–435; and M. Maraqten, 'Writing materials in pre-Islamic Arabia', *JSS* 43 (1998), pp. 287–310 (skins, plants and trees, cloth, metal, bones, potsherds, stones).

nothing to refer to for their decisions and actions except poetry; in it they quarrelled, from it they drew their lessons, through it they vied in virtue, swore oaths with each other, fought each other and offered praise and blame'. Poetry offered a currency in which a wide variety of cultural transactions could be made, and it is in poetry that we can also recover some sense of the pre-Islamic Arabs' conceptions of time and fate. The following lines are credited to ᶜAbīd b. al-Abraṣ, who seems to have belonged to the first half of the sixth century; they are exemplary in both form and content.

> Where are the abodes on the gravelly tract of Rawḥān? Their traces have almost vanished –
> changed by the passing of time.
> I stopped my camel there so that I might question them. Then I turned [the beast] away,
> and tears flowed from my eyes,
> Pouring as if my eyes had surprised me with their tears [like copious rain from] a wintry shower.
> [I remember] the time [lit. 'days'] when my people were the best of ordinary folk to those suffering
> from famine or hardship or imprisonment.
> How excellent were those who played *maysir* [a game of chance] over the slaughtered camel,
> when the wind of winter blew hard and neighbours gathered together;
> When it came to spear-thrusting, they used to dye the points of their spears [with blood];
> And when it came to the clash of swords, they were lions, protective of their cubs;
> And when the shout went up 'dismount', they would rush headlong [to battle on foot] in short
> coats of mail.
> I have remained after they have gone, though I shall not remain forever – for Fortune (*al-dahr*)
> is full of changes and multifarious hues.
> God knows what I do not know about their fate. My memories are of what has gone from me
> at whatever time [it went].

Some doubt attaches to the beginning of the last line, 'God knows'; it may be an interpolation made by a Muslim transmitter of the text. None attaches to the preceding line, where 'Fortune' neatly expresses the fatalism that permeates much pre-Islamic poetry, against which Muḥammad's Qurᵓānic morality was directed.[8]

In an age before books, magazines, radio, television and computers, the task of circulating news, predicting the future, passing on wisdom and practical advice, representing one group's opinion before another, providing entertainment – all of these were discharged by talkers: storytellers, diviners, soothsayers, and tribal spokesmen (the categories overlapped). Orality, put very crudely, *suited* the pre-Islamic Arabs of the Hijaz. Stored in one's head and delivered in the form of

[8] For the tenth-century historian on poetry, see al-Yaᶜqūbī, *Taᵓrīkh* (Leiden, 1883) i, p. 304 (noted already in T. Khalidi, *Arabic Historical Thought in the Classical Period* [Cambridge, 1994], p. 2, where the translation somewhat differs); cf. Ibn Rashīq as translated in S.P. Stetkevych, 'The ᶜAbbasid poet interprets history: three qaṣīdahs by Abū Tammām', *JAL* 10 (1979), p. 49; I draw the translation of ᶜAbīd's poem from A. Jones, *Early Arabic Poetry, Volume I: Marāthī and Ṣuᶜlūk Poems* (Reading, 1992), pp. 58ff.; for fatalism, W. Caskel, *Das Schicksal in der altarabischen Poesie: Beiträge zur arabischen Literatur und zur allgemeinen Religionsgeschichte* (Leipzig, 1926).

sound, poetry and other forms of oral communication are effortless to transport and relatively inexpensive to acquire: a story might cost a meal. Just as important, their content can be adapted to the changing requirements of tribal societies, where one's identity is determined principally by perceived bonds of kinship. In very schematic terms, a tribesman rationalises his social and economic ties to contemporaries by creating or severing ties between supposed forefathers. Those favoured (allies in war; herders who share pasture or water rights) are integrated into a shared past ('we migrated together', 'we fought together', 'we descend from the same man'). Those out of favour are given no or little part in this shared past. And because a tribe's allies naturally change over time, so too do its genealogy and past. More than stubborn written history, oral history suits the pastoral tribesman's way of constructing identity and community. Unlike history books that have to be banned, destroyed or otherwise suppressed, oral history is as dynamic as a society wants it to be.

There is, then, every reason to think that history mattered a great deal to the tribesmen of the Hijaz, and the Qurʾān itself testifies to that: 'Narrate to them the history [or story], so that they reflect' (Q 7:176); 'Has not the history [or story] of those before you reached you, of the people of Noah, and ʿĀd and Thamūd and those after them?' (Q 14:9). But in shape and significance, history for pre-Islamic Arabs differed markedly from history as understood by the annalist or chronographer working within a written medium, not to mention a modern, professional historian. The annalist is produced by a culture that values record keeping and institutionalizes this value in libraries and archives. He may be biased or even disingenuous, but he still shares his culture's view that the past is past and subject to record. If he is a monotheist, he also holds that the world had a beginning in time (Creation) and would have an End. The storyteller in a non-literate and non-monotheist context generally holds an altogether more continuous view of time, and his project is not so much one of recording or transmitting as it is re-inventing. In fact, in the absence of written narrative, established techniques of memorization or professional 'remembrancers' (all of which were apparently lacking in the pre-Islamic Hijaz), the past, by its very definition, is plastic. Whereas written history *can* be made to conform closely to the imperative of the present, oral history *always* conforms to it. Tradition transmitted orally tends in particular towards an hourglass shape, with 'memories' clustering around formative (and frequently legendary) origins and more recent generations (usually fathers and grandfathers). It is true that oral history can extend back three or four generations with some accuracy, but this seems to be the exception rather than the rule, and even in those exceptional cases, what is remembered is generally what is socially significant. What is more, a relatively accurate oral history is predicated on a more or less stable social system, one that holds to old truths and conventions; in societies undergoing rapid social and political change (such as early Islam), oral history tends to be much less accurate. The material may be authentic, at least in that it represents a genuine attempt to make sense of the world, and as such it may interest anthropologists or anthropologically inclined historians. But in this sense it is much more useful as a barometer of social change – especially how people come to terms with the present by reconceptualizing the past – than as a record of what had actually happened.[9]

We shall see that some large part of understanding early Islamic historiography is coming to grips with how, as a bureaucratic empire emerged, oral traditions were complemented and, to some extent, replaced by written history. The transformation of story to history is conditioned not only by bureaucratic habits of record keeping, however. Religious attitudes play a role as well. We can see this most clearly if we briefly compare early Christianity with earliest Islam. The first Christians seem to have been principally interested in Christ's resurrection and its meaning for them, the defining moment in his life being his death. Their belief in his resurrection, rather than their knowledge of his birth or miracles, was what most clearly distinguished Christians from their contemporaries. For their part, it seems that earliest Muslims were principally interested in Muḥammad's charismatic career as God's prophet, the defining moment in his life being his call to prophethood, which is usually said to have occurred when he was 40 years of age. Belief in Muḥammad's prophecy, rather than knowledge of his childhood or career as a merchant, was what distinguished Muslims from other monotheists. And since these were the issues that defined them, they were what earliest Christians and Muslims talked about and passed on. Being central to their identity as Christians and Muslims, they were what they chose to remember.

In both cases, however, believers came up against doubters and sceptics who challenged their views, who demanded to know more about Jesus or Muḥammad: What were their credentials? How do we know that theirs was God's work? Believers also squabbled amongst themselves and challenged each other with all manner of questions. The questions had to be answered, and so they were. Drawing away from a past they actually remembered (the passing of time gave them more freedom to recreate one), and having entered a market of competing ideas and polemics, early Christians and early Muslims eventually came to tell the *whole* story. What they could not remember they duly provided in the form of legends, myths, conjectures and reasonable guesses, all about things that they had had no real memory of, since they had not really mattered before. This explains why Gospel accounts of Jesus' birth, which were first set down in writing about two generations after his death, are so much less reliable as history than accounts of his Passion; while Mark and Acts reflect earlier views and say nothing of Jesus' birth,

[9] Although a great deal has been written about orality, the dearth of contemporaneous evidence makes it hard to know where Hijazi orality stands vis-à-vis other traditions; for a very useful discussion of the African evidence, J.A.S. Evans, *Herodotus, Explorer of the Past: Three Essays* (Princeton, 1981), p. 120 (the Bobangi of Zaire may be the closest parallel); for an argument for an exceptionally long-lived tradition, J. Fadiman, *When We Began There Were Witchmen: An Oral History from Mount Kenya* (Berkeley, 1993) (from the late eighteenth century to the late twentieth); cf. J.K. Davies, 'The reliability of the oral tradition', in L. Foxhall and J.K. Davies, eds., *The Trojan War: Its Historicity and Context* (Bristol, 1984), pp. 87–110; and O. Murray, 'Herodotus and oral history' in H. Sancisi-Weerdenburg and A. Kuhrt, eds., *Achaemenid History II: The Greek Sources* (Leiden, 1997), pp. 93–115; T. Spear, 'Oral traditions: whose history?', *History in Africa* 8 (1981), pp. 165–181.

Matthew and Luke do, because these two later writers saw in it an opportunity to grind theological axes. This is also why Muslim historians began to fill in the details of Muḥammad's pre-prophetic career, proposing a number of inconsistent solutions to a variety of academic questions. In what kind of caravan trade were the Quraysh involved on the eve of Islam? Where and when did these caravans travel? How old, *exactly*, was Muḥammad at the time of his father's death? Unconstrained by actual memory, our sources provide a wide variety of answers to questions such as these (he was still *in utero*; he was six months old; he was eighteen months old). The answers were given because belief now required them. Much like '... the abiding empowerment of the Spirit [that] gave the transmitters of the Jesus tradition a creative freedom', so too were Muslim historians empowered by the spectacular successes of the early community – surely God's proof that the community was acting according to His will – to provide sensible and reasonable answers to questions put by themselves, and others, to their past.[10]

Now by the standards of most historians, this is making things up. In my capacity as historian, I cannot invent a story about the past, even if in good faith I believe it to be true and could claim that it enjoys verisimilitude – that is, that it could very well be true. Nowadays historians who do that are discredited. But there was nothing cynical in a project that generated new biographical 'data' by Christian and Muslim writers. This was because they held to a view of history that differs from ours. As we shall see in chapters 5, 6 and 7, for most Christian and Muslim historians, the purpose of history was generally not to test, probe or explain, nor to provide an accounting for all events that corresponded precisely with what had once happened. On occasion it *could* be some of these, but it was usually many other things, the most common being to teach and inspire by illustrating and exemplifying. For us, then, the significance of these biographical details about Jesus and Muḥammad is not that they provide evidence with which we can more fully reconstruct their lives, but that they reflect a shift in thinking about the past. In other words, they constitute evidence for the history of ideas rather than the history of two people. Details from the pre-prophetic phase of Muḥammad's life began to concern eighth- and ninth-century historians or biographers, who, for whatever reason (curiosity, faith, compulsion, ambition, a patron's commission), tried to reconstruct events to which the earliest Muslims had attached little or no significance, and, therefore, had not chosen to make a part of their oral history. Academic questions such as these, turning as they frequently do on questions of dating, thus signal the transition from tradition to historiography.

[10] For the Gospels and history, I draw on R.E. Brown, *The Birth of the Messiah: A Commentary on the Infancy Narratives in the Gospels of Matthew and Luke* (New York, 1993, updated ed.); for a related controversy about Muḥammad's birth, see M. Lecker, 'The death of the Prophet Muḥammad's father: did Wāqidī invent some of the evidence?', *ZDMG* 145 (1995), pp. 9–27; for an overview of the problems, F.E. Peters, 'The quest for the historical Muhammad', *IJMES* 23 (1991), pp. 291–315, which is reprinted in Ibn Warraq, ed., *The Quest for the Historical Muhammad* (Amherst, New York, 2000), pp. 444–475; the quotation is from J.D. Crossan, *Jesus: A Revolutionary Biography* (San Francisco, 1994), p. xiii.

The distinction between tradition and history is an important one, but it should not be pushed too far. As far as source material is concerned, written history itself need not be based exclusively or even mostly on written materials, be they narratives, documents or records. No less an authority than Herodotus '... managed to produce a very respectable history mainly on the basis of sightseeing and oral history'. In fact, techniques of storytelling are frequently put to use in narrative history, and they may even have had a role in its origins; this, as we shall see, seems to have been true of the Islamic historiographic tradition. As far as perspective is concerned, history can also reflect biases and prejudices, for it, too, can have clear social and political functions: it can instruct, moralize, edify, enthuse and entertain a reader or an audience, and can legitimize and criticize a social order, a ruler or a state. For much of their history, American historians have written less out of any objective disinterest in things past than out of a keen interest in helping forge a national identity, and this seems to have been true not only of their own history, but even of that of the Middle Ages. Even for professional historians, objectivity is only an aspiration, and there are as many examples of bias as there are historians.[11]

If written history shares features with oral tradition, it is still much less pliable than oral tradition, which generally drops out of circulation as soon as it loses its relevance. Revisions to history can certainly be made, and new versions can eclipse old ones, but history is only rarely obliterated. In part this is because stone, clay tablets, papyrus, animal skins, paper and other writing materials outlive human memories, but in equal part because it has its guardians – historians – in whose hands material is constantly recycled for later generations. This book is a case in point: some of what you are reading is drawn from the work of modern historians, but much of it comes from the original sources themselves, and in this way, historical ideas first conceived in the eighth century will survive into the twenty-first. By contrast, we can only know the stories that eighth-century Muslims *told* each other if historians happened to record them in writing.

Composing and collecting

The rise of the historiographic tradition is thus related to the rise of Islam. In the short space of two long generations – the blink of an eye in the slow-moving world of ancient empires and tightly held traditions – the political and religious landscape of the Mediterranean world was redrawn by Arab Muslims, who were responding to what God had ordered them to do. What God had in mind was frequently a

[11] The quotation is from A. Momigliano, 'The place of Herodotus in the history of historiography', in his *Studies in Historiography* (New York and Evanston, 1966), p. 129; on 'Herodotus as field-worker', see Evans, *Herodotus*, pp. 132ff.; on American historians, P. Novick, *That Noble Dream: The 'Objectivity Question' and the American Historical Profession* (Cambridge, 1988); on some recent historiography on the Middle Ages, P. Freedman and G.M. Spiegel, 'Medievalisms old and new: the rediscovery of alterity in North American medieval studies', *AHR* 103 (1998), pp. 677–704.

matter of some disagreement for Muslims, but on one question there came to be a consensus: to 'fight in the way of God' (Qur'ān 19:9 among many other verses) meant spreading monotheism so as to ensure that polytheists converted to Islam and that non-Muslim monotheists, who were permitted to retain their faith, acknowledged the sovereignty of God, represented as He was by the caliphs: early Muslims were less religious missionaries than they were religiously motivated imperialists. From the perspective of Muslim Arabs, then, God was delivering them from the 'ignorance' of pre-Islamic Arabia (the *Jāhiliyya*), and installing them as rulers of most of the known world: between *ca.* 645 and 715 Islamic rule was established in a great swathe of lands that stretches from present-day Mauritania and Spain to the borders of India. Christians and Jews, by contrast, now belonged to obsolete faiths, and although their religious practices were tolerated (and occasionally even encouraged), their exercise of any political authority was unthinkable, since it would have perverted God's will.

Arabs thus moved from the religious and political margins of the Mediterranean world to its centre stage, having become nothing less than instruments of God's plan. This can account for one of the most striking aspects of post-conquest history: the confidence with which the conquerors responded to the cultural challenges posed by those politically subordinated by their rule. For compared to their prosperous, cultured and cosmopolitan neighbours in Byzantium and Sasanian Persia, the conquering Arabs were barbarians, just as Germanic tribesmen had been barbaric compared to the Roman societies they had overrun two centuries earlier. Their political role had been marginal in a region dominated by two superpowers, and they possessed no learning to speak of; if they claimed anything, it was only fearlessness, reckless abandon, and 'obstinate impetuosity', which is as good a translation for 'Jāhiliyya' as any. Unlike the Germanic tribesmen, however, they also possessed religious certainty: God had chosen to speak to one of their own, to do so in their language, and to remain silent thereafter, delegating His authority first to Muḥammad (as His last prophet) and then to His deputies (the caliphs). Possessing both political dominion *and* a cultural confidence born of religious certainty, Muslim Arabs could resist involuntary assimilation into the sophisticated cultural traditions of the Near East, which is generally the fate of barbarian conquerors, such as the contemporaneous Lombards in Italy, or, much later, the Mongols in Iran and Iraq.[12]

So while thirteenth- and fourteenth-century Mongols would quickly adopt the values of the Persian/Islamic culture they had overrun, seventh- and eighth-century Arabs could pick and choose what was on offer, championing what they liked and found useful, and rejecting what they disliked and found useless. From outside of their tradition, they chose the great bulk of classical learning made available through translations from Greek, Syriac (a dialect of Aramaic) and Persian, commissioning works on philosophy, natural science, medicine, mathematics and a

[12] I borrow 'obstinate impetuosity' from S.P. Stetkevych, *The Mute Immortals Speak: Pre-Islamic Poetry and the Poetics of Ritual* (Ithaca and London, 1993), p. 206.

great deal more besides. (Ibn al-Nadīm's catalogue of books and authors bears witness to this explosion in learning.) Much of the practical knowledge was retained, while much of the metaphysics and rationalism was not, since it would eventually prove incompatible with the law and theology that they worked out during the ninth and tenth centuries. From within their own cultural heritage, they championed what made them distinctive within the lettered and monotheist Near East – that is, their orality and language in general, and their storytelling and poetry in particular. During the eighth and ninth centuries Arabic grammar was systematized, Arabic poetry was collected and presented as the pre-Islamic Arabs' greatest cultural achievement, and the Fertile Crescent became increasingly Arabicized.[13]

Command of the Arabic language thus became the *sine qua non* for anyone with aspirations for work in the imperial administration or learning, and its narrative forms were imprinted by what might be called a storytelling rhetoric of orality. In this way, Muslim Arabs did far more than merely supplement the pre-existing cultural traditions of the Near East with Arabic and Islamic learning. They did something altogether more inventive, elevating what is generally on the 'low' or 'popular' register of culture onto the 'high' or 'élite' register of culture. The continuing social significance of orality in the midst of an increasingly lettered and bureaucratic empire is reflected in a number of practices and institutions. These include the *quṣṣāṣ*, 'storytellers', whose work is sanctioned by the Qurʾān, and who held great appeal to urban populations. It is also reflected in the attitudes of many of those who transmitted Prophetic traditions (that is, the traditionists, who are explained more fully in chapter 5), who were loath to permit the writing down of these traditions, arguing that they should be retained in one's head rather than in one's notebook. The survival of orality is also reflected in the continuing preference amongst the lawyers for oral, as opposed to written, testimony (spoken oaths are a prominent feature of the political and social history of Islam).[14]

Of particular importance in understanding the rise of the historiographic tradition is the strikingly *anecdotal* character of Arabic written narrative (both fact and fiction). The crucial Arabic terms are *ḥadīth* and *khabar* (pl. *akhbār*). Both words relate to verbs that express the idea of 'informing', 'reporting', or 'recounting' – that is, telling a story or making a point. Sometimes they are used interchangeably, but whereas the term *ḥadīth* is generally used only in the context of the Prophet's words or actions, *khabar* is used more generically to refer to virtually any kind of account. A *khabar* or a *ḥadīth* is thus a report of some kind or another, and although it can be as short as a line or as long as tens of pages (the latter being extremely rare), it always has a name-tag (figuratively) tied to its beginning; this tag is called

[13] For an overview of the transmission of Greek learning, see F. Rosenthal, *The Classical Heritage in Islam* (Berkeley and Los Angeles, 1975) and D. Gutas, *Greek Thought, Arabic Culture* (London, 1998).

[14] For the storytellers, see K. Athamina, 'al-Qasas: its emergence, religious origin and its socio-political impact on early Muslim society' *SI* 76 (1992), pp. 53–74; and C. Pellat, *Le milieu basrien et la formation de Ǧāḥiẓ* (Paris, 1953), pp. 108ff.

the *isnād*. If the report is a *ḥadīth* from the classical period – that is, from the late ninth century onwards – this *isnād* bears a series of names, which starts with the book's compiler, descends through generations of transmitters, and usually ends with a witness: 'so-and-so told me, on the authority of so-and-so, who said: so-and-so told me, on the authority of so-and-so, who said: I was with the Prophet of God one day, and he said: "Seek knowledge, even as far as in China."' If the report is a *khabar*, the *isnād* may be just as complete, but not necessarily so, since it may include only the name of one of the transmitters, omitting the witness and/or any intervening informants. Thus one might find a *khabar* preceded by the following *isnād*: 'According to Sayf b. ᶜUmar (d. 796), the caliph ᶜUmar ordered Khālid b. al-Walīd [a commander of conquest armies] to Syria'. Here Sayf b. ᶜUmar is an authoritative transmitter, but there is no mention of either witness or intervening names, so the *isnād* is only partial.[15]

The difference between full and partial (or even missing) *isnād*s was held to be crucial by the 'people of *ḥadīth*' (*ahl al-ḥadīth*) who thought very little of how the *akhbārī*s worked. And although the distinction between a *ḥadīth* and a *khabar* was underlined in other ways, there is little to tell them apart in narrative terms: a witness or storyteller recounts an event (or chain of events), and this recounting is transmitted serially and orally (or aurally, when a written account is read or recited to listeners or copyists), eventually finding its place in a written collection. Indeed, *ḥadīth* and *akhbār* works are cut from the same cloth, since they are equally conceived as *collections* or *compilations* of self-contained and independent stories, which are attributed to earlier authorities. It is therefore difficult to speak of 'authorship' for these works, at least in terms familiar to western readers. Classical historians writing in Greek and Latin generally took pains to write in an attractive style, and their work was judged as much for its beauty as for its truthfulness. By contrast, early Muslim historians, following the lead of the jurists, were generally concerned less with composing attractive narrative than they were with collecting assiduously and judiciously, with choosing what to include and in what order to include it. Thus it was the judicious collection – consisting in accounts transmitted on the authority of truthful men and women of an earlier age – that could make the best claim to the truth. From the *ḥadīth* literature, an example is the *Ṣaḥīḥ* of al-Bukhārī (d. 870), who selected the book's 2762 traditions from the 600,000 he says were available to him. From the *akhbār* literature, an example is the *Akhbār al-muwaffaqiyyāt* assembled by his exact contemporary al-Zubayr b. Bakkār (d. 870), which includes 429 *akhbār* (I include here some poetry) from an unknowable number of stories available to him.

In light of these broad similarities, what distinguishes *ḥadīth*s from *khabar*s? Principally, their subject matter. The 'people of *ḥadīth*' were concerned principally with the law, and they collected reports about what the Prophet did or said because nearly everything he did or said could function as legal precedent. Al-Bukhārī, one

[15] For *akhbār* in the sense of *ḥadīth*, see G.H.A. Juynboll, 'Muslim's introduction to his *Ṣaḥīḥ* translated and annotated with an excursus on the chronology of *fitna* and *bidᶜa*', *JSAI* 5 (1984), p. 265.

of the most celebrated of the early *ḥadīth* collectors, adduces the Prophet on a wide number of issues, from marriage, prayer, and fasting to prosecuting holy war and levying taxes; in time, his work would emerge as one of the six most authoritative collections of *ḥadīth*. The interests of those who collected and transmitted *akhbār* were considerably broader and, in the view of the jurists, considerably less weighty. They collected a greater diversity of material (principally stories, but also *bons mots*, aphorisms, lines of poetry) for a variety of reasons: to entertain, amuse, edify, educate, and moralize. Of al-Zubayr b. Bakkār's 429 *akhbār*, we have a fair amount of poetry, but most are stories ranging from the sober ('the sermon delivered by [the first caliph] Abū Bakr after he received the oath of allegiance' [#379] and 'a Christian provides accounts to the caliphs' [#209]) to the curious ('[the sixth caliph] Yazīd b. Muᶜāwiya makes a boon-companion of a monkey' [#200]). The order of these *akhbār* is neither chronological (as it would be in a work of history) nor topical (as it would be in most works of law). Indeed, there is no discernible pattern at all, and this is probably because the social context of the book's composition, unlike that of a *ḥadīth* collection that had to be usable by jurists, did not impose one: stories, told in 'sittings' (*majālis*, after which many *akhbār* works took their names), can be told in just about any order. As one of the tenth century's most celebrated literary compilers (al-Tanūkhī) put it, 'What I have written down comes from what I memorized long ago, mixed with what I have recently heard, without my categorizing it or putting it into ordered sections, because the work's accounts (*akhbār*) can be told in a variety of settings'.[16]

But history cannot, and those collectors of *akhbār* who focused their attention principally (but not exclusively) on past events and ordered them according to an implicit or explicit chronology tended to be called *akhbārī*s and, less frequently, *muʾarrikhūn*. We call them historians and their work historiography.

[16] For an overview of traditions (including al-Bukhārī's), see A. Guillaume, *The Traditions of Islam* (Oxford, 1924; reprinted, Beirut, 1966); and for al-Zubayr, his *Akhbār al-muwaffaqiyyāt* (Baghdad, 1972), and Ibn al-Nadīm, *Fihrist*, pp. 123f. (Dodge, *Fihrist*, pp. 242f.); a typical example of a *majlis* work is Thaᶜlab's *Majālis* (Cairo, 1960); for al-Tanūkhī, his *Nishwār al-muḥāḍara* (Beirut, 1973), i, p. 12 [reading *makān*]; for a translation, D.S. Margoliouth, *The Table-talk of a Mesopotamian Judge* (London, 1922), p. 9.

CHAPTER 2

The emergence of genre

To recapitulate what has been said so far and, in smaller measure, to anticipate what shall follow: the Islamic conquests of the early seventh century ushered in a quite exceptional period of cultural synthesis and experimentation, which was facilitated by Umayyad and Abbasid states that generally tolerated and frequently sponsored non-Muslim and Muslim exchange; in the course of this synthesis, Arabic established itself as the administrative and literary *lingua franca* of what was slowly becoming the Islamic Near East, and forms of Arabic orality (poetry and storytelling) were given literary forms. As far as prose is concerned, by the end of the ninth century the narrative form that had become normative at the micro-level was the self-contained unit (the single *khabar* or *ḥadīth*), attributed (with variable precision) to either a witness of the event or an authoritative collector. At the macro-level, it had become collections of these *akhbār* and *ḥadīth*, selected and assembled by collector-authors, who aspired to being authoritative rather than original, and whose reputations rested on the quality and quantity of their selection.

So most historians would come to follow the model engineered by 'the people of *ḥadīth*': the ideal that triumphed during the ninth century was the ideal of collection rather than composition, and virtually all of the earliest surviving works conform to this description. Two things need to be said about the emerging pattern. The first is that the material available for collection in both *ḥadīth* and *khabar* works being finite and increasingly remote in time, the result was collections that are relatively homogeneous, both in style and in content. This, combined with a widespread enthusiasm for a handful of themes drawn from early history – especially conquest and civil war – means that reading the histories of the early caliphate gives rise to a chronic sense of *déjà vu*: different books often cover the same ground. The second thing that should be said about the pattern – and this point will be made several times during the course of the book – is that it over-simplifies. Not all historians of this early period aimed to compile comprehensive works, and even those historians who worked in this 'collecting mode' were nonetheless keen to relate their stories effectively. Some recent scholarship has shown just how difficult it is to distinguish between fictional and non-fictional styles of storytelling, and, contrary to the conventional wisdom, our historians were not only transmitting and reordering, but recasting – indeed, even inventing. About these and related issues more shall be said later.

To see in some detail how the historiographic tradition arose, we need to cover this ground more carefully. One of our maps is none other than Ibn al-Nadīm's *Fihrist*. By his day, collectors of *akhbār* and *ḥadīth* had been busy for over 200 years, and a vigorous culture of learning and writing had generated a variety of literary forms. Ibn al-Nadīm's Baghdad had shop after shop stocked with this learning and writing, the great bulk of which has long since been lost (that is, destroyed, mislaid or ignored) or mined by subsequent compilers. What the *Fihrist* offers us is thus a snapshot of Islamic learning as it passed from its formative to classical phases, an invaluable tool for documenting a world of learning that was already disappearing in his day, and which is nearly impossible to reconstruct a millennium later. In what follows I propose that the nascent historiographic tradition passed through three phases, each of which I shall take in turn.

But a warning is in order. Since we have so little historiography that can be securely dated to our earliest periods, the reconstruction that follows is necessarily inferential. (Professional Islamicists are used to this kind of hedging, but it should be striking to everyone else.) The scale of our problem can be made clear by comparing things a bit closer to home. The Venerable Bede (d. 735) finished his *Ecclesiastical History of the English People* in a Northumbrian monastery in the year 731. Were it not for this book, we would know almost nothing of eighth-century England, not to mention Ireland and Wales; more precisely, we would be put at the mercy of the material evidence of the time, there being almost no contemporary historical evidence otherwise. What is remarkable about the work is not simply its high quality – the author's vision and acute observations. It is that its quality was recognized so soon after its composition that great care was taken to preserve it. This (alongside a Carolingian 'renaissance') explains a generous tradition of manuscripts, in which figure two very early (late eighth-century) and very accurate copies that may have even been written by two of the author's students. 'Bede's reader', according to the most recent editors, 'has little more need to trouble himself with the details of textual criticism than the reader of Gibbon or Macaulay'. Now at roughly the same time, figures such as ᶜUrwa b. al-Zubayr, al-Zuhrī, Mūsā b. ᶜUqba and Maᶜmar b. Rāshid (the list could be extended), were all assembling biographical material on the Prophet. Meanwhile, others were starting to work out caliphal and annalistic history, filling long pages with accounts of conquest, civil war, and the Abbasid Revolution, and still others would soon turn their attention to arranging material in the *ṭabaqāt* genre. To judge by the surviving quotations alone, their work must have exceeded Bede's output by several factors. But whereas we possess Bede's book in something very much like the form in which Bede himself left it, these quotations *are* all we have, the 'originals' (such as they were) having been lost, with no manuscript evidence, be it early or late, accurate or inaccurate, to work with. Old Arabic manuscripts are occasionally discovered, and the occasional fragment can come to light, but we do not possess anything like the spread of evidence required to see how Islamic historiography formed in the seventh and eighth centuries.[1]

For these and other reasons, the reader is encouraged to compare the following reconstruction of early Islamic historiography with others.[2]

Phase I: *ca.* 610 to *ca.* 730

During this first period, which began with Muḥammad's first revelations and ended in *ca.* 730, the prevalence of orality, so characteristic of the pre-Islamic Hijaz, continued. Those who knew the Prophet would tell stories about him and their experiences alongside him; veterans of conquest battles described their (nearly always glorious) campaigns; successive generations of families would tell family histories. Such, in any case, is what we infer from our later sources, and if the impression is one of continuity, there are elements of some important change at work too. For the stakes were now much higher than they had been in the Hijaz: the state's apologists and critics narrated contrasting accounts of civil wars and rebellions, and professional (that is, paid) storytellers entered into the mix, drawing on the past to criticize those responsible for the present. Just as important, a documentary culture also began to emerge, and there is therefore some reason to think that oral history enjoyed something less than a complete monopoly on the past.[3]

The emerging culture of documentation was triggered principally by state functions (e.g., levying taxes, paying the army, building public works), which grew in complexity during the seventh and eighth centuries, particularly after the Marwānid

[1] For Bede, see *Bede's Ecclesiastical History of the English People*, ed. and trans. B. Colgrave and R.A.B. Mynors (Oxford, 1991, reprint), p. xxxix; and, more generally, G.H. Brown, *Bede the Venerable* (Boston, 1987); information about these and other *sīra* authorities can be found in *EI*^{2}, 'Sīra' (Raven), and M. Kister, 'Sīra', in L.I. Conrad, ed., *History and Historiography in Early Islamic Times: Studies and Perspectives* (Princeton, forthcoming); for an overview of eighth- and ninth-century manuscripts, F. Déroche, 'Les manuscrits arabes datés du iiie/ixe siècle', *REI* 55–57 (1987–9), pp. 343–379; for some early Arabic (legal) manuscripts that have recently come to light, M. Muranyi, *Beiträge zur Geschichte der Ḥadīṯ- und Rechtsgelehrsamkeit der Mālikiyya in Nordafrika bis zum 5. Jh. d.H.* (Wiesbaden, 1997), and idem, *Die Rechtsbücher des Qairawāners Saḥnūn b. Saᶜīd: Entstehungsgeschichte und Werküberlieferung* (Stuttgart, 1999) (which has important things to say about the transmission of legal material in the ninth century); an important *sīra* fragment comes in a papyrus edited by R.G. Khouri as *Wahb b. Munabbih: der Heidelberger Papyrus PSR Heid Arab 23* (Wiesbaden, 1972).

[2] Chief among these are F.M. Donner, *Narratives of Islamic Origins: The Beginnings of Islamic Historical Writing* (Princeton, 1998); E.L. Petersen, *ᶜAlī and Muᶜāwiya in Early Arabic Tradition: Studies on the Genesis and Growth of Islamic Historical Writing until the End of the Ninth Century* (Copenhagen, 1964); A.A. Duri, *The Rise of Historical Writing Among the Arabs*, ed. and trans. by L.I. Conrad (Princeton, 1983; 2nd ed. Odense, 1974); A. Noth, in collaboration with L.I. Conrad (hereafter, Noth/Conrad), *The Early Arabic Historical Tradition*, tr. M. Bonner (Princeton, 1994); and R.S. Humphreys, *Islamic History: A Framework for Inquiry* (Princeton, rev. ed., 1991), pp. 69ff.

[3] Readers who open the 547-page *Arabic Literature to the End of the Umayyad Period* (Cambridge, 1983; Cambridge History of Arabic Literature), ed. A.F.L. Beeston et al., might expect to find a more generous appraisal of written culture in this period, but the tone is set already on pp. 3f., where Beeston speaks of a 'thin trickle of non-inscriptional documents'; there too, Abbasid patronage is considered crucial to literary production.

branch of the Umayyad dynasty took power in the 680s. They are most clearly documented in surviving papyri (in Egypt and, in much smaller numbers, Palestine), coins (copper, silver and gold) and, to a much smaller degree, in inscriptions (the earliest dated road sign that survives was erected in 73/692); there is even some graffiti. Since a great deal of this documentation carried dates, the emerging bureaucracy had the two-fold effect of encouraging literacy and chronological consciousness amongst its Arab élite. It hardly needs pointing out that none of these practices is unique to the early Islamic empire. States generally have an interest in ensuring the predictable and regular discharge of their functions, and this is why they employ bureaucrats to establish, document and even broadcast dates and schedules: in the U.S., Thanksgiving floats around on a Thursday towards the end of November, but almost everyone knows that taxes are *always* due on April 15. Nor should one think that pre-moderns were as chronologically aware as are moderns, surrounded as we are by clocks, schedules, timetables, diaries, and calendars; even a sophisticated chronographer, such as Ibn al-Jawzī (d. 1201), could only approximate the year in which he was born.[4]

What is striking about the early Islamic case is how quickly dating caught on. Some thought was apparently given to a calendar that would start at the Prophet's death in 632, but early Muslims came to agree that it should start with the Hijra, the Prophet's emigration from Mecca to Medina, with the result that year 1 of the Hijra (1 A.H.) corresponds to 622 C.E./A.D.; this would be a lunar calendar, unlike our solar calendar. The choice made sense: as one historian put it, 'Muḥammad's emigration is the divide between truth and falsehood'. Ibn al-Athīr (d. 1233) patiently tells his readers that although some scholars give credit for this calendar to Muḥammad himself, the idea actually belongs to the caliph ᶜUmar (rg. 634–644). Now it is true that the new dating system did not immediately catch on in all media; some early Islamic poetry, for example, seems to preserve a pre-Islamic system. But poetry is notoriously conservative, and there can be no doubt about what system the state was pushing: Hijri dating is attested on a papyrus as early as 22/642, and a generation later on gold and silver (and, more rarely, copper) coins, in addition to a number of inscriptions. Already by the end of the seventh century, Hijri years are cited in Syriac historical works, which were written by Christians living under Islamic rule. The relatively early adoption of Hijri dating may help to explain why seventh-century events are dated with some accuracy by ninth- and tenth-century sources, at least starting in the conquest period (Prophetic history, it

[4] In connecting literacy to administration, 'rather than any abstract desire for education or literature', I follow a broad consensus, exemplified by M.T. Clanchy, *From Memory to Written Record: England 1066–1307* (Oxford, 2nd ed., 1993) (the quotation is from p. 19); for evidence for the growth of the state, F.M. Donner, 'The formation of the Islamic state', *JAOS* 56 (1986), pp. 283–296, his *Narratives of Islamic Origins*, pp. 85ff., and now E. Landau-Tasseron, 'From tribal society to centralized polity: an interpretation of events and anecdotes of the formative period of Islam', *JSAI* 24 (2000), pp. 180–216; for the road sign, the *Corpus Inscriptionum Arabicorum Palestiniae*, vol. 1, ed. M. Sharon (Leiden, 1997), pp. 103ff., and cf. also A. Elad, 'The Southern Golan in the early Muslim period: the significance of two newly discovered milestones of ᶜAbd al-Malik', *DI* 76 (1999), pp. 33–88; for Ibn al-Jawzī, Sibṭ Ibn al-Jawzī, *Mirʾāt al-zamān fī taʾrīkh al-aᶜyān*, viii[2] (Hyderabad, 1952), p. 483.

seems, is more of a problem, since we lack much external control). Our relatively late historians disagree about a variety of things, but their post-Prophetic chronologies are only rarely in dramatic conflict, and they frequently show a real command of death dates. That the break between the Jāhilī and Islamic epochs had already been clearly marked by Hijra dating probably saved later Muslim historians a great deal of work.[5]

Alongside documents produced mainly by and for the nascent tax administration, much of which was staffed by non-Arabs, documentary material of other sorts (e.g. treaties, letters, addresses, sermons) was produced and, to judge by the literature of the ninth and tenth centuries, very occasionally preserved. The most spectacular example is a set of documents drawn up by Muḥammad himself in Medina, which, as transmitted in a number of histories, scholars have misleadingly come to call the 'Constitution of Medina'. Establishing the authenticity of other documents attributed to Muḥammad and the early caliphs has proved much more difficult, and it seems that nearly all have been modified in one way or another, usually edited and touched up to conform to values and conventions of subsequent periods. Letters ascribed to Muḥammad or the caliph ᶜUmar, for example, often assume a military and administrative framework that was only constructed generations later: they more comfortably fit the middle of the eighth century than they do the early seventh. Indeed, we should expect a great deal of editing and redrafting, since many of these were 'living' documents in the sense that they were adduced in political and fiscal disputes (e.g., between taxpayers and tax agents, Muslims and non-Muslims), there being as yet no institutions, such as an archive, that were designed to preserve originals or copies. And about this too there should be little surprise: early documentary material was not archived – that is, duplicates were not made for the purpose of storage – because archival attitudes follow, rather than precede, the mass production of documents. (I leave for later the question of the relative paucity of archives from the pre-Ottoman period.) Aside from exceptional and serendipitous cases, which include the transmission of documentary material by littérateurs usually interested in its style, we must assume that such early documents as survive in the literature of later periods were reworked during their transmission. Put another way, these documents are spurious in that they misrepresent such originals

[5] For Ibn al-Athīr, see his *al-Kāmil fī al-taʾrīkh* (Beirut, 1965), i, p. 10; according to some sources (e.g. al-Suyūṭī's *al-Shamārīkh fī ᶜilm al-taʾrīkh* [Leiden, 1894], pp. 5f.), the caliph ᶜUmar established dating practices after hearing of Yemeni dating traditions, which is unlikely to be true; for one example of conflicting Prophetic chronology, P. Crone, *Meccan Trade and the Rise of Islam* (Princeton, 1987), pp. 224ff.; for poetry ascribed to two early Muslim poets, in which months are proverbially tied to seasons, C.J. Lyall, ed., *The Mufaḍḍalīyāt: An Anthology of Ancient Arabian Odes* (Oxford, 1921–1924), p. 287 (text)/p. 96 (translation) and pp. 332/119f.; the latter is said to belong to Jubayhā (or Jabhā) al-Ashjaᶜī, who, as a contemporary of al-Farazdaq (al-Iṣfahānī, *Kitāb al-Aghānī* [Cairo, 1927–1974], xviii, p. 94), belongs to the late seventh or early eighth century; on chronologies, Donner, *Narratives of Islamic Origins*, pp. 230ff.; for the hard work that Greek historians had to do in order to distinguish the 'Heroic Age' from that of history proper, C.W. Fornara, *The Nature of History in Ancient Greece and Rome* (Berkeley and Los Angeles, 1988), p. 7.

as there were, but they are authentic representations of the (changing) social values that conditioned this process of reworking.[6]

The same thing is presumably true of the name lists that seem to have appeared towards the end of this first phase, and which probably reflect the emerging culture of writing; we have the case of centenarian Shuraḥbīl b. Saᶜd (d. 740), who was accused of fudging his lists in return for payment. With lists circulating such as 'Those Who Fought *alongside* Muḥammad at the Battle of Badr' (the Muslims' signal victory over the Meccans in 624) and 'Those Who Fought *against* Muḥammad at the Battle of Badr' (emphasis added), it is not difficult to see why one might pay to have a grandfather's name removed from one and added to another, particularly since caliphs were known to have inquired about battles such as this. Shuraḥbīl's list happens to appear in the standard biography of the Prophet, and could well have been produced quite early on. Others, which covered a variety of fields (e.g. Companions of the Prophet [usually adult contemporaries], traditionists, judges, and governors) appear in many sources, and probably belong to a secondary period. Thanks to the survival of two Syriac lists of caliphs, one of which is almost certainly based on an Arabic prototype, there is good reason to infer the early eighth-century existence of name lists of caliphs *in the order of their reigns*. If so, lists of caliphs and governors may have functioned as the sequential scaffolding upon which historians of the later eighth and ninth century erected their dynastic chronographies.[7]

So sequential lists may have had a hand in sparking the chronographic tradition, but beyond this, little can be said with much confidence; here it is worth repeating that the rise of historiographic forms is very difficult to reconstruct, since virtually nothing survives from the formative period. Now the literature of the ninth and tenth centuries does frequently ascribe written material (including titles of historical works) to a number of figures in seventh- and early eighth-century caliphal courts, perhaps the best example being ᶜUrwa b. al-Zubayr (d. 712). ᶜUrwa, we

[6] On the 'Constitution of Medina', see R.B. Serjeant, 'The "Constitution of Medina"', *IQ* 8 (1964), pp. 3–16, and Humphreys, *Islamic History*, pp. 92ff.; on documents in the *sīra*, R. Sellheim, 'Prophet, Chalif und Geschichte: die Muhammed-Biographie des Ibn Isḥāq', *Oriens* 18–19 (1967), pp. 46ff. and 73ff. (where they are generally regarded as authentic); cf. Noth/Conrad, *Early Arabic Historical Tradition*, pp. 62ff. (where conquest-era documents are generally regarded as inauthentic).

[7] For Shuraḥbīl, see J. Horovitz, 'The earliest biographies of the Prophet and their authors', *IC* 1 (1927), pp. 552f.; there is some counter evidence, but I follow J. Goody (*The Domestication of the Savage Mind* [Cambridge, 1977]), in seeing listing as a product of literacy; cf. D. Henige, *The Chronology of Oral Tradition* (Oxford, 1974), and Evans, *Herodotus*, pp. 98f.; for Marwān b. Ḥakam's interest in the battle of Badr ('Relate to me the story of Badr!' [*ḥaddithnī ḥadīth Badr*]), al-Ṭabarī, *Taʾrīkh al-rusul wa'l-mulūk* (Leiden, 1879–1901), i, pp. 1313f., which is translated by M.V. McDonald as *The Foundation of the Community* (Albany, 1987; al-Ṭabarī translation, vol. vii), p. 50; the first to recognize the significance of the Syriac lists seems to have been G. Rotter, 'Abū Zurᶜa al-Dimašqī (st. 281/894) und das Problem der frühen arabischen Geschichtsschreibung in Syrien', *Die Welt des Orients* 6 (1971), p. 91; also P. Crone, *Slaves on Horses: The Evolution of the Islamic Polity* (Cambridge, 1980), pp. 213f., notes 99 and 102; and, for lists in the early Islamic tradition, J. Schacht, 'On Mūsā b. ᶜUqba's «*Kitāb al-maghāzī*»', *Acta Orientalia* 21 (1953), pp. 288–300; Noth/Conrad, *Early Arabic Historical Tradition*, pp. 96ff.; and M. Lecker, *Muslims, Jews and Pagans: Studies on Early Islamic Medina* (Leiden, 1995), pp. 135ff.

read, used to converse about history in the mosques of Mecca and Medina, was expert in the Prophet's biography, and even set down accounts of the Battle of Badr in writing for the caliph ᶜAbd al-Malik b. Marwān (rg. 692–705) in the form of a book – indeed, perhaps even an entire *sīra* (or *maghāzī*). In such passages some scholars have seen the beginning of the historiographic tradition. There are good reasons to be cautious about these reports, however. It is not so much that they are inconsistent about the title in question or the contents of this, or any other very early 'book', since inconsistency is a feature of the early tradition as a whole. It is rather that the ascriptions are uniformly late, that such writing as there was in this very early period could only have been carried out against a fairly fierce polemic against writing itself, and, finally, that we know the conventions of writing and authorship to have been in flux a century later. In the present state of our knowledge, there is no reason to doubt that figures such as ᶜUrwa existed, and that they took some interest in the past, circulating stories and (perhaps) even teaching about it. There is less reason to think they exercised any authority as authors (rather than storytellers), much less as recognizable historians.[8]

Phase II: *ca.* 730 to *ca.* 830

It is during this second period that we can begin to speak of Islamic historiography. By 830, biography, prosopography and chronography had all emerged in forms that would remain recognizable throughout the classical period. Historiography, it seems, is therefore about as old as Islamic learning, by which I mean nothing more than producing and classifying knowledge in written form. Like other branches of knowledge, it exploded as part of the late eighth- and early ninth-century boom of learned culture.

As far as historiography is concerned, the period itself is characterized by a tension between an ever-expanding corpus of *akhbār* material, much of which had apparently been put in writing only recently, and the construction of narrative frameworks engineered to contain and order it. We do not fully understand the connection between the two. How does the setting down in ink of oral history relate to the appearance of chronological schemes? Did our historians draw upon a substantial pre-existing corpus of written material, upon which they imposed

[8] For arguments in favour of ᶜUrwa, see Horovitz, 'Biographies', pp. 542ff.; Duri, *Rise of Historical Writing*, pp. 76ff.; and M. Jarrar, *Die Prophetenbiographie im islamischen Spanien* (Frankfurt am Main, 1989), p. 20 ('That ᶜUrwa b. al-Zubayr wrote a work on "maghāzī" is no longer to be disputed'); for telling arguments against ᶜUrwa, E. Landau-Tasseron, 'On the reconstruction of lost sources', in Conrad, ed., *History and Historiography in Early Islamic Times*; cf. G. Schoeler, *Charakter und Authentie der muslimischen Überlieferung über das Leben Mohammeds* (Berlin, 1996), pp. 19ff. and 28ff.; for the caliph ᶜAbd al-Malik forbidding one of his sons from reading *maghāzī*, I. Goldziher, *Muslim Studies*, trans. by C.R. Barber and S.M. Stern (Chicago, 1966), ii, p. 191; for polemics against writing, M. Cook, 'The opponents of the writing of tradition in early Islam', *Arabica* 44 (1997), pp. 437–530; a great deal of useful material is also collected in M.J. Kister, '*Lā taqraʾū l-qurʾāna ᶜalā l-muṣḥafiyyīn wa-lā taḥmilū l-ᶜilma ᶜani l-ṣaḥafiyyīn*: some notes on the transmission of *ḥadīth*', *JSAI* 22 (1998), pp. 127–162.

chronologies? Or were they in the business of both creating *and* ordering the corpus – that is, generating chronological schemes that demanded material, the great bulk of which remained oral?

The answer, one imagines, is some combination of both. On the one hand, many of the titles that date from this period seem to reflect fairly modest historiographic ambitions. Monographs such as 'The Imposter Musaylima' (a contemporary of Muḥammad's who was branded a pseudo-prophet), 'The Death of al-Ḥusayn' (Muḥammad's revolutionary grandson, d. 680), and 'The Battle of the Camel' (656, between Muḥammad's wife ᶜĀᵓisha and his son-in-law, ᶜAlī), were presumably composed largely for political and sectarian purposes. They clearly signal that literature, in addition to orality, had a role to play in politics. But there is no reason to think that these works, many of which give the impression of being shortish partisan tracts – some perhaps not entirely dissimilar to the revolutionary pamphlets of eighteenth-century Paris or Boston – posed any serious problems of chronology or synchronization. One did not have to be a historian to write one of these. On the other hand, this period also produced someone like al-Zuhrī (d. 742), who appears to have been involved in the large and complicated historiographic enterprise of constructing a biography of the Prophet, and who tells us that he is drawing upon multiple authorities, '… each contributing a part of the story, one remembering more of it than another, and I have put together for you what the people told me'. Here we seem to have a glimpse of how ambitious biography eclipsed oral history: to judge by these accounts and what we presume to have been the scheme of his work, al-Zuhrī was a historian by any fair definition of the term.[9]

But there are at least two complications. First, we have no direct access to what al-Zuhrī himself actually wrote, since this and all other quotations survive only in later sources: none of al-Zuhrī's own 'works' (such as they were) remains. In this case, his words are reported by Ibn Isḥāq (d. 761) in his Prophetic biography, the work here transmitted according to the recension (that is, version) of al-Bakkāᵓī (d. 800), itself abridged and vigorously edited by Ibn Hishām (d. 835)! Some of the material credited to al-Zuhrī may be authentic, but some of it is clearly inauthentic, and the hard job of sorting it all out has only recently begun. Second, here, as almost everywhere else one looks in the early tradition, the convention of oral transmission ('what people told me') may misrepresent the transmission of *written* sources: it may be that al-Zuhrī was working from written material, which was transmitted to him aurally, or some combination of written and oral material. Complications aside, there is no reason to doubt that the earliest historians drew on oral sources in large amounts, particularly since the social value of oral testimony must have been held as high as the volume of written narrative still remained relatively

[9] For examples of these titles, see *GAS*, pp. 257ff., and Donner, *Narratives of Islamic Origins*, pp. 297ff.; on the oral or written sources available to Sayf b. ᶜUmar, M. Hinds, 'Sayf b. ᶜUmar's sources on Arabia', in A.M. Abdalla et al., eds., *Sources for the History of Arabia* (Riyadh, 1979), part ii, pp. 3–16 (reprinted in his *Studies in Early Islamic History*, ed. by J. Bacharach et al. [Princeton, 1996], pp. 143–159); on al-Zuhrī, Schoeler, *Charakter und Authentie*, pp. 32ff. (where the surviving material is said to come from private notes).

low. In fact, a similar combination of collecting oral material and ordering it is attested in Muslim Spain, where historiography seems to have emerged about a century later than it did in the Fertile Crescent. Compared to the prestige form of the classical tradition of Greek and Roman historiography, which put the highest value on oral testimony for contemporary history, the choice made by early Muslim historians to rely on oral testimony for *non-contemporary* history is striking, and points towards the value early Muslims and rabbinical Jews placed on oral transmission. Considering the historiographic resources at their disposal, we might say that they made a virtue out of necessity. (Why contemporary history was little cultivated until a secondary period is a separate question, to which we will turn in chapter 5.)[10]

Whatever the precise connection between orality and writing in this earliest phase, we can be fairly certain about its timing: the tradition arose during a late eighth-century boom in learning. The tradition itself suggests that early Abbasid patronage was a crucial factor in this boom, describing how early caliphs directed that Greek and Persian sources be translated into Arabic, that various stories and tales be transcribed into writing, and that Prophetic biographies be written. No less a figure than Ibn Isḥāq himself, who wrote the first great Prophetic biography, is said to have been so commissioned. There is much to recommend the decisive role of this patronage. The early Abbasids were revolutionaries (they had defeated the last Umayyad caliph in 750, and had all but extirpated the Umayyad house) and *arrivistes* to politics and culture more generally (the family had had a very undistinguished history under the Umayyads, and their military power came from an army of non-Arabs from the Islamic East). As a result, they faced lingering opposition, particularly amongst the Shīᶜites of Kufa, along with the doubts and scepticism of an administrative and, to a more limited extent, military élite that had served the Umayyads. Patronizing history thus held out to the Abbasids the prospect of establishing their cultural credentials and legitimizing the violence that had brought them to power. According to some accounts, it is only having received his caliphal commission that Ibn Isḥāq began lecturing to Kufan scholars.[11]

If the Abbasids had good reason to patronize men of learning, they also had the means to pay them, and to make learning well paid more generally, for the social and economic circumstances were favourable for an explosion of learning. Exceptions aside, the Umayyads' cultural horizons were low, their courts peripatetic, and, at least by Abbasid standards, as homogeneous as they were small. Literacy, much less learning, had not yet established itself as a cultural value. But the early Abbasid

[10] For an argument for some authentic al-Zuhrī material, see G. Schoeler, 'Mūsā b. ᶜUqba's *Maghāzī*' in H. Motzki, ed., *The Biography of Muḥammad: The Issue of the Sources* (Leiden, 2000), pp. 67–97; and also Jarrar, *Prophetenbiographie*, pp. 23ff.; for Spain, C. Pellat, 'The origin and development of historiography in Muslim Spain', in P. Holt and B. Lewis, eds., *Historians of the Middle East* (London, 1962), pp. 118–125; and Jarrar, *Prophetenbiographie*.

[11] On the crucial role of Abbasid patronage for Ibn Isḥāq's *sīra*, see Sellheim, 'Prophet, Chalif und Geschichte', pp. 39ff.; and, generally, Donner, *Narratives of Islamic Origins*, pp. 280f.; on revolutionary politics and historiography, J. Lassner, *Islamic Revolution and Historical Memory* (New Haven, 1986).

caliphate coincided with (and, to some extent, was facilitated by) the cresting of an Iraqi economy upon which were based not only the salaries of a military and administrative apparatus of unprecedented scale, but the foundation and explosive growth of their capital and very cosmopolitan city of Baghdad. Here, in a city thronging with newcomers from nearly every conceivable background, learning and the arts could offer those with ambition and talent the opportunity to escape the humblest social backgrounds (such as manumitted slaves taken during conquest, and former peasants) or, for those who already possessed the appropriate skills (priests, Byzantine and Sasanian bureaucrats), to apply them in this new world. It was in this milieu that poets such as Bashshār b. Burd (d. 784) and historians such as Ibn Isḥāq, both grandsons of conquest-era captives, could find their fame and fortune.[12]

It was amidst this economic and cultural explosion that local paper production took root in late eighth-century Iraq, thereby lowering the cost of writing material. (The oldest *surviving* paper manuscript seems to date from 252/866.) Technological determinists might be inclined to emphasize the role of paper production in the explosion of learning, but writing material, especially Egyptian papyrus, had been relatively plentiful, and it took some time for paper to monopolize the market during the ninth and tenth centuries; in any case, other monotheists had managed to get on with their work without it. It might be safer to suggest that the introduction of paper, coming as it did just as the Abbasids were empire building on a massive scale, helped to *accelerate* the movement towards a culture of learning that was at once more widespread and uniform than its Umayyad antecedent. The bureaucratic and administrative machinery introduced by the Abbasids was to some extent predicated on a common body of knowledge to oil its gears; and it was in the prosperous cities of Abbasid Iraq, Iran and Transoxania that this body was put together on paper, which in the long term proved a cheaper medium to produce than papyrus and processed animal skin. Hammering out an imperial law was part of this process, and so too, as we shall see, was the emergence of the principal genres of Islamic historiography. In sum, the Abbasids possessed the motives and the means to patronize learning on some scale, and oversaw the emergence of an altogether larger and more prosperous culture of learning than had the Umayyads. The deepest roots of the historiographic tradition may have lain in Umayyad soil, but this was far too rocky for it to have flourished.[13]

[12] On Ibn Isḥāq, see Ibn Qutayba, *Kitāb al-Maᶜārif* (Cairo, 4th printing, 1981), pp. 491f. (where we are told that his grandfather was taken at ᶜAyn Tamr and then sent off to Abū Bakr); for the first Abbasid caliph ordering that *bons mots* be set down in writing and anthologized, al-Zubayr b. Bakkār, *Akhbār al-muwaffaqiyyāt*, p. 190.

[13] On the introduction of paper, see Pedersen, *The Arabic Book*, pp. 60ff.; G. Endress, 'Handschriftenkunde', in W. Fischer, ed., *Grundriß der Arabischen Philologie, Band I: Sprachwissenschaft* (Wiesbaden, 1982), esp. pp. 275f.; and now J. Bloom, *Paper Before Print: The History and Impact of Paper in the Islamic World* (New Haven, 2001), chapter 2; for the earliest paper manuscript, G.H.A. Juynboll, 'The origins of Arabic prose' in G.H.A. Juynboll, ed., *Studies on the First Century of Islamic Society* (Carbondale and Edwardsville, 1982), p. 255, but cf. E. Kohlberg, *A Medieval Muslim Scholar at Work: Ibn Ṭāwūs and his Library* (Leiden, 1992), p. 85, note 107, which suggests that there may be something a bit earlier.

The great scale of Abbasid learning is reflected just about everywhere. *Akhbārīs* such as Abū Mikhnaf (d. 774) and Sayf b. ᶜUmar, both of whom contributed enormously to the historical tradition, can be credited with about 40 and 30 titles, respectively. The life span of another famous *akhbārī*, Abū al-Ḥasan al-Madāᵓinī, corresponds closely to this phase (he was born in *ca.* 752, and died some time between 830 and 850), and he may have written 200 books. Apparently only two of these survive (and one only in part), but al-Madāᵓinī was a favourite of later historians, and his work, especially on the conquests, survives in long quotations. It is not merely the number of al-Madāᵓinī's titles that is impressive, particularly since many may have overlapped. It is their wide range (we have titles concerning the Prophet's life, the conquests, events of First and Second Civil Wars, 'lives' of governors and rebels, and much, much more), the heterogeneity of forms (narratives, both simple and compound, lists of names and sermons, various collections), and, perhaps most revealing, an apparent hierarchy of versions. The latter include 'The Larger Book of Accounts Concerning the Caliphs', which implies a smaller one, and 'The Shortened Book on the Khārijites' (a sectarian group), which suggests a fuller one. If we are inclined to accept it, evidence of this kind suggests that historical writing had not merely appeared by the early ninth century. It had started to mature.[14]

Al-Madāᵓinī's output is representative of broad trends, and so too of the state of our knowledge. The preceding reconstruction assumes the essential accuracy of relatively late surveys of learning, such as Ibn al-Nadīm's tenth-century *Fihrist*; our understanding of al-Madāᵓinī's conquest work is also mediated by later sources in which quotations happen to survive. Fortunately, we do possess some evidence of higher quality – late copies of works ascribed to crucial figures in late eighth- and early ninth-century scholarship – and these seem to reflect the trends that we have already inferred from mere quotations (for my present purposes, I assume that these works are authentic). So, from almost two generations before al-Madāᵓinī, we have the recently discovered sections of one of Sayf b. ᶜUmar's conquest works; from one generation before him, we have Ibn Isḥāq and his *sīra* (whatever its precise form), along with a three-volume work almost entirely devoted to the last ten years of Muḥammad's life, the *Maghāzī* of al-Wāqidī (d. 823); and from a contemporary of al-Madāᵓinī, Ibn Saᶜd (d. 845), we have an eight-volume survey of learned men and women.[15]

[14] For Abū Mikhnaf, I draw on al-Ṣafadī, *al-Wāfī bi'l-wafayāt*, xxii, pp. 41ff.; and U. Sezgin, *Abū Miḫnaf: Ein Beitrag zur Historiographie des umaiyadischen Zeit* (Leiden, 1971), esp. pp. 99ff.; for al-Madāᵓinī's work in al-Ṭabarī, see G. Rotter, 'Zur Überlieferung einiger historischer Werke Madāᵓinīs in Ṭabarīs *Annalen*', *Oriens* 23–24 (1974), pp. 103–133.

[15] For Sayf b. ᶜUmar's work, see the *Kitāb al-ridda wa'l-futūḥ and Kitāb al-jamal wa-masīr ᶜĀᵓisha wa-ᶜAlī: A Facsimile Edition of the Fragments Preserved in the University Library of Imam Muhammad Ibn Saᶜud Islamic University in Riyadh* (Leiden, 1995); for Ibn Isḥāq's *sīra-maghāzī* in the adaptation of Ibn Hishām, *al-Sīra al-nabawiyya* (al-Saqqā et al., eds., Cairo, numerous reprints), which is translated by A. Guillaume as *The Life of Muhammad* (London, 1955; reprinted, Karachi, 1978); al-Wāqidī, *Kitāb al-Maghāzī* (London, 1966; reprinted, Beirut); Ibn Saᶜd, *Kitāb al-Ṭabaqāt al-kubrā* (Leiden, 1904–1940; Beirut, 1957–1968) (I cite the former throughout).

Al-Madā᾽inī is just one illustration of the explosive growth of historiography. This generated, in turn, trends of its own. Of these, the single most important was the growing specialisation of those circulating *akhbār*, a trend that is reflected in the sharpening of literary genres – including those of history. One of the clearest examples of this sharpening comes from the emerging tradition of Prophetic biography, which is now conventionally called *sīra*; the Arabic word itself means 'the way of proceeding'. Now we shall see that the origins of Prophetic biography are very murky, but there is good evidence to suggest that the genre was first signalled by the term *maghāzī*, a word which means 'campaigns', and, in a more technical sense, the campaigns undertaken against the Meccans by Muḥammad after his emigration to Medina. Why would the generic use of the term *maghāzī* be eclipsed by that of *sīra* in the early ninth century? In part, the answer lies in the increasing volume of learning made available during the latter eighth and ninth centuries, all of which required categorization. Just as *ḥadīth* learning exploded (a traditionist credited with 50 *ḥadith*s in *ca*. 750 would be credited with 900 a century later), producing a range of *ḥadīth* categories, so too did *akhbār* learning explode (the question of Muḥammad's birth date seems to have emerged in this period), producing distinct works of *sīra* and *maghāzī*. The rest of the answer lies in the very traditionism that produced Ibn Masᶜūd's 900 *ḥadīth*s. Ibn Isḥāq lived in an age when knowledge of the Islamic past was still relatively monolithic and modest, and one where Muḥammad's significance had not yet been concentrated in his capacity to provide legal precedents and a cultural paradigm more generally. Al-Wāqidī (d. 823), who seems to have been the first to restrict *maghāzī* to its classical sense of 'campaigns', lived in an age when learning had grown and was continuing to grow by leaps and bounds, and one in which Muḥammad the law-giver had begun to eclipse Muḥammad the charismatic leader of Holy War. What better way to express this shift than in making *sīra* – 'the way of proceeding' – the generic term for his biography? Terminology, like literary genres, reflects social and political history.[16]

Highlighting *sīra* at the expense of *maghāzī* thus echoed the growing attention being paid to Muḥammad's paradigmatic role by Muslim lawyers, and reflected the growing diversification of learning. This explains why figures such as al-Wāqidī are described as expert in *distinct* fields of knowledge: according to one ninth-century authority, al-Wāqidī was 'learned in the *maghāzī*, the *sīra*, the conquests,

[16] My views here on the *maghāzī* and *sīra* are based on M. Hinds, '*Maghāzī* and *sīra* in early Islamic scholarship', in T. Fahd, ed., *La vie du prophète Mahomet* (Paris, 1983), pp. 57–66 (reprinted in Bacharach et al., eds., *Studies in Islamic History*, pp. 188–198), but the argument that the term *sīra* was used from the start has been made; thus Sellheim, 'Prophet, Chalif und Geschichte', p. 43, and Jarrar, *Prophetenbiographie*, esp. pp. 14ff.; for a review, M. Schöller, *Exegetisches Denken und Prophetenbiographie: Eine quellenkritische Analyse der Sīra-Überlieferung zu Muḥammads Konflikt mit den Juden* (Wiesbaden, 1998), pp. 37ff.; the Ibn Masᶜūd number comes from G.H.A. Juynboll, *Muslim Tradition: Studies in Chronology, Provenance and Authorship of Early Ḥadīth* (Cambridge, 1983), p. 29; for the changing significance of Muḥammad during the first two Islamic centuries, P. Crone and M. Hinds, *God's Caliph: Religious Authority in the First Centuries of Islam* (Cambridge, 1987).

and on people's disagreements and agreements on matters of law'. The same trend towards specialization can be followed in other branches of the emerging tradition of historiography. In fact, this description of al-Wāqidī as 'learned in *maghāzī*' comes from Ibn Saᶜd, whose *Kitāb al-Ṭabaqāt al-kabīr* is the earliest surviving example of a large number of *ṭabaqāt* works, that is, compilations of biographical material organized chronologically, according to a more or less flexible measure of what constitutes a generation (the word *ṭabaqa*, which appears in the Qurʾān, means stratum or layer). The book, which has entries on 4,250 persons (including about 600 women), may be the first extant *ṭabaqāt* work, but it certainly was not the first composed. A century earlier, Wāṣil b. ᶜAṭāʾ (d. 748) seems to have written one, as did several early ninth-century authorities, including al-Haytham b. ᶜAdī (d. 822), who is also noteworthy as the first to write an annalistic work of history. Ibn Saᶜd thus stands near the end of the rise of the *ṭabaqāt* tradition, and here, too, one can see the effects of the diversification of knowledge and the rise of traditionalism. Wāṣil b. ᶜAṭāʾ's work, which is modestly entitled 'The Classes of the Learned and the Ignorant', seems to reflect that same monolithic world of learning in which Ibn Isḥāq lived, a world still naïve of academic expertise and specialties (it has been suggested that these two crude categories may point to rival theological camps, but this is unlikely). Within a century, however, the *ṭabaqāt* categories had multiplied and splintered: we now have books that list only poets or singers (and many other groups), that distinguish between lawyers and traditionists, and that confine themselves to certain kinds of transmitters. Works such as these reflect the growing sophistication of Arabic letters in general, and the rise of a rich and variegated historiographic tradition in particular.[17]

Phase III: *ca.* 830 to *ca.* 925

If, as I suggested above, Islamic historiography emerged during that second period of *ca.* 730 to 830, why do I insist on a third? Let us begin with another question.

Assuming for the moment that our eighth- and early ninth-century experts were authors in the common sense of the term – that is, that they wrote works that were then faithfully copied down and transmitted as 'closed' books – we would like to know how much learning was produced in this period, along with precisely what form it was in. Once again, our problem is that we lack direct evidence: although we know that Muslims had begun to write history, only a handful of ninth-century works survives, and, the occasional exception aside, none of these survives in early manuscripts (most manuscripts securely datable to the eighth and ninth

[17] On 'the learned and the ignorant' in a published text of Wāṣil's, see H. Daiber, *Wāṣil ibn ᶜAṭāʾ als Prediger und Theologe* (Leiden, 1988), p. 41; cf. Yāqūt, *Irshād*, iv, pp. 165ff. (on Khālid b. Yazīd, who volunteers that 'I take an interest in books (*kutub*), but I'm not to be counted amongst the learned or ignorant'; we are also told that he was so eager to transmit *ḥadīth*s that if he failed to find anyone appropriate, he would transmit to slave girls); on the *ṭabaqāt* genre and all the subjects it covered, see chapter 4.

centuries are Qurʾāns). There can be little doubt that some early manuscripts *did* survive into later periods. For example, the collection of books assembled by the Shīʿite scholar Ibn Ṭāwūs (d. 1266) included a manuscript with a date of 844 ('a very old copy', in his words), another with the date of 853, and a third with 865. It is true that Ibn Ṭāwūs was a bibliophile, and he may have had an eye for exceptionally significant manuscripts (it is noteworthy that he judges the mid-ninth-century copy to be 'very old'). Still, many other sources of both earlier and later periods make frequent use of early works of history, often citing them by name. In fact, there is every reason to think that many of these had existed in early copies. Ibn al-Nadīm himself says that he read 'in a book, which appears to me to be in an old hand, and which seems to come from the library of al-Maʾmūn' (rg. 813–833). In a biographical notice of one second-century Muslim, al-Maqrīzī (d. 1442) draws on a genealogy written by Ibn al-Kalbī (d. 819), which, he insists, he possesses in an autograph copy; in his *Khiṭaṭ* he also uses a range of sources, many from the earliest stages of the tradition. Both Ibn al-ʿAdīm (d. 1262) and al-Sakhāwī (d. 1497) advertise their learning and libraries by citing works in autograph copies – that is, copies written by their authors. How do we explain why more of these and other copies failed to survive into the nineteenth and twentieth centuries?[18]

Manuscripts disappear for a variety of reasons, and chief among these is that the medium of choice for Arabic manuscripts – paper – is not very durable, especially in the hot and frequently humid climate of the Middle East. We shall see that the choice of paper can go some way towards understanding why so few documents survive. Here it is worth noting (and lamenting) the contrast between this dismal situation and the relatively robust survival of manuscripts in Europe, where parchment and animal skin were the media of choice. Manuscripts disappear for other reasons, too: because they are misplaced, stolen, and deliberately or accidentally destroyed. The twelfth and thirteenth centuries, punctuated as they were by political turmoil in general and the Mongols' catastrophic destruction of Baghdad in particular, seem to have taken a severe toll. The troubles had actually begun even earlier, and they were not limited to Iraq and Iran. A spectacular, but not altogether untypical, case comes in eleventh-century Cairo, where the city's libraries were systematically plundered by soldiers and bureaucrats who had gone unpaid by the Fatimids, rulers of Egypt since 969. We read that 18,000 volumes of science and 2,400 illuminated Qurʾāns were taken away from the caliph's palace in 1068, and that 'in the month of Muḥarram, twenty-five camels loaded with books made their way on a single day from the palace to the house of the vizier', Abū al-Faraj Muḥammad b. Jaʿfar, who was owed 50,000 dinars in back pay. (In this same

[18] For Ibn Ṭāwūs and his old copies, see Kohlberg, *Medieval Muslim Scholar*, pp. 84ff.; for Ibn al-Nadīm, *al-Fihrist*, p. 24 (Dodge, *Fihrist*, p. 41, where the translation is incorrect); for Ibn al-Kalbī's autograph, al-Maqrīzī, *Kitāb al-Muqaffā al-kabīr* (Beirut, 1991), ii, p. 418; for the sources of his *Khiṭaṭ*, A. Guest, 'A list of writers, books and other authorities mentioned by El Maqrīzī in his Khiṭaṭ', *JRAS* (1902), pp. 103–125; for the confusing practice of citing primary works via unacknowledged secondary sources, Landau-Tasseron, 'On the reconstruction of lost sources'.

period a copy of al-Ṭabarī's history could fetch 100 dinars, a considerable sum of money.) The Great Mosque of Damascus, to take one of many other examples, contained several libraries, and it was torched during an uprising.[19]

So Arabic manuscripts were fragile and vulnerable, and perhaps particularly so in the first centuries of Islam, when institutions were still forming. The authoritative works of the later ninth and tenth centuries are preserved in manuscripts that generally date from the twelfth and thirteenth centuries – at the earliest – and little remains even of exceptionally productive and relatively late historiographic traditions, such as that prospering in late Abbasid Baghdad, which culminated in Ibn al-Sāᶜī (d. 1276) and Ibn al-Fuwaṭī (d. 1323). Of course, the fact that the classics of the ninth and tenth centuries *do* survive – and this, even though many were very long, and therefore time consuming and expensive to copy – suggests that matters of taste and fashion were also at work. Manuscript traditions can come to an end not only because paper disintegrates or is consumed by fire or worms, but because the work they record is considered unsound or unsavoury, or made obsolete, outdated or irrelevant by subsequent scholarship, with the result that they lose their market. Pre-modern scribes were no more likely to copy unwanted books than modern-day publishers are to print them, which is why many works disappeared. And precisely this seems to have happened in the late ninth and tenth centuries, when fields of learning were systematized and collections emerged as authoritative.

We have already seen that the great al-Bukhārī (d. 870) was assembling his selection of *ḥadīth* in this period, and alongside that project one can set the historians' selection of *akhbār*. Just as the work of al-Bukhārī and his late ninth- and tenth-century contemporaries sent earlier *ḥadīth* compilations into obsolescence and obscurity, so too did the great historical compilations of the period, which dwarfed earlier efforts in size and prestige. At the start of this period, we have Ibn Hishām, whose version of Ibn Isḥāq's *sīra* would become definitive; towards the middle we have Ibn Saᶜd's *Ṭabaqāt*; and at the end we have Abū Jaᶜfar al-Ṭabarī (d. 923), whose sixteen-volume *History of the Prophets and Kings* became the pre-eminent example of the annalistic tradition. With large-scale and synthetic works such as these, why bother reading (and thus copying) the older and smaller pieces upon which they were based, especially if an earlier author held what had become dubious ideas? Precisely this seems to have been the case with Sayf b. ᶜUmar, who held what became an unpopularly partisan view on the early caliphate, and whose work, aside from one recent and spectacular find, survives almost exclusively in quotations from al-Ṭabarī and other, relatively late, sources.[20]

19 On the destruction of Fatimid libraries, see H. Halm, *The Fatimids and their Traditions of Learning* (London, 1997), p. 77; for background on the violence, Y. Lev, *State and Society in Fatimid Egypt* (Leiden, 1991), pp. 43ff.; for the price of al-Ṭabarī's history, al-Maqrīzī, *Kitāb al-Khiṭaṭ* (Būlāq, 1270 H), i, p. 408; for a translated description of the Great Mosque of Damascus and an account of the fire, H. Sauvaire, 'Description de Damas', *JA* 7 (1896), pp. 185ff. (the fire starts on p. 208).

20 On Sayf's unpopular views, see P. Crone's review of Samarrai's edition of Sayf b. ᶜUmar's *Kitāb al-Ridda wa'l-futūḥ*, *JRAS* (3rd ser.) 6 (1996), pp. 237–240.

Plate 1 The worm-eaten beginning of year 124 in one of the Oxford manuscripts of al-Ṭabarī's *Taʾrīkh* (Bodleian Library, Oxford, MS Marsh 124, fol. 140v).

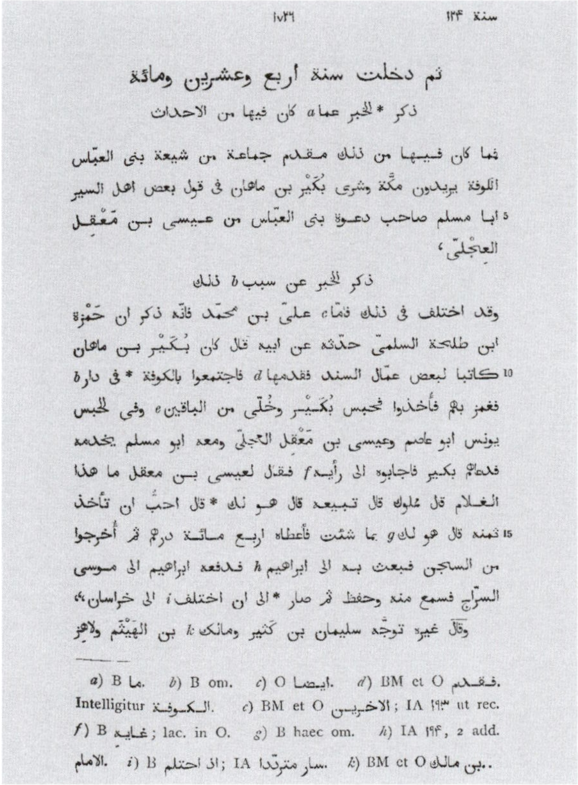

سنة ١٢٤ ١٧٢٦

ثم دخلت سنة أربع وعشرين ومائة

ذكر * الخبر عما *a* كان فيها من الاحداث

فمما كان فيها من ذلك مقدم جماعة من شيعة بنى العبّاس الكوفة يريدون مكّة وشرى بُكَيْر بن ماهان فى قول بعض اهل السير ابا مسلم صاحب دعوة بنى العبّاس من عيسى بن مَعْقِل العِجْلىّ،

ذكر الخبر عن سبب *b* ذلك

وقد اختلف فى ذلك فامّا *c* علىّ بن محمّد فانّه ذكر ان حَمْزة ابن طلحة السلمىّ حدّثه عن ابيه قال كان بُكَيْر بن ماهان كاتبا لبعض عمّال السند فقدمها *d* فاجتمعوا بالكوفة * فى دار *b* فغمز بهم فأُخذوا فحبس بُكَيْر وخُلّى من الباقين *e* وفى الحبس يونس ابو عاصم وعيسى بن مَعْقِل العجلىّ ومعه ابو مسلم يخدمه فدعاهم بكير فاجابوه الى رأيه *f* فقال لعيسى بن معقل ما هذا الغلام قال مملوك قال تبيعه قال هو لك * قال احبّ ان تأخذ ثمنه قال هو لك *g* بما شئت فأعطاه اربع مائة درهم ثم أُخرجوا من السجن فبعث به الى ابراهيم *h* فدفعه ابراهيم الى موسى السرّاج فسمع منه وحفظ ثم صار * الى ان اختلف *i* الى خراسان،

وقال غيره توجّه سليمان بن كَثير ومالك *k* بن الهَيْثَم ولاهز

---

a) B ما. *b*) B om. *c*) O ايضا. *d*) BM et O فقدم. Intelligitur الكوفة. *e*) BM et O الاخرين; IA ١٩٣ ut rec. *f*) B غاية; lac. in O. *g*) B haec om. *h*) IA ١٩٤, 2 add. الامام. *i*) B اذ احتلم; IA سار مترددا. *k*) BM et O بن مالك..

Plate 2 The beginning of year 124 as restored and edited in the Leiden edition of al-Ṭabarī's *Taʾrīkh*, ser. ii, p. 1726.

In this phase, then, we have left behind the age of the relatively brief and single-topic 'monograph' and have entered the age of the large-scale and synthetic collection. The pace at which monographs were eclipsed by collections varies from one subject matter to the next, but the pattern is solid enough. It seems that in the century between 750 and 850 at least fourteen separate works on the battle of Ṣiffīn were composed; in the century between 850 and 950 the number drops to around seven. Monographic *maqtal* works, which recount the death of revered individuals, were composed in large numbers during the eighth and ninth centuries, Abū Mikhnaf apparently writing no fewer than thirteen titles; but the number drops precipitously in the tenth century, and the genre almost died out completely after al-Iṣfahānī (d. 967) wrote his compilation of ᶜAlid martyrologies, the *Maqātil al-Ṭālibiyyīn*. Yet another example can be found in the conquest tradition. The ninth century seems to have been the golden age of conquest monographs, books that brought together conquest accounts of individual cities or provinces in discrete works. Some of these happen to have survived, such as the works of Ibn ᶜAbd al-Ḥakam (d. 870) on Egypt, and al-Azdī (fl. late eighth or early ninth century) on Syria. Most do not, however, having been eclipsed by synthetic conquest works on the one hand, such as al-Balādhurī's *Futūḥ al-buldān* ('The Conquests of the Regions'), and annalistic historiography on the other, such as al-Ṭabarī's. Al-Ṭabarī makes copious and explicit use of the *Futūḥ Khurāsān* ('The Conquests of Khurāsān) by al-Madāʾinī, which must have been a substantial piece of work. For all that al-Madāʾinī was an acknowledged expert, his legacy could hardly rival that of the polymathic al-Ṭabarī, and his *Futūḥ Khurāsān* accordingly perished.[21]

Now it almost goes without saying that the changes should not be overstated. Conquest monographs could come back into fashion in times of intense warfare with Christians, such as during the Reconquista in Spain and the Crusades in Syria and Palestine. Similarly, monographic treatments of the death of the Prophet's grandson, al-Ḥusayn b. ᶜAlī, seem to have been immensely popular not only in the ninth century (we have ascriptions to Abū ᶜUbayda, Abū Mikhnaf, Naṣr b. Muzāḥim, al-Wāqidī and Jābir al-Juᶜfī, among others), but the twentieth, too. (This may be the first time that we should take notice of how conservative the tradition can be, but it will not be the last.) This said, this 'gobbling up' phenomenon – the integration of monographic works into composite and often very large compilations – is a crucial feature of the ninth- and tenth-century tradition, and goes some way towards explaining why so much of the tradition's earlier layers have fallen

[21] On the 'monographs' of the early period, see Petersen, *ᶜAlī and Muᶜāwiya*, pp. 17f. (I borrow the term itself from H.A.R. Gibb, 'Taʾrīkh', *EI*, Supplement [Leiden, 1938], pp. 233–245, which is reprinted in his *Studies on the Civilization of Islam*, ed. S.J. Shaw and W.R. Polk [Princeton, 1962], pp. 108–137); for the works on the battle of Ṣiffīn, I draw on *EI²*, 'Ṣiffīn' (Lecker), but I count Ibn Aᶜtham as an early ninth-century figure, and to this list should be added Muḥammad b. Sulaymān (Abū Jaᶜfar); see al-Laḥjī, *The* Sīra *of Imām Aḥmad b. Yaḥyā al-Nāṣir li-Dīn Allāh* (Exeter, 1990), p. 18; for *maqtal al-Ḥusayn* works, *GAS*, index; Kohlberg, *Medieval Muslim Scholar*, pp. 43 and 254; S. Günther, '*Maqâtil* literature in medieval Islam', *JAL* 25 (1994), pp. 192–212; and idem, *Quellenuntersuchungen zu den 'Maqātil aṭ-Ṭālibiyyīn' des Abū'l-Farağ al-Iṣfahānī (gest. 356/967)* (Hildescheim, 1991).

away: why we are left with what al-Balādhurī and al-Ṭabarī preserved of al-Madāʾinī's conquest work, rather than al-Madāʾinī's work itself, and with what Ibn Isḥāq-Ibn Hishām preserved of al-Zuhrī's work, rather than al-Zuhrī's work itself.[22]

How did the 'gobbling up' take place? It was once held that ninth- and tenth-century authorities were involved in a more or less straightforward project of collecting, selecting and arranging the available *akhbār* according to their sound judgment and narrative scheme (such as it was). They were authoritative, it was thought, chiefly because they were such ambitious and indefatigable compilers, and their works such comprehensive surveys. This view was convenient for two reasons. First, in characterizing these authorities as (mere) collectors, it accorded with the disdain that some Orientalists felt towards Islamic learning in general and Islamic traditionalism in particular: there was little original going on, it was thought. Second, it accorded with one of the principal methods followed by textual historians in the nineteenth and much of the twentieth century, the *Quellenforschung* ('research into sources') that underpinned European scholarship on the Hebrew Bible and New Testament. It thus gave Islamicists a tool with which they might dig into texts in order to identify, isolate and excavate earlier works that had been deposited in later ones. Although varieties of *Quellenforschung* continue to produce important results, it has also come in for criticism, some of which is fair: there is little to be gained from seeing the chapters in al-Balādhurī's monumental *Ansāb al-ashrāf* ('Genealogies of the nobles', a genealogical work filled with historical material) as 'in great part nothing more than the monographs, the "books", of Abū Mikhnaf and al-Madāʾinī'. In the words of M.G.S. Hodgson, one of a small handful of iconoclastic Islamic historians of the twentieth century, some scholars may be guilty of what he called 'reductivism' – 'the habit of mind of those historians who occupy themselves, indeed, with a great piece of work, but who treat it as merely the sum of ingredients that are not great'.[23]

Certainly anyone who has written history can only marvel at the variety and number of al-Ṭabarī's sources: by any reasonable standard, he was an extraordinarily resourceful scholar. It is not only the scale of his work that is marvellous, however. Just as impressive is its overall coherence. It is a hugely ambitious narrative that begins with creation and ends with the year 915, and which pivots around the birth of Islam: the career of the Prophet, the conquests and early caliphs – the culmination of God's will for human history. It is precisely this coherence that gives rise to the suspicion that al-Ṭabarī was doing more than merely collecting and arranging. In fact, it is now becoming clear that he and his contemporaries

[22] On some Crusader-dated conquest works, see below; a recent work on the Prophet's grandson is ʿAbd al-Razzāq al-Muqarram's *Maqtal al-Ḥusayn* (Qum, *ca.* 1990).

[23] One example of literary excavation is W. Hoenerbach, *Waṯīma's Kitāb ar-Ridda aus Ibn Ḥağar's Iṣāba* (Wiesbaden, 1951); on al-Balādhurī's chapters, S.D. Goitein's introduction to the *Ansāb al-ashrāf*, v (Jerusalem, 1936), p. 16; on 'reductivism', M.G.S. Hodgson, 'Two pre-modern Muslim historians: pitfalls and opportunities in presenting them to moderns', in J. Neff, ed., *Towards World Community* (The Hague, 1968), pp. 64f.

were doing much more than that. Late ninth- and tenth-century compilers impressed their vision upon the material not merely by selecting and arranging pre-existing *akhbār*, but by breaking them up, by rephrasing, supplementing and composing anew. Hodgson was right more than 30 years ago: al-Ṭabarī *was* an author.

So assembling and building large-scale historical narratives during the ninth and tenth centuries were by no means inevitable or 'natural' steps in the emergence of the tradition. And although al-Ṭabarī was certainly an indefatigable collector, he was much more than that. A particularly striking feature of this stage in the tradition, which seems to have been at work in both the biographic and chronographic traditions, is the fragmenting of (relatively) long narratives into shorter accounts that were now prefaced by *isnād*s. We can see this in Sayf b. ᶜUmar (d. 796), whose work had earlier been available to modern scholars only as transmitted by historians of the ninth and tenth centuries (or later), but some of which has recently been edited on the basis of a unique manuscript: here the narrative is altogether more continuous than one finds it as cited in the later compilations. Works that resisted this move towards relatively short, *isnād*-equipped narrative were sometimes even flagged as such: thus al-Dīnawarī's (d. 891) *Kitāb al-Akhbār al-ṭiwāl* ('Book of Long Accounts'), which eschews *isnād*-equipped *akhbār*s in favour of the synthetic voice of the single historian. We shall have more to say about *isnād*s and traditions later; here it suffices to note that from the changes apparently at work in the ninth century – the fragmenting of extended narratives, and the widespread use of *isnād*s – one might infer the transition to a new rhetoric of historical narrative, one conditioned by standards set by the increasingly influential traditionists. Now it is true that there were alternatives to this traditionist historiography. Al-Masᶜūdī (d. 956), who was deeply antipathetic towards traditionists in general, did not use *isnād*s, and it may not be coincidental that he, virtually alone amongst practising historians in this period, seems to have regarded historiography as a 'well ordered *and* firm science' (emphasis added – Arabic has no italics). But however much we may value al-Masᶜūdī's approach, especially his catholic and urbane tastes, the later tradition expressed its own preferences by steering clear of his work: it is a very rare historian (such as the exceptional Ibn Khaldūn) who admits his approval of what al-Masᶜūdī was doing. The same thing can be said of similarly iconoclastic histories, such as the *History* of al-Yaᶜqūbī (d. *ca.* 900) which is all but invisible in the later tradition, not simply because it eschewed *isnād*s, but because it presented a Shīᶜite view of the caliphate; his *Geography*, which betrays none of his own beliefs, *was* used by later authors. It would be al-Ṭabarī's model – emphatically traditionalist, moderate and catholic – that would dominate, at least in the short term.[24]

[24] The recently published fragment of Sayf's corpus is the *Kitāb al-ridda wa'l-futūḥ and Kitāb al-jamal wa-masīr ᶜĀʾisha wa-ᶜAlī*; on the fragmentation of narrative more generally, Donner, *Narratives of Islamic Origins*, pp. 258f. (and for al-Ṭabarī's 'master narrative', pp. 127ff.); on al-Dīnawarī's *al-Akhbār al-ṭiwāl* (Leiden, 1888), Duri, *Rise of Historical Writing*, pp. 68f.; and Petersen, *ᶜAlī and Muᶜāwiya*, pp. 159ff.; on how the rise of traditionism made early accounts obsolete, J. Bellamy, 'Sources of Ibn Abī 'l-Dunyā's *Kitāb Maqtal amīr al-muʾminīn ᶜAlī*', *JAOS*

Clearly much was changing in this period, and yet the preceding reconstruction still understates the degree of ninth-century change. This is because I have assumed that lost specimens of eighth- and early ninth-century historical narrative were principally organized into discrete works ('books', 'titles') more or less accurately ascribed to named authorities ('authors'). In other words, I have assumed that early Islamic learning was created and transmitted much like later Islamic learning was. But what *were* the cultural practices of writing and transmitting early on, and how were these practices applied in the various forms of narrative? We know the *Ecclesiastical History of the English People* as Bede's book because Bede was working in a culture that more or less shared our understanding of authorship, and put in place institutions to ensure that books, once written, remained inviolably their authors', rather than their copyists', works. In practice, this meant that scribes trained in all the required skills (especially grammar and penmanship) laboured in monastery libraries and scriptoria (copying rooms) producing manuscript copies whose accuracy not infrequently lies somewhere between a present-day computer scanner and an electronic copying machine. Put another way, a given combination of attitudes, procedures and writing technologies will produce particular kinds of texts and textual traditions, while other combinations produce other kinds of texts and textual traditions. And although a related combination eventually did establish itself amongst Muslim scholars, producing a tradition of not dissimilarly 'authored' books fairly accurately transmitted by copyists, this took some time.

How much time is a matter of some debate, but given that writing itself only began to complement orality during the late seventh and early eighth centuries, we might suppose that notions of authorship familiar to us would crystallize some time thereafter. In fact, the most careful work, much of which is based on the biographical and legal material, suggests that 'authorship' can be said to have crystallized only during the ninth century. According to some scholars, the crucial point came in the early ninth century, while, according to others, it came in the latter part of the century; at least in part, the answers depend on the texts and genres being read. In any case, behind this crystallization we have something else. Far from being 'authored' and 'published' – that is, books with fixed contents that were more or less faithfully transmitted – many of our earliest titles seem to have originated as scholars' and students' notebooks and copybooks, which were initially circulated privately among fellow students, scholars and friends. Having been subject to nearly all manner of altering, these works would then slip (intentionally or unintentionally) into broader circulation, oftentimes only emerging as 'books' some time well after their reputed 'authors' had died. Naturally, a protracted process of composition such as this produces not one, single 'original' version, but a clutch of versions, none of which might have been recognizable to its purported 'author'. Faithful only in the loosest sense to what an authority intended to say, these

104 (1984), p. 16; on history as a science (ᶜ*ilm*), al-Masᶜūdī, *Murūj al-dhahab wa-ma*ᶜ*ādin al-jawhar* (Beirut, 1962–1979), i, p. 12, which is translated by C. Barbier de Meynard and J.B. Pavet de Courteille (rev. by C. Pellat) as *Les prairies d'or* (Paris, 1966–1997), i, p. 4; see also A. Shboul, *Al-Mas*ᶜ*ūdī and his World* (London, 1979), p. 37 (for his low opinion of the traditionists).

'transmitters' were not simply taking liberties with texts: they were *generating* the texts themselves. According to this model of writing in early Islam, Ibn Isḥāq did not 'author' an authoritative version of the *sīra* that is ascribed to him, and, barring some fantastic discovery that shatters this model, we shall never know, nor be able to reconstruct, any 'original' of his. What we can say, however, is that his authority *acquired* a more or less stable set of forms in its three main recensions, the most important of which was preserved and adapted by Ibn Hishām.[25]

We can say something more about the work that was written two generations later, and we are still dealing with a very creative mode of transmission. Perhaps the best example of the early ninth-century state of affairs comes from al-Haytham b. ᶜAdī (d. 822), whom we have already met as the first to organize *akhbār* according to an annalistic scheme. Although not a single volume of his work has survived, later compilers and historians preserve a very large volume of *akhbār* whose *isnād*s identify him as the account's originator. How much of this material is genuinely al-Haytham's? The picture is more complex than one might have thought. On the one hand, there does not seem to have been any wholesale inventing on the part of his transmitters. Unlike so many of the semi-legendary figures of the previous century, al-Haytham does seem to have written widely and authoritatively on a variety of topics: a recognizable corpus of al-Haytham material *does* survive. On the other hand, the *isnād*s certainly cannot guarantee the authenticity of all the material ascribed to him, because al-Haytham's 'transmitters' frequently redacted, shaped and otherwise modified his material for a variety of reasons. In this case there is apparently no bad faith involved, although the ascription of material to earlier authorities for polemical purposes was not uncommon. It is more that these 'transmitters' felt free to redact and adapt the very material they were preserving. They were transmitting according to the rules of transmission that were normative in their day.[26]

[25] On authorship and Ibn Isḥāq, see Schoeler, *Charakter und Authentie*; 'Schreiben und Veröffentlichen'; M. Muranyi, 'Ibn Isḥāq's *Kitāb al-maġāzī* in der *riwāya* von Yūnus b. Bukair', *JSAI* 14 (1991), pp. 214–275; R. Sellheim, 'Muhammad's erstes Offenbarungserlebnis: zum Problem mündlicher und schriftlicher Überlieferung in 1./7. und 2./8. Jahrhundert', *JSAI* 10 (1987), pp. 1–16; L.I. Conrad, 'Recovering lost texts: some methodological issues', *JAOS* 113 (1993), pp. 258–263, which is reprinted in Ibn Warraq, ed., *The Quest for the Historical Muhammad*, pp. 476–485; D. Wasserstein, 'Ibn Ḥazm on names meet for the caliphs', *Cahiers d'onomastique arabe* 1988–1992 (1993), pp. 61–88.

[26] On al-Haytham b. ᶜAdī, see S. Leder, *Das Korpus al-Haiṯam ibn ᶜAdī (st. 207/822): Herkunft, Überlieferung, Gestalt früher Texte der aḫbār Literatur* (Frankfurt am Main, 1991); idem, 'Authorship and transmission in unauthored literature: the *akhbār* attributed to al-Haytham ibn ᶜAdī', *Oriens* 31 (1988), pp. 67–81, and 'Features of the novel in early historiography – the downfall of Xālid al-Qasrī', *Oriens* 32 (1990), pp. 72–96; for the blurry line between authorship and transmission in al-Madāʾinī, Rotter, 'Überlieferung', pp. 110f.; on redactional activity earlier on, E. Landau-Tasseron, 'Processes of redaction: the case of the Tamīmite delegation to the Prophet Muḥammad', *BSOAS* 49 (1986), pp. 253–270; and for the same activity later on, J. Ashtiany Bray, '*Isnād*s and models of heroes: Abū Zubayd al-Ṭāʾī, Tanūkhī's sundered lovers and Abū 'l-ᶜAnbas al-Ṣaymarī', *Arabic and Middle Eastern Literatures* 1 (1998), pp. 7–30.

CHAPTER 3

Consequences and models

By the end of the ninth century, the state of historiographic affairs was still dynamic, but discernible patterns were now in place, and we are far enough along that the trajectory has begun to flatten. It is worthwhile to remind ourselves of two important changes that have taken place.

First, the explosive growth of historical narrative in the eighth and early ninth centuries – the historians of ninth-century Baghdad probably produced more narrative history in a week than all of contemporaneous France or Germany could produce in a year – was followed by a period of authoritative collecting and pruning, which produced the great bulk of the surviving texts. This final period is certainly the most spectacular, but in design these works followed patterns set already during what I have called phase II (*ca.* 730–830), and it is here that the origins of Islamic historiography seem to lie. If the earliest *akhbār* literature was dominated by relatively narrow, single-issue 'monographs' with short shelf-lives, it was the insight of our first historians to recognize that for the ever-growing past to be recorded, it required more plastic forms of narrative. It is precisely this flexibility that explains why other schemes of historical narrative, such as *futūḥ* (works on the great Islamic conquests), *manāqib* (works on the virtuous life and times of leading figures, usually jurists), and *maqātil* (works on the deaths of revered figures, especially Shīᶜite Imams) would be sidelined: they had had and would continue to have their champions, but they could not compete with synthetic chronography in its three principal forms.

Second, the authority of original writers – that is, recognizable 'authors' – had emerged in historiography, as it had in the law and belles-lettres. In other words, composition and transmission were increasingly disentangled. The process may have begun as early as the late eighth century, but we reach a watershed only in the middle of the ninth, perhaps already in the generation of al-Madāᵓinī (d. 843), and certainly in that of al-Balādhurī (d. 893). Of course, there would always be a measure of continuity in the ways historians wrote and published. For example, many historians would continue to 'publish' their works not by writing them out and having copyists execute finished copies, but rather by lecturing or dictating from their notes or drafts. (A not entirely dissimilar process has recently produced a posthumous set of *Lectures on Shakespeare* by W.H. Auden, reconstituted principally from lecture notes taken by a favoured student and friend.) Then, as now, scholars changed their minds over time, and students misconstrued, neglected and conflated lessons (I can only imagine what this book would look like if it originated in a reconstruction along these lines). Whatever the case, the result was multiple recensions, and these remained a feature of the historiographic tradition for as long as we can trace things. Continuities aside, however, there is still a world of difference between Ibn Isḥāq on the one hand, and al-Balādhurī on the other. The former was an authority whose work was eclipsed by what became a normative version (Ibn Hishām's); the latter was an author-historian whose work copyists copied.[1]

What explains these fundamental changes? In what follows, we shall look at some of the mechanisms and influences that were at play; we shall then turn to the consequences they have for reconstructing early Islamic history.

The significance of ninth-century change

Here it must be stressed that more was at work than just the insight of individual historians, however industrious, resourceful and clever they may have been. The rise of the historiographic tradition, whether or not it was triggered by caliphal patronage, was a deeply political process. For the setting down of (versions of) oral history into writing must have been part of a larger reorganizing and focusing of social power, as knowledge became identified with writing and texts, and thus increasingly concentrated in the pens of those who generated and explained these texts, be they the Qurʾān, *ḥadīth* or *akhbār*. What has been called a 'logocentric community' – a society organized around the written word – was emerging. Whatever the immigrant tribesman may have thought about his conquest past, it could now be put at variance with written versions, which, by their very definition, were the preserve of the same urban élites that claimed his taxes (and the Abbasids were far more enthusiastic about taxing fellow Muslims than the Umayyads had been). It was one thing for a Kufan to embellish some family history by crowing (often at the expense of the Basrans) about his heroic participation in a Kufan conquest, but when a historian collated Kufan conquests with Basran conquests, integrated the resulting collation into a work on the conquests as a whole, and, finally, integrated this putative conquest work into a universal history, the end product is unmistakably imperial in design. Individual history, tribal history, local history, Islamic history – a great deal depends on perspective, and perspective is what our historians were imposing on their narratives. So, too, genealogy: it was one thing for a tribesman to claim descent from some distant forefather, while another, who

[1] For an example of a relatively late history that exists in two very different recensions, one of which may preserve a draft, see L. Guo, *Early Mamluk Syrian Historiography: Al-Yūnīnī's Dhayl Mirʾāt al-Zamān* (Leiden, 1998), pp. 28ff.; Auden's lectures are reconstituted in his *Lectures on Shakespeare*, ed. by A.C. Kirsch (Princeton, 2001).

shared fields or battles with him, claimed descent from the same. It was a very different thing when a professional genealogist arranged all his data to show that two settler-soldiers, one in Arabia and the other in Iraq, were somehow related (or unrelated).[2]

So the amalgamation of disparate and fragmented accounts into the large, synthetic works of the mid-ninth century represents more than an ingenious solution to a thorny problem of how to organize all the material made increasingly available to historians through the passing of time and the production of knowledge. It marks a massive project of rethinking history, in which contesting visions and versions of the past were integrated (and, to a large degree, harmonized) according to an imperial project. Unpleasant and controversial history was occasionally suppressed, an early example being the revolutionary excesses of the Abbasids: of the horrific slaughter of the Umayyad family undertaken by the Abbasids, al-Ṭabarī, writing as he was in Abbasid Baghdad, says not a single word, while an anonymous eleventh-century history written in Spain, which lay outside of Abbasid control, describes the violence in some detail. Far more often, controversial history seems to have been preserved, recast and naturalized into a more or less eirenic vision of the Islamic past. Material concerning early sectarian groups, such as the Shīʿites and Khārijites, apparently existed in copious amounts, and much of it was initially transmitted by Shīʿites and Khārijites. Since the bulk of it survives only in synthetic works written by and for tolerant Sunnis with catholic tastes, however, it is frequently recast in terms sympathetic to the Sunni cause. And Sunnis being closest to political power, the result, more often than not, is a benign Sunni triumphalism, which legitimizes through historical narrative what Shīʿites and Khārijites alike considered illegitimate rule.[3]

Organizations of knowledge are never neutral or natural, and they always say something about the organizer and his culture. So, too, genres, which do not emerge accidentally. We shall see that Persian and Christian models may have exercised some influence upon the nascent tradition, but it is hard to imagine that Muslim historians would have produced universal histories on the scale that they did, were it not for the position given to Muḥammad in the monotheist lineage that extended back through Abraham to Adam, and the absolutist claims of the caliphate itself,

[2] On the construction of history when tribes and states collide in the modern Middle East, see A. Shryock, 'Popular genealogical nationalism: history writing and identity among the Balqa tribes of Jordan', *Comparative Studies in Society and History* 37 (1995), pp. 325–357; and idem, *Nationalism and the Genealogical Imagination: Oral History and Textual Authority in Jordan* (Berkeley and Los Angeles, 1997); for a discussion of the early Islamic case, H. Kennedy, 'From oral tradition to written record in Arabic genealogy', *Arabica* 44 (1997), pp. 531–544; the phrase 'logocentric community' comes from M.G. Carter, 'Language control as people control in medieval Islam: the aims of the grammarians in their cultural context', *al-Abhath* 31 (1983), p. 72.

[3] On writing and culture, see, for example, J. Goody, *The Logic of Writing and the Organization of Society* (Cambridge, 1986), esp. pp. 16ff.; and D. Olson, *The World on Paper: The Conceptual and Cognitive Implications of Writing and Reading* (Cambridge, 1994); for the argument that Arabic, unlike pre-Carolingian Latin, was well equipped for logic, P. Saenger, *Space between Words: The Origins of Silent Reading* (Stanford, 1997), esp. pp. 123ff.; the Spanish source is the *Akhbār majmūʿa*, ed. and trans. as *Ajbar Machmuâ* (Madrid, 1867), pp. 47ff.

which ruled, either directly or indirectly, so much of the civilized world (Adam is counted as a caliph in the Qurʾān, and the early caliphs presented themselves as the heirs of the prophets). Although writing in a universalist mode certainly disposed the historian to legitimize the *institution* of the (Sunni) caliphate, which is probably why universal histories would in the long run prove as popular among Sunnis as they would prove unpopular among Shīʿites, it did not necessarily dispose the individual historian to legitimize any *individual* caliph. In fact, a recent study has shown just how much universal history of the early Abbasid period was deeply critical of members of the ruling house. Little wonder: what better way to call a caliph or vizier to account than to profile his actions against the backdrop of history? Chronography, written as it so often was by jurists, is in this sense comparable to jurisprudence, which can fairly be described as a system of thought designed to express the community's corporate ideals and limit the absolutist excesses that states are disposed to commit. Indeed, it might be said that it is historical narrative – frequently no more than a record of civil war, usurpation and more civil war – that most clearly highlights the gap between the ideal once realized under the leadership of the Prophet and the early rulers on the one hand, and the compromised present on the other. We would probably go too far in following one scholar of Biblical history, who held that historical writing appears 'when the actions of kings are viewed in the larger context of the people as a whole, so that it is the larger national history that judges the king and not the king who makes his own account of history'. But it is still fair to see much jurisprudence and chronography as complementary ways of expressing opposition to state power. In sum, early Abbasid attempts to patronize history for apologetic purposes seems to have succeeded only in part, and chronography would lend itself to *Kaiserkritik* of various kinds.[4]

The rise of synthetic chronology is thus related to the rise of traditionalism on the one hand, and the rise of an imperial tradition on the other, which are issues that we shall explore more fully in chapters 5, 6 and 7. Here it bears remembering that things *could* have developed differently. In fact, from the perspective of year 800, one might have thought that the future lay not in the sober and eirenic traditionalism exemplified by al-Ṭabarī or al-Balādhurī, but in the less sober (and sometimes epic) narratives of al-Azdī al-Baṣrī and Ibn Aʿtham al-Kūfī, both writers of conquest monographs where romantic heroism is as prominent as a careful chronology is absent. Conquest works such as these, much like the Prophetic biography of Abū al-Ḥasan al-Bakrī, which in some form also seems to belong to the ninth century, are characterized by storytelling narrative styles that would be elbowed aside (if not entirely eliminated) by what emerged as the normative tradition, leaving their authors in almost total obscurity and their transmission histories especially complex. Despite the rough treatment these texts received at the hands

[4] The recent book is T. El-Hibri, *Reinterpreting Islamic Historiography: Hārūn al-Rashīd and the Narrative of the ʿAbbāsid Caliphate* (Cambridge, 1999); on jurisprudence as opposition to government, N. Calder, 'Friday prayer and the juristic theory of government: Sarakhsī, Shīrāzī, Māwardī', *BSOAS* 49 (1986), p. 39; on kings and history, J. Van Seters, *In Search of History: Historiography in the Ancient World and the Origins of Biblical History* (New Haven, 1983), p. 2.

of many *fuqahāʾ* and early Orientalists (al-Bakrī was called a liar), they can shed some light on the background for later trends – not only the (re)appearance of 'legendary' conquest works of the twelfth and thirteenth centuries falsely ascribed to ninth-century compilers such as al-Wāqidī, but the spread of 'popular' epics that are still performed today. Perhaps even more important, they supply a standard against which we can judge some of the changes that would take place within the dominant tradition itself. For already in Ibn Isḥāq-Ibn Hishām we have the seeds of Prophetic miracle making that would flower in the later *sīra* tradition, just as some of the legendary features of Mamluk chronography and biography echo the exploits of conquest-era commanders in al-Azdī and Ibn Aᶜtham. That these alternative trends were marginalized says something about the intellectual authority of traditionalism.[5]

The origins of the tradition: some problems and solutions

There were, then, good reasons why historians settled into their patterns. The task that remains here is to try to discern the cultural ingredients available to those historians who were composing the foundational genres of chronography, biography and prosopography. The question is conventionally framed in terms of indigenous 'inspiration' and exogenous 'influences'; both models assume that pre-Islamic Arabs were naïve of sophisticated historiography. Although this is an inadequate way of approaching the problem, I shall begin by criticizing the internalist argument.[6]

Three factors internal to the Islamic tradition are commonly adduced to explain the rise of historical thinking (and, by implication, historiographical forms). First, it has been pointed out that the Qurʾān locates man within a universal sequence of events (Creation, a series of prophets, Muḥammad's revelation, the Day of Judgment), knows of several historical events (including a battle between the Persians and Byzantines), distinguishes between the true signs and promise of God and 'the [mere] fables of the ancients', and even teaches that 'men of understanding' can derive lessons from the past (Q 12:111). The revelation, so it is argued, impressed

[5] For a ninth-century dating of al-Azdī al-Baṣrī and his *Futūḥ al-Shām* (the preferred ed. is Calcutta, 1854), see now S. Mourad, 'On early Islamic historiography: Abū Ismāᶜīl al-Azdī and his *Futūḥ al-Shām*', *JAOS* 120 (2000), pp. 577–593, which builds upon L.I. Conrad, 'Al-Azdī's history of the Arab conquests in Bilad al-Sham: some historiographical observations', in M.A. Bakhit, ed., *Proceedings of the Second Symposium on the History of Bilād al-Shām during the Early Islamic Period up to 40 A.H./640 A.D. Vol. 1* (Amman, 1987), pp. 28–62 (for contrasts with the prevailing ninth-century tradition, pp. 46f.); Ibn Aᶜtham's work is the *Kitāb al-Futūḥ* (Hyderabad, 1968–1975); for al-Bakrī, B. Shoshan, *Popular Culture in Medieval Cairo* (Cambridge, 1993), pp. 23ff.; on the later 'legendary' conquest works, R. Paret, 'Die legendäre futūḥ-Literatur', in *La poesia epica e la sua formazione* (Rome, 1970), pp. 735–749; for two published ps.-Wāqidī works, see the *Futūḥ al-Shām* (Calcutta, 1854), and the *Taʾrīkh futūḥ al-Jazīra wa'l-Khābūr wa-Diyār Bakr wa'l-ᶜIrāq* (Damascus, 1996); on the popular epics, M.C. Lyons, *The Arabian Epic: Heroic and Oral Story-telling: Volume 1: Introduction* (Cambridge, 1995), and P. Heath, *The Thirsty Sword: Sīrat ᶜAntar and the Arabic Popular Epic* (Salt Lake City, 1996).

[6] A brief summary can be found in M. Springberg-Hinsen, *Die Zeit vor dem Islam in arabischen Universalgeschichten des 9. bis 12. Jahrhunderts* (Würzburg, 1989), pp. 12ff.

a vision of history upon early Muslims, and historical thought is thus as early as the Qurʾān itself. Second, it has been suggested that since narratives of pre-Islamic battles (called *ayyām*, literally, 'days'), which were recorded and collected in early Islam, bear a strong resemblance to early historical narrative, there may be a genetic relation between the two; allied with genealogy, the collection and narration of these *ayyām*, it is thought, acted to crystallize historical thought. Third, it has been argued that *ḥadīth* learning played a decisive role, fostering critical and historical thinking: for *ḥadīth* learning called not only for the collection of Prophetic accounts, but the careful evaluation of their authenticity according to criteria that were (at least in part) chronological, and we know that many of the early *akhbārīs* were *ḥadīth* collectors and transmitters.

Did the Qurʾān, these 'battle-day' narratives, or Prophetic traditions instill some kind of historical spirit in eighth-century Muslim writers, to whom we can credit the earliest historical works? It is all possible – and all very problematic. If we leave aside an unexplained gap (since historical material only began to be organized during the early to mid-eighth century, one would need to explain why the Qurʾān exercised its decisive influence only at a secondary stage), it still remains difficult to hold to a Qurʾānic inspiration. The Qurʾān's concerns are principally moral, and its view of the past instrumental and didactic. Here chronology as such plays no important part, the past being flattened, a platter on which moral choices have always been (and always will be) offered to man. Concerns such as these may certainly have given impetus to the emergence of a linear and sequential view of the past, but not for the sophisticated historiography of the early Abbasid era. The Bible also exhorts its readers and listeners to 'remember' events, such as the enslavement of the Israelites (Deuteronomy 5:15), but these passages can hardly explain the rise of historiography amongst Jews and Christians. The argument for the role of 'battle days' is similarly strained, since the first collections of these narratives appeared alongside, and in some instances only *after*, our earliest examples of history. In any event, here, too, a clear and developed sense of chronology is entirely absent: these narratives preserve a great deal of tribal and geographical material, and from some of it one can infer sequence, but sequence is very different from chronology. What, finally, about the influence of *ḥadīth*? Even if we choose to overlook the fact that the emergence of the *ḥadīth* is as obscure as the emergence of historiography, the earliest historians seem to have ignored many of the rules of transmission that the traditionists were busy laying down, such as using the *isnād*. As we have already seen, *ḥadīth* standards seem to have been imposed on history writing at a secondary stage. Although it is certainly possible that the preservation and patent fabrication of accounts intended to form the basis for a timeless and immutable law could inspire chronological rigour in narrative that is often concerned with change, we have no evidence that it actually did.[7]

[7] On Qurʾānic history, compare Khalidi, *Arabic Historical Thought*, pp. 8ff., and N. Abbott, *Studies in Arabic Literary Papyri I: Historical Texts* (Chicago, 1957), pp. 6ff. with Donner, *Narratives of Islamic Origins*, p. 80 (whom I follow); cf. also Rosenthal, *History*, pp. 27f.; M.Z. Brettler, *The Creation of History in Ancient Israel* (London and New York, 1995), pp. 136f.; cf. E. Meyer's conclusions (*Der historische Gehalt der Aiyām al-ʿArab* [Wiesbaden, 1970], esp. p. 5).

The historian's sources may be oral, but historical thinking – disciplined, coherent and transmitted historical thinking – is a textual phenomenon, and there is accordingly little hope of finding it before textuality took hold. As one ancient historian has put it, 'evidence from the past, the past as a source of paradigms, is one thing. History as a systematic study, as a discipline, is another thing'. That Muslim historians, such as Abū Shāma (d. 1267), anchored their project in the Qurʾān and in the Prophet's *sunna* says far more about the power of traditionalism than it does about the actual origins of the tradition.[8]

Of course there is no reason to doubt that learned Muslims of the earliest period felt the currents of history: indeed, all religions organized around a revelation root themselves in history. Already in what seems to be a very late seventh-century letter, which is preserved in much later sources, we have elements of the 'salvation history' so familiar to us in the ninth- and tenth-century tradition. Nor is there any reason to doubt that many of the unlearned felt these currents too, living as they did in a world of constant reminders of the past: everything from pharaohs' pyramids and tombs, Greek and Roman theatres and baths, Sasanian palaces and Byzantine churches, to members of the Persian gentry, strutting around in their silk finery, tonsured monks in their drab and dirty wool, and curious pillar saints, perched 50 feet in the air. Monuments of empires past were far thicker on the ground of the seventh-century Near East than they are in the twenty-first, and early Muslim imperialists were quick learners. Surviving monuments, such as the Dome of the Rock in Jerusalem and a palace in the Syrian desert, which is known as Quṣayr ʿAmra, tell us that already by the late seventh and early eighth centuries the Umayyad state had begun to represent itself as the heir to a monotheist and Hellenistic past, and this both privately and publicly. Thus Quṣayr ʿAmra boasts a quite striking fresco that represents six kings, four of which can be securely identified: Caesar (Byzantine), Khusraw (Sasanian), Roderic (Visigothic) and the Negus (Ethiopian). It is tempting to see in these cultural artifacts some precursors to the combination of pre-Islamic history and legend that would eventually find its way into universal histories and Prophetic biographies.[9]

So there is no question that many early Muslims thought historically. But this scarcely makes them historians. Rather than trying to identify the origins of historical *thinking* in the murky decades of the late seventh and very early eighth centuries, we might examine those historical schemes adopted in the late eighth and early ninth, when biography and prosopography (the latter, in this period, still synonymous with the *ṭabaqāt* scheme) emerged alongside chronography – that is, when inchoate historical ideas crystallized into literary form.

8 The ancient historian is M.I. Finley, 'Myth, memory and history', in his *The Use and Abuse of History* (London, 1990, reprint), p. 12; for Abū Shāma's views, see his *Kitāb al-Rawḍatayn fī akhbār al-dawlatayn* (Cairo, 1956), i[1], p. 2.

9 For the late seventh-century letter, see J. van Ess, 'Das *Kitāb al-irǧāʾ* des Ḥasan b. Muḥammad b. al-Ḥanafiyya', *Arabica* 21 (1974), pp. 20–52; an influential study of monuments and history is D. Lowenthal, *The Past is a Foreign Country* (Cambridge, 1985); for discussions and descriptions of the Quṣayr ʿAmra fresco, O. Grabar, 'The painting of the six kings at Quṣayr ʿAmrah', *Ars Orientalis* 1 (1954), pp. 185ff.; and now G. Fowden, *Empire to Commonwealth: Consequences of Monotheism in Late Antiquity* (Princeton, 1993), pp. 143f.

Although one might speculate that Prophetic *sīra* owes some indirect or refracted debt to the vibrant, Late Antique tradition of Christian hagiography, there is no clear evidence for it. Moreover, insofar as early biography was Prophetic and early prosopography was concerned with recording *ḥadīth* transmitters, one might be attracted to an internalist model that puts the rise of the Prophet's *sunna*, preserved as it was by *ḥadīth* transmitters, at the centre of both. 'The origins of Arabic biographical literature lie in the criticism of (Prophetic) Tradition', as one scholar put it plainly, and by biographical literature, he meant both biography *and* prosopography. The problem, however, is two-fold. First, early biography was not exclusively Prophetic; we shall come to several non-Prophetic examples. Second, early prosopography was not exclusively concerned with *ḥadīth* transmitters: it is reasonable to presume that the interests of our earliest apparent prosopographer Wāṣil b. ᶜAṭāᵓ – rationalist theologian that he was – lay outside of traditions, and here it is also noteworthy that the next attributed *ṭabaqāt* work, the *Ṭabaqāt al-shuᶜarāᵓ* of Yazīd b. Mubārak al-Yazīdī (d. 818), was about poets rather than traditionists. Both, it should be noted, date from a period when the Prophet's legislative authority as transmitted through *ḥadīth* had not yet been clearly established. In fact, considering how robust biographical and even autobiographical writing would become amongst non-traditionists and non-Sunnis in general, one might even suspect that at least some of it arose *despite* the indifference of the Sunni traditionalist establishment.[10]

Although the *ṭabaqāt* scheme appears to be *sui generis*, and in some respects does seem closely related to the emblematically Islamic practice of attaching chains of transmission to legal and historical reports, the rise of Prophetic *sunna* does not accommodate all of the evidence, and cannot fully account for the rise of either biography or prosopography. The rise of biographical writing, therefore, must have something to do with the rise of *the individual* in the late eighth and ninth centuries, rather than with the rise of *an individual* (the Prophet), as tribal affiliations faded as a result of sedentarization, urbanization and assimilation more generally. Meanwhile, the emergence of prosopography must owe a great deal to the increasing professionalization and group-consciousness of the same period, in which the *ḥadīth* transmitters played a leading – but not the only – part.

The case of chronography

We are on firmer ground when it comes to the rise of chronography. To begin with, there is some reason to think that of the two dominant forms – caliphal

[10] The quotation comes from O. Spies, *Beiträge zur arabischen Literaturgeschichte* (Leipzig, 1932), p. 1; for the *ṭabaqāt* titles, see I. Hafsi, 'Recherches sur le genre «*Ṭabaqāt*» dans la littérature arabe, I, II, III', *Arabica* 23 (1976), pp. 227–265; 24 (1977), pp. 1–41 and 150–186; and G. Makdisi, '*Ṭabaqāt*-biography: law and orthodoxy in classical Islam', *IS* 32 (1993), pp. 371–396, both as corrected by C.F. Robinson, 'al-Muᶜāfā b. ᶜImrān and the beginnings of the *ṭabaqāt* literature', *JAOS* 116 (1996), pp. 114–120.

chronography and annalistic chronography – the former appeared first, particularly since much early annalistic work seems to have been based on histories organized according to caliphal reigns. Already with Ibn Isḥāq we have a purported *History of the Caliphs* (*Ta*ᵓ*rīkh al-khulafā*ᵓ), and he predeceases the earliest annalist, al-Haytham b. ᶜAdī, by some 60 years; Abū Maᶜshar (d. 786), to whom another *Ta*ᵓ*rīkh al-khulafā*ᵓ work is attributed, also predeceases al-Haytham b. ᶜAdī by nearly 40 years. (The earliest extant work in this genre seems to belong to Ibn Māja [d. 886].) Moreover, insofar as these two genres reflect a *Sitz im Leben*, it might be suggested that the scheme seems to fit an early Abbasid context, when caliphal power was at its apogee. The scheme itself may be explained as an expansion of skeletal lists of caliphs, which we know from the Syriac tradition to have been circulating in the middle of the eighth century, and whose use in the mature tradition is frequently betrayed. Indeed, listing – not only caliphs, but also governors, judges and other officials – appears to have been amongst the *akhbārī*s' earliest enthusiasms, and one which survived the rise of the synthetic forms of the ninth century.[11]

Such is one model – lists of caliphs with regnal dates, expanded into chronographies ordered according to caliphal reigns – that might explain the appearance of caliphal chronography at the end of the eighth century. And since caliphal chronography poses awkward problems of narrative, as we shall see in chapter 4, it is not hard to see why annalistic history might emerge as an attractive alternative in the ninth century. If one is similarly inclined towards an internalist, rather than externalist, explanation for the rise of annalistic chronography, there is another model to follow: the emergence of literary form (the chronicle – what I have called here 'annalistic chronography') from regularly dated public records (the annal) or regularly dated private records (the diary). Of the two, diary keeping is the more promising, there being no clear evidence for city or imperial annals in early Islam akin to the *tabulae pontificum* of Rome of the third century C.E., nor, for that matter, any clear sign of the city records that seem to lie behind the emergence of the Syriac tradition. Unfortunately, the practice of diary writing in this period requires a great deal more research.[12]

[11] On lists, see chapter 2 above, and for one tenth-century example, G. Conrad, *Abū'l-Ḥusain al-Rāzī (-347/958) und seine Schriften: Untersuchungen zur frühen damaszener Geschichtsschreibung* (Stuttgart, 1991), pp. 23ff.; Donner, *Narratives of Islamic Origins,* pp. 182ff.; Ibn Māja's *Ta*ᵓ*rīkh al-khulafā*ᵓ was published in Beirut, 1979.

[12] On the relative dating of caliphal and annalistic history, see C.F. Robinson, 'The study of Islamic historiography: a progress report', *JRAS* (3rd ser.) 7 (1997), pp. 222ff.; on annals and history in the Christian tradition, B. Croke, 'The origins of the Christian world chronicle', in B. Croke and A.M. Emmett, eds., *History and Historians in Late Antiquity* (Sydney, 1983), pp. 117ff., which is reprinted in idem, *Christian Chronicles and Byzantine History, 5th–6th Centuries* (London, 1992); idem, 'City chronicles in Late Antiquity', in G. Clarke, et al., eds., *Reading the Past in Late Antiquity* (Sydney, 1990), pp. 165–203, which is also reprinted in *Christian Chronicles*; and, for the origins of Syriac historical writing in local annals, W. Witakowski, *The Syriac Chronicle of Pseudo-Dionysius of Tel-Maḥrē: A Study in the History of Historiography* (Uppsala, 1987), p. 77; for the argument in favour of the diary's role in the rise of the early Islamic tradition, G. Makdisi, 'The diary in Islamic historiography: some notes', *History and Theory* 25 (1986), pp. 173–185; and for an argument in favour of the diary's role in a much later Islamic tradition, M. Cook, 'The historians of pre-Wahhābī Najd', *SI* 76 (1992), pp. 165ff.

So much for internalist arguments. Other historians have proposed that the earliest Muslim historians became familiar with historiographic forms from non-Muslim annalists. For not only is there good evidence for an exchange of historiographic ideas amongst Muslims, Christians and Jews during the eighth and ninth centuries, but Islamic sources from the tenth make their debt to Christian histories explicit. We even have the 'spectacular' case of Orosius' *Historiae adversus paganos*, which was translated into Arabic in tenth-century Spain. Is it possible that the nascent tradition, evolving towards chronographic solutions of its own, may also have drawn upon non-Islamic schemes that were in circulation in the eighth and ninth centuries?[13]

Muslims certainly *exported* both historical material and historiographic forms. We know, for example, that rabbis took up the *ṭabaqāt* scheme from their Muslim counterparts, and that well-placed Christians such as Theophilus of Edessa, the 'astronomer royal' of the caliph al-Mahdī (rg. 775-785), wrote a history that drew, among other things, upon Islamic material. In fact, Theophilus stands near the beginning of a series of Christian and Jewish astrologers who found favour in the caliphs' courts, well-placed *importers* of the Sasanian enthusiasm for astrological history. The earliest signs of this enthusiasm survive from the middle of the eighth century, but horoscopes may have been cast for caliphs of the late seventh century, and we can occasionally see how Sasanian astrological history was assimilated into Islamic chronography. Such is the case, for example, when eighth-century collections of horoscopes organized according to a variety of dating systems are naturalized in ninth-century caliphal histories. In addition, we know that the Sasanians produced a respectable tradition of chronicles (Greek writers mention them in the sixth century), and some of these may have been translated into Arabic already during the caliphate of Hishām b. ᶜAbd al-Malik (rg. 724–743). It has been suggested that this Persian historiographic tradition, at the centre of which stood the king, may have influenced the regnal mode of Islamic chronography.[14]

[13] On the debts of the historiographic tradition, compare Duri, *Rise of Historical Writing,* p. 60 (the translations from Greek and Syriac contain 'nothing to indicate' that Greek and Syriac historiography 'had any effect on historical writing') and B. Radtke, 'Towards a typology of Abbasid universal chronicles', *Occasional Papers of the School of Abbasid Studies* 3 (1991), p. 12: ('At best, one may speak of concurrent developments and vague influences') with Rosenthal, *History*, pp. 71ff. (where lots of inferential evidence for 'borrowing' is adduced, which is the most one can hope for in the circumstances); cf. Van Seters, *In Search of History*, p. 81; 'spectacular' is H. Busse's word in his 'Arabische Historiographie und Geographie', in H. Gätje, ed., *Grundriß der Arabischen Philologie, Band II: Literaturwissenschaft* (Wiesbaden, 1987), p. 270, citing G. Levi Della Vida, 'La traduzione araba delle storie di Orosio', *al-Andalus* 19 (1954), pp. 257–293; for more eighth-century evidence for Christians drawing on Islamic accounts, K.B. Wolf, *Conquerors and Chroniclers of Early Medieval Spain* (Liverpool, 1999; 2nd ed.), p. 27.

[14] For the rabbis' adoption of the *ṭabaqāt* scheme, see Abraham Ibn Daud, *The Book of Traditions (Sefer ha-qabbalah)*, ed. and trans. G.D. Cohen (Philadelphia, 1967), esp. pp. liff.; Muslim access to the Persian historical tradition is made especially clear in the case of al-Masᶜūdī, *Kitāb al-Tanbīh wa'l-ishrāf* (Leiden, 1893), p. 106 (where the author sees in the city of Iṣṭakhr 'a huge tome' that covers the sciences, history, topography and politics), and, more generally, Shboul, *Al-Masᶜūdī and his World,* pp. 102ff. and J.S. Meisami, *Persian Historiography to the End of the Twelfth Century* (Edinburgh, 1999), p. 9; for early evidence for the role of the caliph al-Mahdī, S.P. Brock, 'Two letters of the Patriarch Timothy from the late eighth century on translations from Greek', *Arabic*

A case can also be made on the Christian side of things. We have reports that histories in the Eusebian tradition were being translated during the reign of al-Manṣūr (rg. 754–775), and it seems that one Muslim apocalyptic text, perhaps written about 780, is the 'reworking' and translation of a Christian version written in Syria. The case for Byzantine (that is, Greek) influence is weaker than that for the Syriac variety, especially because Byzantine historical writing seems to have been moving away from chronography during the seventh and eighth centuries towards other forms, such as saints' lives. It is also weakened by the geographic shape of the early Islamic tradition. Had Greek influence upon Muslim chronographers been decisive, we might expect that these chronographers would have exercised greater influence in Syria, and that Syrian Muslims might have outpaced their Iraqi colleagues. Quite the opposite is the case, however. Early Islamic Syria did produce some historiography, much of which has come to light only recently, but it cannot compare with the Iraqi output.[15]

In sum, there is reasonable evidence for an evolution from caliphal list to caliphal history and for non-Muslim inspiration for the appearance of annalistic chronography: it may be that historiographic ideas rode piggy-back on the heavy traffic of Sasanian and Christian learning, which began to flow into the caliphs' courts in the eighth century. The latter is what we might otherwise expect: other historiographic traditions have enjoyed jump-starts in precisely the same way, and, after all, it was not just booty and tax revenues that fell into the hands of early Muslims, but the accumulated inheritance of several Near Eastern chronographic traditions, of which the Christian and Jewish contributions were only the most recent deposits. This used to be called 'borrowing', a once-respectable term that is now frequently taken to imply that Muslims, short on ideas of their own, were forced to reach outside of their own tradition, or, even worse, that they were nothing more than the passive recipients of foreign ideas. This is to misunderstand things entirely. Clearly, we are not dealing with borrowing in the sense that I might borrow a neighbour's car, which I would be expected to return, or a cup of sugar, which would leave me with an obligation to reciprocate in kind: Muslim and non-Muslim were not neighbours with adjoining houses and separate possessions. They may have been at frequent odds over matters great and small, and to say that they always interacted in some kind of symbiotic harmony is going altogether too far. Still, Christians, Jews, Muslims and Zoroastrians (I count here only those making real and durable contributions to learned culture) lived in a shared world of texts and scriptures, and this was particularly the case in the early, formative period,

Sciences and Philosophy 9 (1999), pp. 233–246; and, for astronomical history, D. Pingree, 'Historical horoscopes', *JAOS* 82 (1962), pp. 487–502; S. Stern, 'Abū ᶜĪsā ibn al-Munajjim's chronography' in S. Stern, et al., eds., *Islamic Philosophy and the Classical Tradition* (Oxford, 1972), pp. 437–466.

[15] For the apocalypse, see M. Cook, 'An early Islamic apocalyptic chronicle', *JNES* 52 (1993), pp. 25–29, and cf. his 'The Heraclian dynasty in Muslim eschatology', *al-Qanṭara* 13 (1992), pp. 3–23; on the state of Byzantine historiography, M. Whitby, 'Greek historical writing after Procopius: variety and vitality', in Cameron and Conrad, eds., *Byzantine and Early Islamic Near East I*, pp. 25–80.

before Muslims generated a distinct tradition of their own. Christians wrote Syriac history in part based on Islamic sources, in some cases even using Hijri dating; Greek historians followed Syriac historians in writing according to a Eusebian model; Jews, as we have already seen, appropriated the emblematically Islamic *ṭabaqāt* genre. If the venerated traditions could 'borrow' in these ways, why not the upstarts, perhaps especially for polemical purposes? If the culture of early Islamic Iraq was anything, it was cosmopolitan and eclectic.[16]

Consequences

The reconstruction of early Islamic historiography described above is intended to lay the foundation for an understanding of later Islamic historiography, to which we shall presently turn. But it has obvious consequences for understanding early Islamic *history*, and it may therefore be valuable to examine precisely what these are. For although questions about the reliability of the early tradition (particularly the *sīra*) had been raised as early as the 1920s, and scholars have long had their doubts about Sayf b. ᶜUmar, a sharp turn towards scepticism was taken in the 1970s and 1980s. Since then, the consensus about how to reconstruct this period – indeed, about the prospect that it *can* be reconstructed in any real detail – has broken down almost completely, with the result that relatively little seventh- and early eighth-century history has been written over the last 25 years or so.

There is no way around the fact that what we know of eighth- and much ninth-century narrative consists in what later authorities thought worth collecting and preserving. Some of these later authorities belong to the generations that immediately followed, but others belong to much later periods, even the thirteenth, fourteenth and fifteenth centuries. We consequently find ourselves at two removes from the earliest events themselves, in a historiographic 'décalage' of the most disorienting sort. It is true that the gap between event and record in early Islam is relatively narrow compared with our source material for the ancient Israelites, which usually dates from several centuries after the facts they purport to relate; it is also true that non-Islamic sources put at our disposal far more corroborating information about earliest Islam than do the non-Christian sources for Jesus and his movement. For these and other reasons, it is very unlikely that the tide of scepticism that has washed over early Islamic studies will ever rise so high that the outlines of a historical Muḥammad will be washed away. This said, the loss of the tradition's earliest layers has been nothing short of catastrophic, in the provocative words of one historian, a 'historiographic failure on the grandest scale imaginable'. Aside from the Qurᵓān and a small handful of exceptions, modern historians are

[16] The Greek historian is Theophanes, on whom I follow C. Mango, 'The tradition of Byzantine chronography', *Harvard Ukrainian Studies* 12–13 (1988–89), p. 369; for the view that the *isnād* may have Rabbinic origins, Cook, 'The opponents of the writing of tradition in early Islam', pp. 508ff.

robbed of virtually any literary evidence composed within natural memory of the great moments of early Islam: Muḥammad's preaching amongst the polytheists of Mecca; his move to Medina, in which he established his community and from which he prosecuted war against the Meccan opposition; the fractious succession struggles and civil wars of the seventh century; the slow rise of a revolutionary movement in the east, and the precipitous collapse of the Umayyads to Abbasid armies in 749–750.

And this, of course, is just to mention the spectacular. Would that we knew something of the mundane, the background noise against which we might judge all this clamorous change: how pagan pastoralists, having jumped on the opportunities that conversion presented, negotiated the difficult processes of sedentarization and assimilation; how garrison settlements were transformed into thriving cities; how social élites secured, maintained or lost their élite status amidst all the change. To these and many, many other questions our texts do give answers, but they do so at such a geographic, temporal and cultural remove from the events in question that far from being primary sources, they actually constitute secondary or tertiary sources, which, standing precariously upon the unsteady foundations of oral tradition, often tell us more about their date of composition than they do about the events they purport to relate. Little wonder, then, that a great deal of modern scholarship is currently concerned as much with historiographic questions – can early material be identified within this late corpus? – as it is with the actual history that the tradition is supposed to reflect. This book is a case in point.[17]

So in al-Haytham b. ᶜAdī, we once had a secure link between the lost world of the eighth century and the surviving sources of the late ninth and tenth, through which we could reasonably reconstruct Umayyad and even pre-Umayyad history in some detail. Now we are not so sure. What does it mean that our source material developed in such a discontinuous fashion, and that isolating and reconstructing works in their 'original' or 'authoritative' forms is almost certainly chimerical? It may be that we know much less than we thought we knew about the religious and social history of the first Islamic century, but we certainly know far more about how second- and third-century Muslims handled their history – what they thought about it, and how they wrote about it. And although translating historiographical

[17] For Israelite history, see I. Provan's review article, 'The end of (Israel's) history?' *JSS* 42 (1997), pp. 283–300; for the non-Christian sources on Jesus, R.E. Van Voorst, *Jesus Outside the New Testament: An Introduction to the Ancient Evidence* (Grand Rapids, 2000); I borrow 'décalage' from J. Chabbi, 'La représentation du passé aux premiers âges de l'historiographie califale', in R. Curiel and R. Gyselen, eds., *Itinéraires d'Orient: hommages à Claude Cahen* (Bures-sur-Yvette, 1994; *Res Orientales* vi), p. 25; the provocative historian is J. Howard-Johnston in the translation of Sebeos, *The Armenian History Attributed to Sebeos*, trans. by R.W. Thomson with commentary by Howard-Johnston (Liverpool, 1999), ii, p. 243; the argument for the obliteration of authentic historical material has never been put more effectively than L.I. Conrad, 'The conquest of Arwād: a source-critical study in the historiography of the early medieval Near East', in A. Cameron and L.I. Conrad, eds., *The Byzantine and Early Islamic Near East I: Problems in the Literary Source Material* (Princeton, 1992), pp. 317–401.

insights into positive historical knowledge is considered naïve by some, there are no signs within the field of classical Islamic history that the project will be abandoned any time soon: nearly all practitioners still believe that our sources refer to a past that can be reconstructed.[18]

In this respect, classical Islamic studies is fortunate to have remained relatively free of the occasionally ugly debates currently raging in other fields, in which 'positivist' historians – that is, those who believe that our sources are referential to a past – fight it out with their critics, either 'anti-representationalists' who hold that that they do not, or otherwise 'post-modern' historians who hold that all representations are essentially hegemonic. The debate in Islamic studies turns not so much on the philosophical question of whether history is knowable, but on how far back into the earliest period we can recover it, and how we should go about doing so. The reconstruction I have presented so far will be considered unduly sceptical by those who retain a largely *isnād*-based faith in the authenticity of the early tradition, and who accordingly make a series of positive affirmations: writing *did* appear early on; early figures *were* authors (and frequently real historians too); their work *was* transmitted more or less faithfully through *isnād*s; therefore the origins of Islam *can* be recovered in real detail. It should be clear by now that those who do not share the same faith in the *isnād* system generally negate all these affirmations, arguing that the first century or so is recoverable only insofar as we can use a variety of sources, Islamic and non-Islamic, literary and material. To discern the character of Umayyad administration, for example, one might do more than read Abbasid-era representations of how it was intended to function, however detailed they may appear. One might do well to collect and interpret a substantial and contemporaneous corpus of gold, silver and copper coins, for these coins (many of which bear dates and mint-names) can tell us where and at what speed the state's machinery was running, in addition to something of how the Marwānids themselves thought to represent themselves. To understand the nature of the Umayyad caliphate, for another, more controversial example, one might consider not what the *ᶜulamā'* of the ninth century said of it, but some contemporaneous (or near contemporaneous) documentation, such as surviving coins, poems, and letters preserved in later sources.[19]

[18] For three very different and very influential books, see A. Noth, *Quellenkritische Studien zu Themen, Formen und Tendenzen frühislamischer Geschichtsüberlieferung* (Bonn, 1973) (Noth/Conrad, *Early Arabic Historical Tradition*); P. Crone and M. Cook, *Hagarism: The Making of the Islamic World* (Cambridge, 1977); and J. Wansbrough, *Quranic Studies: Sources and Methods of Scriptural Interpretation* (London, 1977).

[19] Some sense of the battles raging elsewhere can be found in P. Joyce, 'History and post-modernism I', *Past and Present* 133 (1991), pp. 204–209; and for three recent instalments in the debate, see P. Zagorin, 'History, the referent, and narrative: reflections on post-modernism now', *History and Theory* 38 (1999), pp. 1–24, K. Jenkins, 'A post-modern reply to Perez Zagorin', *History and Theory* 39 (2000), pp. 181–200, and P. Zagorin, 'Rejoinder to a post-modernist', *History and Theory* 39 (2000), pp. 201–209; for the early Muslim understanding of the caliphs on the basis of these documentary and quasi-documentary sources, Crone and Hinds, *God's Caliph*.

Here it must be stressed that these alternative sources are far from a panacea. When we have them, coins can only tell us so much, and the earliest securely datable issues first appear in the final decades of the seventh century; in many regions they are only spotty. For all its virtues, archaeology is a far better barometer of long-term processes, such as patterns of settlement and land use, than it is of political change. Archaeologists have recently discovered in southern Jordan the palace complex in which the Abbasids almost certainly plotted their revolution against the Umayyads, but the discovery has so far made no appreciable impact on our understanding of this revolution, and there is no reason to think that it will: the beautiful ivory carvings do not tell us what the Abbasids thought of the Umayyads. Nor will reading what Christians wrote in Syriac or what Jews wrote in Hebrew deliver us from the problem of bias, even if they, unlike the surviving Islamic sources, were contemporaneous (or at least relatively early). No less than Muslims writing their history, Christians and Jews had their own axes to grind, and unlike Muslims, virtually without exception they were bystanders and foreigners, writing at both a geographic and cultural distance from the events they were recording. We shall never find a seventh- or eighth-century Syriac text that offers us anything like a disinterested portrayal of Muḥammad's prophetic mission, and we only very rarely find non-Arabic accounts – written, as they almost invariably were, outside of Arabia – that manifest any real understanding of how the early Islamic state actually worked. The value of the non-Islamic material therefore lies not so much in systematic descriptions of Islam as in the occasional glimpse of lived Muslim practice, and it should generally be used alongside, rather than instead of, the Islamic tradition.[20]

There is no question, then, of abandoning the Islamic tradition in favour of other source materials, be they literary or material: properly understood, ten pages of al-Ṭabarī's work probably have more to teach us about Islamic history than 100 pages of the great twelfth-century Patriarch-historian, Michael the Syrian, the author of an invaluable Syriac history. Indeed, it is precisely to the difficulty of properly understanding al-Ṭabarī that much of a generation's scholarship has been devoted. On this point, there should be no confusion. Despite what one occasionally reads, most scholars who take a sceptical position on the authenticity of the early Islamic tradition do so not merely because the early sources are biased (all sources are biased in one way or another), and certainly not because they hold some grand conspiracy theory, according to which ninth-century Muslims systematically suppressed the facts of their origins, thereupon inventing a replacement set. Serious historians do not hold conspiracy theories about the rise of Islam. They question the early tradition because they hold that cultural norms are subject to

[20] For the palace complex in Jordan, see J.P. Oleson, et al., 'Preliminary report of the al-Humayma Excavation Project, 1995, 1996, 1998', *Annual of the Department of Antiquities of Jordan* 43 (1999), pp. 411–450; for a systematic treatment of the non-Islamic sources, R. Hoyland, *Seeing Islam as Others Saw It: A Survey and Evaluation of Christian, Jewish and Zoroastrian Writings on Early Islam* (Princeton, 1997).

history, and early Islamic history being a time of great social change, that these norms changed, too. That the prevailing norms of early Islam valued the adaptation, redaction and reformulation of historical narrative, rather than the preservation of inert, historical data, certainly makes our present work more difficult. But it is far more important to see that they were part of the very dynamism that made early Islam so spectacularly adaptive and inventive. To make these early authorities objective and reliable transmitters of Islam's origins is not simply anachronistic: it underestimates the creativity of early Muslims.[21]

[21] The secondary literature occasionally speaks of 'falsification', but this should not be taken to mean intentional lying; cf. the comments by Landau-Tasseron, 'Redaction', pp. 262f. (the 'natural result of the presuppositions and formulaic thinking....'); on the originality and creativity of the Islamic legal literature, N. Calder, *Studies in Early Muslim Jurisprudence* (Oxford, 1993), pp. 198ff. (it is worth noting that one of the field's most sceptical historians saw early Muslim legal thinking and writing as much more dynamic and creative than did his fiercest critics).

CHAPTER 4

Three categories: biography, prosopography, chronography

We have seen that by the end of the ninth century Islamic historiography had generated three principal ways of organizing historical narrative – what I have called biography, prosopography and chronography. Few would dispute that we now have works of *sīra*, *ṭabaqāt* and *taʾrīkh*, even if questions might be raised about precisely when our earliest examples were put down in their final form. The text of Ibn Saᶜd's *Ṭabaqāt*, for example, was 'closed' only decades after his death, and so, too, the history of Medina written by ᶜUmar b. Shabba (d. 878), which apparently was put into its final form by one of his students; other texts also carry on beyond the deaths of their authors. (In all such cases, I shall ignore the possibility of redaction, assuming that a given work's published form reflects the design of its author.) What may be controversial is how I have defined my categories, and the significance I attach to them. I therefore owe my readers an explanation. Accordingly, this chapter serves to explain these terms and to elaborate on form and genre. (Readers who are familiar with the genres in question may wish to move directly to chapter 5.)[1]

Historiography and sources for history

By historiography, I have been speaking of prose representations of the past in which chronology, whether explicit or implicit, is an essential feature. This definition is in some measure inspired by the terminology of the tradition itself: it is hardly for nothing that writers generally reserved the terms *akhbārī*, *ahl al-sīra* (or *siyar*) and *muʾarrikh* for those who worked in one or another of the three forms, and virtually all the authors discussed here are mentioned, or would have been mentioned, by Ibn al-Nadīm in chapter 3 of his *Fihrist*. Nor is it coincidental that the works under discussion here are the bread and butter of modern historical

[1] For the post-mortem dating of Ibn Saᶜd's *Kitāb al-Ṭabaqāt*, see C. Melchert, 'How Ḥanafism came to originate in Kufa and traditionalism in Medina,' *Islamic Law and Society* 6 (1999), p. 325; on ᶜUmar b. Shabba's, S. Günther, 'New results in the theory of source-criticism in medieval Arabic literature', *al-Abhath* 42 (1994), p. 12, and *GAS*, pp. 345f.; ᶜUmar b. Shabba's work is the *Taʾrīkh al-madīna al-munawwara* (Beirut, 1990).

research into medieval Islam, at least as it has been practised by most historians. Every work I shall mention has something to teach us about how Muslims lived and thought in the medieval period, even if the lessons are not always immediately understood. For example, many historians of the first two centuries of Islam now believe that Ibn Hishām's Prophetic biography may have less to tell us about its apparent subject – the life and times of the Prophet Muḥammad – than it does about Umayyad and early Abbasid attitudes towards prophecy, religious law, and rulership, all of which are revealed in how the events are represented. Some Abbasid political narratives, for their part, may have less to say about Abbasid politics than they do the historians' ethical concerns about the societies in which they lived. Historians are often loath to admit that the first thing to be asked of a narrative of the past is what it says about its present.[2]

So the definition of historiography in operation here in part reflects the plain fact that historiography is the *sine qua non* of our research. But like the three-part typology of biography, prosopography and chronography, which aims to draw distinctions that are otherwise obscured, the term 'historiography' is also intended to be heuristic: despite all their differences, we shall see that chronography, biography and prosopography share a common history. The same thing cannot be said of other narratives of the past, and so 'historiography', as used in this book, excludes such backward-looking genres as genealogy, geography, heresiography (writing about schools of thought – sectarian, religious and philosophical), Qurʾānic exegesis, legal writing of various kinds (including *ḥadīth*), belletristic prose (especially essays on historical topics), in addition to others too numerous to mention. To varying degrees, works written in these genres are rooted in the very same deeply historical impulse – that sense of belonging to and making human history – that helped propel much of the historiographic enterprise itself. Some were even written by men whom I shall appropriate as historians, even if the tradition does not recognize them as such. Perhaps most important to most historians nowadays, all can be very profitably put to use in order to reconstruct the past. The geographical writing of the tenth century, for example, offers precious information on patterns of trade and on the natural and human geography of the Islamic world, not to mention some invaluable help in working with historiographic sources that presume their readers' familiarity with thousands of toponyms. Lexical and grammatical exegesis of an obscure passage in the Qurʾān, to take a very different example, may seem an unlikely source for social history, but if handled deftly, it can shed some light upon how social groups saw themselves. Works such as these may also share common sources with historiography proper (such as the case of Qurʾānic commentaries), and *akhbārī*s often drew upon them for their histories (such as the case of geography). And since the most *comprehensive* collection of accounts was

[2] On attitudes towards Muḥammad's life (rather than data for its reconstruction), see U. Rubin, *The Eye of the Beholder: The Life of Muḥammad as Viewed by the Early Muslims: a Textual Analysis* (Princeton, 1995), and idem, *Between Bible and Qurʾān: The Children of Israel and the Islamic Self-image* (Princeton, 1999); on some Abbasid political narratives, El-Hibri, *Reinterpreting Islamic Historiography*.

frequently considered the best, the practising historian can find himself tracking down parallel accounts of a single event in multi-volume works of history, law and belles-lettres. For these and other reasons, there should be no doubt that these sources are immensely important to modern historians; they belong in any *Handbuch* of Islamic history.[3]

This is not a *Handbuch*, however, and I am accordingly liberated from any responsibility to historians-to-be. (Their needs have in any case been addressed elsewhere: there is no shortage of bibliographies and guides to the sources of Islamic history.) For all their usefulness to modern historians, these works do not qualify as historiography. They fail not merely because the Islamic tradition fails to identify their authors as historians, but because they organize narrative in a fashion that subordinates chronology. The tenth-century geographers, for example, offer a more or less systematic and generally synchronic survey of the Islamic world – and sometimes beyond it. It is the *foregrounding of chrononology* at the organizational level that historiography makes a habit of doing, which is why tenth-century chronography is altogether more useful than tenth-century geography for reconstructing patterns of settlement and urban change in the eighth and ninth centuries. To be sure, there are soft edges around a solid chronographic core. We shall presently see that some varieties of Prophetic biography – what I shall call 'devotional biography' – do precious little with chronology. Similarly, in forsaking chronological for alphabetic arrangement, one of the trajectories of the prosopographical tradition clearly sacrifices chronology for the sake of convenience. Even so, 'fuzzy borders do not imply that a phenomenon lacks distinctive character', as one literary critic put it. And for all its faults, the typology proposed here makes some sense of what may be, aside from its sheer size, the most striking feature of the Arabic prose tradition: how author-compilers circulated more or less autonomous narrative units (*akhbār* and *ḥadīth*) across its varieties of narrative, collecting, copying, recasting, reframing, supplementing and reordering them according to a fairly limited and stable repertoire of schemes. Why this should be so is a question that will concern us later; suffice it to say here, we shall have frequent occasion to see how the concern for chronology underpins these historiographical modes.[4]

The operating definition of historiography is therefore produced by a number of considerations. And that is how definitions always are. As I suggested in chapter 1, categories are not intrinsic to narrative: in reading, thinking and writing, we impose them, and where one draws a line between jurisprudence and historiography can say as much about the scholar drawing the line as it does about the texts themselves. That I am a historian may not be unrelated to the fact that I count the *ṭabaqāt* as a historiographic form, while one student of Islamic law has counted it as one of (his) three varieties of legal writing. Now one does not have to be a

[3] On how to squeeze some social history out of Qurʾānic exegesis, see R.P. Mottahedeh, 'The Shuʿûbîyah controversy and the social history of early Islamic Iran', *IJMES* 7 (1976), pp. 161–182.
[4] The literary critic is R. Alter, *The Pleasures of Reading in an Ideological Age* (New York, 1996), p. 29.

historian to see the problems in the latter judgment, such as the title ascribed to Wāṣil b. ᶜAṭāᵓ, in addition to a plethora of non-legal *ṭabaqāt* works. But being a historian certainly helps, just as it helps one to argue away the obvious overlap between *ḥadīth* and *akhbār*: compilations of Prophetic *ḥadīth* often include sections on *maghāzī*. Honest scholars will admit that their training and perspective condition their understanding of texts: how one distinguishes between 'fictionalized history' and 'historicized fiction' will usually turn on whether one is interested in facts or fiction. The question is not idle, and we shall return to it in chapter 8. But honest scholars will equally insist that some schemes accommodate all the available evidence more effectively than others, which is a professional historian's way of saying that they are better. So what is proposed here attempts to accommodate evidence, rather than identify truths, and I am mindful that I operate according to the rules of my profession rather than the laws of nature.[5]

This – the historical contingency of classifying narrative – is of course no less true of the Islamic tradition itself. Ibn al-Nadīm's categories illuminate the state of tenth-century historiography, which is why I have made abundant use of his *Fihrist*. Seeing how Muslim critics organized narrative is an extremely useful thing, particularly as an antidote to lazy assumptions we may make on the basis of nineteenth- and twentieth-century traditions of our own, which have tended to champion chronography at the expense of other historiographical forms. 'Historians write history; gentlemen write biography', it was once said: Ibn al-Nadīm had the good fortune to be naïve of this smug pseudo-distinction. But Ibn al-Nadīm's categories remain Ibn al-Nadīm's, and however 'authentic' they may be, they carry authority not because they touched any essential nerve in the literary tradition, but because they were transmitted by the tradition: his book, copied, recopied, read and cited by later authorities (such as Yāqūt), became a 'classic'. He cannot tell us what historiography 'was', nor can anyone else. 'The term *taᵓrīkh* ("History") signifies a branch of learning that is concerned with research regarding the occurrences which take place in time, in the intention of establishing their character, and their place in time'. Such is the point of view of al-Sakhāwī (d. 1497), and I should hardly like to suggest that it is wrong. But aside from the fact that it is very late (and therefore inadmissible as evidence for the formative period of the tradition), it is pushed along by an apologetic undercurrent that is nearly as old as Islamic historiography itself. We shall see that al-Sakhāwī was arguing the case for chronography at a time when traditionist taboos on historiography were breaking down.[6]

So it is not enough to recycle indigenous categories, since they cannot guide us towards any single, 'authentic' meaning of texts or genres. As historians, all we

[5] For another way of classifying narrative, see F. Malti-Douglas, 'Texts and tortures: the reign of al-Muᶜtaḍid and the construction of historical meaning,' *Arabica* 46 (1999), pp. 313–336; and S. Leder and H. Kilpatrick, 'Classical Arabic prose literature: a researchers' sketch map', *JAL* 23 (1992), pp. 2–26; for the view that the *ṭabaqāt* belong to *fiqh* literature, N. Calder, 'Law' in S.H. Nasr and O. Leaman, eds., *History of Islamic Philosophy* (London, 1996), pp. 979–998; for a literary approach to *ḥadīth*, M. Speight, 'Narrative structures in the *ḥadīth*', *JNES* 59 (2000), pp. 265–271.

[6] On the transmission history of Ibn al-Nadīm's *Fihrist,* see S. Leder, 'Grenzen der Rekonstruktion alten Schrifttums nach den Angaben im *Fihrist*' in *Ibn an-Nadim und die mittelalterliche arabische Literatur*, pp. 21f.; on al-Sakhāwī's definition, Rosenthal, *History*, p. 273.

can aim to do is to recover some of the different ways that Muslims understood these texts and genres, and, whenever possible, to see how some understandings were made to dominate over others, according to the political, academic and cultural context in which they were generated and transmitted. Those are the main tasks of the historian; the rest is either criticism or taste.

Three categories

To classify historiography into chronography, biography and prosopography is to propose a typology. Like all typologies, this one marks *ideal types*, the cardinal points of a compass, one with which we can get our bearings, and to which all historiographic works somewhere point, *but no single one directly*. In practice this means that most of the books written after that enormously experimental and creative period of *ca.* 730 to 850 conform to one of the three, and the scholar who cultivated more than one generally did so in separate works. But other works do not fit so neatly: we should expect some cross-fertilization, and hybrids do appear. For example, in two recently published works that belong to the ninth century, the *Taʾrīkh* of the Spaniard ᶜAbd al-Malik b. Ḥabīb (d. 853) and the *Kitāb al-Maᶜrifa wa'l-taʾrīkh* of the Persian Yaᶜqūb b. Sufyān al-Fasawī (d. 890), we have works that combine chronography (in these cases, annals) with prosopography (*ṭabaqāt*). The scheme seems to have been abandoned in the tenth century, and it is therefore tempting to argue their significance away on the ground that they are too early to count. But the fact is that even some of the purest examples of chronography we possess incorporate lists (e.g. of judges, governors, those who led the Pilgrimage) and also mention the deaths of worthies (especially members of the Prophet's family and traditionists); this incipient prosopography within chronography would later flourish in the twelfth century, in the *Muntaẓam* of Ibn al-Jawzī, where capsule biographies close each year's entry. Another apparently aberrant text can be found in Ibn Saᶜd's multi-volume *ṭabaqāt*, a prosopography that opens with a Prophetic *sīra*, since *sīra* and prosopography would generally go their separate ways. Once again, however, we see that texts have the habit of entangling themselves: biographers of eponymous jurists (such as al-Ṣaymarī, d. 1045) might close with a brief *ṭabaqāt* section, while relatively late *ṭabaqāt* works not infrequently devote opening sections to fairly extensive biographical treatments of these same eponyms (such as Ibn Abī Yaᶜlā, d. 1131): *ṭabaqāt* and biography intertwine. In sum, most works do sit squarely within a given category, but this is less important than the fact that we can find a given work's essential orientation on our metaphorical compass.[7]

[7] The *sīra* material in Ibn Saᶜd's *Ṭabaqāt* occupies the first two volumes of Sachau's Leiden edition of 1904–1940; ᶜAbd al-Malik b. Ḥabīb's work was published in Madrid, 1990, and al-Fasawī's in Beirut, 1981 and Medina, 1410 H; on the former, see Jarrar, *Prophetenbiographie*, pp. 110ff., and *GAS*, p. 362, and on the latter, *GAS*, p. 319; al-Ṣaymarī's work is the *Akhbār Abī Ḥanīfa wa-aṣḥābihi* (Hyderabad, 1974; reprinted, Beirut, 1976); Ibn Abī Yaᶜlā's is the *Ṭabaqāt al-Ḥanābila* (Cairo, 1952).

This is because the tradition would end up by being relatively conservative. These three modes of organizing narrative, having crystallized in the middle of the ninth century, turned out to be experiments in chronology so successful that they would remain the prestige forms of the tradition throughout the medieval and pre-modern period, in some cases even to this day. Anyone familiar with ninth-century chronography that describes the Abbasid empire can feel at home in nineteenth-century chronography that describes the Napoleonic invasion of Egypt, just as anyone familiar with Ibn Hishām's adaptation of Ibn Isḥāq's *sīra* will know his way around twentieth-century epitomes of Ibn Hishām. By this I certainly do not mean to suggest that Muslim historians stopped thinking in the middle of the ninth century. We shall see that they would continue to write mountains of narrative, to innovate in language and subject matter, to cross-fertilize and produce hybrids, and, by the late fourteenth and fifteenth centuries, to argue their case for chronography with some real success. The tradition has a measure of dynamism for the simple reason that historical writing attracted restless and ambitious minds, authors who recognized that historical narrative could function in a number of ways (not merely to record, but to entertain, legitimize, criticize and inspire), and who challenged themselves to respond to, update, outstrip or otherwise improve upon their predecessors' work. 'Social control, pious conviction, reflective logic, virtuoso display, intellectual curiosity', all these had a hand in an ongoing reshaping of the historiographic tradition. Still, as much as they innovated, Muslim historians innovated within a framework erected in this foundational period; the prestige forms of historical narrative weathered all the change.[8]

This relative conservatism is what we should expect of historians working during late antiquity and classical Islam. Far from being revolutionary or brilliantly original (this was left to the poets and belletrists, who took the risks and reaped the rewards), the most daring sought the same, relatively modest goal that was pursued by ancient historians – that is, to be 'incrementally innovative', either to write somehow distinctively within a recognizable genre, or to compose within sight of commonly held conventions. That may appear to be faint praise, but in societies that were as deeply traditionalist as the ones in which these historians were working, it is saying a great deal. In the next chapter we shall see what traditionalism was, and what it meant to write history in a society in which traditionalism was the prevailing mode of thought. It remains in this chapter to survey biography, prosopography and chronography. Biography having pride of place in the emergence of the tradition, we can start there.[9]

[8] I borrow 'social contol … intellectual curiosity' from Calder, *Studies*, p. 200.

[9] I borrow the phrase 'incrementally innovative' from J. Marincola, *Authority and Tradition in Ancient Historiography* (Cambridge, 1997), p. 14.

Biography

'An account of the life of a man from birth to death is what I call biography', wrote A. Momigliano, one of the greatest Roman historians of the last century, and it is hard to find fault with the simple dictum, particularly since he proceeded to qualify it severely. The prestige form of Islamic biography of this description came to be Prophetic biography, and by this, one usually understands Ibn Isḥāq's *Sīra* in the version of Ibn Hishām, since the tradition itself so regularly insists upon it. But Prophetic writing did not end with the death of Ibn Hishām in 835. Moreover, there are other terms for biographical writing, and biographers wrote about a variety of men, some within the religious establishment and some outside of it. There was, at least by Momigliano's definition, a great deal of biography (and, as we shall see, a fair amount of autobiography) in classical Islam, and upon all this material some categories can be imposed.[10]

In speaking of biography and prosopography I have already made a crucial distinction, and one that is mirrored in the tradition itself: a single-subject and stand-alone biography is conventionally called a *sīra*, while one that is embedded in a compilation of capsule biographies is called a *tarjama*. Now one cannot always anticipate the contents of a book by its title: prosopographies, to take what may be the most common example, are sometimes called *taʾrīkh*s, the term that is conventionally associated with chronography. What is more, there is some real overlap between the two categories of *sīra* and *tarjama*, which is why other surveys consider both biographical. Such is the case in formal terms. What were initially short *tarjama*s would eventually grow to considerable size, so much so, in fact, that they could no longer be accommodated within multiple-*tarjama* prosopographies. The result was independent *tarjama* works – that is, single-subject, stand-alone biographies. Such is also the case in approach: biography and prosopography share attitudes towards their subjects and conventions of description that are as strange to modern readers as they are typical in late antique literature, be it in Greek, Latin or Arabic. This being particularly striking to moderns accustomed to forensic biography and self-revealing autobiography, it requires some explanation.

For the most part, we now expect a biographer to get under the skin of his subject, to explain how and why he is in some way unique or exceptional – to show, perhaps most important of all, how he came to be who he was. Since we generally hold personality ('character') to be the product of experience and accumulated influence, professional biographers usually aspire to identify and assess as many of these experiences and influences as possible, particularly during the early – and formative – period of their subjects' lives: the most recent instalment in a

[10] The great Roman historian is A. Momigliano, *The Development of Greek Biography: Four Lectures* (Cambridge, Mass., 1971), p. 11; cf. now G.W. Bowersock, 'Momigliano's quest for the person,' *History and Theory* 30 (1991), pp. 27–36; on the biographical impulse in early historiography in general, M. Cooperson, *Classical Arabic Biography: The Heirs of the Prophets in the Age of al-Maʾmūn* (Cambridge, 2000).

multi-volume biography of Gustav Mahler, which covers a handful of years, runs to some 1,000 pages. Muslim biographers and prosopographers, by contrast, were generally interested not so much in what made their subjects unique as in what made them exemplary, and they favoured in their modes of characterization the external (appearance, speech, the sequence of events and actions) over the internal. When we are made privy to the thoughts of a defeated and forlorn governor, riding tragically (and comically) upon a donkey, his feet dragging along the ground, we are getting something very special. Far from seeing character as contingent and dynamic, biographers usually saw character as determined and fixed, a general rule that is tested, rather than broken, by the infrequent exception. Two examples can suffice.[11]

The first is a biography of Saladin (d. 1193), which was written by Bahāʾ al-Dīn Ibn Shaddād (d. 1235). As the chief judge of Saladin's army, Ibn Shaddād enjoyed direct access to his subject, whose words he repeatedly cites, and he experienced first-hand many of the events of his book. No doubt he had ample opportunity to put all manner of questions to Saladin. But Ibn Shaddād did not share our modern view that childhood and adolescence are formative influences, and of Saladin's parents, family, friends and tutors – the collectivity of human contact that we would hold responsible for conditioning the man Saladin would become – we hear virtually nothing. (It is true that Ibn Shaddād advertises his work as a *mukhtaṣar*, but the word should not be taken literally here; it actually signals the false modesty of an ambitious historian.) The point of Ibn Shaddād's biography is not to understand how Saladin became the man he became; it is to portray him as the archetypical holy warrior. This is why, in scarcely ten lines, the author moves from his subject's birth in the Iraqi town of Takrit to his first great career break, when he received the patronage of Nūr al-Dīn b. Zanjī (rg. 1146–1174), the ruler of northern Iraq and Syria; from that point on, we move from battle to glorious battle, watching Saladin repulse the Crusaders. And because this literary patterning – Saladin's representation as *mujāhid* ('crusader') extraordinaire – has clear echoes in the art and architecture of the time, we can be sure that it is not *merely* literary, but plays one part in a broader political programme of the state. As a chronographer of the period said of the Ayyubids (rg. 1169–1260), the dynasty that Saladin had established in Syria and Egypt:

> In this book I have compiled accounts of the kings of the Banū Ayyūb [Ayyubids] and all their qualities (*maḥāsin*) and virtues (*manāqib*). For they are greater kings than those who have preceded them and more magnificent in ruling. God delivered holy Jerusalem

[11] A useful introduction to biography in a similar context is P. Cox, *Biography in Late Antiquity: A Quest for the Holy Man* (Berkeley and Los Angeles, 1983), where the distinction drawn between 'chronological' and 'topical' biography (pp. 57f.) has influenced the typology proposed here; for the third volume on Mahler, H.-L. de la Grange, *Gustav Mahler: Vienna, Triumph and Disillusion (1904–1911)* (Oxford, 2000); cf. the contrasting remarks in D.F. Reynolds, ed., *Interpreting the Self: Autobiography in the Arabic Literary Tradition* (Berkeley and Los Angeles, 2001), pp. 36ff.; for the forlorn governor, al-Balādhurī, *Ansāb al-ashrāf*, ivb (Jerusalem, 1938), p. 109.

> from the hands of the infidels through them, and he laid low through their swords the necks of the heretics. They purified the Egyptian domains of the innovations of the Bāṭinīs [the Ismāᶜīlī Shīᶜtes], and [re]established the foundations of the true Muslim religion (*arkān al-milla al-ḥanafiyya*)....[12]

The same concern to exemplify can be traced in portraits drawn of men of learning. Here too, in a second example, we can see that biography was selective, and that modelling was intended not merely to edify or inspire, but to produce social and institutional consequences. Thus, the biographies of Aḥmad b. Ḥanbal (d. 855) offer something less than a full discussion of their subject's life: one might begin at birth and end at death, but, aside from developing the hagiographic themes of piety and asceticism – themes of growing significance to late ninth- and tenth-century audiences – these events function as little more than a frame, inside of which sits a detailed and elaborate treatment of the event that transformed Aḥmad into the traditionists' hero: his defiant resistance against the inquisition imposed by the Abbasid caliph al-Maᵓmūn (rg. 813–833), the narrative of which fills about nine-tenths of the work as a whole. Portraying Aḥmad as the hero of the traditionists' resistance against the caliph's rationalizing programme – indeed, as an emblematic figure of opposition to the state's abuse of power and its usurpation of the scholars' authority in matters of religion – served not merely the traditionist cause, but the nascent Ḥanbalī school of law itself. Whose eponym could trump Aḥmad, who, alone amongst the eponyms of the four law schools that survived, had the good fortune to endure the caliph's torture? Little wonder that the event gave its name to another of the earliest biographies of Aḥmad, *Dhikr miḥnat al-imām Aḥmad b. Ḥanbal*, 'Account of the inquisition of the imam Aḥmad b. Ḥanbal', by Ḥanbal b. Isḥāq (d. 886). As one historian has said of biography in late antiquity, 'The biographical process of creating an ideal character out of the historical data of a man's life suggests that it is the philosophical and historical stance of the biographer, rather than of the subject himself, that dominates the composition of the biography'. It is this approach to biography, which, already in the ninth century, consists in the selective enumeration of 'glorious exploits' (*manāqib*), *maḥāsin* ('excellences') and 'virtues' (*faḍāᵓil*) of foundational figures, that seems to have provided a model for the dynastic biographies of the Ayyubid and Mamluk

[12] Bahāᵓ al-Dīn Ibn Shaddād's *Sīrat Ṣalāḥ al-Dīn* (*al-Nawādir al-sulṭāniyya wa'l-maḥāsin al-Yūsufiyya*) was published in Cairo, 1962, and translated by D.S. Richards as *The Rare and Excellent History of Saladin* (*al-Nawādir al-sulṭāniyya wa'l-maḥāsin al-Yūsufiyya*) (Aldershot, 2001); on the work, see D.S. Richards, 'A consideration of two sources for the life of Saladin', *JSS* 25 (1980), pp. 46–65; on Saladin and the *jihād*, M.C. Lyons and D. Jackson, *Saladin: The Politics of the Holy War* (Cambridge, 1982), and C. Hillenbrand, 'Jihad propaganda in Syria from the time of the First Crusade until the death of Zengi: the evidence of monumental inscriptions' in K. Athamina and R. Heacock, eds., *The Frankish Wars and their Influence on Palestine* (Bir Zeit, 1994), pp. 60–69; the chronographer is Ibn Wāṣil in his *Mufarrij al-kurūb fī akhbār Banī Ayyūb* (Cairo, 1953), i, p. 1.

periods. The figures were generally of two kinds: caliphs (Muᶜāwiya, ᶜUthmān, ᶜAlī, Muᶜāwiya) and jurists (Abū Ḥanīfa, al-Shāfiᶜī, Aḥmad b. Ḥanbal).[13]

Sīra and, as we shall presently see, *tarjama*, thus share a selective approach to biography, and they usually appear as complementary terms for complementary forms. They need not so appear, however. Indeed, *sīra* could mean a variety of things, particularly during the first three centuries of Islam, before Ibn Hishām's *sīra* of the Prophet had become so influential. 'Life' was certainly among them, and, according to Ibn al-Nadīm (among others), many of the earliest specimens were about caliphs (Abū Bakr [rg. 632–634], Muᶜāwiya [rg. 661–680], al-Manṣūr [rg. 754–775], al-Maʾmūn [rg. 813–833], al-Muᶜtaḍid [rg. 892–902] and al-Muktafī [rg. 902–908]), and aspiring caliphs, too (thus the Prophet's grandson Ḥusayn). It is equally clear, both from purported titles and usage more generally, that the term *sīra* (or its plural, *siyar*) could also describe a *life and its related times*, such as *Sīrat al-Furs* ('Sīra of the Persians'), and this is presumably why 'the people (*ahl; aṣḥāb*) of the *siyar*' frequently appears as a synonym for *akhbārī*s – 'historians'. Behind these eighth- and ninth-century usages, there seems to lie an even earlier one, that of 'manifesto', such as appears in relation to a document (*kitāb*) written by Jahm b. Ṣafwān for the rebel al-Ḥārith b. Surayj in 746, which is mentioned in later sources. This latter sense of *sīra* seems to have been lost to the Sunnis during the ninth century, when it was all but obliterated by that of 'biography', and it apparently survived only among non-Sunnis, such as the Ibāḍī Khārijites of present-day Oman, who would continue to call their religious epistles *sīra*s well into the classical period.[14]

There are other, related problems of terminology, not the least of which is the practice of some modern editors to impose titles of their own upon their editions. The biography of Aḥmad b. Ḥanbal that so selectively treats his life was apparently assembled by one of his sons, Abū al-Faḍl Ṣāliḥ (d. 878); and although it was recently published as a *sīra*, there does not seem to be any traditional attestation for the title. In addition, Prophetic *sīra*s are occasionally extracted from chronographies, and then published separately as *sīra*s: two examples come from the *al-Bidāya wa'l-nihāya* of Ibn Kathīr (d. 1373) and the *Taʾrīkh al-Islām* of al-Dhahabī (d. 1348). It is true that in the manuscript culture of the pre-modern Islamic world

[13] For the biographies of Aḥmad b. Ḥanbal, see below and Ḥanbal b. Isḥāq, *Dhikr miḥnat al-imām Aḥmad b. Ḥanbal* (Cairo, 1977); Cooperson, *Arabic Biography*, pp. 107ff.; cf. N. Hurvitz, 'Biographies and mild asceticism: a study of Islamic moral imagination', *SI* 85 (1997), pp. 41–65; (and cf. the biographical transformation of a Crusading man of action into a reclusive holy man in G. Spiegel, *The Past as Text: The Theory and Practice of Medieval Historiography* [Baltimore, 1997]); on the significance of the 'inquisition', *EI*², 'Miḥna' (Hinds); on characterization through sequence, Ashtiany Bray, '*Isnād*s and models of heroes,' pp. 13f.; the quotation is from Cox, *Biography*, p. 37; for *manāqib* and *faḍāʾil* works about these caliphs and jurists, see *GAS*, index.

[14] For several uses of *sīra* and *siyar*, see Hinds, '*Maghāzī* and *sīra*'; Jarrar, *Prophetenbiographie*, pp. 4ff.; Schöller, *Exegetisches Denken*, pp. 43ff.; Ibn al-Farrāʾ, *Kitāb Rusul al-mulūk* (Beirut, 1972), p. 36 (*aṣḥāb al-siyar*); for *ahl al-siyar* = *akhbārī*s, al-Ṭabarī, *Taʾrīkh*, ii, p. 1269; al-Azdī al-Mawṣilī, *Taʾrīkh al-Mawṣil* (Cairo, 1967), p. 25; for al-Ḥārith b. Surayj, al-Ṭabarī, *Taʾrīkh*, ii, p. 1918; and for Ibāḍī Khārijite epistles, P. Crone and F. Zimmermann, *The Epistle of Sālim b. Dhakwān* (Oxford, 2001).

copyists might choose to copy only one part of a multi-volume work, rather than the cumbersome (and expensive) whole. It is also true that a teacher might teach a single section from a multi-volume work, be it his or someone else's. In conventions such as these, one might find a precedent for the modern practice of extracting and retitling. All of this said, we should try to distinguish between those works that were called *sīra*s in their day (or well before ours, in any case) and those that we have chosen to call *sīra*s.[15]

So Prophetic biography enjoys pride of place in the Islamic tradition, and Ibn Hishām's version of Ibn Isḥāq's *sīra* enjoyed pride of place within Prophetic biography: as we shall see in chapter 10, it generated a tradition of redacting, commenting and epitomising. Just how faithful Ibn Hishām was to Ibn Isḥāq is a question that scholars have pondered over. The evidence being so exiguous, there is no clear answer (we have already seen that the very existence of an authoritative 'original' by Ibn Isḥāq is itself very problematic). How faithful later sources were to Ibn Hishām and the style of Prophetic biography he represented is easier to judge: their fidelity depended much on their purpose. Here we arrive at some distinctions that we must draw within the biographical tradition.

In typological terms, Ibn Hishām's biography is deeply chronographic. He begins with Muḥammad's genealogy and birth, ends with his death, and has chronology serve as the guiding hand throughout the entire work; he often pauses to pin down problems of dating and sequence. This attention to chronology should not be confused with objectivity: much is legendary and miraculous (Muḥammad bears the 'signs of prophecy' as a small child), and already the dogma of Muḥammad's perfection seems to have taken some hold. But compared to later Prophetic biographies, the legends and miracles are quite restrained: Ibn Hishām seems to have had more of an appetite for lists than he did for legends. More important is the fact that the legends are all firmly embedded in the carefully ordered and oft-measured folds of his life and times. In short, this is sophisticated historical writing by any reasonable definition. The same thing cannot be said of other (and, on the whole, much later) works of Prophetic biography, which can usefully be called 'devotional biography'. A representative example is the *Shifāʾ* of the Andalusian al-Qāḍī ʿIyāḍ (d. 1149), an immensely popular compilation – indeed, arguably the single most popular Prophetic biography of the entire tradition. But its popularity ends at the historian's door. For here miracles and legends run riot, and the historical Muḥammad – Ibn Hishām's pragmatic and resourceful Muḥammad, the engaging figure who improvises responses to events, good and bad – is eclipsed by a fully mythologised and altogether more static Perfect Man. Because he is timeless, chronology as much as disappears as a narrative feature, replaced by a catalogue of encomia: in works such as this one, we are very much

[15] Ṣāliḥ's '*Sīra*' of Aḥmad b. Ḥanbal was published in Alexandria, 1981 and Riyadh, 1995; Ibn Kathīr's '*sīra*' was published in Cairo in 1966, and was translated by T. Le Gassick as *The Life of the Prophet Muhammad* (London, 1998–2000); al-Dhahabī's was published in Beirut in 1981 (and here its extraction is acknowledged); Ibn Kathīr's *al-Fuṣūl fī sīrat al-rasūl* (Beirut, 1993) does appear to have been an independent work.

on the margins of the historiographical corpus. Between these two poles of chronographic and devotional biography, represented in the first instance by Ibn Hishām and in the second by al-Qāḍī ᶜIyāḍ, lie mixed works, in which chronology yields to a topical arrangement. An example is the *Bahjat al-maḥāfil wa-bughyat al-amāthil* by al-ᶜĀmirī (d. 1488). The first of its two parts, which relies heavily upon Ibn Isḥāq's 'large *sīra*', consists of a chronological treatment of the Prophet's genealogy, birth, career and death. The second leaves chronology behind, and catalogues his glorious sobriquets, his virtues, exemplary character, and miracles. The same tension – between chronographic particularism on the one hand, and timeless universalism on the other – is also present in non-Prophetic *sīra*.[16]

Prosopography

I have already suggested that whereas biography is about exemplary or otherwise distinctive individuals, prosopography compiles and organizes those items of biographical data that mark an individual's belonging to a group. Biographies accentuate the individual; prosopographies make individuals members. For reasons that should become clear in chapter 7, these groups are almost without exception groups of élite individuals, such as those who possessed religious merit (Companions of the Prophet), a particular type of knowledge (philosophers, traditionists) or skill (Qur'ān reciters). Some of these groups, such as the schools of legal thought, generated powerful ties of loyalty, and in these cases, the members felt a correspondingly powerful (if not necessarily exclusive) sense of membership. In other cases, such as the 'notables' (*aᶜyān*) who are the subject of Ibn Khallikān's prosopography, there was no such social sense of membership, since the only criterion for inclusion was celebrity itself: a famous poet may follow a caliph, and a jurist, a philosopher. Here the category is literary. As we have already seen, our earliest *ṭabaqāt* works seem to date from the late eighth and early ninth century; like so much of the early tradition, they were written in Iraq.

Just as some works of biography point more clearly in the direction of chronography than others, so, too, do some works of prosopography. This is particularly so in the case of *ṭabaqāt* works, where group members are organized into cohorts of successive generations, the length of which can vary from several years to several decades: one of our earliest surviving *ṭabaqāt* works was written by Muslim b. al-Ḥajjāj (d. 875), where we have have three *ṭabaqa*s; by the time we reach the *Kitāb al-Ṭabaqāt al-Shāfiᶜiyya* by Ibn Qāḍī Shuhba (d. 1448), we have 29. And just as some biography points away from chronography, so, too, does some prosopography. Already with the 'Great History' (*al-Taʾrīkh al-kabīr*) of al-Bukhārī (d. 870)

[16] The only systematic analysis of Ibn Isḥāq remains Sellheim, 'Prophet, Chalif und Geschichte'; on al-Qāḍī ᶜIyāḍ's biography (including a rough measure of its popularity) see chapter 6; al-ᶜĀmirī's work was published in Medina, 1969; cf. the *Bidāyat al-saʾūl fī tafḍīl al-rasūl* (Beirut and Damascus, 1983) of Ibn ᶜAbd al-Salām al-Sulamī (d. 1262) and the *Khulāṣat al-siyar fī aḥwāl sayyid al-bashar* (Delhi, 1343 H) of Muḥibb al-Dīn al-Ṭabarī (d. 1295).

we have what amounts to a very long list of names (it has entries on over 12,000 traditionists), arranged in roughly alphabetical order (this and similar works often begin with Muḥammad, in deference to the Prophet). In the tenth century we have the appearance of the *muᶜjam*, which is the term generally used for alphabetically arranged compilations. The term 'biographical dictionary' is often employed to describe both the *ṭabaqāt* and *muᶜjam* genres, but I shall use it only for the second. I include therein all prosopographies alphabetically ordered, regardless of their title or how faithful their arrangements are to the actual Arabic alphabet.[17]

Both *ṭabaqāt* and proto-*muᶜjam* works thus have their origins in the ninth century. Both, moreover, can be regarded as one of the clearest signs (along with non-historiographic compilations of miscellaneous data) of the mania for lists that characterizes medieval Arabic literature in general, and early *sīra* in particular. It has been suggested that the listing features inherent in genealogy may explain its origins (if not the mania itself), but this does not take us very far, since genealogy as a written practice emerged alongside historiography. Be this as it may, alongside al-Bukhārī's *al-Taʾrīkh* one can set the *ṭabaqāt* works of Khalīfa b. Khayyāṭ (d. 854) and Muslim b. al-Ḥajjāj, which are even sparer: often just bare names (or even just a single name) slotted into the appropriate generation. Even chronographers aspiring to concision seem to let themselves get carried away by their lists, al-Yaᶜqūbī's *History* being a good case in point. Or did they? The answer turns on how much sense we can make of particular lists and of the listing phenomenon as a narrative technique more generally. On the first of these, some good progress has been made. The criteria for inclusion in al-Bukhārī's lists, for example, seem to be related to the emerging criteria of the *ḥadīth* sciences (we have other ninth-century evidence that this science was fairly well developed, too); for these and other reasons, we can surmise that although *ḥadīth* criticism cannot explain the appearance of prosopography, it certainly gave an impetus to its elaboration. On the second question, relatively little progress has been made, at least not beyond pointing out that listing *is* a narrative strategy. One may presume that part of its attraction was in showing off: the more lists one had to hand and, similarly, the longer one's lists, the greater one's industry and knowledge. In an academic tradition that revered accumulated knowledge (traditionists often crowed about how many *ḥadīth*s they had memorized), listing made good sense.[18]

[17] Muslim b. al-Ḥajjāj's *Kitāb al-Ṭabaqāt* was published in Riyadh, 1991; the most recent edition of Ibn Qāḍī Shuhba's *Kitāb Ṭabaqāt al-Shāfiᶜiyya* is Cairo, 1998, but here I cite Hyderabad, 1978; al-Bukhārī's *al-Taʾrīkh al-kabīr* was published in Hyderabad, 2nd ed., 1958, on which see C. Melchert, 'Bukhārī and early hadith criticism', *JAOS* 121 (2001), pp. 7–19; for an early *muᶜjam* work by Abū Yaᶜlā (d. *ca.* 920), H. Schützinger, 'Abū Yaᶜlā al-Mauṣilī. Leben und Lehrerverzeichnis (*Kitāb al-Muᶜǧam*)', *ZDMG* 131 (1981), pp. 281–296 (for more examples of this sub-genre, in which a scholar lists his teachers, see below, and *GAS*, pp. 170f.).

[18] Khalīfa b. Khayyāṭ's *Ṭabaqāt* was published in Damascus, 1966; on al-Bukhārī's criteria, Melchert, 'Bukhārī and early hadith criticism'; for more early evidence, M. Muranyi, 'Zur Entwicklung der *ᶜilm al-riǧāl*-Literatur im 3. Jahrhundert d.H.', *ZDMG* 142 (1992), pp. 57–71; on listing as a narrative strategy, M. Robinson Waldman, '"The otherwise unnoteworthy year 711": a reply to Hayden White', *Critical Inquiry* 7 (1981), pp. 784–792.

i. Biographical dictionaries

If listing is a feature common to many of the historiographic genres, it certainly finds its apotheosis in the biographical dictionaries, which, as we have seen, might reasonably be defined as name lists, annotated (often generously) and arranged in accordance with the compilers' design and purpose. As time passed, producing more and more notable Muslims and increasingly ambitious historians, works could grow to truly gargantuan sizes. The original version of the *History of Damascus* by Ibn ᶜAsākir (d. 1176), which has been recently published in no fewer than 70 volumes, seems to have been considerably larger than what we now possess – perhaps 16,000 folios in total, all covering figures with one connection or another to the city of Damascus. Another local dictionary, which, like Ibn ᶜAsākir's, was modelled upon the fourteen-volume *History of Baghdad* by al-Khaṭīb al-Baghdādī (d. 1071), is the *History* of Aleppo by Ibn al-ᶜAdīm (d. 1262); it probably consisted of some 8,000 folios, and included entries on 8,000 people. *Al-Wāfī bi'l-wafayāt* ('The Complement to the *Wafayāt* [obituaries]') by al-Ṣafadī (d. 1363) is one of several works intended to continue and complement the first dictionary of notable men of all varieties, which was assembled by Ibn Khallikān (d. 1282); now published in over 30 volumes, it contains about 5,500 biographical notices. *Al-Durar al-kāmina fī aᶜyān al-miʾa al-thāmina* ('Hidden pearls about the notables of the eighth [Islamic] century') by Ibn Ḥajar al-ᶜAsqalānī (d. 1449) was the first dictionary to compile notices of figures who had died in a single century (several would follow); it finds room for more than 5,000 such figures. A work devoted to the following century, al-Sakhāwī's *al-Ḍawʾ al-lāmiᶜ li-ahl al-qarn al-tāsiᶜ* ('The Light Shining upon the People of the Ninth Century'), is relatively modest in size but remarkable for its range: in addition to prominent figures from the worlds of learning (both religious and literary), politics and administration, 'be they Egyptian, Syrian, Hijazi, Yemeni, Byzantine, or Indian, in the East and West', al-Sakhāwī covers non-Muslims from within the Islamic world.[19]

The building block of these huge edifices is the capsule biography written in the third person, whose coverage and size depend on the purpose and range of the host prosopography, be it a dictionary or a *ṭabaqāt* work. Put a different way, all varieties of prosopography offer highly selective biographical notices, and what is selected from the available biographical data conforms to the designs of the compiler. In prosopographies of traditionists, such as Ibn Ḥajar's *Tahdhīb al-tahdhīb*, the conventions are designed principally to deliver information necessary for *ḥadīth* criticism, a sub-field of the *ḥadīth* sciences that generated several sub-genres;

[19] On prosopographies in general, see P. Auchterlonie, *Arabic Biographical Dictionaries: A Summary Guide and Bibliography* (Durham, 1987); on Ibn ᶜAsākir and Ibn al-ᶜAdīm in particular, D. Morray, *An Ayyubid Notable and his World: Ibn al-ᶜAdīm and Aleppo as Portrayed in his Biographical Dictionary of People Associated with the City* (Leiden, 1994), pp. 10f. and 144f.; Ibn ᶜAsākir's *Taʾrīkh madīnat Dimashq* was published in Beirut, 1998; al-Khaṭīb al-Baghdādī's *Taʾrīkh Baghdād* in Cairo, 1931; Ibn al-ᶜAdīm's *Bughyat al-ṭalab fī taʾrīkh Ḥalab*, in Damascus, 1988; Ibn Ḥajar's *al-Durar al-kāmina fī aᶜyān al-miʾa al-thāmina*, in Cairo, 1349 H; for al-Sakhāwī's programmatic statement, his *al-Ḍawʾ al-lāmiᶜ li-ahl al-qarn al-tāsiᶜ* (Cairo, 1355 H), i, p. 5.

Plate 3 Two tables of contents in a volume of Ibn Khallikān's *Wafayāt al-aᶜyān* (Bodleian Library, Oxford, MS Pococke 338, fols. 1v and 2r), which starts with 'Maḥmūd' and carries through the letters 'n', 'h', 'w' and 'y'; each box contains the name of a subject, the bolder script indicating a change of letter.

among these are dictionaries of trustworthy transmitters (*thiqāt*) and dictionaries of weak transmitters (*ḍuᶜafāʾ*). Since there were thousands – indeed, tens of thousands – of transmitters, some good, some bad, others indifferent, all transmitting to each other from one end of the Islamic world to the other, what mattered in this discipline was the *precise* identity of the individual in question, his standing as transmitter, and when and where he lived (aliases were sometimes used in the case of especially weak transmitters). The conventions thus usually call for a full name (including variants), provenance (often indicated by the *nisba* adjective that forms part of the name), reputation (expressed either by a technical term such as 'trustworthy' or 'weak', and/or an authority's opinion or a vivid anecdote), an account of training and career (which, in the case of undistinguished transmitters, is usually boiled down to names of traditionists) and, if the data is available, a death date.[20]

An entirely typical (though admittedly brief) example of a relatively undistinguished transmitter can be drawn from the twelve-volume *Tahdhīb al-tahdhīb* ('Refinement of the Refinement'), a work that seems less curiously entitled when one realizes that it is based in large part upon the 35-volume *Tahdhīb al-kamāl fī asmāʾ al-rijāl* ('The Refinement of the Complete [Book] on Men's [read: transmitters'] Names') by al-Mizzī (d. 1341). (I have inserted numbers for the sake of clarity.)

> (1) ᶜAbd al-Jalīl b. Ḥumayd al-Yaḥṣubī, Abū Mālik al-Miṣrī. (2) He transmitted [*ḥadīth*] on the authority of al-Zuhrī, Yaḥyā b. Saᶜīd al-Anṣārī, Ayyūb al-Sakhtiyānī, ᶜAbd al-Karīm Abū Umayya and Khālid b. Abī ᶜImrān. (3) From him transmitted Ibn ᶜAjlān, who was a contemporary of his, Mūsā b. Salama, Ibn Wahb, Abū Nāfiᶜ b. Yazīd and Yaḥyā b. Ayyūb, [all] Egyptians. (4) Al-Nasāʾī said: 'There is nothing wrong with him'. (5) Ibn Ḥibbān mentioned him [in his book entitled] *The Trustworthy Ones* (*al-Thiqāt*) (6) Ibn Yūnus said: 'He died in year 148'. (7) I say: Aḥmad b. Rishdīn said, on the authority of Aḥmad b. Ṣāliḥ: he is trustworthy.

The first sentence gives us his name, which, in including two *nisba* adjectives (Yaḥṣubī and Miṣrī), tells us his tribal affiliation (the Yaḥṣub) and provenance (Miṣr = Egypt); equipped with this information, we are unlikely to confuse him with any other ᶜAbd al-Jalīls. The second gives us some teachers, amongst whom we find al-Zuhrī (d. 742), already introduced in chapter 2 as a *sīra* specialist; the third sentence provides some students' names. We can accordingly place our ᶜAbd al-Jalīl in a sequence of transmitters, and combining what we know from (1) and (3), we begin to sense that he forms part of an Egyptian tradition. The fourth, fifth and seventh sentences state his reputation as a transmitter; 'There is nothing wrong with him' (4) is a technical phrase used in the criticism of transmitters, and Ibn Ḥibbān's work (5) is an example of the sub-field of *ḥadīth* criticism. The sixth sentence gives us a death date of 148, which started in February of 765 CE and ended in February of 766; the relative sequence provided by (1) and (2) is corroborated, and now yields to an absolute date. What this means is that anyone who claims to have heard a *ḥadīth* from ᶜAbd al-Jalīl after 148 is either confused or

[20] On Ibn Ḥajar's work, see below.

lying. This may sound cynical, but it is not: prosopographers were defending (or impugning) the reputation of *ḥadīth* authorities as much as they were defending the integrity of *ḥadīth* transmission itself.[21]

Such, then, are the sort of answers that much traditionist prosopography is designed to supply. Other kinds of prosopography offer different answers in similarly formulaic ways. Historians are naturally free to ask questions of their own, and because works of prosopography are by convention both formulaic (the capsule biographies provide comparable data) and massive, they lend themselves particularly well to quantitative approaches. Where did the learned men of Mamluk Cairo come from? What roles did women have in Islamic societies? What professional activities did learned men engage in? At what rate did the indigenous population of Iran convert to Islam? While chronography is usually silent on these and related questions, the biographical dictionaries have offered answers. Of course treating prosopographies as data banks is not without its risks, especially if the answers are taken to be representative for society at large. Since the data all comes from a self-selected slice of the social and political élite, the more tightly a question focuses directly upon that élite, the more likely its answers are to be correct. And here it bears reminding ourselves that these are second or third-order questions. In answering the first order question – *how* do the texts say what they say? – relatively little has been done, so our understanding of prosopographical texts as texts (rather than data banks) remains poor.[22]

Here it should be pointed out that although the third person is the voice that prevails in these prosopographies – and, indeed, in biography and chronography as well – passages in the first person do often appear. (To distinguish these from stand-alone autobiographies, I shall refer to them as autobiographical passages.) The shift can produce narratives that are far more complex than the preceding example, and produce fairly revealing autobiographical passages. An example can be drawn from al-Khaṭīb al-Baghdādī's *History of Baghdad*. Eleven lines into his entry on Ibn Shāhīn (d. 995), al-Khaṭīb al-Baghdādī cites Ibn Shāhīn himself, who describes in the first person how he came to learn of his own genealogy and birth date (he read them on some papers [*kutub*] of his father's). He also says something of his early training ('As far as I can remember, the first time I wrote *ḥadīth* down

[21] The biography is translated from Ibn Ḥajar al-ᶜAsqalānī, *Tahdhīb al-tahdhīb* (Hyderabad, 1327 H), vi, p. 106; al-Mizzī, *Tahdhīb al-kamāl* (Beirut, 1992), xvi, p. 398 (where several other sources are given, including Ibn Ḥibbān al-Bustī's *al-Thiqāt* and al-Bukhārī's *al-Taʾrīkh al-kabīr*); for contentious biographers and prosopographers, E. Dickinson, 'Aḥmad b. al-Ṣalt and his biography of Abū Ḥanīfa', *JAOS* 116 (1996), pp. 406–417.

[22] For prosopographies as data banks, see C. Petry, *The Civilian Elite of Cairo in the Later Middle Ages* (Princeton, 1981); R. Roded, *Women in Islamic Biographical Collections: From Ibn Saᶜd to Who's Who* (Boulder, 1994); M.L. Avila, *La sociedad hispanomusulmana al final del califato: aproximación a un estudio demográfico* (Madrid, 1985); H. Cohen, 'The economic background and the secular occupations of Muslim jurisprudents and traditionists in the classical period of Islam', *JESHO* 13 (1970), pp. 16–61; R. Bulliet, 'A quantitative approach to medieval Muslim biographical dictionaries', *JESHO* 13 (1970), pp. 195–211; in general, Humphreys, *Islamic History*, pp. 189ff.; for prosopographies as texts, Malti-Douglas, 'Dreams, the blind, and the semiotics of the biographical notice'; eadem, 'Texts and tortures'; and H.E. Fähndrich, 'The *Wafayāt al-aᶜyān* of Ibn Khallikān: a new approach', *JAOS* 93 (1973), pp. 432–445.

in my own hand was in the year 308, when I was eleven'). This last biographical detail now sets al-Khaṭīb off in an autobiographical direction of his own. He first tells his reader of three men, all former teachers, who also first started writing *ḥadīth* down at the age of eleven. The first lived to the age of 103, the second to 90, and the last to 80 (such longevity was considered unexceptional for *ḥadīth* transmitters); al-Khaṭīb volunteers the fact that he led the prayers at all of their funerals. He then turns to his own birth and describes how – and here we begin to understand why he has digressed so much – he came to 'hear' *ḥadīth* at the very same age of eleven. Only now does he return to Ibn Shāhīn, in order to survey his prodigious literary output: reportedly over 300 volumes, several of which survive. So the author's third person yields to the subject's first person, and this yields to the author's first person, an intermingling of narrative that one imagines is not unrelated to the point of the digression itself: the names of traditionists may change, but the pattern of learning amongst its membership is unchanging.[23]

ii. *Ṭabaqāt* works

Some of the preceding applies to *ṭabaqāt* works. The capsule biography, conventionally written in the third person, functions as the principal narrative unit, arranged in this case in successive cohorts. (There are some *ṭabaqāt* works in which the 'classes' represent categories of excellence, rather than chronological cohorts; I leave these aside.) If most *ṭabaqāt* works catalogue men of learning, there is the occasional exception, one being a dynastic history of the Ayyubids by Aḥmad b. Ibrāhīm al-ᶜAsqalānī (d. 1471), in which members of the ruling house are organized by *ṭabaqāt*. Although *ṭabaqāt* works did not reach the massive size of many *muᶜjams*, many were still large, multi-volume works that assembled thousands of these capsule biographies: Ibn Saᶜd's, for example, includes over 4,000 subjects, of whom around 600 are women. And just as one *muᶜjam* might inspire continuations and complements, so, too, did some *ṭabaqāt* works: Ibn Abī Yaᶜlā's history of the Ḥanbalites, the *Ṭabaqāt al-Ḥanābila*, was continued by Ibn Rajab (d. 1392), and Ibn Rajab was epitomized by al-ᶜUlaymī (d. 1521). There are at least two contrasts that should be drawn, however. First, whereas Ibn Khallikān opened the way for a series of encyclopaedic biographical dictionaries in which celebrity itself was the criterion for inclusion, the *ṭabaqāt* tradition remained exclusive: we have *ṭabaqāt* works on virtually every important discipline in Islamic letters (especially poets, philologists, jurists, and traditionists), but none that encompasses all of them. One might surmise that the impulse to organize material along these lines was satisfied otherwise: in the first instance, in the marriage of chronography and prosopography effected by Ibn al-Jawzī (where generous biographical notices end each annual entry); in the second, in the appearance of the 'centennial dictionaries'

[23] Aḥmad b. Ibrāhīm al-ᶜAsaqalānī's work is the *Shifāᵓ al-qulūb fī manāqib banī Ayyūb* (Baghdad, 1978); al-Khaṭīb al-Baghdādī, *Taᵓrīkh Baghdād*, xi, pp. 265ff.; on Ibn Shāhīn, *GAS*, pp. 209f. (several of the titles listed have been edited since 1967); on autobiographical passages, see H. Kilpatrick, 'Autobiography and classical Arabic literature', *JAL* 22 (1991), pp. 1–20; and Reynolds, ed., *Interpreting the Self*.

first introduced by Ibn Ḥajar. The second point of contrast is altogether more interesting. Whereas alphabetically ordered *muᶜjam* works subordinate chronology for the sake of convenience, and sit on the margins of historiography as a result, chronologically ordered *ṭabaqāt* works sit squarely at its centre. This means that in addition to whatever role they played as works of reference, they made claims about history. In fact, the appeal of the *ṭabaqāt* went well beyond their academic utility. They came to have a social function, particularly in the formation of the legal schools, all of which outfitted themselves with *ṭabaqāt* and *ṭabaqāt*-related histories during the ninth and early tenth centuries: it seems that no more than two *ṭabaqāt* works were written during the late eighth and early ninth centuries; by the early eleventh, by which time these schools of law had crystallized and learning had professionalized, one count puts the number at 28.[24]

We can understand something of the social function of the *ṭabaqāt* if we look briefly at works associated with one of the most celebrated of all medieval *madrasa*s (institutions of higher Islamic learning), that of the Niẓāmiyya in Baghdad, founded by the Saljuk vizier, Niẓām al-Mulk (d. 1092). It is worth noting that among the works of its first appointee, Abū Isḥāq al-Shīrāzī (d. 1083), is the *Ṭabaqāt al-fuqahāʾ*, which he seems to have finished shortly after 1060, and that among those of a successor, ᶜAbd al-Wahhāb al-Fārisī (d. 1106), is another prosopography, the *Taʾrīkh al-fuqahāʾ*. Both are histories of jurists. Al-Shīrāzī, who advertises his work as an abridgment (or a concise statement), makes clear in his introduction that he intends it to be used for the purposes of identifying and dating the lifetimes of men of learning; in other words, it could be taken to be a reference work for lawyers. But from this point of view, the work seems to fall short in at least two respects: al-Shīrāzī fails to provide death dates for many of those who figure in his book, and although the overall scheme of the work is chronological, within individual sections the arrangement is chronologically untidy. Incomplete and dishevelled, the work is too blunt an instrument for the very exacting job of measuring the accuracy of *isnād*s.[25]

Whatever its imperfections as a work of reference, the book functions effectively as a work of programmatic history, and this in two ways. First, al-Shīrāzī's is a survey of the key jurists of *all* the main schools, and this at a time when others had begun to write *ṭabaqāt* works that were particular to individual schools: in this context of increasing inter-school rivalries, this was a work of conciliation. Second – and here the work illustrates a feature common to a great number of *ṭabaqāt* works – his book anchors the learning of the day in the knowledge of authoritative figures of the past. For a member of one of the four (or in this case, five) legal schools, this naturally meant the Companions to the Prophet on the one hand, and the founding figures of these legal schools, on the other. Al-Shīrāzī's history is

[24] Ibn Rajab's *Dhayl ᶜalā ṭabaqāt al-Ḥanābila* was published in Cairo, 1953; al-ᶜUlaymī's *Mukhtaṣar ṭabaqāt al-Ḥanābila* in Damascus, 1921, and Beirut, 1983; for the count, see Makdisi, '*Ṭabaqāt*-biography', p. 374.

[25] Or, as Makdisi put it ('*Ṭabaqāt*-biography', p. 387): 'His *Ṭabaqāt* was meant to be studied, not to be used primarily as a reference book.'

actually concerned with scholarly filiation, rather than *ḥadīth* transmission. Whereas real genealogies claim to chart the transmission of genes, this genealogy claims to chart the transmission of doctrine. And just as tribal genealogies are schematic – only important tribesmen are mentioned, particularly those who initiate important sub-lineages – so, too, does this genealogy generally include only those learned men who made significant contributions of one kind or another. There was no point for a prosopographer such as al-Shīrāzī to include *every* learned man, any more than there was for a genealogist to include every tribesman, no matter how modest his contribution to the life of the tribe. It was by studying under a Shāfiᶜī and, more important, by practising law according to transmitted Shāfiᶜī doctrine, that one was counted a Shāfiᶜī. So what mattered was not that every lawyer be mentioned, but that every important lawyer be related to a founding father. Thus we read that al-Shīrāzī himself studied under Abū al-Ṭayyib al-Ṭabarī (d. 1058; not to be confused with the chronographer Abū Jaᶜfar al-Ṭabarī), who had studied under Abū al-Ḥasan al-Māsarjisī (d. 998), who had studied under Abū Isḥāq al-Marwazī (d. 951), who had studied under Ibn Surayj (d. 918), who is described by al-Shīrāzī as none other than the greatest follower of the master himself, al-Shāfiᶜī (d. 820). A similar pattern is followed by al-Sulamī (d. 1021) in his *ṭabaqāt* of Sufis; the final generation of his 103 biographies includes his grandfather and his teacher.[26]

Chronography

Of all the historiographic forms, chronography has nearly always commanded the most respect on the part of modern historians. The *Mukhtaṣar fī akhbār al-bashar* ('The Abridged Work on Accounts of Humankind') by Abū al-Fidāᵓ (d. 1331) was translated into Latin as early as 1754, and the rise of nineteenth-century historicism and Oriental philology combined to produce not only the first detailed reconstructions of Islamic political history, such as G. Weil's five-volume *Geschichte der Chalifen* ('History of the Caliphs', 1846–1862), but the first (and, in some cases, still authoritative) editions of several essential works in Islamic chronography. A partial list includes Ḥamza al-Iṣfahānī's *Taᵓrīkh sinī mulūk al-arḍ* (1844), al-Maqrīzī's *Kitāb al-Sulūk li-maᶜrifat duwal al-mulūk* (Paris, 1845), al-Wāqidī's *Kitāb al-Maghāzī* (1855), Ibn al-Athīr's *al-Kāmil fī al-taᵓrīkh* (1876), al-Masᶜūdī's *Murūj al-dhahab* (1877), al-Yaᶜqūbī's *Taᵓrīkh* (1883), al-Dīnawarī's *al-Akhbār al-ṭiwāl* (1888), and finally – the crowning achievement – al-Ṭabarī's *Taᵓrīkh* (1901). It is true that Orientalists were not entirely exclusive in their commitment to chronography, since the Prophetic biography by Ibn Hishām (1864) and the prosopography by Ibn Saᶜd (1904–1940) found their editors. These are very early,

[26] Abū Isḥāq al-Shīrāzī, *Ṭabaqāt al-fuqahāᵓ* (Beirut, 1970); for al-Shīrāzī and the *taᶜaṣṣub* of his time, I draw on E. Chaumont, '*Kitâb al-Lumaᶜ fî uṣûl al-fiqh* d'Abû Isḥâq al-Šîrâzî (m. 476–1083), Introduction, édition critique et index', *Mélanges de l'Université Saint-Joseph* 53 (1993–1994), pp. 22f.; and for the school and many of these figures, see C. Melchert, *The Formation of the Sunni Schools of Law, 9th–10th Centuries C.E.* (Leiden, 1997), chapter 4; for al-Sulamī, J. Mojaddedi, 'Legitimizing Sufism in al-Qushayri's *Risala*', *SI* 90 (2000), pp. 39ff.

however, and the occasional exception aside, the profession would focus its energies much less upon those works that enjoy cultural significance within the Islamic tradition, such as later Prophetic biography and the monumental prosopographical tradition, than it would upon the sources that could answer the questions professional historians wanted answered. In the nineteenth century this meant establishing a political chronology and emphasizing origins and beginnings. Many of the profession's great works of reference (such as the first edition of the *Encyclopaedia of Islam*, which was published between 1913–1936, and E. von Zambaur's *Manuel de généalogie et de chronologie pour l'histoire de l'Islam*, which appeared in 1927), were based squarely upon the works of chronography that had been edited during the nineteenth and early twentieth centuries.

Now we shall see that relative to other forms of historiography, chronography fared poorly, so it is probably the case that the edited corpus of Islamic historiography exaggerates chronography's significance within the tradition. Here it is enough to note that there were two principal kinds of chronography: annalistic history (*taʾrīkh ʿalā al-sinīn*), in which narrative is organized by lemmas (headings) ordered according to Hijra years, and caliphal history (*taʾrīkh al-khulafāʾ*), in which it is organized by the reigns of successive caliphs: these generally begin with the accession of a caliph and end with his death. As we have already seen, caliphal history seems to have emerged first, perhaps arising from lists of caliphs, which are attested already in the early eighth century. Caliphal history would always labour in the shadow of the mammoth annalistic tradition, but it was reasonably productive, and seems to have enjoyed its heyday in the ninth, tenth and eleventh centuries. In addition to histories of caliphs proper, early on the genre produced universal histories, such as al-Yaʿqūbī's *Taʾrīkh* and al-Masʿūdī's *Murūj al-dhahab*, and histories of viziers and secretaries, such as the *Kitāb al-Wuzarāʾ wa'l-kuttāb* of al-Jahshiyārī (d. 942). There are also a number of later examples, such as the *al-Inbāʾ fī taʾrīkh al-khulafāʾ* of Ibn al-ʿImrānī (d. 1184) and the *Taʾrīkh al-khulafāʾ* of al-Suyūṭī (d. 1505); here one might also include the *Kitāb al-Fakhrī* by Ibn al-Ṭiqṭaqā (fl. late thirteenth century), which is organized by dynasties. We also have to take account of the occasional hybrids, one being the anonymous late eleventh-century *Kitāb al-ʿUyūn wa'l-ḥadāʾiq*, where annalistic dating is interleaved within regnal chapters. Another example is the historical section of the *Kitāb al-Awrāq* by Muḥammad b. Yaḥyā al-Ṣūlī, in which dates are assigned within regnal chapters.[27]

[27] Surviving sections of al-Jahshiyārī's *Kitāb al-Wuzarāʾ wa'l-kuttāb* were published in Cairo, 1938 and Beirut, 1964, the latter as *Nuṣūṣ ḍāʾiʿa min kitāb al-wuzarāʾ wa'l-kuttāb*; parts of the second section of the anonymous *ʿUyūn* were published in the nineteenth century, and these editions include that of Leiden, 1869, which was published as *Fragmenta Historicorum Arabicorum*; two sections of the fourth part were published as the *Kitāb al-ʿUyūn wa'l-ḥadāʾiq fī akhbār al-ḥaqāʾiq*, iv[1] (Damascus, 1972), where a review of the publishing history can be found at pp. ix-xiii, and iv[2] (Damascus, 1973); the anonymous *Taʾrīkh al-khulafāʾ* (Moscow, 1967) also seems to belong to the eleventh century; cf. also the anonymous *Nubdha min kitāb al-taʾrīkh* (Moscow, 1960); al-Ṣūlī's work has been (partially) edited as the *Akhbār al-Rāḍī lillāh wa'l-Muttaqī lillāh* (Beirut, 1935), and translated by M. Canard as *Histoire de la dynastie abbaside de 322 à 333/933 à 944 (Akhbâr al-Râḍî billâh wa-l-Muttaqî billâh)* (Algiers, 1950); some of the previously unpublished material is now available in a partial ed., St. Petersburg, 1998.

What were the attractions in writing in this mode, rather than annalistically? It is striking that so many examples come from the frontier of historical writing that is adjacent to *adab* literature, while traditionist chronographers, by contrast, seem to have been inclined towards the annalistic form. We have, then, an important matter of implicit emphasis – it might be said that caliphal history represents the sovereign as the ordering force of history itself – and one wonders if this is not unrelated to the culture and economics of court patronage. Certainly there were also prosaic reasons. One is that it relieved the historian of working out precise chronologies, a task that was especially difficult when his material may have come to him without dates. 'Jaᶜfar served as secretary during al-Muᶜizz's reign, before his brother died': this (hypothetical) example would suit a caliphal history fine, but begs too many questions for the annalistic historian. The historian writing caliphal history has a relatively easy task in synchronizing such disparate materials as he has: he need only know during which reign they occurred. Taken together, these features suggest that regnal chronography suited those whose interests lay less in chronology than in character and culture.

Of course organizing narrative by caliphal reigns also had its disadvantages. Just as an event might extend over two successive years, causing problems for historians writing in the annalistic mode, history did not pause while one caliph succeeded another: an event that began during one caliph's reign might end during his successor's. Al-Maqrīzī solves one such problem in his *Sulūk* by discussing a two-year battle in the course of a single year's entry (755 H/1354–1355 C.E.), because 'narrating it as a continuous sequence is clearer and more useful to the reader'. And how was one to treat periods of political turmoil, when no single individual could be said to rule? Al-Yaᶜqūbī handled the turmoil of the Second Civil War (*ca*. 685–692) by lumping together under a single rubric 'the reigns [lit. 'days'] of Marwān b. al-Ḥakam, ᶜAbd al-Allāh b. al-Zubayr and some of the reign of ᶜAbd al-Malik'. He solved al-Maqrīzī's problem by beginning his account of the reign of ᶜAbd al-Malik (685–705) with a reminder to his readers of some earlier passages, and there he lays bare a strikingly pragmatic definition of the caliphate itself:

> We have already given the account of how ᶜAbd al-Malik was given the oath of allegiance during the reign of Ibn al-Zubayr, of how the provinces were in upheaval, and of how each had been overrun … in addition to other matters that are part of the narrative framework (*nasaq*) of Ibn al-Zubayr's reign. For some have argued that the caliphate rightfully belongs to whomsoever controls the two sanctuaries in Mecca and Medina and leads the pilgrimage. For this reason we placed the account of Marwān and some of the reign of ᶜAbd al-Malik in the midst of the account of Ibn al-Zubayr.[28]

Ibn al-Zubayr had filled the political vacuum caused by the dissolution of Sufyānid Umayyad authority in 683, coming to control much of Arabia and Iraq; his reign (he minted coins and appointed governors) was put to an end by ᶜAbd al-Malik in 692.

[28] Al-Maqrīzī, *Kitāb al-Sulūk li-maᶜrifat duwal al-mulūk* (Cairo, 1958), ii, p. 914; al-Yaᶜqūbī, *Taʾrīkh*, ii, p. 321.

So caliphal chronography had its attractions, one of which was that it was forgiving as far as chronology was concerned. In this respect it contrasts sharply with annalistic chronography, where chronological precision appears to have been highly prized, thus giving rise to a practice of further sub-division; such is the case, for example, in the very little that remains of al-Musabbiḥī's chronography, where each annual entry is sub-divided into monthly entries. The nature of annalistic narrative will become clearer if we take a brief look at the entry on year 96 (September 714–September 715) in the *Kitāb al-Taʾrīkh* of Khalīfa b. Khayyāṭ, which is the last year of the reign of the caliph al-Walīd b. ʿAbd al-Malik (rg. 705-715). This annalistic history is significant only because it is the earliest we possess; neither the author, who merits only two lines in Ibn al-Nadīm's *Fihrist*, nor his short book, which tells us little that we do not otherwise know from the later tradition, is noteworthy otherwise. As is so frequently the case, the work survives in a single (and in this case, Moroccan) copy, which preserves the recension of the work transmitted by Baqī b. Makhlad (d. 889), a Cordovan scholar who would have picked it up during his travels in Iraq. Khalīfa himself seems to have been poorly travelled by the standards of his day, and there is no reason to think that he journeyed to the west. The entry on year 96 is composed of four unequal parts, the first and fourth of which I translate. The numbers, paragraphing and italics are also mine.[29]

> 1. In it al-Walīd b. ʿAbd al-Malik b. Marwān [the caliph] died. Al-Walīd b. Hishām, on the authority of his father and grandfather and ʿAbd Allāh b. al-Mughīra, on the authority of his father, and Abū al-Yaqẓān, and others [all] informed me that al-Walīd died on Thursday in the middle of the month of Rabīʿ I, someone else saying (*wa-qāla baʿḍuhum al-ākhar*) year 96, at the age of 44. Sulaymān b. ʿAbd al-Malik [his brother and successor] led the prayers [at his funeral]. Yaḥyā b. Muḥammad related to me, on the authority of ʿAbd al-ʿAzīz b. ʿImrān, on the authority of Muḥammad b. ʿAbd Allāh b. al-Muʾammal al-Makhzūmī, who said: al-Walīd was born in Medina in year 45. He [also] said: He died at the age of 51. Ḥātim b. Muslim said: at the age of 49; Sulaymān b. ʿAbd al-Malik led the prayers. His reign was nine years, five months and [a few] days long. The oath of allegiance was then given to Sulaymān b. ʿAbd al-Malik b. Marwān. His mother was Wallāda bt. al-ʿAbbās, who was the mother of al-Walīd b. ʿAbd al-Malik.
>
> 2. Signalled by the rubric 'Identification of the appointees (*ʿummāl*) of al-Walīd b. ʿAbd al-Malik and al-Ḥajjāj' [the latter being the governor of all of the eastern provinces and al-Walīd's *de facto* lieutenant], this section consists of two sets of lists: a list of provincial governors, leaders of the pilgrimage, leaders of the campaigns along the Byzantine frontier, and of various positions in the court and bureaucracy; and a very short list of provincial judges [as caliph, al-Walīd exercised both civil and legal authority in the capital]. It is roughly five times the length of section 1.

[29] The single fragment of al-Musabbiḥī was published in Cairo, 1978 as *al-Juzʾ al-arbaʿūn min akhbār Miṣr*; Khalīfa's *Taʾrīkh* has been edited in Damascus, 1967, Baghdad, 1967 (with a second ed. in Beirut, 1977, which I cite, pp. 309ff.), and Beirut, 1995 (whether the last is independent of the first two is not clear); for Khalīfa's entry, Ibn al-Nadīm, *Fihrist*, p. 288 (Dodge, *Fihrist*, p. 559), and *GAS*, p. 110.

3. Signalled by 'And in year 96', this section provides three very brief accounts, each introduced by the same phrase 'And in this year…'. The first two are administrative matters; the third is the killing of the celebrated general and governor, Qutayba b. Muslim.

4. 'In year 96, Ibrāhīm al-Nakhaᶜī died at the age of 53, and [also] Ibrāhīm b. ᶜAbd al-Raḥmān b. ᶜAwf and Maḥmūd b. al-Rabīᶜ al-Khazrajī. Sulaymān b. ᶜAbd al-Malik dispatched Maslama b. ᶜAbd al-Malik to lead the summer campaign. Abū Bakr b. Muḥammad b. ᶜAmr b. Ḥazm led the pilgrimage. In it al-ᶜAbbās b. al-Walīd led raids and conquered [an apparent corruption follows]. Bishr b. al-Walīd [also] led raids, but returned [to Syria], al-Walīd having died. In it Jidār was wounded, while he was with him [Bishr] in Byzantine territory.

The entry exemplifies several features of Khalīfa b. Khayyāṭ's work and the annalistic tradition more generally. We can begin with formal features.

The first is that the annalistic scheme can accommodate, accordion-like, as little or as much material as the historian wishes to include. In the three editions of Khalīfa's *Taʾrīkh*, the entry on year 96 varies in length from four to nine pages, the latter when printed in an exceptionally generous format. By contrast, al-Ṭabarī's entry for the same year comes in at about 36 pages in the very densely printed Arabic of the standard edition, which amounts to at least twenty times the length of Khalīfa's. While Khalīfa pauses for five lines on Qutayba's death, al-Ṭabarī devotes over twenty pages to the same topic, drawing on a wide variety of sources, and integrating eye-witness accounts, speeches and poetry; in the entry as a whole, Khalīfa cites no poetry, while al-Ṭabarī cites approximately 100 lines. In all this variety we come to a second feature of the annalistic genre: more than in biography or prosopography, here we typically find a great heterogeneity of materials. On this score, Khalīfa exemplifies the early tradition's enthusiasm for lists. Between the second section, 'Identification [lit. "naming"] of the appointees of al-Walīd and al-Ḥajjāj', and the fourth, much of which we might infer was drawn from lists very similar to those cited in the second, we have what amounts to over 75 per cent of the total entry. Lists remain discernible in al-Ṭabarī's account, but listing as a narrative technique has now greatly receded in prominence, except in the closing section of each year: in form, there is little difference between Khalīfa's fourth section and al-Ṭabarī, *Taʾrīkh*, ii, p. 1305, which lists various administrative appointments, dismissals and deaths. We saw that this residual dating section would later be expanded, when Ibn al-Jawzī married chronography and prosopography by concluding each annual entry with lengthy obituaries. This format would be taken up and elaborated by later historians, such as al-Yūnīnī.[30]

Comparing Khalīfa's entry on year 96 with al-Ṭabarī's sheds light on other features that are common to chronography. One is the family *isnād* (al-Walīd b.

[30] Al-Ṭabarī's entry begins on ii, p. 1269 and ends on p. 1305, which is translated by M. Hinds as *The Zenith of the Marwānid House* (Albany, 1990; al-Ṭabarī translation, vol. xxiii), pp. 218–230, and D.S. Powers, *The Empire in Transition* (Albany, 1989; al-Ṭabarī translation, vol. xxiv), pp. 3–29; for the suggestion that Ibn al-Jawzī picked up the idea from a teacher, G. Makdisi, *Ibn ᶜAqīl et la résurgence de l'Islam traditionaliste au xiᵉ siècle* (Damascus, 1963), p. 24; on al-Yūnīnī, Guo, *Early Mamluk Syrian Historiography*, pp. 83f.

Hishām relates on the authority of his father and grandfather, and ᶜAbd Allāh on the authority of his father al-Mughīra) and a form of the collective *isnād* (also illustrated in 1). Another is emphasis through arrangement, a technique much favoured by traditionist-historians who only grudgingly expressed their own opinions at all explicitly. Both historians thus *begin* their entries with the year's most important event: the death of the caliph. It is this same traditionist-inspired reticence that explains their high tolerance for contrary evidence. Khalīfa is content to report, rather than resolve, three views on al-Walīd's age at his death (44, 49 or 51). And lest we explain this away by noting that pre-moderns rarely made a habit of noting dates of birth, al-Ṭabarī teaches us that things are not so simple. Here, as so often in his history, he draws our attention to disagreement at the very beginning of his account: not only do his sources disagree about al-Walīd's age, but they disagree about the length of his reign. Whereas Khalīfa had given us only one option ('nine years, five months and [a few] days', al-Ṭabarī gives us no fewer than four: one month short of ten years; nine years and seven months; eight years and six months; nine years, eighth months and two days. It is one thing to neglect birth dates, but quite another to neglect dates of accession, particularly since the same sources that record these kind of disagreements take care to note those very dates of accession. One can only conclude that preserving disagreement – indeed, even accentuating it – is an important feature of traditionist historiography, which in this respect, as in others, seems to have been produced by the same conventions and attitudes that produced comparable legal discussions of jurists' disagreements. Al-Ṭabarī himself authored one such work, his *Kitāb Ikhtilāf al-fuqahā*ᵓ (or: *ᶜulamā*ᵓ) ('The Disagreements of the jurisprudents [or: scholars]'). That historians so frequently preserve conflicting reconstructions has been taken to suggest a general rule: while we moderns take it for granted that the historian's task is to isolate that single reconstruction that describes most accurately a given event in the past, medieval Muslim historians held an inclusive and catholic view of the past, which accommodated multiple reconstructions. Now it may be premature to formulate this as a general rule, but it is a striking fact that while al-Ṭabarī, the historian, preserves and presents disagreement after disagreement in his *History*, al-Ṭabarī, the exegete and jurist, almost always tells us exactly what to make of points of Qurᵓānic interpretation and law. What this says about history is a point that shall occupy us in later chapters.[31]

[31] A fragment of al-Ṭabarī's *Ikhtilāf* work was edited by J. Schacht as *Das konstantinopler Fragment des Kitāb Iḫtilāf al-fuqahā*ᵓ *des Abū Ǧa*ᶜ*far Muḥammad b. Ǧarīr aṭ-Ṭabarī* (Leiden, 1933); I draw the contrast between al-Ṭabarī as historian and al-Ṭabarī as exegete-jurist from C.F. Robinson, 'al-Ṭabarī', in M. Cooperson and S.M. Toorawa, eds., *Arabic Literary Culture, 500–925* (The Dictionary of Literary Biography; Detroit, 1978–; forthcoming); on multiple truths, Malti-Douglas, 'Texts and tortures'.

PART II

Contexts

CHAPTER 5

Historiography and traditionalism

Most people now take it for granted that history writing is distinctive from other kinds of non-fictional writing, that history is a discrete discipline of learning, and that the goal of the historian is to uncover, record and explain the past. Unlike 'literature', which is produced in the creative and imaginative mind of the fiction writer, history writing is held to be subject to commonly shared rules and conventions of evidence and argument. This is why the historian, unlike the novelist or poet, has to be *trained*. During his apprenticeship (the Ph.D.), the historian-to-be acquires the skills and techniques of the trade, such as the ability to read a foreign language or a documentary style, along with attitudes towards evidence and argument – in short, his approach and temperament. He then begins to produce work, and although his ideas may accord with or differ from the received wisdom, they are almost invariably expressed within an accepted idiom, such as the examined thesis, reviewed monograph or article, whose conventions reflect the underlying principles of his profession, and distinguish it from other kinds of written narrative.

This book is a case in point. It is a work of professional history not simply because it discusses the past (so does today's newspaper), but because it does so in conventional ways. It is published by an academic press that frequently publishes professional history and *never* publishes fiction (at least knowingly). Meanwhile, my footnotes and bibliography assert my training and industry, and point to the debt I owe to fellow practitioners, upon whose work this work is partly based. Other genres signal themselves in other ways. Books about the past that are written within what might be called a sub-genre of fictional prose, the historical novel, are at least in part signalled as such because they sport bibliographies but generally *dispense* with footnotes. Deleting footnotes is one of the ways that an academic book is tailored or retrofitted for a larger, non-academic audience. Professional historians say something like 'As a trained historian, I play by my guild's rules: believe me, and if you're not sure, feel free to check my notes'. Historical novelists say something like 'Believe me: I'm not making *all* of this up'.[1]

[1] On the footnote, see A. Grafton, *The Footnote: A Curious History* (Cambridge, Mass., 1997, rev. ed.); for one historical novelist who is blunt about his method, see the author's note to J. Rathbone, *The Last English King* (London, 1997).

This book's conventions thus reflect how I want you, the reader, to respond to what I, as historian-author, think. Now we shall see that Muslim historians also followed conventions to signal things to their readers, such as modest prefaces, bibliographies and abbreviations. Whatever its literal accuracy, the *isnād* certainly endows the accompanying *khabar* with professional authority – the aural learning of the author-compiler, transmitted according to professional standards; the *isnād* tells the reader that the qualified traditionist is not telling mere *stories*. The point to be made here is that the conventions and principles that I follow as a professional historian are relatively new. Most date from the late eighteenth and nineteenth centuries, when the definition of literature was increasingly restricted, and when historiography was cut away from other branches of literature. The surgery was closely related on the one hand to the emergence of science as the principal focus of social authority in western societies, and to the professionalization of teaching and writing in history on the other. Only in this period did historians begin to see themselves as practising a real discipline, and to make historiography more clearly distinct from other forms of past narration. In particular, historiography was now patterned after the natural sciences, and this definition of 'history as (social) science', despite a great deal of criticism, continues to hold in many quarters today. According to this model, the historian's work is to be based on clear distinctions between evidence (data), argument (method) and conclusions (results). Just as knowledge of the physical universe grows, so, too, our knowledge of the past: the field as a whole moves forward only insofar as one historian's results are verified or falsified by another. In this model, historiography is to be forensic, and its paradigmatic form is autopsy – the critical examination of something or someone of the past.[2]

So this is all relatively new. And before this patterning took place – indeed, for as far back as knowledge had been classified – writing about the past was usually considered just another kind of writing, and was frequently understood as a branch or sub-genre of literature, rather than a discipline in its own right, as theology and law typically were. Insofar as history was held to make any truth claims at all, these were held in low regard (sometimes even contempt) by philosophers and scripturally minded monotheists, to whom the truth lay elsewhere – in dialectic, revelation, or some combination of both. As a branch of literature with no real tools to probe or examine, historiography was usually judged on aesthetic and moral grounds. Was it beautiful, clever, entertaining or inspirational? Did it teach the right lessons? This is the context in which the great bulk of pre-modern history was written, and the one in which a figure as familiar as Gibbon (d. 1794) was writing his history (and bestseller), the *Decline and Fall of the Roman Empire*. Gibbon, writing as he was before history had fully established itself as an independent discipline, is said to have given more thought to the *way* he was going to write history than to the subject about which he proposed to write, and as it turned out,

[2] There are many criticisms of this model; for one, see P. Veyne, *Writing History* (Middletown, 1984), pp. 87ff.

the work would ultimately be valued less for its historical insights than for its exemplary style. Not entirely unlike many works of Arabic literature that modern historians appropriate as works of Islamic historiography (such as Ibn Qutayba's *Kitāb al-Maᶜārif* and *ᶜUyūn al-akhbār*), it was a literary masterpiece, a repository from which 'classical scholars and persons of correct, "enlightened" attitude would cull a few lapidary pages ...'[3]

Muslims were heirs to the classical and monotheistic traditions of the Near East, and these traditions brought with them attitudes toward historiography. The translation movements of the eighth, ninth and tenth centuries made available to Muslim thinkers Aristotle's disdain for history, and in Arabic prescriptions that follow an Aristotelian model, historiography scarcely figures at all. Since it generated no truths, it was considered dispensable. The philosophers' disdain for history cannot explain very much, however, because their ideas remained marginal to the mainstream Islamic tradition. Far more important was Islamic traditionalism. It is within this traditionalist culture that history was understood and recorded, and in part because of traditionalism that a discrete discipline of history took so long to develop. Even more than training in the law or rhetoric conditioned the historical perspectives of lawyer-historians writing in Greek and Syriac, training in traditionalism tended to condition the way that most Muslim historians viewed their task, particularly in the early period, when prescriptive attitudes were being formed. To understand the shape of the Islamic historiographic tradition, we therefore need to understand something about Islamic traditionalism.[4]

Traditionism and traditionalism

Put very schematically, traditionalist cultures such as medieval Islam and Rabbinic Judaism hold that knowledge is better *conserved* than it is *created*. In particular, they hold that the best kind of knowledge is the wisdom of pious and inspired forefathers, which, whether recorded in their day or generated retrospectively by subsequent generations, can validate and guide the experience of the present. As

[3] On the divorce of history from literature, see the 'Introduction' to R.H. Canary and H. Kozicki, eds., *The Writing of History: Literary Form and Historical Understanding* (Madison, 1979), from which the quotation comes; cf. the essays in S. Leder, ed., *Story-telling in the Framework of Non-fictional Arabic Literature* (Wiesbaden, 1998); for views on Gibbon, P. Brown's comments in the '*SO* debate: the world of late antiquity revisited', *Symbolae Osloenses* 72 (1997), p. 5; and L. Braudy, *Narrative Form in History and Fiction: Hume, Fielding, and Gibbon* (Princeton, 1970).

[4] On Aristotle's disdain for history and its transmission into the Islamic tradition, B. Radtke, *Weltgeschichte und Weltbeschreibung im mittelalterlichen Islam* (Beirut and Stuttgart, 1992), pp. 145ff.; M. Mahdi, *Ibn Khaldûn's Philosophy of History* (London, 1957), pp. 138ff.; Rosenthal, *History*, pp. 30ff.; a convenient overview of the relevant surveys of learning can be found in W. Ouyang, *Literary Criticism in Medieval Arabic-Islamic Culture: The Making of a Tradition* (Edinburgh, 1997), pp. 25ff.; for the influence of rhetorical training on classical historians, T.P. Wiseman, 'Practice and theory in Roman historiography', *Historia* 66 (1981), pp. 375–393, and J. Harries, 'Sozomen and Eusebius: the lawyer as church historian in the fifth century', in C. Holdsworth and T.P. Wiseman, eds., *The Inheritance of Historiography, 350–900* (Exeter, 1986), pp. 45–52.

distrustful of creativity as they are convinced of the inerrancy of those who came before them, traditionalists are generally critical about the present and nostalgic about a 'golden age' when men, acting in accordance with fresh truths, accomplished great things. They do not revere the past; they revere *a* past, and although the length and character of this past differ from culture to culture, there is always an ever widening gap between the time of inspiration (or revelation) on the one hand, and the present time of decay, on the other. The task they set for themselves is thus to remain anchored to the secure ground of this inspired past, and this falls to those who are said to follow in the footsteps of the pious forefathers: in other words, the men (and, less frequently, the women) who exemplify these attitudes and possess the skills required for transmitting, rather than innovating. This generally means conservative-minded men with very good memories, or, since the past can serve as a programme for revolutionaries, one might rather say conserving-minded men. This last contrast – between those who actually transmit *ḥadīth*s (the *muḥaddithūn*) and those who embrace the values of traditionalism more generally – can be neatly preserved in the English 'traditionist' and 'traditionalist'. Nearly everyone in classical Islam, save speculative theologians and philosophers, came to have a traditionalist perspective, and this is why speculative theologians and philosophers generally experienced a mixture of hostility and disdain.[5]

In the Islamic case, God had made His will manifest to man in the form of His revelation (the Qurʾān) and the model (or 'path', *sunna*) of His Prophet Muḥammad. A 'golden age' was accordingly defined by the beginning of Muḥammad's recitations of the Qurʾān (about 610 AD) and the deaths of those who witnessed (or directly heard about) his model behaviour (as late, it is sometimes held, as the middle of the eighth century), and whose views were accordingly held to be paradigmatic. An overlapping 'golden age' was also constructed in political terms. For example, al-Jāḥiẓ (d. 868), a rationalist who in this instance demonstrates just how prevalent traditionalist attitudes were, defined the 'first generation' (*al-ṭabaqa al-ūlā*) as:

> The era of the Prophet, on whom be peace and prayers, Abū Bakr and ᶜUmar, may God be pleased with them, and 6 years of the caliphate of ᶜUthmān, may God be pleased with him, when they [the early Muslims] acted according to the true monotheism and pure sincerity, with concord and complete agreement as regards the Book [the Qurʾān] and *sunna*. At that time, there was nothing in the way of offending action or scandalous innovation, no act of disobedience, envy, rancour or rivalry [or: strained interpretation].

This is a common view, which reflects the trauma of ᶜUthmān's assassination and the civil war that followed it. Although some (particularly the Shīᶜites) might take issue with the specifics, nearly everyone agreed that things were better back in the early days. A widely circulated saying of the Prophet expresses things neatly enough: 'The best people are my generation, then those who follow them, then those who follow them.'[6]

[5] I borrow the distinction between conservative and conserving from Goody, *Logic of Writing*, p. 20.

[6] For al-Jāḥiẓ's words, see his *Risāla fī al-Nābita* in the *Rasāʾil al-Jāḥiẓ* (Cairo, 1965), ii, p. 7; and C. Pellat, 'La «Nâbita» de Djâhiz: (un document important pour l'histoire politico-religieuse de l'Islâm)', *Annales de l'Institut des Études Orientales* (Algiers) 10 (1952), p. 310.

It appears that the Qurʾān was set down in writing within a generation of the Prophet's death, but the *sunna* initially took the form of oral *ḥadīth*s, these being written down only later, perhaps starting in the second third of the eighth century. By the early ninth century, the Qurʾān and *sunna* had come to complement each other as the foundations of Islamic law, the *sharīʿa*. And, much more so than dogma, it was the transmitted law that mattered, since fidelity to the law – nothing less than a detailed translation of God's providential guidance into the language of prescribed and proscribed human actions – that conditioned the believer's fate. It is true that theology enjoyed some favour early on, and that some jurists flirted with a law based not so much on traditions as individual reasoning and discretion. It is also true that there was some resistance early on to adducing traditions for generating the law. But by the end of the tenth century, theology had been thoroughly marginalised, while traditionalism had come to enjoy a virtual monopoly on jurisprudence, and conditioned nearly all branches of knowledge (philosophy never gained more than a cult following). The 'science of traditions', which meant compiling, editing and commenting upon reports of the Prophet's words and deeds, including their transmitters, had become the prestige activity of Islamic scholarship. In time, the *isnād* would even become an organizing principle of education more generally. Without any qualifying adjectives, 'knowledge' (*ʿilm*) meant knowledge of traditions, and those who possessed such knowledge were the *ʿulamāʾ* (literally 'those who know'), a term which came to denote the religious élite in general.[7]

This learning was substantial: the 'science' of *ḥadīth* was equipped with a system of criticism that categorized both the individual transmitter (as 'trustworthy', 'acceptable', 'weak', 'mendacious', etc.) and the text of the *ḥadīth* itself. Here the jurists engineered the immensely influential and pragmatic concept of *tawātur* ('corroboration'), which means the parallel transmission of texts from witnesses and transmitters, the greater number of parallel versions, the more trustworthy being the text. On this count, the Qurʾān scored very high, so high indeed that there were no doubts about the text itself, aside from variant readings: it was God's speech. Most of the transmitted *ḥadīth* that formed the *sunna* scored less well, but never so poorly as to imperil the fundamentals of the faith. They may not have generated certain knowledge (as did the Qurʾān), but properly vetted and mutually corroborating *ḥadīth* were held to be so *probably* true that only the quarrelsome could oppose their use. We have seen that many historians came to play by the traditionists' rules, collecting assiduously and prefacing the accounts they had

[7] Nearly every textbook on Islam has something to say about traditionalism, but for general discussions, see J. Fück, 'Die Rolle des Traditionalismus im Islam', *ZDMG* 93 (1939), pp. 1–32, which is translated in M. Swartz, ed. and trans., *Studies on Islam* (New York and Oxford, 1981), pp. 99–122; W. Graham, 'Traditionalism in Islam: an essay in interpretation', *Journal of Interdisciplinary History* 23 (1993), pp. 495–522; for those theoretically inclined, A. Al-Azmeh, 'Muslim genealogies of knowledge', *History of Religion* 31 (1992), pp. 403–411 ('The space connecting precedent and consequent is a space of filiation, their connection a genealogy'); for some early resistance to traditions, M. Cook, 'ʿAnan and Islam: the origins of Karaite scripturalism', *JSAI* 9 (1987), pp. 161–182; for examples of men endowed with especially long memories, L.T. Librande, 'The scholars of Hadith and the retentive memory', *Cahiers d'onomastique arabe* 1988–1992 (1993), pp. 39–48.

collected with the *isnād*s so favoured by the people of *ḥadīth*: here, too, claims to represent the truth were to be based on the piety and trustworthiness of the transmitters. Still, the *akhbārī*s were nearly always considered poor at *ḥadīth* transmission, since their broken, incomplete or collective *isnād*s ran afoul of the *muḥaddithūn*'s standards.[8]

So Muḥammad set the standard: as the Andalusian polymath Ibn Ḥazm (d. 1063) wrote, 'whosoever desires good in the next world, understanding of this world, sound comportment, possession of all the best qualities, and realization of all the virtues, let him follow the example of Muḥammad.' But precisely how and when Muḥammad's views came to be held as authoritative is a topic of some real disagreement amongst modern scholars. There is a wide range of opinion. At one end stand those who hold that his views were authoritative in his time and faithfully transmitted thereafter. The *isnād*, so it is argued, is an accurate record of the transmission history of *ḥadīth*s, and in the main these are as authentic or inauthentic as medieval authorities thought they were, provided one also controls for obvious legends and anachronisms. The words or deeds of Muḥammad and many of his contemporaries – in short, the facts of primitive Islam – are thus recoverable. At the other end of the spectrum stand those who think that early Islam conforms to a pattern discernible in other religious traditions, according to which definitive ideas and systems of thought (such as Prophetic *sunna*) emerge only slowly, and who, drawing on a range of textual evidence as well, consequently argue that *ḥadīth*s are generally inauthentic (the word used is usually 'spurious'). To be more precise: these critics hold that the *isnād* system was fully assembled only after jurists had taken up many of their positions on legal questions, and that, in any event, they cannot guarantee the accurate transmission of texts from one generation to the next. Far from documenting the transmission of legal material over time, *isnād*s dating from the earliest period were produced only retrospectively, in order to legitimize views first held in the Umayyad and Abbasid periods. It is conceded that some *ḥadīth*s *may* come very close to words uttered by the Prophet, that many scholars were acting in accordance with what they held to be the Prophet's intentions, and that some *isnād*s can be traced back as far as the early eighth century. But none of this can be cause for assuming the *general* reliability of a corpus that stabilized only in the ninth century, by which time oral transmission had been eclipsed by written transmission, the capital of the caliphate had moved from Medina to Damascus to Baghdad, and four civil wars and one revolution had taken place. The 'facts' expressed by the *ḥadīth*, the critics hold, are not historical facts about early Islam, but sociological facts of what the community held to be true about early Islam.[9]

8 On corroboration in the Qur'ān and *sunna*, see the typical remarks in Ibn al-Athīr, *Usd al-ghāba* (Būlāq, 1871), i, p. 2; in general, B. Weiss, 'Knowledge of the past: the theory of *tawâtur* according to Ghazâlî', *SI* 61 (1985), pp. 81–105.

9 For Ibn Ḥazm, see his *Kitāb al-Akhlāq wa'l-siyar,* which is edited and translated by N. Tomiche as *Épître morale* (Beirut, 1961), p. 23 (Arabic and French); for a useful overview of the *ḥadīth* literature from a neo-traditional perspective, M.Z. Siddiqui, *Hadith Literature* (Cambridge, 1993); cf.

The alert reader will suspect that my views are in sympathy with the critics, but it is more important to know that it was only during the ninth century that the 'science of traditions' crystallized, when jurists recognized that spurious *ḥadīth*s were circulating in large numbers. The Prophet's inspired contemporaries had accurately transmitted his *sunna*, but scholars with sectarian and political axes to grind were now forging on a massive scale. The solution was to examine the *isnād*s, identifying weak transmitters (the forgetful, impious, the corrupt) and implausible or impossible links (such as when an Iraqi traditionist was given to transmit from an Egyptian, the two men never having left their native lands); texts that were unacceptable on legal or theological grounds were also rejected. It was in this way that al-Bukhārī isolated his 2,762 traditions from the corpus of 600,000, and the product of all this editing activity was a number (usually put at six) of authoritative collections. That so much attention was paid to the transmitters and relatively little to the text of the *ḥadīth*s is striking to non-traditionalists, but the approach makes a great deal of cultural sense. By what criteria could one distinguish between authentic and inauthentic reports of Muḥammad's words and wisdom, since, as God's Prophet, he knew the future? A keen student of Prophetic *ḥadīth*s might query an amazing prediction (such as, for example, of the Abbasid Revolution in 750) or an apparent anachronism: how was it that the Prophet could mention *sulṭān*s 'since there were no sultans in his days'? But the student would be mistaken, because he failed to understand, as one authority put it, that 'the apostle of God had predicted with prophetical insight everything that is going to happen until the hour of resurrection'. What is more, the paradigmatic force of Muḥammad's judgments makes a great deal of cultural sense – and not simply because he was so charismatic and successful. The Qur'ān actually offers little in the way of substantive law, and most of the 500 or so relevant verses address a relatively narrow range of issues. Meanwhile, Muḥammad, who eventually came to be considered the last of the prophets, had a prophetic career of some twenty years, ample time to spell out his views on a wide range of issues. To Sunnis, his model therefore came to represent God's last detailed communication to man before the Day of Judgment. What else should have served as a blueprint for a society that was undergoing great political and social change?[10]

In holding that knowledge was to be preserved, rather than created, and that the agents of preservation were to be authoritative figures from the increasingly

W. Hallaq, *A History of Islamic Legal Theories* (Cambridge, 1997), chapter 1; for a concise summary of the critical position, J. Schacht, 'A revaluation of Islamic traditions', *JRAS* (1949), pp. 143–154, which is reprinted in Ibn Warraq, ed., *The Quest for the Historical Muhammad*, pp. 358–367; for variations on Schacht's work, Juynboll, *Muslim Tradition*, which is quite close to Schacht, and H. Motzki, *Die Anfänge der islamischen Jurisprudenz: ihre Entwicklung in Mekka bis zur Mitte des 2./8 Jahrhunderts* (Stuttgart, 1991), the results of which he summarizes in 'The *Muṣannaf* of ᶜAbd al-Razzāq al-Ṣanᶜānī as a source of authentic *aḥādīth* of the first century A.H.', *JNES* 50 (1991), pp. 1–21, and updates in his *The Origins of Islamic Jurisprudence: Meccan Fiqh before the Classical Schools* (Leiden, 2001).

[10] For the keen student, see Goldziher, *Muslim Studies*, ii, p. 143.

remote past, traditionalists do not rule out the potential for change. The law was reinterpreted, reformulated and refined throughout the medieval period. As the world changed (usually slowly, it must be said), the law had to change, too. Even so, there is no way around the fact that traditionalism does limit the territory in which discovery can be made to a handful of foundational texts and hermeneutic techniques, and that it is at some odds with the rationality and freedom of thought that are conventionally held at least partially responsible for the technological and political hegemony of the modern West. (Again, this is not to say that Muslim jurists exercised no rationality in their work; it means only that they held that reason *alone* could never generate the law.) Little wonder, then, that some modernizing Muslims have tried to loosen traditionalism's hold on religious authority, by proposing, for example, to derive the law exclusively from Qurʾānic principles, abandoning the more or less fixed codes specified by the *ḥadīth*s. For a variety of reasons, they have not got as far as they would have liked.[11]

It is not hard to understand why. One need not be a traditionalist to believe that the model for a successful present should be a remote and glorious past, particularly in a post-colonial context: after all, even prosperous and progressive cultures can be given to deep nostalgia. Nor, perhaps, should one make too much of the post-colonial irony that those who now denounce Western influence most ferociously tend to have been produced by the more or less secularizing educational systems that were introduced by colonial powers. For it was these systems that undermined the culture of memorization and textual commentary so valued by the traditionalists, thus liberating neo-conservative Islamists to call for a 'return' to a 'traditional' Islam that most pre-modern traditionists would not have recognized. It is more important to note that Europe had the good fortune to experience the eclipse of medievalism and rise of science and modernity on pretty much its own terms, and one of the products of the successful transition has been the rise of Biblical criticism, which, among other things, provided a 'scientific' basis for faith. Far from undermining faith, historical criticism as undertaken by Christians and Jews could be said to confirm it, by discerning the historical process of God's relation to man: His miracles may have been sacrificed, but His providence has survived, reinterpreted as a progressive force in human history. The Islamic world has had none of this good fortune, and those who have challenged the traditionalist consensus (arguing, for example, for a historically critical approach to the Qurʾān), have suffered for it. One result is the unhappy state of affairs in which the study of early Islamic history currently finds itself, with virtually all the critical-historical research taking place in the West.[12]

[11] On the continuing vitality of Islamic law throughout the medieval period, see B. Johansen, *Contingency in a Sacred Law: Legal and Ethical Norms in Muslim Fiqh* (Leiden, 1999), and W. Hallaq, *Authority, Continuity and Change in Islamic Law* (Cambridge, 2001); on traditionalism in the modern period, D. Brown, *Rethinking Tradition in Modern Islamic Thought* (Cambridge, 1996).

[12] On the rise of Biblical criticism, see J. Rogerson, *Old Testament Criticism in the Nineteenth Century: England and Germany* (London, 1984) and M.S. Massa, *Charles Augustus Briggs and the Crisis of Historical Criticism* (Minneapolis, 1990); a recent restatement of the critical position can be found

Whatever the fate of Islamic traditionalism in the future, here we need to understand why it was such an attractive idea in the ninth and tenth centuries. Why build an imperial law in the Fertile Crescent upon the sayings of Muḥammad, who, having become God's Prophet, never left Arabia? In part, the answer can be found in the experience of the Arabs themselves. Predicated as it was on a rigorous command of Arabic language and grammar, traditionalism asserted the distinctively Arab character of God's final monotheism and the enduring significance of Arabic learning for its understanding – and this at a time when the social barriers between Arab and non-Arab were disintegrating, and effective political power was falling into the hands of non-Arabs (armies of non-Arab slave soldiers made their first appearance in the middle of the ninth century). Like the annual pilgrimage and the consensus that the Qur^ʾān was untranslatable from the Arabic, traditionalism kept Muslims moored to their Arabian origins. God had spoken to Muḥammad in a 'clear Arabic tongue' (Qurʾān 16:103 and 26:195), and there is good reason to think that Muḥammad was first understood as an Arabian, rather than universalist, prophet. This incipient Arabo-centrism was ultimately overcome, but it was not completely effaced.

More than this, traditionalism functioned to blunt and redirect the forces of particularism, which emerged as the caliphate fragmented politically during the late ninth and tenth centuries. If the collapse of the caliphate as a political unity was to some degree inevitable – no one has managed to generate long-term solutions to all the challenges there were in ruling a multi-ethnic empire from the Atlas mountains to the Indus valley – no one could have predicted what would replace it. The empire yielded to a trans-regional commonwealth of Islamic culture, which, as much as the glorious days of imperial unity, was responsible for generating so many of the institutions and practices characteristic of Islamic civilization, such as the institutions of higher learning (the *madrasas*) and Sufi brotherhoods. And what made this commonwealth meaningful and sensible was in large measure the tradition-based system of law: the requirement of Arabic language training for Arab and non-Arab alike, of travelling to the heartlands of the early caliphate (the Fertile Crescent and Arabia) for the purposes of the oral transmission of *ḥadīth*, and entrance into one of four schools of legal thinking (Ḥanbalī, Ḥanafī, Shāfiʿī and Mālikī), each named after eighth- and ninth-century eponyms, each copying, commenting and epitomizing the seminal texts these authorities had written, but all reading a more or less common set of authoritative collections. It was into this regime that élites could send their sons, thereby making academic colleagues out of Persians, Turks and Arabs, be they from Morocco, Iraq or Afghanistan. It was this regime that conditioned the conduct of local politics, too. When the élites of Persian cities such as Nishapur disagreed about town politics, they tended to

in Ibn Warraq, ed., *The Quest for the Historical Muhammad* (Amherst, New York, 2000), chapter 1; see also M. Arkoun, *Rethinking Islam*, ed. and trans. by R.D. Lee (Boulder, 1994), pp. 35f. (on Qurʾānic scholarship); and, for some criticisms of Orientalist studies of Islamic law, A. Laroui, *Islam et histoire: essai d'épistémologie* (Paris, 1999), pp. 69ff.; cf. R.S. Humphreys, 'Modern Arab historians and the challenge of the Islamic past', *Middle Eastern Lectures* 1 (1995), pp. 119–131.

express their disagreements as Ḥanafīs and Shāfiᶜīs, and when the Ḥanafīs and Shāfiᶜīs disagreed about how to interpret the law, they still shared the same collections of *ḥadīth*.[13]

Traditionalism was therefore more than an intellectual tradition: it was a way of ordering society. As one anthropologist has put it, one can no more conceive of Islam without the *ᶜulamāʾ* than one can conceive of Latin Christianity without Gregory, or Hinduism without caste.[14]

The consequences of traditionalism

What did it mean to write history in a traditionalist culture? One thing should be obvious: writing history in a culture that attached so much value to the past was an important thing – indeed, a powerful thing, since the past was held as a model for the present. This said, there is no necessary connection between the value that a society places upon history and the amount or character of the historiography that it produces. History played much less of a role in the self-understanding of the classical Greeks than it did for the Jews, and yet it is to the Greeks that we owe paradigmatic forms of historiography, while the Jews as much as abandoned what is conventionally categorized as historiography in the second century C.E., only returning to it in the sixteenth. In other words, since traditionists and traditionalist-historians revered *a* past rather than *the* past, it is hardly enough to say that traditionalism produced historiography, and that Muslims were prolific historians because most were dyed-in-the-wool traditionalists. Muslim historians cultivated *particular* kinds of Islamic history in *particular* ways. In what follows, I describe how traditionalism influenced historiography during the first four centuries of Islam, beginning here with form and style, and then turning to genre. I finish the task in the next chapter, when I turn to court-produced historiography.[15]

There can be no doubt that the single most distinctive feature of Islamic historiography is the *khabar-isnād* unit, which, transmitted, transformed, compiled and arranged according to a variety of formats, functions as the building block of large-scale historical works. Although we shall see that much changed during the eleventh and twelfth centuries, this remains true throughout the classical period: *khabar*-historiography would be complemented, rather than eclipsed, by other narrative techniques. That this is so says something about the conservatism of the tradition,

[13] For a summary overview of these schools, see J. Schacht, 'The schools of law and later developments of jurisprudence', in M. Khadduri and H.J. Liebesny, eds., *Law in the Middle East I: Origin and Development of Islamic Law* (Washington D.C., 1955), pp. 57–84; and Melchert, *The Formation of the Sunni Schools*; the preceding has comments on epitomizing, as does J.E. Brockopp, 'Early Islamic jurisprudence in Egypt: two scholars and their *mukhtaṣars*', *IJMES* 30 (1998), pp. 167–182; on Nishapur, R. Bulliet, *The Patricians of Nishapur* (Cambridge, Mass., 1972).

[14] The anthropologist is C. Geertz, *Islam Observed: Religious Development in Morocco and Indonesia* (Chicago, 1968), p. 3.

[15] For the contrast between the Greeks and Jews, see A. Momigliano, *The Classical Foundations of Modern Historiography* (Berkeley and Los Angeles, 1990), pp. 18ff.

or, put somewhat differently, about an enduring consensus that whatever new directions historiographic forms might take, the project should remain tethered to the traditionalist principles it had embraced during the ninth century, when the *khabar-isnād* unit was adopted as the fundamental unit of narration. The past was to be captured as a compilation of single snapshots, each either 'taken' by a witness to the event itself or transmitted by someone who had received it from him. Insofar as it had any bearing, the truthfulness of these snapshots much more frequently turned on the judgment of the witness and/or transmitter than it did upon the plausibility of the event itself, and the task of the historian lay principally in selecting these snapshots according to one or another set of criteria and to compile them according to one or another arrangement. The results were a passion for collection and arrangement, and a correspondingly taciturn authorial voice. If we describe Arabic prose narrative as a continuum, at one end of which stand the mute traditionist-transmitters of the law, and at the other stand the outspoken belletrists, historiography is to be situated between the two, its position oscillating according to time and fashion. During the formative period, it moved towards and remained near the traditionist pole; during the classical period, it moved towards the centre and sometimes further towards the belletrists.[16]

The preceding can be restated in terms of style and tone. Historians of the formative period generally took their task seriously, went about it soberly, and expected their readers to do the same: Arabic literature can be farcical and comical, but there is little comedy in historiography. They also wrote clearly and plainly, which is not as obvious as it may sound. Both in its syntax and morphology, Arabic is a relatively plastic language, which, in the hands of an ambitious and talented author, can produce poetry and prose of great effect. Already in the eighth century we have evidence for complex prose styles, which seem to have been associated with chancery figures, and in the middle of the ninth century, Iraq could boast prose stylists of extraordinary gifts, authors who took advantage of all the language had to offer; parallelism, assonance and rhyme were favoured techniques. Now there is no question that most historians commanded the philological skills required to write in these higher registers of language, nor, to judge from how often and how much attractive poetry and complex documentary Arabic they integrated into their histories, is there any question that they were attracted to it. An address given by the caliph ᶜUthmān is characterized by complex parallelism at the level of syntax and sense, by repetition, association, antithesis and a variety of other rhetorical techniques – and we only know of it because al-Ṭabarī preserved it; indeed, it is probably fair to say that he preserved it precisely *because* of its rhetoric. After citing a stirring and difficult speech given in year 75/694–695 by al-Ḥajjāj, the governor of Iraq, al-Ṭabarī writes very much as the linguist and philologist whom we can recognize in the great exegesis of the Qurʾān, glossing several of the most obscure words and images, and citing apposite poetry to clarify things.

16 On the 'ḥadīth format' and 'atomistic quality' of the early tradition in particular, see Donner, *Narratives of Islamic Origins*, pp. 255ff.

But for all their interests and abilities in ambitious language of this kind, the fact remains that early historians still chose not to compose in these higher registers (unless one argues that it was *they*, rather than the caliph or governor, who composed the speeches, which they put into the mouths of ʿUthmān and al-Ḥajjāj). Instead, the historians opted for the same, relatively economical and transparent academic style that prevailed amongst the traditionists. Much as compiling (rather than composing) marks the historians' respect for the traditionalist ethos, so, too, do the transparency and relative homogeneity of their style reflect that ambivalence about originality and individuality. This would change, and we shall see that the change was effected in part by outsiders to the traditionalist establishment.[17]

So in approach and tone, historiography seems to have been deeply influenced by the traditionalist ethos. Things become even clearer when we turn to the historians' fields of inquiry, where traditionalism's reverence for *its own past*, combined with a corresponding indifference towards the present, seems to have conditioned the historiographic project. Chronography is a case in point. The very occasional exception aside, throughout the early period the *akhbārī*s usually sacrificed contemporary history in their devotion to the early, foundational moments of Islamic history. Even though he had an enormous amount of material at his disposal, al-Ṭabarī only reluctantly says much about his own day: no more than about 10 per cent of his monumental *Taʾrīkh* is concerned with contemporary history. Meanwhile, many historians said nothing at all, concentrating upon the Glorious (such as Prophetic history and the great conquests of the seventh century), the Tragic (especially the Civil War of the 650s) or the Curious (the genealogist Ibn al-Kalbī is a fine example of the latter, having specialized in all manner of antique arcana, including a book on famous horses). A catalogue has recently been made of the most prominent historians and their titles until the end of the second Islamic century (*ca.* 820), and not a single one of the themes enumerated there reflects an enthusiasm for contemporary history.

This is a remarkable way of going about things, not so much because it runs counter to classical norms (which were in any case exceptional), but because it is counter-intuitive. When we describe, we are apt to describe what we know best, and what we know best is what we know by direct experience rather than received wisdom. Indeed, this is exactly how other, non-Muslim historians were working. At the very time that Syriac historians working in the Near East very summarily gathered early material in order to be able to devote the bulk of their narrative to detailed discussions of contemporary history, Muslim historians were doing quite

[17] For humour in Arabic letters, a place to start is F. Rosenthal, *Humour in Early Islam* (Leiden, 1956); ʿUthmān's address is discussed in A.F.L. Beeston, 'Parallelism in Arabic prose', *JAL* 5 (1974), pp. 134–146; on the evolution of prose styles, A.F.L. Beeston, *Samples of Arabic Prose in its Historical Development* (Oxford, 1977); for al-Ṭabarī's gloss (*tafsīr*), see his *Taʾrīkh*, ii, pp. 866ff., which is translated by E. Rowson as *The Marwānid Restoration* (Albany, 1989; al-Ṭabarī translation, vol. xxii), pp. 16ff.; precisely because there is relatively little individuality in it, relatively little work has been done on the early historians' style; for one example, W. Fischer, 'Die Prosa des Abū Miḫnaf,' in R. Gramlich, ed., *Islamwissenschaftliche Abhandlungen* (Festschrift for F. Meier) (Wiesbaden, 1974), pp. 96–105.

the opposite, moving faster the closer they got to their own day. We *can* find an enthusiasm for contemporary history in this period, but we find it amongst the poets rather than the historians. Might it be that the historians were playing it safe? It is true that ventilating upon (the manifest decline of) the present might have proven risky, and the poets did occasionally pay for their honesty; it is also true that criticism of the political order can be expressed very effectively when recast in narratives of foundational moments. But the imbalance between past and contemporary history cannot be fully explained in terms of potential persecution. For one thing, the religious establishment was not so vulnerable as that; in fact, we shall see in chapter 8 that most states were relatively weak, while the social élites that produced most of our historians were fairly resilient. For another thing, the historians failed to produce *all* varieties of contemporary history in the early period, whether harshly critical or fulsomely panegyric. Traditionalism, rather than persecution, seems to explain the historians' aversion to the present.[18]

This is why the same sensitivities were at work in other forms of historiography. In chapter 4 we saw that traditionist prosopography was immensely productive, and that this productivity can be explained not merely with reference to its utility for *ḥadīth* criticism, but as a contribution to the crystallization of the schools of law. We also saw how one example, al-Shīrāzī's *History of the Jurists*, is a highly selective and programmatic work, which seems to offer an exceptionally inclusive and catholic vision of juristic activity at a time when inter-school controversies and rancour were on the rise. So prosopography was a vehicle for traditionalist debate, and it exemplifies, especially in its size, traditionalism's values and aspirations. Here it is crucial to note its distinctive shape: al-Shīrāzī stops his retrospective survey of jurists short of his own generation. In fact, this prosopographical ban on the present had been long standing. Already in Ibn Sa^{c}d's time prosopographers had shied away from including contemporaries in their works, limiting their coverage to figures who were authoritative and dead. Indeed, the logic of traditionalism meant that being authoritative generally meant being dead. Schools of thought typically formed after their eponyms passed away, a good example being none other than the 'Jarīrī' school of law, which followed the teachings of 'Ibn Jarīr' al-Ṭabarī, the figure whom we know principally as a historian, but whom Ibn al-Nadīm classified primarily as a jurist. Originality was as uncomfortable as emulation was natural, and this explains why the very traditionalists who shied away from championing contemporaries were the same traditionalists who claimed to transmit, rather than compose. What could *they* possibly have to offer?[19]

Similar things can be said of autobiography, which is commonly described as biography in the first person. This is true enough. Much less frequently noted is the

[18] For the catalogue, see Donner, *Narratives of Islamic Origins*, pp. 141ff.; cf. the themes discussed in Noth/Conrad, *Early Arabic Historical Tradition*, which is principally concerned with conquest narrative; a contemporaneous Syriac historian is the anonymous author of the so-called *Zuqnin Chronicle*, on which see below; for some contemporary history in verse, S.P. Stetkevych, *Abū Tammām and the Poetics of the ^{c}Abbāsid Age* (Leiden, 1991), Part II.

[19] For the short-lived Jarīrī school, see Melchert, *The Formation of the Sunni Schools*, pp. 191ff.

fact that autobiography is, by its very definition, contemporary history. The two ingredients made for a combination that was especially distasteful to the traditionalist. For what could offend his sensitivities more than an autobiographer – a narrator who, in recording the contemporary history of his own life (if only schematically and stereotypically), proposed that *it*, rather than the accumulated tradition to which he was heir, was worthy of emulation? No surprise, then, that it was left to non-traditionalist rationalists and iconoclasts (philosophers, mystics and Ismāᶜīlī Shīᶜites), such al-Muḥāsibī (d. 857), Ḥunayn b. Isḥāq (perhaps; d. 877), al-Ḥakīm al-Tirmidhī (d. *ca.* 910), Ibn Sīnā (Avicenna; d. 1037) and al-Muᵓayyad fī al-Dīn al-Shīrāzī (d. *ca.* 1078) to monopolize the field of early autobiographical writing in Arabic. Another recent catalogue lists 21 specimens of autobiographical writing that date from the ninth, tenth and eleventh centuries. Now several of these are problematical ascriptions to now-lost works, but amongst those that remain, there is not a single independent autobiography that can be securely credited to any historian, much less anyone working at or near the heart of the traditionalist establishment. As we shall see, it was only in the thirteenth and fourteenth centuries that traditionalist historians did finally come around to writing autobiographies in any number, and when they did, they frequently wrote in the third person. The technique recommended itself not merely through its familiarity to them – after all, *biography* had a long and reputable tradition – but because it allowed the autobiographer to put himself at some distance from his immodest subject.[20]

What follows from the preceding is this: the trajectory of the historiographical tradition conventionally described as 'mainstream', which leads from Ibn Isḥāq through al-Wāqidī to al-Ṭabarī, owes much of its success to its embrace of the ethos and tools of Islamic traditionalism, which set the cultural tone during the eighth and ninth centuries. The exercise of rationalism and individual discretion was to be subordinated to reports reliably transmitted by predecessors: the knowable past was not inferred, but preserved. Put another way, 'rational deductions' and 'mental elucidations' (the words are al-Ṭabarī's) had no role to play in generating knowledge of the past. Moreover, there was a past, and then there was *the* past, and in practice this meant following the traditionists' reverence for the paradigmatic beginning and a corresponding indifference to contemporary history.

[20] Al-Muḥāsibī's autobiographical writing was first made part of the history of Arabic autobiography by F. Rosenthal, whose 'Die arabische Autobiographie', *Studia Arabica* 1 (1937), pp. 1–40 (for al-Muḥāsibī, see pp. 11f.) is a classic discussion; al-Ḥakīm al-Tirmidhī's autobiography, which seems to be the first to survive in any more than fragmentary form, is published in his *Kitāb Khatm al-awliyā*ᵓ (Beirut, 1965), pp. 14ff.; it is translated by B. Radtke and J. O'Kane in *The Concept of Sainthood in Early Islamic Mysticism* (Richmond, 1996), pp. 15–36, and discussed by B. Radtke, *al-Ḥakīm at-Tirmiḏī: ein islamischer Theosoph des 3./9. Jahrhunderts* (Freiburg, 1980), pp. 1–11 (where reference is also made to van Ess's fragments of al-Muḥāsibī's autobiography); work on Ḥunayn's purported autobiography (which survives in Ibn Abī Uṣaybiᶜa) begins with Rosenthal ('Autobiographie', pp. 15ff.) and continues with M. Cooperson, 'The purported autobiography of Ḥunayn ibn Isḥāq', *Edebiyât* n.s. 7 (1997), pp. 235–249; there are several translations of Ibn Sīnā's, one of which is W. Gohlman, *The Life of Ibn Sina* (New York, 1974); al-Muᵓayyad's was published in Cairo, 1949; for another Ismāᶜīlī memoir, W. Madelung and P. Walker, *The Advent of the Fatimids: A Contemporary Shiᶜi Witness* (London, 2000); the catalogue is Reynolds, ed., *Interpreting the Self*, pp. 256ff., which includes translations of several of the above.

The *akhbārī*s, some of whom were themselves practising jurists and *ḥadīth* transmitters, duly adopted the *isnād* – the emblematic tool of the *ḥadīth* trade – and also the *ṭabaqāt* form, which, whatever its genetic links with *ḥadīth* criticism, became closely associated with traditionist institutions. But historiography would eventually emerge from the traditionists' shadow, and non-traditionalist historiography would come to complement traditionalist forms. We can begin to see how this happened by returning to the *isnād*.[21]

1000 to 1500: New directions

Whatever its utility in the short term, the *isnād*, like other traditionist tools, was poorly suited for the job of crafting history in all its forms. It was one thing to identify witnesses for the relatively circumscribed arena of Prophetic activity (twenty years or so in the Hijaz), but quite another for conquest battles in Spain, not to mention the career of Alexander the Great. Was one to limit the scope of history to those events for which one could identify and quote an eyewitness? In addition, there were considerations of scale and style. In lengthy works, complete or even incomplete *isnād*s could occupy an enormous amount of valuable space (paper was not free) and consume a copyist's expensive time (abbreviations were introduced, but these hardly addressed the problem). Moreover, in works of *any* length, *isnād*s could be regarded as narrative intrusions, brakes all too often applied on the reader's momentum. Lengthening *isnād*s taxed the paper manufacturer, the copyist and the reader's attention and patience.

One solution was to eliminate the *isnad*s altogether, which, in the modern idiom, amounts to dispensing with footnotes. This can be done, but it requires a trusting (or lazy) reader and a historian with enough confidence to risk colleagues' criticisms. Another solution was to combine the *isnād*s, to synthesize discrete versions of the same event into a single account: modern historians have called this the 'collective' *isnād* or 'combined' report. Traditionists might take offence at this practice too, since it risked blurring lines of transmission and – perhaps more important – endowed authors with more authority than these traditionist-transmitters thought seemly. We read that one second-century *muḥåddith* took al-Wāqidī (d. 823) to task on these grounds, insisting that he transmit the accounts in his *maghāzī* work separately, disentangling the constituent *akhbār*, each with its own appropriate *isnād*. Although the *muḥaddith* was duly warned of the results, the end of the anecdote still packs a punch: 'He [al-Wāqidī] disappeared for a week and then brought us [the *muḥaddith*, speaking in the first person plural] the [story of the] Uḥud expedition in twenty volumes. So we said: "Let's go back to the earlier scheme."'[22]

[21] The translation of al-Ṭabarī's words is borrowed from Mahdi, *Philosophy of History*, p. 136.

[22] For al-Wāqidī, his critic, and how some early historians handled *isnād*s, see M. Lecker, 'Wāqidī's account on the status of the Jews in Medina: a study of a combined report', *JNES* 54 (1995), pp. 15–32, and Donner, *Narratives of Islamic Origins*, pp. 264ff.

In fact, the historians knew exactly what they were doing. As the past grew longer with the unfolding of time, it became obvious that historiography could not sustain the traditionists' standards, nor did it have to follow the traditionists' rules. The monumental history of al-Ṭabarī, which is furnished with all the *isnād*s that this well-placed jurist could muster, quickly established itself as the standard universal history, being cited and continued by successive generations of historians. Yet it also shows the limitations of a method developed according to the traditionists' standards, and this is why it was epitomized rather than emulated by many later tenth-century historians, as Ibn al-Nadīm tells us it was, writing within two generations of the master's death. Some, then, opted for the first solution outlined above, which was to eliminate *isnād*s altogether, the most notable of these being Ibn al-Athīr (d. 1233), who drew copiously on al-Ṭabarī for the early period (the second solution did not prove as popular). From this perspective, al-Ṭabarī's work marks the culmination of the early chronographic tradition not because subsequent historians failed to live up to his standard, but because they had the good sense to see that his approach was no longer workable. Put differently, the traditionists had realized during the ninth century that the time had come for selecting and pruning; the historians learned the same lesson in the tenth, and they applied it not only to their material, but to method as well. This is not to say that all historians would henceforth dispense with the *isnād*. For many, historical knowledge, as before, would be produced through the transmission of discrete accounts, and no attempt would be made to rebuild the tradition atop the rationalism proposed by al-Mas^{c}ūdī. Like it or not, his was a dead end: historiography would remain far more traditionalist than most modern historians would have wished it. But it is certainly fair to conclude that the winds were changing. For whereas marginal figures (such as al-Ya^{c}qūbī and al-Dīnawarī) had eschewed the *isnād*s, now figures in the twelfth- and thirteenth-century mainstream were doing the same. Historiography was becoming an altogether more assertive activity, and its practitioners now possessed the confidence to generate new forms and explore new themes. It is starting in this period that many historians began to free themselves from the traditionists' sensitivities and taboos.[23]

There are several signs of this new confidence. One is language. A relatively homogeneous rhetoric of historical description gives way to a relatively heterogeneous one, in which the highest and lowest registers of language are now used. Insofar as adopting more ambitious narrative styles (including rhyming) signals a challenge to the traditionalist ethos, the historians made the challenge only in the eleventh century. Perhaps our earliest and clearest evidence comes from a history of the reigns of Sebüktigin and Maḥmūd, two members of the Ghaznavid dynasty, which ruled present-day eastern Iran, Afghanistan and northern India from 977 to 1186; it was written by Abū Naṣr al-^{c}Utbī (d. 1036). The following relates Maḥmūd's reaction to his father's death and the succession of his brother to power,

[23] For Ibn al-Nadīm on al-Ṭabarī, see the *Fihrist*, pp. 291ff. (Dodge, *Fihrist,* pp. 563ff.).

and comes as close as one might reasonably hope to the elaborate and convoluted style of the Arabic original:

> The amir Sayf al-Dawla [Maḥmūd's title] was at a loss how to deal with what had befallen him; for he found gentleness more attractive than crudeness, preferred mending over rending, inclined to blandishment rather than contention and complaisance rather than confrontation, chose kindness over harshness, and 'saved cauterization as the last resort in an illness' [a proverb]. But when the star of forbearance set, and the robe of decorum grew threadbare, he prepared to 'approach the matter by the front door' [a Qurʾānic allusion] and to restore that which had been snatched from him to its proper place ... Then he marched out with his élite slave troops, his infantry, and the commanders charged with obeying his orders, and reached Herat [in present-day Afghanistan], where he continued to send letters to Ismāʿīl [his brother], mixing promises and threats, and enticements and deterrents, inviting him alternatively to despair and hope, and warning him against landing himself in a position of regret and shame. But all this made not a date-stone's difference, and failed to unravel a single strand from the braided rope of Ismāʿīl's stance ... [24]

Al-ʿUtbī provides a spectacular example, which anticipates one of the directions in which the Persian historical tradition would eventually travel. And, once again, we should not exaggerate things: historical rhetoric did not change beyond all recognition, and for every historian who exploited Arabic fully by writing in its highest registers, there are a dozen who would not. But now a new set of styles do appear, complementing the 'collecting mode' of the previous period, and although this is especially true amongst those most closely tied to the chancery and the court, even those with traditionist credentials might take it up. Ibn al-Athīr is a case in point. He is at once a traditionist prosopographer who compiled the *Usd al-ghāba fī maʿrifat al-ṣaḥāba* ('The Lion of the Thicket Concerning Knowledge of the Companions'), and, as we have already seen, a chronographer. Indeed, nearly everything in his *Kāmil* seems designed to secure the broadest possible audience: *isnād*s were eliminated, and difficult passages in al-Ṭabarī's original were either omitted or glossed, the obscure poetry being cut out nearly altogether. By every reasonable standard, the work was a great success, and Ibn Ḥajar even seems to have given some thought to writing a continuation of it. To complement this work, Ibn al-Athīr also wrote a deeply panegyric chronography of the Atabegs of Mosul, his patrons, and in several of its passages the stylistic contrast with the *Kāmil* could hardly be more striking. Here, in this work of court panegyric, we can sometimes find that very ornate and forbidding chancery style of historical narrative: as much as the *Kāmil* seems to be intended for a broad audience, this dynastic history seems intended only for the court.[25]

24 I draw the ʿUtbī translation from E.K. Rowson, 'History as prose panegyric: al-ʿUtbī and the beginnings of euphuistic historiography' (unpublished typescript); for ʿUtbī, see Meisami, *Persian Historiography*, pp. 53ff.; and cf. L. Richter-Bernburg, *Der syrische Blitz: Saladins Sekretär zwischen Selbstdarstellung und Geschichtsschreibung* (Beirut, 1998), pp. 137ff.

25 For Ibn Ḥajar's interest in the *Kāmil*, see his *al-Muʿjam al-mufahras* (Beirut, 1998), p. 419; Ibn al-Athīr's *al-Taʾrīkh al-bāhir fī al-dawla al-atābakiyya* was published in Cairo, 1963 and Baghdad, 1963.

So the linguistic possibilities of historical prose were opening up to historians in this period, and they would continue to do so in ensuing periods. Just as the highest registers were used, so, too, were lower ones. The appearance of non-standard Arabic in historical prose, particularly the vernacular, is conventionally associated with Mamluk historiography of the fourteenth and fifteenth centuries, good examples being the Egyptian Ibn al-Dawādārī (d. 1335) and the Syrian Ibn Ṣaṣrā (fl. late fourteenth or early fifteenth century), although we have some good examples of it in earlier and less formal historical compositions, such as the 'memoirs' of Usāma b. Munqidh (d. 1188). From this, too, we might infer that historians no longer felt compelled to uphold the traditionists' linguistic standards by archaizing their actors' speech and excluding non-standard forms from third-person narrative. Even if non-classical Arabic is not entirely unknown in historical prose of the earlier period, in some Mamluk chronography it becomes nearly normative, forming part of a new rhetoric that was at once linguistically more ambitious and thematically less constrained by classical standards. Indeed, what had been unseemly – an interest in the fantastic, the miraculous and strange – now becomes fairly commonplace.[26]

Alongside these changes in language and tone, there emerges a relatively robust tradition of contemporary history, the earliest signs of which are discernible in chronography. It should come as no surprise that the agents of change seem to have come from outside of the traditionalist establishment. Already with Muḥammad b. Yaḥyā al-Ṣūlī (d. *ca.* 950), we can see how littérateurs, who had never been shy about relating the present, might dabble in contemporary history; at the end of the tenth and early eleventh century, it was left to other figures marginal to the establishment, such as the iconoclastic Ibn Miskawayh (1030) and successive members of the (mostly pagan) Ṣābiʾ family of historians, to cultivate contemporary history on some scale. In fact, Ibn Miskawayh clearly brought to his contemporary history (the *Tajārib al-umam*, 'The Experiences of Nations') a philosophical and ethical programme that owed little to traditionalism and much to the very rationalism that the traditionists had rejected, arrogating to himself the authority to judge the veracity of his informants, and frequently writing in the first person.[27]

What explains the change? During the eleventh and twelfth centuries many historians were trained and worked not as traditionists, but as secretaries and

[26] The classic statement on the new rhetoric of Mamluk historiography, 'die Literarisierung der Geschichtsschreibung', belongs to U. Haarmann, 'Auflösung und Bewahrung der klassischen Formen arabischer Geschichtsschreibung in der Zeit der Mamluken', *ZDMG* 121 (1971), pp. 53ff.; and also his *Quellenstudien zur frühen Mamlukenzeit* (Freiburg im Breisgau, 1969), pp. 159ff.

[27] More will be said of the Ṣābiʾ family below; for now, see (the fragments of) Hilāl al-Ṣābiʾ's *Tuḥfat al-umarāʾ fī taʾrīkh al-wuzarāʾ* (London, 1904); for the exceptional Ibn Miskawayh, his *Tajārib al-umam* (fragments edited in London, 1921 and now Teheran, 1987–), and his exceptional times, see J. Kraemer, *Humanism in the Renaissance of Islam: The Cultural Revival during the Buyid Age* (Leiden, 2nd rev. ed., 1993), pp. 222ff. and M. Arkoun, *L'humanisme arabe au ivᵉ/xᵉ siècle: Miskawayh, philosophe et historien* (Paris, 2nd rev. ed., 1982); on the ethical in historiography, J.S. Meisami, 'Dynastic kingship and the ideal of kingship in Bayhaqi's *Tarikh-i Masᶜudi*', *Edebiyât* n.s. 3 (1989), pp. 57–77.

bureaucrats, with the result that they brought to their historical work much of the linguistic virtuosity that their training had produced and their patrons, who were living in a highly competitive, post-imperial and thus polyfocal world, now demanded. So the courts, covetous of the prestige and legitimacy that the historians could offer, seem to have exercised a decisive influence on the course of the historiographic tradition. We have already seen that the court lay behind al-ᶜUtbī's and Ibn al-Athīr's panegyric histories; the latter wrote his *Bāhir* to edify al-Qāhir, the son of Nūr al-Dīn Arslān (d. 1210). Meanwhile, contemporaries such as ᶜImād al-Dīn al-Iṣfahānī (d. 1201) and Bahāᵓ al-Dīn b. Shaddād (d. 1235) were writing fawning biographies of Saladin. In fact, the period is characterized by an altogether cosier relationship between historians and the courts of ambitious dynasts: we have no fewer than three near contemporary biographies of al-Ẓāhir Baybars (rg. 1260–1277) – a quite unprecedented attempt to fashion and refashion the image of a ruling house.[28]

What we have, then, is an explosion of contemporary history during the twelfth and thirteenth centuries. Not all of it can be explained by court patronage. The field was now open for a different kind of prosopography – contemporary prosopography. To be sure, the taboo had not always been respected: Ibn al-ᶜAdīm (d. 1262), who followed in the footsteps of Ibn ᶜAsākir (d. 1176) and al-Khaṭīb al-Baghdādī (d. 1071), had held that allowances might be made for those contemporaries of exceptional celebrity. In the event, he failed to uphold the principle, which suggests that the rules were loosening up, but it is only with al-Ṣafadī (d. 1363) that we have a prosopography devoted entirely to contemporaries, the *Aᶜyān al-ᶜaṣr wa-aᶜwān al-naṣr*. The same trends are present in autobiography – that combination of contemporary history and self-aggrandizement, which was doubly distasteful to the traditionists. Whereas autobiography had earlier been cultivated only by outsiders (or at least those very familiar with rationalist models marginalized by the legal tradition), now it is cultivated by historians with traditionalist credentials. Thus Abū Shāma (d. 1267) inserts in his annalistic history *Dhayl ᶜalā al-Rawḍatayn* an autobiographical notice in the third person, a practice that would be followed by Ibn Ḥajar in the *Rafᶜ al-iṣr ᶜan quḍāt Miṣr*; later al-Suyūṭī would write an autobiography with considerably less trepidation.[29]

So traditionalist-historians were now writing contemporary prosopography (in which they frequently inserted autobiographical notices), while fellow historians

[28] On Ibn al-Athīr's patronage, see D.S. Richards, 'Ibn al-Athīr and the later parts of the *Kāmil*: a study of aims and methods', in D.O. Morgan, ed., *Medieval Historical Writing in the Christian and Islamic Worlds* (London, 1982), pp. 76–108; on al-Ẓāhir Baybars, P.M. Holt, 'Three biographies of al-Ẓāhir Baybars', in Morgan, ed., *Medieval Historical Writing*, pp. 19–29; and J. Sublet, *Les trois vies du sultan Baïbars* (Paris, 1992).

[29] On Ibn al-ᶜAdīm, see Morray, *Ayyubid Notable*, esp. 11f., note 37; in general, Reynolds, ed., *Interpreting the Self*; on Abū Shāma, J.E. Lowry, 'Time, form and self: the autobiography of Abū Shāma', *Edebiyât* n.s. 7 (1997), pp. 313–325, which is one of several articles on Arabic autobiography in an issue devoted exclusively to the topic; and L. Pouzet, 'Remarques sur l'autobiographie dans le monde arabo-musulman au moyen âge', in U. Vermeulen and D. de Smet, eds., *Philosophy and Arts in the Islamic World* (Louvain, 1998), pp. 97–106 (which surveys autobiographical fragments in general).

were sniping at each other and sometimes even praising each other. Al-Ṣafadī even goes so far as to champion a fellow historian (al-Dhahabī, d. 1348) at the *expense* of the *ḥadīth* transmitters: 'he had none of the rigidity of the *muḥaddithīn*' – they may seem perfectly tame to us now, but in the fourteenth century these were fighting words. (We shall see in chapter 9 that it was in this period that professional camaraderie and rivalry develop.) It was not just al-Ṣafadī who had the courage to take the critics on and to argue systematically for the project. Thus al-Sakhāwī (d. 1497) was bold enough to write a work of polemic, *al-Iᶜlān bi'l-tawbīkh li-man dhamma ahl al-taʾrīkh* ('The Public Denunciation of those who Criticize History'). History is now championed as a science, even if exactly what it is remains to be spelt out: 'the term *taʾrīkh*', al-Sakhāwī writes, 'signifies a branch of learning that is concerned with research regarding the occurrences which take place in time, in the intention to establish their character, and their place in time'. By this period we can also begin to see the signs of historiographic schools, such as we have, for example, in Almohad and Merinid North Africa in the thirteenth and fourteenth centuries and in Mamluk Syria.[30]

It is hardly coincidental that this later, more confident period also produced the *Muqaddima* of Ibn Khaldūn (d. 1406), the most theoretically sophisticated programme of historical thought produced by any pre-modern historian, be he Christian, Muslim or otherwise. The *Muqaddima* – the programmatic 'Introduction' to his universal history – was not merely a work of great insight, however. It was a hugely personal piece of research, based on his own reflection and opportunistic reading, and nothing in his formal education, which he describes in – fittingly enough – an autobiography, prepared him for the undertaking. This, as we have seen, is because the standard course of education had been tailored by traditionists to produce more traditionists, rather than historians of universal chronicles.[31]

[30] For the sniping, see A. Darrāǧ, 'La vie d'Abū'l-Maḥāsin Ibn Taġrī Birdī et son oeuvre', *Annales Islamologiques* 11 (1972), pp. 163–181, and W. Popper, 'Sakhāwī's criticism of Ibn Taghrī Birdī', *Studi Orientalistici in onore di Giorgio Levi Della Vida* (Rome, 1956), pp. 371–389; for al-Ṣafadī's praise of al-Dhahabī, Ibn Ḥajar, *al-Durar al-kāmina fī aᶜyān al-miʾa al-thāmina*, iii, p. 337 (*jumūd al-muḥaddithīn*); the Sakhāwī translation is from Makdisi, 'The diary in Islamic historiography: some notes', p. 179; sections from al-Sakhāwī's *Iᶜlān* and al-Kāfiyajī's *al-Mukhtaṣar fī ᶜilm al-taʾrīkh* are translated in Rosenthal, *History*; for the North African schools, M. Shatzmiller, *L'historiographie mérinide: Ibn Khaldūn et ses contemporains* (Leiden, 1982); for the Syrian school (and salutary remarks on the Egyptian), L. Guo, 'Mamluk historiographic studies: the state of the art', *MSR* 1 (1997), esp. 37ff., and *Early Mamluk Syrian Historiography*, pp. 81ff.

[31] Ibn Khaldūn's *Muqaddima* was translated by F. Rosenthal as *The Muqaddimah: An Introduction to History* (New York, 1958; 2nd, corrected ed., Princeton, 1967; abridged ed., Princeton, 1969); the bibliography on Ibn Khaldūn is naturally very large, but note might be made of M. Brett, *Ibn Khaldun and the Medieval Maghrib* (Aldershot, 1999) (collected articles); A. Cheddadi, *Peuples et nations du monde: la conception de l'histoire, les Arabes du Machrek et leurs contemporains, les Arabes du Maghreb et les Berbères* (Paris, 1986) (translations and interpretation); and A. Al-Azmeh, *Ibn Khaldun in Modern Scholarship: A Study in Orientalism* (London, 1981).

CHAPTER 6

Historiography and society

We have seen that historiography occupied an ambivalent position in the classical Islamic world of letters. The traditionalist establishment was enthusiastic about Prophetic biography and traditionist prosopography, which reinforced traditionalist values and institutions, and could serve as auxiliary tools for understanding and verifying *ḥadīth*. Meanwhile, later chronography and non-Prophetic biography (including autobiography) were on the margins of their programme. We are reminded that historiography reflects cultural values. Biography and autobiography became attractive literary genres during the Renaissance because they put the individual at the centre of the historical process. Historiography in general became popular in nineteenth-century Europe because it expressed the idea of *progress* towards a future full of promise. By contrast, later chronography and contemporary biography were less attractive to many traditionalist Muslims because they did little or nothing to *conserve* that part of the past that really mattered.

The point should not be overstated. Compared to theology or philosophy, both of which could engender downright hostility on the part of the establishment, historiography fared well. The practice of history writing may not have enjoyed the prestige accorded to jurisprudence, but historians were never ostracized; some of their books may have been neglected, but they were not burned. Now it is true that some reports actually do attach opprobrium to the study of the *maghāzī*: Aḥmad b. Ḥanbal is supposed to have said that *tafsīr* (exegesis of the Qur᾿ān), *malāḥim* (accounts of the battles that would usher in the End) and *maghāzī* were without any foundation. What probably bothered Aḥmad was not the study of *maghāzī* as such, however, but rather that its experts failed to meet his exacting standards for transmission. In fact, some of the earliest compendia of Islamic law include sections on the *maghāzī*. Authors institutionalized in texts what professors of higher learning would eventually institutionalize in the curriculum of the *madrasa*.[1]

[1] For Aḥmad b. Ḥanbal's attitudes towards *maghāzī*, see Goldziher, *Muslim Studies*, ii, pp. 191f.; sample compendia are Ibn Abī Shayba, *al-Muṣannaf* (Beirut, 1989), viii, pp. 3ff. (an intriguing assortment of *akhbār* grouped under the rubric of *ta᾿rīkh*) and pp. 434ff. (*maghāzī* material to the caliphate of ᶜAlī); ᶜAbd al-Razzāq al-Ṣanᶜānī, *al-Muṣannaf* (Beirut, 1972), v, pp. 313ff. (*maghāzī* material to the caliphate of ᶜUmar); al-Bukhārī, *al-Ṣaḥīḥ* (Leiden, 1862–1908), iii, pp. 52ff.

So Muslims were deeply committed to early Islamic history, and what happened in the seventh century would have enduring effects on Muslim self-identity. Whereas late antique Christians quarrelled about Christology, Muslims quarrelled about the conduct of seventh-century Muslims as it was remembered and recorded in history. Those who exemplified the orthodoxy of their days – figures such as al-Ṭabarī, Ibn al-Jawzī and al-Suyūṭī – found time in their day to write chronography, and even had it been left to the parochial edge of the traditionalist establishment, historiography would not have remained as underdeveloped amongst the *ᶜulamāᵓ* as it would remain amongst the rabbis, with whom the traditionists shared a great deal in common. Convincing proof of that can be found in the monumental prosopographical tradition of the *ᶜulamāᵓ*, the likes of which the rabbis never produced (we have already seen that the rabbis seem to have borrowed the *ṭabaqāt* form from Muslim contemporaries). Rabbinical texts are typically indifferent to dates, with the result that generating a chronology typically turns on a given rabbi's relationships with masters, contemporaries and students. It adds up to very little. 'Historical events of the first order are either not recorded at all, or else they are mentioned in so legendary or fragmentary a way as often to preclude even an elementary retrieval of what occurred'. Islamic prosopography, by contrast, provides not only the relational data, but fairly bristles with dates: birth dates (sometimes), death dates (almost always); divergences are almost invariably recorded.[2]

All of this said, we are left with a problem. Given the traditionalists' ambivalence, how do we explain the sheer monumentality of the chronographic tradition? Why is it that universal and post-Prophetic history was cultivated so successfully? The answers take us away from the religious milieu strictly speaking, and into the social and political world of medieval Islam. That Muslim historians produced such an outstanding chronographic tradition has much to do with the fact that Islam, unlike traditionalist Judaism, was spectacularly successful in its political missionizing, especially in creating a broader culture of politics and learning. As great imperialists, Muslims became great historians. Blinkered traditionists might dominate the religious establishment, but they could hardly prevent scholars from reflecting on the past or jurists from moonlighting as historians. Most crucial of all, they could hardly dictate literary tastes or proscribe historiography from the broader market of learning and culture. And there, amongst princes, administrators, bureaucrats, scribes, secretaries, and patrons of various sorts, all varieties of historical narrative were in great demand. In sum, parochial traditionalism and

[2] The quotation is from Y.H. Yerushalmi, *Zakhor: Jewish History and Jewish Memory* (Seattle and London, 1982), p. 18; for more on the Rabbis' indifference to history, Brettler, *The Creation of History in Ancient Israel*, p. 2 ('there was no question more meaningless or boring than the purpose and usefulness of an exact description of what actually transpired'); W.S. Green, 'What's in a name? – the problematic of "rabbinic biography"', in W.S. Green, ed., *Approaches to Ancient Judaism: Theory and Practice I* (Missoula, 1978), pp. 77–96; cf. J. Neusner, 'Judaic uses of history in Talmudic times', in A. Rapoport-Albert, ed., *Essays in Jewish Historiography* (Middletown, CT, 1988) (= *History and Theory*, Beiheft 27), esp. p. 32; on the similarities, C. Hezser, *The Social Structure of the Rabbinic Movement in Roman Palestine* (Tübingen, 1997), where one can usually replace 'Rabbinate' with '*ᶜulamāᵓ*'.

cosmopolitan imperialism came together in forging the classical historiographic tradition.

In this chapter I finish the task of outlining the cultural status of history writing in the classical Islamic world. While traditionalist prosopography was produced as needed by schools of law that were autonomous from the state, and examples of softer-edged Prophetic biography (what I have called 'devotional biography') were in near constant demand by literate Muslims at large, we shall see that chronography and chronographic *sīra* can often be associated with states and courts. The same pattern can be expressed in chronological terms: whereas traditionalism would always form the backbone of Islamic learning, the tradition of bureaucratically influenced historical writing would complement tradition-based historiography during the eleventh and twelfth centuries. What this means is that we shall have to examine in more detail the thorny problem of patronage, perspective and audience.

Measuring audience

Like other forms of book learning, historiography was produced for an audience of readers and listeners who were well off and lived in cities and towns – in short, the social and political élite who could, if so inclined, dispose of both their money and time in consuming it. Accurate or representative numbers for these readers are impossible to come by for the medieval period, but there is no reason to think that they differed dramatically from that of early twentieth-century Morocco, where about 10–20 per cent of the urban male population was literate – perhaps some 4 per cent of the adult male population in total. (Here it bears remembering that there are different standards and kinds of literacy and numeracy, all socially conditioned in one way or another. In classical Islam, as elsewhere, the ability to read did not guarantee the ability to write, and this helps to explain the crucial role played by scribes, who mastered both sets of skills.) Whatever the precise numbers, for most of our period readers in the Islamic Near East would have been far more numerous than they were in contemporaneous Europe. But who read the great tomes of historiography that were being written?[3].

The question is hard to answer. Nowadays we can know a great deal about how readers respond to books, about who they are and what they do, why they buy the books they buy, how much they are willing to pay, and where they go to buy them. All this information is collected by publishers as a matter of course, but anyone who can read the newspaper has access to a surprisingly detailed measure of readers' tastes. The very organization of bestseller lists (fiction; non-fiction;

[3] I borrow the statistics from D.F. Eickelman, 'The art of memory: Islamic education and its social reproduction', *Comparative Studies in Society and History* 20 (1978), p. 492; on the varieties of literacy, see A.K. Bowman and G. Woolf, eds., *Literacy and Power in the Ancient World* (Cambridge, 1994), *passim*; for one example of a reader who could not write, al-Balādhurī, *Futūḥ al-buldān* (Leiden, 1866), p. 472; for a complementary discussion on the status of historiography, Rosenthal, *History*, pp. 30ff.

'self-help') suggests broad trends, and the particular data contained (the sales figures) are a precise and dated record of the relative popularity of titles (some climbing, some falling), in addition to overall performance (total sales from date of publication). On the basis of bestseller evidence alone, future historians will be able to reconstruct a detailed picture of what books were read, and how politics and culture influenced readers' appetites (and vice-versa). Since they will certainly have much more than that – everything from readers' diaries and library circulation records to book reviews and transcripts of radio and television talk shows – they will be able to say how much we read, how we responded to the books we read, and why. The evidence for medieval Islam is altogether slimmer – so slim, in fact, that historians, naturally predisposed to thinking more about how history is written than about how it is understood, have generally said little at all about audience. I shall outline this evidence in descending order of its value in answering the question to hand.

We may lack bestseller lists and market research, but we do possess a wide range of material, much of which has scarcely been tapped by modern historians. One category is the medium upon which narrative is recorded: manuscripts can yield valuable information about when, why and by whom they were copied, read, heard, transmitted or owned. Information such as this comes in a variety of forms. Colophons, which are statements about the production of a book (or part of one) that scribes wrote at the end of what they had copied, can often tell us the name of the scribe in question, the date when he finished his work, and (much less often) even the name of a commissioning patron. Some manuscripts also bear *ijāza*s, 'certificates of audition' (on which see chapter 9), and these can provide the date and place of a 'hearing', in addition to the names and numbers of those involved; sometimes a single manuscript will even bear a number of such *ijāza*s, which allow us to measure its readership over several generations. Finally, most manuscripts bear marks, signatures and notes made by readers and their owners (not unlike our *ex libris*: '[this] is among the books of so-and-so'), and transfers of ownership ('this book came to so-and-so from so-and-so').[4]

What light can these practices shed on works of historiography? It is from manuscript marks and notes that the editor of the historical section of the *Awrāq* of Muḥammad b. Yaḥyā al-Ṣūlī (d. 950) can conclude that his Cairene copy circulated amongst a large number of scholars from the seventh to the ninth Islamic centuries. Marginal notes written in one of the copies of an anonymous eleventh-century caliphal history suggest that it could claim at least one Khārijite and Shīᶜite reader. It is intriguing to know from an *ijāza* that Ibn Sayyid al-Nās (d. 1334), a biographer of the Prophet, studied the text (fittingly enough on the Prophet's life) of one of the manuscripts of Ibn Saᶜd's *Ṭabaqāt* that Orientalists

[4] On manuscript marks, see Endress, 'Handschriftenkunde', pp. 288ff.; for a very interesting compilation of *ijāza*s, S. Leder, Y.M. al-Sawwās and M. al-Ṣāgharjī, *Muᶜjam al-samāᶜāt al-Dimašqiyya* (Damascus, 1996); on colophons in general, R. Şeşen, 'Esquisse d'une histoire du développement des colophons dans les manuscrits musulmans' in F. Déroche and F. Richard, eds., *Scribes et manuscrits du Moyen-Orient* (Paris, 1997), pp. 189–221.

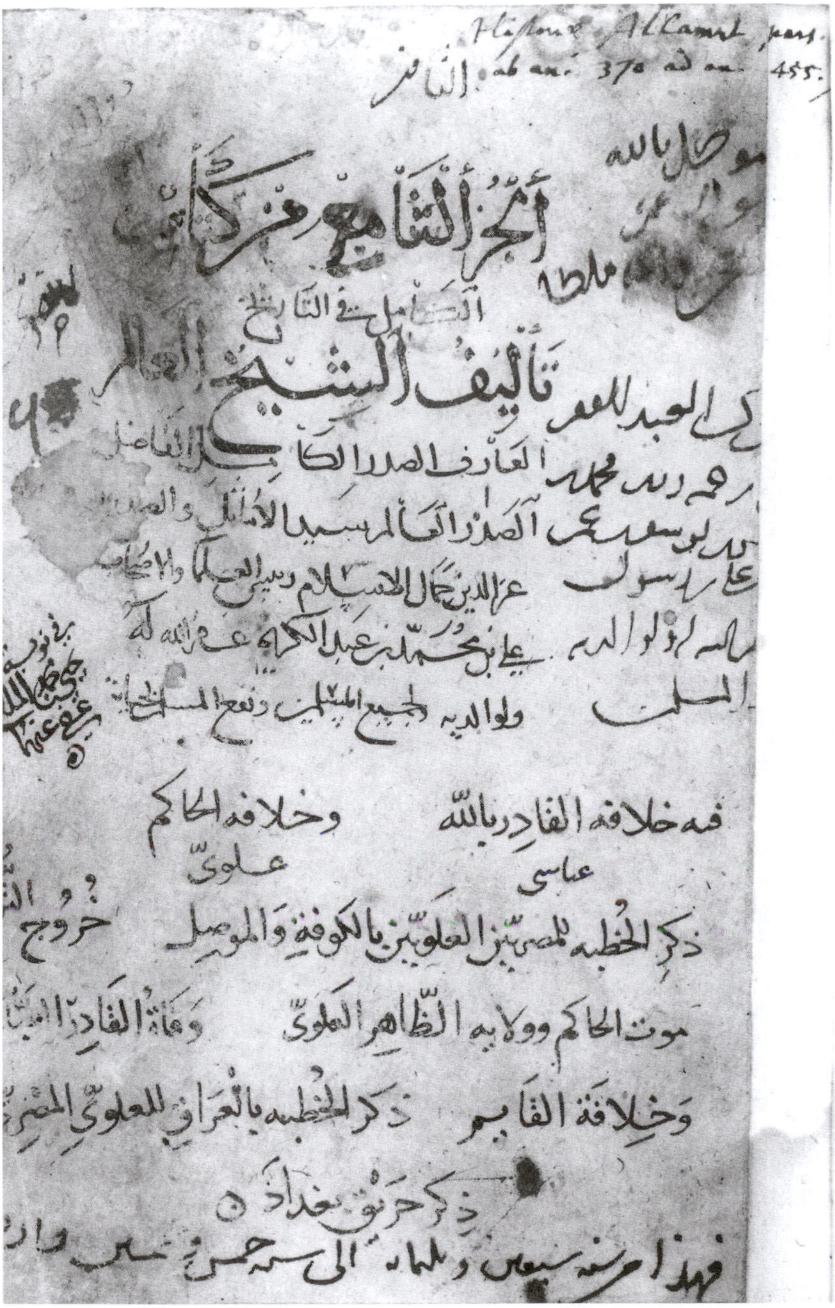

Plate 4 The incipit of the ninth part of a manuscript of Ibn al-Athīr's *al-Kāmil* (Bodleian Library, Oxford, MS Pococke 73 fol. 1r), which gives the volume's contents (in two different hands) and bears owners' marks.

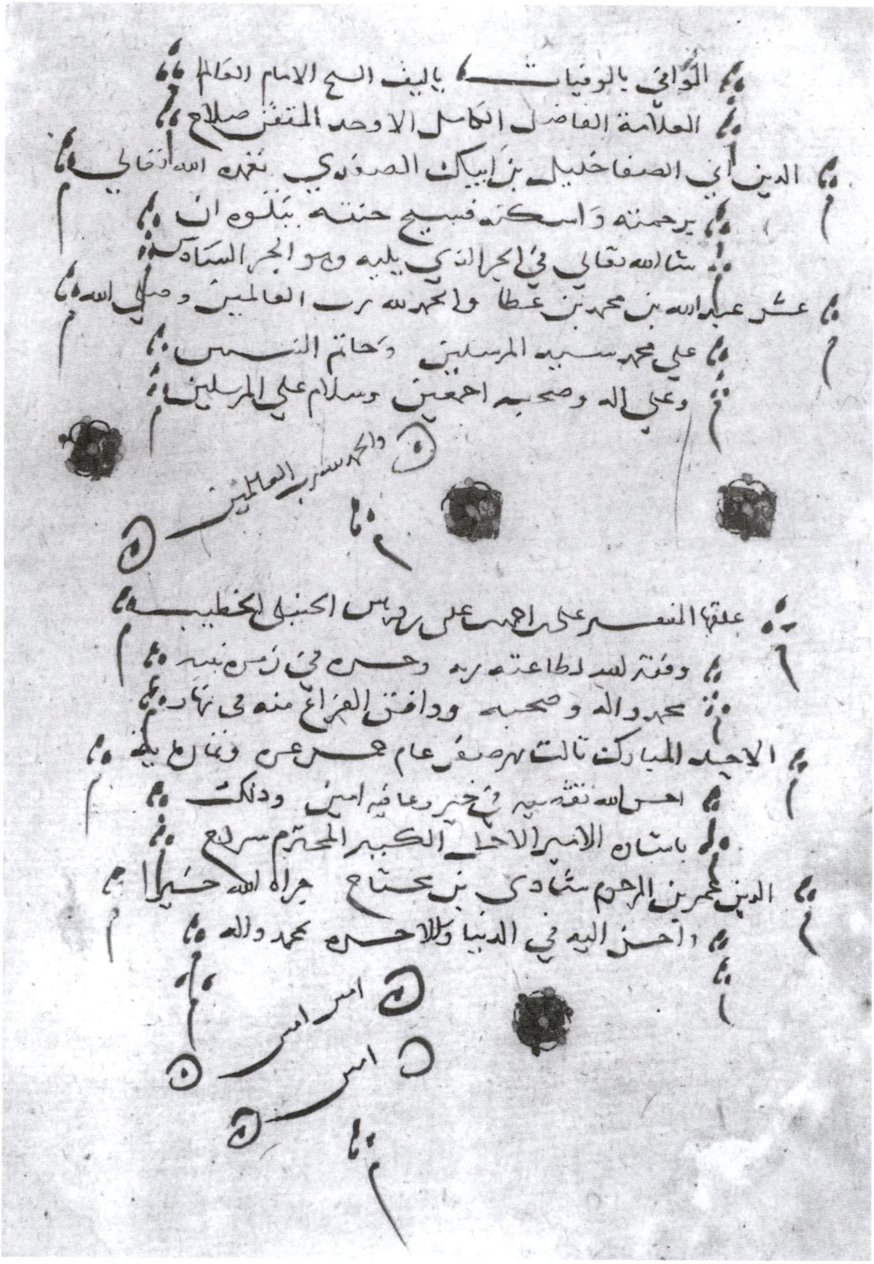

الوافي بالوفيات تأليف الشيخ الامام العالم
العلامة الفاضل الكامل الاوحد المتقن صلاح
الدين ابي الصفا خليل بن ايبك الصفدي تغمده الله تعالى
برحمته واسكنه فسيح جنته يتلوه ان
شا الله تعالى في الجز الذي يليه وهو الجز السادس
عشر عبد الله بن محمد بن عطا والحمد لله رب العالمين وصلى الله
على محمد سيد المرسلين وخاتم النبيين
وعلى اله وصحبه اجمعين وسلام على المرسلين
والحمد لله رب العالمين
علقه الفقير [illegible] الحنبلي الخطيب
[illegible]
محمد واله وصحبه ووافق الفراغ منه في نهار يوم
الاحد المبارك ثالث شهر صفر عام [illegible]
احسن الله تقضيه بخير وعافية امين وذلك
باشارة الامير الاجل الكبير المحترم [illegible]
الدين عبد الرحيم [illegible] جزاه الله خيرا
واحسن اليه في الدنيا والاخرة بمحمد واله
امين امين امين

Plate 5 Folio 142v of a manuscript of al-Ṣafadī's *al-Wāfī bi'l-wafayāt* (Bodleian Library, Oxford, MS Arch. Seld. A.25), which concludes with an especially full colophon: we have the name of the copyist, the date when he finished copying it, and the name of a commissioning patron.

would use almost 600 years later in assembling the standard edition of the work: we also know from whom he got it and where it went. It is similarly worth noting that al-Maqrīzī consulted the Escorial manuscript that preserves a small fragment of al-Musabbiḥī's history. Ṭhree of these examples are in line with many others, which suggest that the pool of historiographic manuscripts may always have been fairly shallow. A colophon on one of the copies of the huge prosopography of Damascus (the *Taʾrīkh madīnat Dimashq*, 'History of Damascus') by Ibn ᶜAsākir (d. 1176) tells us that it was copied by the great-grandfather of the historian al-Birzālī (d. 1339), who was working in a Damascus *madrasa*; it also tells us that he was working from a copy written by one of the author's sons. The note thus says something about copying: that one of Ibn ᶜAsākir's sons copied his father's work is typical of the culture of book production. It also says something about one Damascene *madrasa*'s attitudes towards prosopography. In this instance we can understand why the book was copied where it was copied: the work champions Damascus as a centre of learning, and it does so in a deeply traditionalist manner. In fact, Ibn ᶜAsākir's *History* is notable in precisely this respect. While other historians of his period had dispensed with the *isnād*s, he was retaining them. (Townsfolk liked to hear about their towns; we know that al-Khaṭīb al-Baghdādī lectured from his *Taʾrīkh Baghdād* in Baghdad.)[5]

Just as notes written upon a manuscript reveal something about its copying and reception, so, too, does the shape of a book's manuscript tradition help us understand its relative popularity. Now this is a very rough measure, since serendipity has something of a role to play in the survival of manuscripts, and larger books were copied less frequently than shorter ones. For these and a variety of other reasons, we should probably operate on the assumption that manuscript collections reflect the spread and number of books once in circulation about as accurately as coin collections reflect the circulation of coinage – that is, very poorly indeed. And while numismatists can turn to the horde evidence, which can give a more accurate account of circulation patterns, historians have no such control. We can still reach relative conclusions, however. One is that lots of people read Prophetic biography. That close to 100 copies of a twelfth-century *sīra* survive in two Cairo collections alone suggests that this particular work (the *Shifāʾ* of the Qāḍī ᶜIyāḍ) was wildly popular. And this does seem to have been the work's reputation amongst medieval authorities: multiple copies of the *Shifāʾ*, its epitomes and commentaries, can be

[5] For a discussion of a fairly typical manuscript and its notes, see R. Guest's edition of al-Kindī's *Kitāb al-Wulāh wa-Kitāb al-Quḍāh* (London, 1912), pp. 47f.; for al-Ṣūlī, his *Akhbār al-Rāḍī lillāh*, pp. *wāw* and *rāʾ* (where the marks are transcribed); the anonymous history is the *Kitāb al-ᶜUyūn wa'l-ḥadāʾiq*, iv[1], p. xiv; for the *ijāza* in one of the copies of Ibn Saᶜd's *Ṭabaqāt*, the 'Einleitung' (p. xli) in vol. iii of the Leiden, 1904–1940 edition; for al-Maqrīzī and al-Musabbiḥī, p. *dhāl* of the introduction to al-Musabbiḥī's *al-Juzʾ al-arbaᶜūn min akhbār Miṣr*; for the Birzālī example, *The Catalogue of the Arabic and Persian Manuscripts in the Oriental Public Library at (Bankipore) Patna* (Patna, 1908–1940), xii, p. 145; for another historian copying Ibn ᶜAsākir in a Damascus *madrasa*, I. ᶜAbbās, *Shadharāt min kutub mafqūda fī al-taʾrīkh* (Beirut, 1988), pp. 190f.; for al-Khaṭīb, Yāqūt, *Irshād*, i, p. 246; for how much colophons in another Near Eastern tradition have to offer to the historian, A. Sanjian, *Colophons of Armenian Manuscripts, 1301–1480: A Source for Middle Eastern History* (Cambridge, Mass., 1969).

found in manuscript collections within and outside of the Islamic world. Such a work seems to have claimed far larger an audience than could chronography and non-Prophetic biography. For an exceptionally popular work of historical topography, al-Maqrīzī's *Khiṭaṭ*, produced about 170 surviving copies *in total*, while other histories are very poorly preserved. One biography of Saladin, for example, survives in only two Oxford manuscripts – and this, only in part. As we have already seen several times, chronographies not uncommonly survive in single, incomplete copies.[6]

Of course these works appeared relatively late in the tradition. When one goes back further in time, copies of chronographies become even rarer still. Although al-Ṭabarī's history once existed in hundreds of copies (al-Musabbiḥī, who died in 1029, is said to have had access to an autograph), not a single surviving copy is complete. Here we do come upon a striking contrast. The Arabic original of al-Ṭabarī's *History* was completed at some point in the second decade of the tenth century, perhaps in 915; the Persian version was commissioned and executed within two generations of this Arabic original. But whereas we lack that single, complete manuscript of the Arabic, copies of the Persian versions (there are several) are almost innumerable, and include several illustrated examples. Some of the popularity may be explained by the tastes of a Persian-reading audience, to whom Balᶜamī's adaptation had much to offer; but it also seems that size mattered: being a fraction of the length of the Arabic, the Persian version was faster – and therefore cheaper – to copy out. There are other striking exceptions, too, such as al-ᶜUtbī's *al-Kitāb al-Yamīnī*, which survives in what, relative to comparable works of history, is a staggering number of copies, perhaps over 100. Here, once again, there is a ready explanation: the number is probably to be explained by the author's linguistic virtuosity, rather than any lingering attachment to Sebüktigin, Maḥmūd of Ghazna or the Ghaznavids, for in addition to Persian and Turkish translations, it generated several philological commentaries. Another exception is the cluster of ps.-Wāqidī conquest works, which seem relatively well represented in the manuscript traditions.[7]

Manuscript evidence is the closest we can get to the modern bestseller list, which tells us what people actually read, or short of that, what they intended to read or wanted people to think they read (everyone knows that bookshelves can be

6 Al-Qāḍī ᶜIyāḍ's *al-Shifāʾ* has been published several times, including Cairo, 1977, and translated by A.A. Bewley as *Muhammad Messenger of Allah: ash-Shifa of Qadi ᶜIyad* (Granada, 1991); the Cairo number comes from the edition's introduction; cf. the number of mss. in Berlin (W. Ahlwardt, *Verzeichnis der arabischen Handschriften* [Berlin, 1877–1899], ii, pp. 602ff.) (4); Paris (M. de Slane, *Catalogue des manuscrits arabes* [Paris, 1883], i, pp. 349f.) (4); London (A.G. Ellis, *Catalogue of the Arabic Books in the British Museum* [London, 1894], i, p. 770) (6); Dublin (A.J. Arberry, *A Handlist of the Arabic Manuscripts* [Chester Beatty] [Dublin, 1955–1964], viii, index '*al-Shifāʾ*') (5+ copies); cf. also Ḥājjī Khalīfa, *Kashf al-ẓunūn* (Leipzig, 1835–1858), v, pp. 56ff.; the 'exceptionally popular chronography' is al-Maqrīzī's *Khiṭaṭ*, and for the number I follow A.F. Sayyid, 'Early methods of book composition: al-Maqrīzī's draft of the *Kitāb al-Khiṭaṭ*', in Y. Dutton, ed., *The Codicology of Islamic Manuscripts* (London, 1995), p. 95.

7 For al-Musabbiḥī, see al-Maqrīzī, *Kitāb al-Khiṭaṭ*, i, p. 408; for the Persian Ṭabarī mss, E. Daniel, 'Manuscripts and editions of Balᶜamī's Tarjamah-i tārīkh-i Ṭabarī', *JRAS* (3rd ser.) 2 (1990), pp. 282–321; for a description of the Ṭabarī manuscripts and the first edition, F.-C. Muth, *Die Annalen von aṭ-Ṭabarī im Spiegel der europäischen Bearbeitungen* (Frankfurt am Main, 1983), chapter 1 and, for Balᶜamī, chapter 2; for al-ᶜUtbī, *GAL* I, p. 314 and *SI*, pp. 547f.; for ps.-Wāqidī, *GAS*, pp. 294ff.

filled with books that their owners have no intention of opening). There is also a related body of evidence, which describes (rather than documents) what libraries or individuals had once possessed. Descriptions of semi-public libraries, which were founded by dynasts and patrons and usually open to interested scholars and readers at the discretion of the librarian, often make mention of histories, particularly large-scale works, and occasionally note that some were held in multiple and specially commissioned copies. One Fatimid library is said to have contained some 1,220 manuscripts of al-Ṭabarī's *Taʾrīkh*. The figure is probably fantastic, and almost certainly refers to individual volumes rather than complete copies; even so, it says something about states' interest in universal chronography – and how much has apparently been lost. It seems that private collections generally found less room for multi-volume histories than did these well-endowed semi-public libraries; one imagines that expense and size explain the pattern. One thirteenth-century survey of the collections of Aleppo counts little history among its 915 works, but dynastic biography fares relatively well. One fourteenth-century scholar from Jerusalem seems to have paid little attention to the explosion in Syrian and Egyptian historical writing that was taking place around him. One seventeenth-century mosque-library in North Africa is typical enough: it is made up overwhelmingly of Qurʾāns, Qurʾānic studies, and books of law; it seems to have contained a small handful of history books.[8]

What survives otherwise from the pre-modern Islamic world is of a different order: rather than documenting what books people actually read, copied or owned, it indirectly models or deliberately prescribes what it was thought they *should* read. Thus Ibn Ḥajar al-ʿAsqalānī (d. 1449) starts a catalogue of his own reading and training with al-Bukhārī's *ḥadīth* collection, moving from there through various works of traditionism and jurisprudence, and only eventually arriving at a number of *sīra* and *maghāzī* works (chronography hardly appears at all). In his long list of *ca.* 300 works, al-Suyūṭī (d. 1505) puts *adab* ('literary culture') and *taʾrīkh* at the end. In addition to these and other prescriptions, we have two twelfth-century reading lists, the first compiled by the same al-Qāḍī ʿIyāḍ whose Prophetic biography was so popular, the second by an otherwise obscure native of Qazwīn, a city in western Iran. Here historiography fares about as well.[9]

[8] For libraries in general, see Y. Eche, *Les bibliothèques arabes* (Damascus, 1967), and M. M. Sibai, *Mosque Libraries: An Historical Study* (London and New York, 1987, which is not always entirely reliable); much remains useful in O. Pinto, 'The libraries of the Arabs during the time of the Abbasides', *IC* 3 (April, 1929), pp. 210–248; also Kohlberg, *Medieval Muslim Scholar,* pp. 71ff.; for a description of the 'house of knowledge' of the Fatimid imam-caliph al-Ḥākim (rg. 996–1021), Halm, *The Fatimids and their Traditions of Learning*, pp. 71ff.; for the Aleppo survey, P. Sbath, *Choix de livres qui se trouvaient dans les bibliothèques d'Alep* (Cairo, 1946) (*Mémoires de l'Institut d'Égypte* 49); for the Jerusalem scholar, U. Haarmann, 'The library of a fourteenth century Jerusalem scholar', *DI* 61 (1984), pp. 327–333; for the North African library, G. Deverdun, 'Un registre d'inventaire et de prêt de la bibliothèque de la mosquée ʿAli ben Youssef à Marrakech daté de 1111 H./1700 J.-C.', *Hespéris* 31 (1944), pp. 55–60.

[9] Ibn Ḥajar's work is *al-Muʿjam al-mufahras*, where the appearance on p. 77 of Sayf b. ʿUmar's *Kitāb al-ridda wa'l-futūḥ* is anomalous – and intriguing; al-Suyūṭī's testimony comes in the *Ḥusn al-muḥāḍara fī akhbār Miṣr wa'l-Qāhira* (Cairo, 1863), pp. 153ff.; for al-Qāḍī ʿIyāḍ's list, his *al-Ghunya: fihrist shuyūkh al-Qāḍī ʿIyāḍ* (Beirut, 1982); for the Qazwīnī list, A.J. Arberry, *A Twelfth-Century Reading List* (London, 1951).

The status of history writing: conclusions and consequences

What sense can we make of this evidence? First, we can infer that historiography (in general) and chronography (in particular) were produced and consumed at lower rates than other forms of learned narrative, particularly the tradition-based law. The point can also be expressed in words that anticipate conclusions we shall reach about who patronized and read chronography in real quantities: works produced by and for courts generally fare poorly compared to texts produced for a wide audience, especially school texts, since then, as now, textbooks sold well. Here the curriculum of the *madrasa*s, the colleges of (religious) learning that emerged during the tenth and eleventh centuries, spreading from Iran and the east to Egypt, Syria and beyond, is immediately relevant. It almost goes without saying that the curriculum could differ from place to place and time to time, but a general pattern is still discernible. As a place run by and for jurists, the *madrasa*'s curriculum made ample room for those disciplines that underpinned jurisprudence, such as the Qurʾānic 'sciences' (principally exegesis and variant readings of the text), *ḥadīth*, and dialectic (formal argumentation), modest room for Prophetic *sīra*, and very little (or no) room for non-Prophetic biography and chronography. In including Prophetic history and excluding non-Prophetic history, this curriculum can be seen to institutionalize the contents of the standard compendia of law, based squarely as it came to be upon the Prophet's paradigmatic actions; as we have already seen, these included *maghāzī* sections. Lacking a firm foothold in the *madrasa*s, then, historiography could command only a relatively small market of readers. And lacking opportunities to teach history, historians resorted to writing history in their spare time. It was apparently as a moonlighter, rather than a teacher, that al-Ṭabarī wrote his universal history, working diligently every night. One supposes that he used artificial lighting of one kind or another, but al-Bukhārī is said to have moonlighted quite literally, writing his *al-Taʾrīkh al-kabīr* (*Great History*), he tells us, at night by the Prophet's tomb – apparently an already venerable cliché.[10]

Why it is that little room was made in institutions of learning for universal histories is no harder to explain for late antique Muslims than it is for any other late antique tradition. To traditionists and hard-core traditionalists – those who determined the *madrasa* curriculum – later chronography was irrelevant, and writing contemporary history was hubristic and irreverent. Whether this caliph ruled from Damascus or that one from Baghdad, whether a vizier fell from grace through the plotting of this or that rival, whether an army marched up a river valley in spring or summer – to the traditionist, all this made no difference in the long run.

[10] On the beginnings of the *madrasa,* see H. Halm, 'Die Anfänge der madrasa', *ZDMG* Supp. 3 (1977), pp. 438–448; the papers collected in N. Grandin and M. Gaborieau, eds., *Madrasa: la transmission du savoir dans le monde musulman* (Paris, 1997); S.A. Arjomand, 'The law, agency, and policy in medieval Islamic society: development of the institutions of learning from the tenth to the fifteenth century', *Comparative Studies in Society and History* 41 (1991), pp. 263–293; for the status of *sīra*, Schöller, *Exegetisches Denken*, pp. 71ff.; for al-Ṭabarī's moonlighting, Yāqūt, *Irshād*, vi, p. 456; for the moonlighting al-Bukhārī, *EI*², 'al-Bukhārī' (Robson).

It is true that the believer might learn something from the litany of apostasies, civil wars, heresies, and military defeats that fill the histories, and this was occasionally conceded; but one hardly needed thousands of pages of history for this. After all, the consequences of unbelief had already been made clear by God in the Qurʾān and *sunna*.

In the light of this first conclusion, a second – that historians did not advertise their interest in history, nor did others do it for them – should hardly surprise. Prescriptive reading lists of various kinds told us that, and biographies often point in the same direction. Muḥammad b. Saḥnūn (d. 849), son of the scholar conventionally credited with introducing the Mālikī law school into North Africa, was prolific, and amongst the 100 (or so) works ascribed to him were a six-volume *taʾrīkh* and a seven-volume *ṭabaqāt* work. But just as al-Ṭabarī is known in Islamic scholarship primarily as a jurist and exegete, rather than as the historian who produced thirteen volumes of densely printed Arabic text, one would hardly know from the biographical notices that Ibn Saḥnūn was a historian either. As one of his biographers put it, 'there was no one more learned in the sciences than he: he composed works in all the sciences *and* on the Prophet's battles and history (*wa-fī al-maghāzī wa'l-taʾrīkh*)'. And just as individual historians hesitated to advertise their interest in history, so too were they loath to signal any group identity or, for that matter, to form schools of thought. In writing a *ṭabaqāt* work, that survey of membership organized according to successive generations, virtually every occupation, profession and social identity worthy of note in classical Islamic history did precisely this, from jurists, grammarians, lexicographers, traditionists, Qur'ān reciters, poets, Sufis, Shiʿites, Muʿtazilites, littérateurs, philosophers and singers to Ḥanbalīs, Shāfiʿīs, Mālikīs and Ḥanafīs – every one, that is, save history writing.[11]

Why is it that we lack a *ṭabaqāt al-akhbāriyyīn* or a *ṭabaqāt al-muʾarrikhīn*? Since so many of these *ṭabaqāt* works memorialize interests or skills (rather than professions), the historians' failure cannot be argued away on the grounds that they were nearly always employed in some other capacity: just *writing* history would have been enough. There is no away around concluding that insecurities were at work. Lacking a method that was distinct from traditionism (many were targeted for traditionists' barbs about several of their methods), and mindful of the ambivalent status of historiography in the traditionalist establishment to which many of them belonged, our historians deliberately kept their heads low during much of the classical period. This ambivalence goes a long way towards explaining the apologetic tone of so many histories' introductions. The unpleasant truth is that modern historians are apt to exaggerate the social and intellectual significance of their premodern counterparts. And were it not for kingly and princely courts and the

[11] On Muḥammad b. Saḥnūn, see the editor's introduction to the *Kitāb Ādāb al-muʿallimīn* (Algiers, 1973), pp. 39ff.; and the anonymous *Kitāb al-ʿUyūn wa'l-ḥadāʾiq*, iv^1, pp. 12f. (twenty works on *al-siyar* and four on *al-taʾrīkh wa'l-ṭabaqāt*); cf. G. Lecomte, 'Le livre des règles de conduite des maîtres d'école par Ibn Saḥnūn', *REI* 21 (1953), pp. 77–105; for a meticulous reconstruction of his father's work and its reception in North Africa, Muranyi, *Die Rechtsbücher des Qairawāners Saḥnūn b. Saʿīd*.

patronage they offered, their status would have been even lower. In what follows, I shall try to demonstrate this.[12]

Courts and culture

To measure the importance of courts and their influence upon readership more generally, we may begin with the *Mafātīḥ al-ᶜulūm* ('The Keys to the Sciences'), a prescriptive account of learning that was written in *ca.* 997 by Muḥammad b. Aḥmad al-Khwārizmī for the vizier of Nūḥ b. Manṣūr (rg. 976–997), the ruler of the Samanid dynasty, which controlled Khurasan and Transoxania (present-day eastern Iran and Uzbekistan) from the city of Bukhara. Al-Khwārizmī seems to have had in mind an audience of secretary-clerks and secretary-clerks-to-be for the Samanid state. The book is divided into two sections, the first on the 'sciences of Islamic law', by which is meant those fields of learning that are Arabic and Islamic in inspiration and practice, and the second on the 'sciences of the foreigners', by which is meant those that were naturalized into the Arabic-Islamic world from outside it, e.g., philosophy, logic, medicine, arithmetic, geometry, astronomy and astrology, music, mechanics and alchemy. History (here called *akhbār*) is located in the first of these two sections, occupying the last place in a list naturally headed by jurisprudence. Other surveys, such as the works by Ibn Qutayba (d. 889), al-Nuwayrī (d. 1332) and al-Qalqashandī (d. 1418), also recommend a command of history to the aspiring secretary or bureaucrat. In fact, the theme appears very early, already in a letter quoted by al-Jahshiyārī in his tenth-century history of viziers and secretaries, which he credits to ᶜAbd al-Ḥamīd (d. 750), the secretary to the last Umayyad caliph, Marwān II. There we read that secretaries should command the Arabic language and script, in addition to knowledge of 'the reigns (or battles; *ayyām*) of the Arabs and non-Arabs, and stories of them and their accounts' (*aḥādīthahā wa-siyarahā*).[13]

In fact, the examples can be multiplied. Another tenth-century authority, Ibn Farīghūn, recommended Persian and Islamic history for the lessons it taught, and

[12] For criticisms, see E. Landau-Tasseron, 'Sayf ibn ᶜUmar in medieval and modern scholarship', *DI* 67 (1990), pp. 1–27; and Lecker, 'Wāqidī's account on the status of the Jews in Medina', pp. 20ff.; cf. al-Madāᵓinī, who was considered truthful in *ḥadīth* transmission only when he transmitted on the authority of trustworthy transmitters (*thiqāt*) – in other words, he lacked good judgment; see al-Ṣafadī, *al-Wāfī bi'l-wafayāt*, xxii, p. 41.

[13] For a brief outline of al-Khwārizmī's prescription, see Rosenthal, *Classical Heritage*, p. 54; C.E. Bosworth, 'The terminology of the history of the Arabs in the Jāhiliyya according to Khwārizmī's "Keys of the sciences"', in S. Morag, ed., *Studies in Judaism and Iran Presented to Shelomo Dov Goitein on the Occasion of his Eightieth Birthday* (English volume) (Jerusalem, 1981), pp. 27–43 (reprinted in C.E. Bosworth, *Medieval Arabic Culture and Administration* [London, 1982]); and for *adab* and history, Khalidi, *Arabic Historical Thought*, pp. 83ff.; on the surveys more generally, C. Pellat, 'Les encyclopédies dans le monde arabe', *Cahiers d'histoire mondiale* 9 (1966), pp. 631–658; for al-Qalqashandī, his *Ṣubḥ al-aᶜshā* (Cairo, 1964), i, p. 479 (where *sīra* finds a place in the 'domestic economy' [*tadbīr al-manzil*], which naturally falls at the very end of his survey); also G. Wiet, 'Les classiques du scribe égyptien au XVᵉ siècle', *SI* 18 (1963), pp. 41–80; I draw upon al-Jahshiyārī, *Kitāb al-Wuzarāᵓ wa'l-kuttāb*, pp. 73ff.

was among the few who found room for history in a broader theory of knowledge. Some viziers, one learns in a history intended for a general readership (the *Fakhrī*), were even of the view that kings should not be left to read historiography (*siyar*; *tawārīkh*), precisely *because* they might learn something. Of the history available to teach lessons and guide rulers, Persian history seems to have enjoyed pride of place, particularly in those courts in the Islamic East, where so much of the thinking and ruling was being done by Persian or Persianophile dynasties. From this perspective we can see that there is nothing accidental or inevitable about the way that al-Ṭabarī's great universal chronography passed from Arabic into Persian: it was translated by none other than the vizier to ᶜAbd al-Malik b. Nūḥ, ruler of the same Samanid state that commissioned al-Khwārizmī's work. 'I have translated it into the Darī Persian language,' al-Ṭabarī's translator (Balᶜamī, fl. 963) tells his reader, 'so that *subjects and authorities* can share in reading and learning from its knowledge and to facilitate studying it' (emphasis added). One Buyid *amīr* was chastened by the politically astute Maḥmūd of Ghazna for having failed to read his Ṭabarī.[14]

Why do these manuals for bureaucrats-to-be prescribe a knowledge of history? It is because the states they hoped to serve had things to learn. Amongst those who ruled – the kings, princes, governors, and administrators, all of whom set the cultural tone during the tenth and eleventh centuries – chronography was read because it had lessons to teach about everything from just rulership to administrative geography. Even the most deeply pious might concede that Muḥammad's *sunna* – his model way of doing things, enshrined in the *ḥadīth* – had little specific to teach men in power about creating or maintaining a polity and social order. By contrast, the patrimony of Near Eastern imperial history, which, in varying amounts, the historians both transmitted and created, could offer example after example, from Alexander the Great through to the most recent caliph. This – the didactic function of historiography in the world of politics – explains why the fields of history first prescribed by al-Khwārizmī (of the Greeks, Persians, Byzantines, Yemenis and early caliphs) are precisely those fields that teach political lessons; that he also includes the stray definition or two, e.g., 'Īlīyā is the city of Jerusalem' (by his time, Jerusalem had come to be known by its Arabic name, al-Quds), also suggests that his audience of secretaries was expected to make sense of an increasingly obscure terminology for their patrons.

If the courts played a role in patronizing historiography, its readership went well beyond rulers and those who served them. In the cosmopolitan cities of the Islamic middle ages, to be a man of culture and learning was to command not only the ability to express oneself in a refined and grammatically sound Arabic, but

[14] For Ibn Farīghūn, see Rosenthal, *History,* pp. 34f. and Meisami, *Persian Historiography,* p. 8; on kings and history, Ibn al-Ṭiqṭaqā, *al-Fakhrī* (Cairo, 1923), pp. 9ff.; on the Ṭabarī translations, see E. Daniel, 'The Samanid "translations" of al-Ṭabarī', in H. Kennedy, ed., *Al-Ṭabarī: A Muslim Historian and His Work* (Princeton, forthcoming) (where the political circumstances are emphasized), and Meisami, *Persian Historiography,* pp. 23ff.; for Maḥmūd of Ghazna, Ibn al-Athīr, *al-Kāmil*, ix, pp. 371f.

sufficient material to make doing so worthwhile. Although poetry often enjoyed the most prestige, knowledge of history was packed in the cultural baggage that one was supposed to carry, a source of stories and figures on which to draw in conversation and debate, and through which allusive literature could be made meaningful in quiet reading. In other words, it formed part of what was called *adab* – that combination of skills, attitudes and knowledge that distinguished the learned amateur from the boorish ignoramus. Historical events and anecdotes were frequently the topic of conversation and dictation in circles of learned men. The *Laṭāʾif al-maʿārif* ('The Book of Curious and Entertaining Information') of al-Thaʿālibī (d. 1038) is filled with historical accounts, and includes a section on 'diverse items of curious and striking information of the Prophet, Quraish and rulers of the Arabs' – a mélange of anecdotes and lists (e.g., 'the notorious liars of Quraish'; 'the great commanders who were one-eyed', etc.). According to one authority, as late as the nineteenth century, the thirteenth-century historian Ibn al-Athīr was among the three authors most frequently adduced in learned discussion in Mecca. Now chronography was nearly always a source for aphorisms and *bons mots*, but it also came to be the source for real pleasure, too. Here we can return to al-ʿUtbī, the Ghaznavid historian whom we met earlier:

> Over the generations authors and men of letters have composed works about their times and the vicissitudes of fortune they have witnessed, according to their stylistic abilities and the share of eloquence granted their wits and fingers. Then Abū Isḥāq Ibrāhīm b. Hilāl al-Ṣābiʾ [d. 994; see chapter 9] wrote his book called the *Tājī* on the history of the Dailamites, which he bedecked in the finery of his bewitching words and arrayed in the vestments of his brilliant rhetoric; he loosed the knot of eloquence with the phrases he tied together, and brightened the face of stylistic elegance with the dark ink he put to paper ... I am thus obliged ... to provide the people of Iraq with a book on this subject [i.e., a history of Maḥmūd], Arabic in language and secretarial in style, which they may adopt as a companion for wakeful nights, and friend both at home and when traveling.

One late twelfth- and early thirteenth-century biographer of Saladin makes it clear that he, like Gibbon, saw his project in literary terms, and envisioned a highly literate audience: 'In this book I have given shares both to the literati who watch for brilliant purple passages and to those with historical interests who look out for embellished biographies'.[15]

Historiography was thus held to entertain and enthral, and much as it had lessons to teach the politician and bureaucrat about the world, it had lessons to teach the individual about himself. 'One should read histories (*tawārīkh*), study biographies and the experiences of nations,' ʿAbd al-Laṭīf al-Baghdādī (d. 1231) tells his reader, 'because in this way it is as if one transcends his short lifetime to

[15] For *akhbār* in circles of learning and definitions of *adab*, see G. Makdisi, *The Rise of Humanism in Classical Islam and the Christian West* (Edinburgh, 1990), pp. 163ff.; al-Thaʿālibī's book has been translated by C.E. Bosworth as *The Book of Curious and Entertaining Information* (Edinburgh, 1968); I draw the ʿUtbī translation from Rowson, 'History as prose panegyric'; on Ibn al-Athīr's popularity, Richards, 'Ibn al-Athīr', p. 94 (citing Hurgronje); I draw the quotation in Saladin's biography from D.S. Richards, 'ʿImād al-Dīn al-Iṣfahānī: administrator, littérateur and historian', in M. Shatzmiller, ed., *Crusaders and Muslims in Twelfth-Century Syria* (Leiden, 1993), p. 143.

live alongside the communities of the past, to become their contemporaries and intimates, and to know the best and worst of them. Your conduct (*sīra*) must be that of the earliest generation, so read the biography of the Prophet, emulate his deeds and states, follow in his footsteps, and model yourself upon him as much as possible and to the best of your abilities.' ᶜAbd al-Laṭīf was a man of exceptionally wide interests and abilities, and the work that records his advice may not have been widely read. But the advice was certainly not unique to him, nor was he unique in writing about himself for the purpose of setting an example for others. Al-Kalāᶜī (d. 1237) writes that one of the goals of his brief work of Prophetic biography is to whet the reader's appetite for more (inspiring) stories about Muḥammad. Usāma b. Munqidh's *Kitāb al-Iᶜtibār* is conventionally translated as 'Memoirs', but the Arabic here rather means 'teaching by example', and this is precisely what the text is about. It thus tells us a great deal about the Crusaders (their surgeons were butchers; they were immodest in the bath-houses, etc.) and, no doubt more important to its intended audience, the fortitude before God that Usāma exemplified.[16]

It was thus to a non-specialist audience – men with broad interests and catholic minds, but little expertise or time to spare – that a large industry of popularizing history was geared. Products of this industry can be found almost everywhere in the Islamic world, and they seem to have emerged already in the late ninth century, when historical compendia, such as Ibn Qutayba's *Kitāb al-Maᶜārif* appeared. In his *Murūj al-dhahab*, al-Masᶜūdī (d. 955) left the ambitious reader with a multi-volume work, which is the epitome of an even larger work; in his *al-Tanbīh wa'l-ishrāf* (perhaps to be translated as 'The Reminder/Memory-jogger and Summary Overview'), he left one modest volume for everyone else. So, too, did Ibn al-Sāᶜī (d. 1276), who wrote a multi-volume history of the caliphate and also an epitome, in his words, 'a brief notebook, a modest tome' (*daftar mukhtaṣar wa-sifr muqtaṣar*). Arabic literature had grown so voluminous that amateurs could hardly be expected to master history's details. Reading all of Ibn al-Athīr's volumes, or even all of Ibn Hishām's increasingly obscure biography, was hard work. Already in the late tenth or very early eleventh century, one master of Arabic prose was of the view that 'lengthy books are boring'. Many historians were alert to their readers' impatience: the anonymous eleventh-century author of an Abbasid history announces his intention in his rhyming introduction 'to abandon prolixity and avoid expansion'.[17]

[16] For ᶜAbd al-Laṭīf's advice, see Ibn Abī Uṣaybiᶜa, *ᶜUyūn al-anbāʾ fī ṭabaqāt al-aṭibbāʾ* (Beirut, 1965), p. 692; cf. G. Makdisi, *The Rise of Colleges: Institutions of Learning in Islam and the West* (Edinburgh, 1981), pp. 88f.; and C. Cahen, ''ᶜAbdallatif al-Baghdadi, portraitiste et historien de son temps: extraits inédits de ses mémoires', *BEO* 23 (1970), pp. 101–128; for al-Kalāᶜī, *al-Iktifāʾ* (Beirut, 1997) p. 8, on whom see, Jarrar, *Prophetenbiographie*, pp. 224ff.; on Usāma's *Kitāb al-Iᶜtibār*, D.W. Morray, *The Genius of Usāma ibn Munqidh* (Durham, 1987).

[17] The Masᶜūdī title translation belongs to G.M. Wickens, 'Notional significance in conventional Arabic "Book" titles: some unregarded potentialities', in C.E. Bosworth et al., eds., *The Islamic World from Classical to Modern Times: Essays in Honor of Bernard Lewis* (Princeton, 1989), pp. 369–388; for Ibn al-Sāᶜī, his *Mukhtaṣar akhbār al-khulafāʾ* (Cairo, 1309 H); on boring books, F. Rosenthal, '"Of making many books there is no end": the classical Muslim view', in G.N. Atiyeh, ed., *The Book in the Islamic World* (Albany, 1995), p. 43; I draw the introductory remarks from the anonymous *Nubdha min kitāb al-taʾrīkh* (Moscow, 1960), f. 236a.

So history, particularly as written up in encyclopedias, potted versions, even put in verse, was intended to reach a wide audience of cultured Muslims. Distilling history to the essentials, and packaging it for wide readership, seem to have been particularly cultivated in Muslim Spain. It was there that the Cordovan Ibn ᶜAbd Rabbihi (d. 940) compiled *al-ᶜIqd al-farīd* ('The Precious Necklace'), a large compendium of all that the cultured man was to know, in which figure two historical sections (#15 and #16), alongside others on 'generous men' (#3), 'proverbs' (#7), 'speech of the bedouins' (#11) and 'food and drink' (#24). Although the work is filled with material imported from the Islamic East, Ibn ᶜAbd Rabbihi naturally gives special prominence to Umayyad figures who had special appeal in Spain. It was also in Muslim Spain that Ibn Ḥazm (d. 1063), basing himself on an epitome of the Prophet's life, wrote an epitome of his own, which is approximately one-sixth the size of Ibn Hishām's (already-reduced) version of Ibn Isḥāq. He also wrote a series of what might fairly be called 'bluffer's guides' to history, including a nine-page history of the early conquests and a twenty-page history of the caliphs to the reign of al-Qāᵓim (rg. 1031–1075). Works such as these may also have functioned as reference works for scholars who needed quick access to simple information. Finally, it was there too that al-Kalāᶜī wrote his digest of Ibn Isḥāq's life of the Prophet, stripping away the elements he considered non-essential, and replacing them with his own selection of prose, genealogy and poetry. Medieval audiences required not only that standard works be condensed, but that they be periodically refreshed.[18]

The case of chronography: patronage and politics

We have seen that in the traditionist programme (if such a generality can be hazarded) historiography fared poorly compared to those disciplines that lay at the heart of the Islamic sciences – particularly language and grammar, both intended to service the proper understanding of scripture and *ḥadīth*, and thus the law – and that later chronology enjoyed some appeal amongst rulers and ruled alike. In other words, historiography as a whole was conditioned not merely by the snobbery of the traditionists, but the utilitarianism of the administrators and the cultural aspirations of much of the urban élite. This latter point requires some explanation and expansion.

Politics and learning may seem to be distinct things, but learning is expensive, it does not just come into being on its own, nor do men of learning survive or prosper on their own. Far from it: a learned class is predicated on a political and economic system that creates surplus revenues upon which it can draw, these usually taking the form of salaries and stipends awarded by state (the court; the

[18] On Ibn ᶜAbd Rabbihi and his sources, see W. Werkmeister, *Quellenuntersuchungen zum Kitāb al-ᶜIqd al-Farīd des Andalusiers Ibn ᶜAbdrabbih (246/860–328/940)* (Berlin, 1983); on Ibn Ḥazm's potted histories, his *Rasāᵓil Ibn Ḥazm al-Andalusī* (Beiruit, 1987), ii, *passim*.

bureaus) or private institutions. If men of learning depended either directly or indirectly upon states, it is because states stood to benefit. For in addition to possessing a capable military and a reasonably efficient administration, to rule effectively for any length of time required translating the power to coerce into the legitimate right to govern. In practice this meant putting in place an ideological and cultural programme that was designed for members of the court and state, in addition to those social élites (usually landowners and merchants) who, for whatever reason, lay outside of the ruling establishment. The programme naturally varied from circumstance to circumstance, but virtually all rulers claimed to possess (either directly or by proxy) a divine mandate, and presented themselves as upholders of God's law, suppressors of heresy and rebellion, builders of cities, and patrons of learning and high culture – in sum, guardians of the good life in this world (and sometimes even guarantors of the good life in the next), behind whom non-ruling élites should throw their support.

Put at its crudest, then, rulers commissioned histories and supported historians because they wanted to learn history's lessons, and because they wanted others to be part of a matrix of learning and culture. What they wanted, in other words, was for their subjects to have a stake in their political fortunes. Although men of learning and culture can occasionally turn into revolutionaries – 'philosophical concepts nurtured in the stillness of a professor's study could destroy a civilization', as one philosopher put it – this is rare, or at least rarer than successful revolutionary movements that are successful in part because they dismantle or re-engineer the cultural system they inherit. The political quietism of pre-modern learned élites is as close to a historical truism as one can get, one illustrated no less well by a number of non-Islamic cases. The historian had an especially important role to play in this self-presentation, since historiography offered a medium through which states could broadcast claims about the past, present or future, legitimize themselves and undermine their critics.[19]

These, then, are the general principles that underlie how and why pre-modern states supported learning and historiography. We may now ask a series of questions of our tradition. Did Muslim rulers patronize historiography? If so, how much, in what forms, and why? Did they commission the writing of their *own* history, and, if so, can it can be regarded as comparable to those imperial traditions (such as the Chinese), in which 'official histories' were regularly produced and published by employees of the state bureaucracy?

We can begin with the last two questions. The commissioning of dynastic histories is certainly well attested in medieval Islam, and becomes a striking feature of Islamic historiography from the twelfth century on, when Ayyubids and Mamluks had courtiers write (usually deeply panegyric) biographies and chronographies. We shall see that the Buyids commissioned a history by one of the Ṣābiʾ chronographers, and al-Ẓāhir Baybars (rg. 1260–1277) was the subject of no fewer than

[19] The words are Isaiah Berlin's, *The Proper Study of Mankind: An Anthology of Essays* (London, 1997), p. 192.

three biographies. How early this practice extends is hard to say. Extant examples take us back into the tenth century: Ibn al-Dāya (d. *ca.* 945), for example, wrote a biography of Aḥmad b. Ṭūlūn, an independent-minded governor of Egypt, and al-Jahshiyārī (d. 942) quotes directly from an autograph copy of a history of the Abbasid caliphs written by Muḥammad b. Aḥmad b. ᶜAbd al-Ḥamīd (d. 900), the grandson of the late Umayyad courtier whom we met earlier. In an anecdote about the famous *chanteuse* Shāriya (d. 870) we read of domestic slaves carrying 'caliphs' lives' (*siyar al-khulafāʾ*) in large tomes (*dafātir*); the impression is that these were prepared in and for the court. In any event, what is clearer is official diary-keeping at a much later period, such as the *mutajaddidāt* set down by al-Qāḍī al-Fāḍil (d. 1200), who was a high-ranking secretary in Saladin's administration. Meanwhile, the Chinese case, in which historiography was produced by bureaucrats trained and employed primarily or even exclusively for the task, is quite exceptional, and although Islamic states embraced learning in several ways (employing scholars, founding libraries and a variety of institutions of learning), they never fully absorbed it, even in the heyday of the bureaucrat-historian, such as Ibn Miskawayh. Networks of learning thus interlocked and overlapped with the administrative and military grids that powered medieval Islamic states – jurists could become judges, and genealogists, fawning biographers – but they remained distinct from them. We shall have more to say on how historians made their living in chapter 9.[20]

If dynastic chronography and non-Prophetic biography were two varieties of historiography that states commissioned – and here we return to our first two questions – chief amongst the others were universal history and Prophetic biography. As Balᶜamī's introduction to his translation of al-Ṭabarī's *History* tells us, 'I have translated it into the Darī Persian language so that *subjects and authorities* can share in reading …' But what were they to learn?

The caliphal history written by Ibn al-ᶜImrānī (d. 1184) makes one answer clear. He begins by offering formulaic prayers for Muḥammad, the 'four Rightly Guided caliphs' (that is, his four successors, Abū Bakr, ᶜUmar, ᶜUthmān and ᶜAlī), the Abbasid dynasty, and, last but not least, his patron, the caliph al-Mustanjid (rg. 1160–1170), 'may God strengthen Islam and the Muslims through the endurance of his rule'. Of the Umayyads, who ruled between the 'four Rightly Guided caliphs' and the Abbasids, we read scarcely a thing, and this is because Ibn al-ᶜImrānī views them as usurpers who interrupted a succession of legitimate caliphs: 'I shall begin with the master of human kind and the intercessor on the day of judgment [i.e., Muḥammad], then the four leaders after him, then those Umayyads

[20] On official histories in China, see Twitchett, *The Writing of Official History under the T'ang*; for Ibn al-Dāya, al-Balawī, *Sīrat Aḥmad b. Ṭūlūn* (Cairo, 1939), p. 100; for al-Jahshiyārī's account, the *Kitāb al-Wuzarāʾ wa'l-kuttāb*, p. 281, ᶜAbbās, *Shadharāt*, pp. 207ff., and *GAS*, p. 321 (for Muḥammad himself); for the tomes, al-Iṣfahānī, *al-Aghānī*, xvi, p. 15; for the authorities' repeated attempts to entice al-Ṭabarī into service, C. Gilliot, 'La formation intellectuelle de Tabari (224/5–310/839–923)', *JA* 276 (1988), pp. 201–244; for *tajaddada* 'to happen' (and *mutajaddidāt*, 'happenings'), which survive in Abū Shāma's *Kitāb al-Rawḍatayn*, cf. ᶜAbd al-Laṭīf al-Baghdādī, *Kitāb al-Ifāda wa'l-iᶜtibār* (Damascus, 1983), p. 81, and Abū al-Fatḥ's Samaritan chronicle, *Kitāb al-Taʾrīkh* (*Annales Samaritani*) (Gotha, 1865), p. 4 ('events', 'happenings').

to whom power was arrogated, until just rule [literally, 'the truth'] returned to his [Muḥammad's] family, reverting to those most entitled to it, these being the family of the Prophet.' The volume of a broadcast such as this is quite loud – the Abbasid house, unlike the Umayyad, exercises the legitimate right to rule – and brings to mind earlier Abbasid histories, such as an eleventh-century fragment, according to which 'a blessed turning [of dynasties – that is, the Abbasid Revolution] returned affairs to their proper place'. It is perhaps louder still elsewhere: in the hands of their biographers, Ayyubid and Mamluk *usurpers* become legitimate *successors*. But it need not be so loud, nor was the task of legitimizing dynastic rule left entirely to chronology. When Abbasid-era biographers of the Prophet place the forefather of the ruling, Abbasid house at a crucial meeting with the Prophet (ᶜAqaba, traditionally dated to 621), they were legitimizing Abbasid rule itself, based as it (partially) was on the intimacy of this relative to the Prophet.[21]

History writing is a potent source of legitimacy and criticism not simply because it can deliver particular versions or reconstructions of the past. It can also reflect (or impose) ways of thinking about time, about change, about how the individual relates to the state, and the state to the world. Thus it is one thing to write Prophetic biography that ends with the Prophet's death, and another to write Prophetic biography that runs, as a spring into a river, into caliphal history. Similarly, it is one thing to write history according to an annalistic scheme inaugurated by Muḥammad's Hijra, in which a transcendent dating system functions as the organizing principle. It is quite another to write history according to the reigns of specific caliphs and successive dynasties, in which the caliphs – their dates of accession and deaths – quite literally make history. The genre is still chronographic, but chronography consists in the rhythm of death and succession, and caliphal biographies take on special prominence. I have already suggested that the appearance of dynastic chronography may owe something to the absolutist caliphate of the early ninth century. Here we should note that Ibn al-ᶜImrānī chose this form of chronography, and in his hands it functions to underpin an apologetic programme, which corresponds quite neatly to the more assertive Abbasid politics of the 1150s and 1160s, when the caliphs had some success pushing back the power of their Saljuk overlords in Iraq. In a history commissioned by an Abbasid caliph, it is perhaps little wonder that the Abbasids, described by Ibn al-ᶜImrānī as 'his [Muḥammad's] cousins, inheritors of his knowledge, trustees of his revelation, those who discharge his *sunna*, the divinely guided, the people of mercy and compassion', are tied so closely to the Prophet himself.

In the hands of Ibn al-ᶜImrānī, historiography thus has a clear apologetic function. Historiography could also function programmatically. And the deeper one dug into early history, the richer the soil for cultivating a programme for the

[21] For Ibn al-ᶜImrānī, see his *al-Inbāʾ fī taʾrīkh al-khulafāʾ* (Leiden, 1973), p. 43; and Cooperson, *Arabic Biography*, pp. 62ff.; for the 'blessed turning', the anonymous *Nubdha min kitāb al-taʾrīkh*, f. 236a; on Mamluk usurpers and apologia, see P.M. Holt, 'The presentation of Qalāwūn by Shāfiᶜ b. ᶜAlī', in Bosworth et al., eds., *Essays in Honor of Bernard Lewis*, pp. 141–150.

present. In Prophetic chronography we can see that the Prophet's life functioned as an enormously powerful paradigm for political activism and warfare, perhaps especially at moments of high ideological temperature, and that historiography of even the most remote and specialized variety is *always* informed in one way or another by history itself.

Earlier we saw that *sīra* scholarship can be associated with caliphal patronage offered by the earliest Abbasids: the political uses of learning are something the Abbasids seem to have understood from the start, whereas the Umayyads seem to have learned the lesson too late. The pattern survives the early period, experts in chronographic *sīra* from al-Zuhrī (d. 742) to al-Suhaylī (d. 1185) and Ibn Sayyid al-Nās all appearing to have been close to the ruling establishment. Al-Suhaylī, for example, laboured in obscurity until he was offered the patronage of the Almohad ruler Abū Ya^cqūb Yūsuf (rg. 1163–1184), for whom he would write his Prophetic biography/commentary, *al-Rawḍ al-unuf* during the last three years of his life. As Ibn Kathīr put it acidly, 'He was ascetic and poor, but great wealth came to him at the end of his life from the master of Marrakesh.' In fact, it is nearly impossible to avoid the conclusion that the Almohads of North Africa and Spain (rg. 1130–1269) recognized the ideological utility of Prophetic biography in their war with the Christians of Spain, for it seems to have been precisely for this war that they commissioned another work of early history, the *Kitāb al-Ghazawāt wa'l-futūḥ* ('Book of [Prophetic] campaigns and conquests') by Ibn Ḥubaysh (d. 1188). Al-Andalus, as one eleventh-century historian writing there put it, was 'the place for *jihād*'. In much the same way, Saladin had works on *jihād* written for his cause against the Crusaders: ᶜImād al-Dīn al-Iṣfahānī even claimed that Saladin could not stop himself from reading the volume he had written for him. One fourteenth-century Mamluk would have *ḥadīth*s about the *jihād* read out to him while on campaign. It is tempting to think that a reasonable timeline of Muslim-Christian crusading and counter-crusading might be inferred from the shape of the historiographic tradition alone: a rise in Prophetic biographical writing of the chronographic variety suggests that a struggle against unbelievers was underway.[22]

So history could provide a model for the present. The modern historian generally reads Prophetic *sīra* as a *description of Muḥammad's life*; the medieval Muslim reader generally read it as a *prescription for his own life*. For ᶜAbd al-Laṭīf al-Baghdādī, the *sīra* prescribed a life of piety and fear of God. For others, it might

[22] On the Umayyads' failure to produce much historiography, see Chabbi, 'La répresentation du passé', pp. 34f.; on al-Zuhrī and the question of patronage, M. Lecker, 'Biographical notes on Ibn Shihāb al-Zuhrī', *JSS* 41 (1996), pp. 21–63; al-Suhaylī's *al-Rawḍ al-unuf fī sharḥ al-sīra al-nabawiyya* was published in Cairo in 1967 (Abū Yaᶜqūb Yūsuf's patronage is as much as acknowledged in the preface to the work, p. 30); for Ibn Kathīr's comment, *al-Bidāya wa'l-nihāya* (Beirut reprint of Cairo, 1932–1977), xii, p. 318; cf. Ibn Khallikān, *Wafayāt al-aᶜyān* (Beirut, 1968–1972), iii, p. 144; on al-Suhaylī, his *Rawḍ*, and *jihād* in Spain, Jarrar, *Prophetenbiographie*, pp. 176ff. and 244ff.; on Ibn Ḥubaysh, Landau-Tasseron, 'On the reconstruction of lost sources'; the eleventh-century historian is the anonymous compiler of the *Akhbār majmūᶜa*, pp. 27f.; for the fourteenth-century Mamluk (Sanjar al-Dawādārī, d. 1300), U. Haarmann, 'Arabic in speech, Turkish in lineage: Mamluks and their sons in the intellectual life of fourteenth-century Egypt and Syria', *JSS* 33 (1988), p. 98.

mean taking up arms for God's cause against His enemies. Precisely who these enemies were naturally depended on one's point of view: Prophetic biography remained programmatic precisely because it was plastic enough for near-continual recycling: the enemies need only be 'associators', *mushrikūn*, that is, among those who 'associated' people or idols with God. In this potency there is a good parallel between Prophetic *sīra* and those books of the Bible, particularly Exodus, which served as a model for reformist and revolutionary movements for other monotheists. Two final examples can illustrate this and several preceding points.

Muḥammad b. ʿAbd al-Wahhāb (d. 1792) was the founder of the Wahhābī reformist movement, the strict form of Ḥanbalī Islam that had a hand in producing modern Saudi Arabia; he also had a son named ʿAbd Allāh b. Muḥammad b. ʿAbd al-Wahhāb (d. 1826). Both were learned men who wrote Prophetic *sīra*s, which were based to varying degrees upon Ibn Hishām; and both *sīra*s reflect the political and ideological context of their composition. Compared with the son's *sīra,* a thoroughly academic work that sits solidly in a near 1,000-year-old tradition of epitomizing biographies, the father's is idiosyncratic. Not only does he cite far fewer of the standard sources than his son, but whereas the son concludes his *sīra* with the death of the last of the 'four Rightly Guided caliphs' (and the death of the son of the last of these, al-Ḥasan b. ʿAlī), the father carries on well after it. To year 60 of the Hijra (the death of Yazīd b. Muʿāwiya) he writes annalistically; thereafter he organizes his material by caliphal reign, until al-Maʾmūn (rg. 813–833), 'who imposed a great number of creedal trials upon the believers. He translated the Greeks' books of philosophy, went public with the view of the createdness of the Qurʾān, imposed it upon people and tested Aḥmad b. Ḥanbal and other imams'. Why would he end there? Muḥammad b. ʿAbd al-Wahhāb's beautifully teleological handling of Prophetic biography – history starts with Adam, leading through Muḥammad to Aḥmad b. Ḥanbal – is manifestly Ḥanbalī, because the Ḥanbalīs celebrated Aḥmad's heroic resistance against al-Maʾmūn and his rationalizing programme. But it is more than that. It forms part of a radical Wahhābī reading of history (and one that went well beyond *sīra*). The Prophet's biography mattered in the nineteenth century not simply because Muḥammad b. ʿAbd al-Wahhāb claimed that the Muslims of his day had fallen into *shirk* – the 'associationism' of polytheism – that was comparable to that of Muḥammad's day, but because Wahhābī apologists patterned their telling of Muḥammad b. ʿAbd al-Wahhāb's movement directly upon that of the Prophet himself, making, for example, his move from the Najd to the town of Dirʿiyya nothing less than Muḥammad's Hijra. His opponents responded within the same time-tested territory of description and meaning: Muḥammad b. ʿAbd al-Wahhāb is made none other than Musaylima, a pseudo-prophet and one of Muḥammad's most notorious enemies. Historical writing of this variety combines description and prescription.[23]

[23] On Exodus as model, see M. Walzer, *Exodus and Revolution* (New York, 1985); the *Mukhtaṣar* of Muḥammad b. ʿAbd al-Wahhāb was published in Beirut, 1995, that of ʿAbd Allāh b. Muḥammad b. ʿAbd al-Wahhāb in Cairo, 1379 H; on Wahhābī history and historiography, E. Peskes, *Muḥammad b. ʿAbd al-Wahhāb im Widerstreit: Untersuchungen zur Rekonstruktion der Frühgeschichte der Wahhābiyya* (Beirut, 1993).

CHAPTER 7

God and models of history

Modern historians of the medieval Islamic world frequently complain about the radically uneven coverage of their sources. They especially complain that Muslim historians chose to tell us so little about non-élites in general and rural non-élites in particular. Why is this so? Answering this question takes us some way towards understanding how pre-modern Muslim historians saw and described their world. And in large part this means understanding the roles in history that pre-modern historians gave to God.

Part of the explanation can be found in the identity of their audience, since well-off townspeople then, like well-off townspeople now, liked to read about themselves, or at least about what was familiar to them: even the exotic stories of *1001 Nights*, though ultimately Indian and Iranian in inspiration, were 'naturalized', the main characters becoming honorary Baghdadis in the course of their translation and adaptation from Persian into Arabic. One's sources also dictate one's story, and well-placed historians are apt to have worked with accounts that were produced in the élite circles to which they themselves belonged, and in which they enjoyed courtly appeal. Among the many well-placed informants quoted by al-Balawī in his tenth-century biography of Ibn Ṭūlūn was the governor's chief interrogator – surely a man in possession of some good information. Ibn Miskawayh tells us at one point that he was present when one wretch was beaten by the vizier (we are not given to understand exactly why). In one biographical notice about Hilāl b. al-Muḥassin al-Ṣābiʾ (d. 1055) we read that his history was especially valuable because both he and his uncle served in the Buyid administration, and accordingly had access to the state's innermost secrets. Near the beginning of al-Masʿūdī's section on the caliph al-Rāḍī (rg. 934–940), which is based on a number of court informants, stands an extended discussion of chess and backgammon, which were among the court's favourite pastimes. Would that we knew as much about tax farming in tenth-century Iraq as we do about board games.[1]

[1] For the interrogator, see al-Balawī, *Sīrat Aḥmad b. Ṭūlūn*, p. 130; for Ibn Miskawayh, his *Tajārib al-umam*, ii, p. 184; for the Ṣābiʾ historian, al-Qifṭī, *Akhbār al-ḥukamāʾ* (Cairo, 1326 H), pp. 77ff.; for al-Masʿūdī's discussion, the *Murūj al-dhahab*, v, pp. 218ff. (drawing on al-Ṣūlī); on the silence of Muslim historians on rural history, Humphreys, *Islamic History*, pp. 284ff.; for an impressive bibliography on chess, R. Wieber, *Das Schachspiel in der arabischen Literatur von den Anfängen bis zur zweiten Hälfte des 16. Jahrhunderts* (Walldorf-Hessen, 1972).

The historian's access to information and his audience's tastes are certainly important factors, but none of the preceding can account for the intrepid or resourceful historian, much less the odd iconoclastic one, and even those who bucked the historiographic trends of their day (such as, in many respects, al-Mas^{c}ūdī) generally evinced little or no interest in non-élites. So we must look elsewhere for a fuller explanation. We can find it if we consider what Muslim historians thought important. The principal reason why historians focused on the urban, consuming élite was that its experience was seen to possess a great deal of meaning, whereas that of the producers (in a pre-industrial society consisting largely of the rural peasantry and herders of several varieties) and the non-producers (nearly always identified as such, e.g., drifters, urban riff-raff, country bandits) were seen to possess much less meaning. For the most part, history was made by important people who lived in cities.

No better example of the striking selectivity of the historiographic tradition can be found than in early Abbasid Syria, a topic about which our (mostly Iraqi) Islamic tradition says relatively little. Indeed, were it not for the testimony of a single late eighth-century Syriac history, which was written by an anonymous monk living in a modest monastery situated in the countryside, we would never know how deeply that countryside had been affected by Abbasid taxation: villages were deserted, graves robbed, children sold into slavery. Why does our Syriac source have so much to say? There is no question of his being a better historian than his Muslim counterparts; by virtually every standard, he is a worse one. The doleful details were of significance for our monk not because he had a catholic view of history, but because they were part of a world that he knew intimately, and, unlike the goings-on of Islamic cities, one that made real sense to him. In chronicling how the heavy 'Israelite yoke' (Islamic rule) bore down upon his fellow Christians, he was chronicling God's punishment, which He was inflicting because of the Christians' sins (heresy, divisiveness, greed). The events having no real significance for Muslim historians living in the cities, they ignored them. In fact, even when social forces are identified in the countryside, such as they frequently were in the form of rebels and nomads, it was still in the cities that they conquered that proper history – that is, a meaningful and important past – was made. We have descriptions of a spectacular slave rebellion in the late ninth century, which give some sense of the dreadful tasks these slaves were set in lower Iraq (clearing the land of heavily salinated soil in order to bring it back into cultivation). But it seems that the events were recorded in detail because their leader ('the wicked', as he usually appears in the sources) made the mistake of marching them into the city of Basra, which never fully recovered from the destruction; little wonder that some later historians might refer to him as 'master of the Zanj, who rebelled in Basra' (*ṣāḥib al-zanj al-khārij bi'l-Baṣra*). Had he remained in the rural wastes, we would almost certainly know much less about him and his movement. It certainly never produced a historian to tell its side of the story.[2]

So historiographic coverage must be explained with reference to sources, audience and perspective. It is the last of these that I should like to explore in this chapter. In particular, I should like to show that Muslim historians have so much to say about city élites and so little to say about what now interests social and economic historians because they held to a model of history that differs from ours. And since models of history are related in one way or another to models of the world, we can start with a few comments about their world.

The alterity of medieval Islam

Let us begin with a single *khabar*, that self-contained building block of historical narrative. It is an attractive piece, which illustrates particularly well the role of chance, patronage and loyalty in ascending the social ladder in a very unpredictable world, in this case during the reign of Hishām b. ᶜAbd al-Malik (rg.725–745). As is so often the case in traditionalist historiography, the account appears in slightly different forms in a number of sources. It is also entirely typical in its uneven style. We begin slowly and deliberately: the scene is set in Syria, we are made privy to the protagonists' dialogue, and are given precise details (orders given to subordinates; gifts). A break (both narrative and physical) then takes place between the two principals, and we accelerate madly, first to Iraq, then Iran, in order to arrive at an edifying and instructive reunion back in Syria. This telescoping of time is characteristic of much chronography.

> Bakr b. al-Haytham related to me on the authority of ᶜAbd al-Razzāq, on the authority of Ḥammād b. Saᶜīd al-Ṣanᶜānī, on the authority of Ziyād b. ᶜUbayd Allāh, who said: I went to Syria, and while I was [waiting] at the door of [the caliph] Hishām, someone came out. He asked, 'Who are you, young man?', and I told him: 'A man from the people of Yemen: I am Ziyād b. ᶜUbayd Allāh b. ᶜAbd Allāh al-Ḥārithī'. [At this] he smiled, saying: 'Come with me'. Pointing to his men, he then said to me: 'Tell my men that the Commander of the Faithful [i.e., the caliph Hishām] has appointed me as governor, ordered me to travel [to my new post], and has deputized someone to escort me [out of the camp].' 'Who, in God's mercy, are you?' I asked, [to which] he responded: 'Khālid b. ᶜAbd Allāh al-Qasrī', and then, 'Let him have the wrap from my cloak and the yellow nag of mine.' I was given them, and then he said to me: 'If some day you hear

[2] The Syrian source is the so-called *Zuqnin Chronicle*, the relevant part of which has recently been retranslated into English by A. Harrak as *The Zuqnin Chronicle, Parts III and IV, AD 488–755* (Toronto, 1999); on the history it recounts, C. Cahen, 'Fiscalité, propriété, antagonismes sociaux en Haute-Mésopotamie au temps des premiers ᶜAbbāsides d'après Denys de Tell-Mahré', *Arabica* 1 (1954), pp. 136–152; for one of the slave accounts, the anonymous *Kitāb al-ᶜUyūn wa'l-ḥadāʾiq*, iv¹, pp. 18ff.; and for the appellation, Abū Shāma, *Kitāb al-Rawḍatayn fī akhbār al-dawlatayn* i² (Cairo, 1962), p. 515; for a history of this movement, A. Popovic, *La révolte des esclaves en Iraq au IIIᵉ, IXᵉ siècle* (Paris, 1976), now translated into English by L. King as *The Revolt of African Slaves in Iraq in the 3rd/9th Century* (Princeton, 1999).

> that I have been appointed governor of Iraq, then join me [there].' Nowhere in Hishām's camp was there anyone of handsomer cloak, nor anyone of nobler carriage than I.
>
> In no time at all, it was announced that Hishām had appointed Khālid as the governor of Iraq. So I set off, having engaged the paymaster to retain my stipend until I returned, and went to Iraq. When I came to Khālid in Kufa [the capital of Iraq] and greeted him, he granted me some dinars and a garment worth 600 dinars. Then one day he asked me, 'Ziyād, do you know how to write?', and I responded, 'No: I can read, but I cannot write.' He then slapped his forehead, exclaiming: 'By God, of the ten reasons I wanted you [in my employment], you possess only one!' So he purchased a slave who was both [fully] literate and numerate, sent him to me, and he taught me enough that I could read well and write [to a lower standard]. Then he sent to me a letter from his agent [over the taxes] of al-Rayy [near modern-day Tehran], and I read it out. He was pleased by this, and he said: 'I hereby appoint you over his post.' So I departed and came to al-Rayy, whereupon I arrested the agent of the land tax. He had it relayed to me that the Commander of the Faithful would never appoint an Arab over the land tax, and I responded by showing him nothing but disdain. So he said 'Take 300,000 dirhams from me, and leave me be,' and I took up my post. Later I would write to Khālid, 'I have grown to miss the Commander [that is, Khālid], so let him summon me back to him.' When I returned to him, he appointed me over his security force.

This is a world of tribes and political factions: when asked who he is, Ziyād starts with his factional identity ('from the people of Yemen') and then gives his tribal affiliation through genealogical self-description ('Ziyād b. ᶜUbayd Allāh b. ᶜAbd Allāh al-Ḥārithī'). This is also a world where a man can make something of himself, provided that he understands that success comes through good fortune, effective patronage and stubborn loyalty: the best client is the client, who, having achieved great things, still retains his loyalty to his patron. (Khālid's gesture – slapping his forehead in frustration – is an endearing reminder that despite all that separates us from eighth-century Syria, some things defy change.)[3]

It is one of the features of self-affirming modernity that we tend to exaggerate how different we are from our pre-modern counterparts: the 'invention' of the Middle Ages had much to do with nineteenth-century nationalism, but the knights in shining armour retain their fascination because they are emblematic of a world of rank and stasis that we left behind for one of equality and progress. This said, we do see the world and history in ways that would confound Ibn al-Nadīm. Equipped with a vocabulary of social description that derives from an economically industrialized, politically liberal and secularizing western world of the nineteenth and twentieth centuries, we now see the economy, society, and government (whatever its precise form) as conceptually separate spheres, each of which is given to operate according to principles or patterns that history (or other kinds of social analysis) has tried to discern, and which come together in conditioning the experience of men – that is, autonomous and more or less free-thinking men. The subject the historian chooses to write about invariably suits the model he has

[3] I draw the account from al-Balādhurī, *Ansāb al-ashrāf*, vib (Jerusalem, 1993), pp. 158f.; for other sources, Crone, *Slaves on Horses*, p. 55 (where it is summarized).

chosen, either implicitly or explicitly, to follow. Those historians who hold a materialist understanding of historical change, for example, privilege economic processes over political ones, seeing élite politics and ideology as a function of competition over material resources: only within such a model does it make much sense to write histories of the proletariat or working class. And although different historians emphasize different spheres to explain historical change, the point is that they *do* try to explain, and this by constructing (or following) models of how these spheres relate and interact, and by adducing more or less proximate causes for the events in question. At least for the professional historian, it no longer suffices to speak of Fate, Providence or Progress, indeed any other universal that, in failing to reflect the segmented world of factors, influences and models we construct to make sense of the world, relieves him of the task of explaining men's actions.

Medieval Muslim historians, in this respect much like other pre-modern historians, naturally lacked our modern terms of social description. They generally conceived of the world in more monolithic – or, as one might prefer to say, more 'integrated' – terms. Neither the economy nor society was clearly distinguished from the political order, and the laws of politics, which usually boiled down to acting justly or unjustly, were understood to determine economic and social life. This political order was God's design. It had been established to effect His will, first in broad strokes under Muḥammad's small polity in Medina, and then elaborated more fully by his successors, the 'four Rightly Guided caliphs'. At its apex sat one of his (real or figurative) descendants, the Abbasid caliph (or sultan), who, in the very act of holding office, enjoyed what has been aptly called the 'presumptive satisfaction of God' (at least according to the Sunnis), and who, by appointing governors, commanders and judges, legitimized the activities of the state. (In our account, Khālid al-Qasrī is the appointee of the caliph Hishām, and enjoys his legitimacy, while Ziyād is Khālid's and enjoys his.) Prosecuting war, regulating the market place, raising taxes, settling law – all these took place (at least in theory) under the legitimizing penumbra of the caliph's authority (in formative Islam) or, later, that of the law (the *sharīᶜa*), which he safeguarded.

For all that it claimed to represent, the state itself was usually very small by modern standards. For the most part, we live as individuals in powerful states; pre-modern Muslims generally lived as members of communities (tribes, kinship groups, families) in relatively weak states. Armies typically numbered in the tens of thousands at their very largest, and the reach of state power was made short not only by the lack of manpower and a variety of technological constraints (transportation and communication were particularly difficult), but a lack of ambition. The rhetoric of rule was often absolutist, but the state's politics were usually pragmatic. The power to coerce or persuade was extended only over those areas that produced more revenue than they cost the state to coerce or persuade (campaigning armies, policing and taxing are expensive activities), which in practice meant that marginal or unproductive land, such as desert, steppe and mountains, which together amount to most of the Near East, experienced little state power. Power thus tended to be concentrated in the cities and their immediate hinterlands and also, at least in moments of exceptional strength, along its main roads. Insofar as the proportionately huge population of the state's subjects had any role in this system, it was only to produce an agricultural surplus large enough above subsistence level to justify the bother of taxing. The cities lived off the land, centres of consumption much more frequently than production, and the contrast between city and country was predictably stark. Even within the cities, this was a world where differences were clearly drawn and hierarchy prevailed, where signs of social ranking were nearly ubiquitous by modern standards: everything from clothing and housing to how one spoke, the horses one rode and the food one ate (Khālid al-Qasrī's first act of patronage towards Ziyād is to grant him conspicuous clothes and a fine mount). It was a world where one knew one's place, and where moving up the social ladder was extremely infrequent, since, as we have seen, it required not only real ability, but usually some combination of fortune and patronage. It was a world where innovation and originality were usually resisted, and where nothing essential was supposed to change. It made a great deal of sense.[4]

God and history

Historians were part of this world of traditional roles and clear hierarchies: they reflected, recorded and recreated it. In a polity where the caliph or sultan claimed a divine right to rule, power was to be effected from the top down. The (usually) silent engine propelling human history was thus neither progress nor class conflict, nor even individual self-interest, but rather God's will, effected directly (typically through breaks in the natural order – miracles) or, much more frequently, through the agency of élite individuals, such as prophets, kings, commanders, governors, pretenders, schismatics and rebels. God may not appear in our edifying story about Ziyād b. ᶜUbayd Allāh's career, but He is still there, the ultimate patron who has chosen Hishām to act as the patron of Khālid al-Qasrī, himself the patron of our loyal and pluckish narrator.

To say that God's will was the engine of history is not to suggest that men were considered mere puppets strung from His hands. According to a theology worked out during the tenth and eleventh centuries, men were given to act as agents of their own free will by acquiring the responsibility of acts created by God. They were rewarded and punished accordingly, always in the Next World, and often in this one too. An omnipotent and omniscient God did not release man from the obligation to act in accordance with His command and to eschew that which was

[4] On the size of some early Islamic armies, see H. Kennedy, *The Armies of the Caliphs: Military and Society in the Early Islamic State* (London, 2001), *passim*; I borrow the phrase 'presumptive satisfaction of God' from R.P. Mottahedeh, 'Some attitudes towards monarchy and absolutism in the early Islamic world of the eleventh and twelfth centuries AD', *Israel Oriental Studies* 10 (1980), p. 90; on the crucial importance of patronage, idem, *Loyalty and Leadership in an Early Islamic Society* (Princeton, 1980); and, for some of the salient features of pre-modern societies more generally, P. Crone, *Pre-industrial Societies* (Oxford and Cambridge, Mass., 1989).

repugnant – which is a gloss on the ubiquitous injunction of *al-amr bi'l-maᶜrūf wa'l-nahy ᶜan al-munkar*, the command to do right and the prohibition from doing wrong. This explains why so many historians presented their work as a record of human choices, from which their readers were to draw the appropriate lessons. History taught these lessons (or 'admonitions', Ar. *ᶜibra*, pl. *ᶜibar*), a word that appears frequently in titles, such as those of Usāma b. Munqidh, Ibn Khaldūn and al-Dhahabī, and an idea that appears even more frequently in introductions to historical works.

Similarly, that God's will is the engine of history does not mean that Muslim historians failed to acknowledge the interplay of what we would call natural forces, or social, economic and political factors. Historians often did take note of economic processes (rising prices is a favourite), for which they sometimes provide material causes, such as famine, and consequent effects, such as the unpopularity of a governor, or the breaking-off of a siege. In his entry on year 1048 C.E., Ibn al-Athīr describes the all-too-familiar sequence of famine (people were forced into eating carrion) and epidemic (what with people weakened and sickened by eating carrion); he also specifies the exact prices of certain foodstuffs, such as pomegranates, almonds and cucumbers. But these were symptoms, rather than causes. That the economy or climate worked independently of, much less counter to, God's will, was virtually unthinkable: historians understood the world to be an integrated and ordered whole, all its occupants being subject to God's sovereignty. Just rulers enjoyed God's favour and witnessed peace and prosperity. But when the fish rotted, it rotted from the head down: an unjust governor appointed rapacious tax collectors, who, in over-taxing, might rob the farmers of the seed corn they needed for the following year, which would mean famine. The whole system fell out of balance. As the author of one fourteenth-century history of Damascus puts it: 'When the sultan is unjust, injustice spreads in the land and the people become weak; rights are suppressed; they become addicted to wrongdoing and they pervert weights and measures. Thereupon blessing is withheld and the heavens are prevented from giving rain; the seeds dry up and cattle perish, because of their withholding charity and because false oaths have spread among them. Cunning and stratagems increase in their midst …'[5]

All this may sound very strange and foreign to us, but here it is particularly important to note that pre-modern Muslim historians were anything but alone in holding a God-centred model of history. In the contemporaneous Christian worlds (both East and West) 'secular' historical writing on the classical model was nearly always on the margin, elbowed aside during late antiquity by much the same God-centred view of history. Christian historians may have found Islamic history distasteful, but the model it followed would have made perfect sense to them. What is distinctive about Islamic historiography is not that God's will is seen to determine

[5] For Ibn al-Athīr's entry, see his *al-Kāmil*, ix, p. 541; for the Damascene historian, Ibn Ṣaṣrā, *A Chronicle of Damascus, 1389–1397* (*al-Durra al-muḍī'a fī al-dawla al-ẓāhiriyya*), ed. and tr. by W.M. Brinner (Berkeley, 1963), pp. 191f.; for God's commands, M. Cook, *Commanding Right and Forbidding Wrong in Islamic Thought* (Cambridge, 2000).

history, nor that God makes His will manifest through human and natural events – Christian historians of the time wrote in much the same way, granting to God much the same explanatory position in their tradition as He enjoyed in the Islamic. What *is* distinctive about the tradition is the meaning it attaches to these events and, perhaps to a lesser extent, the way that God was made to work on earth.

A case in point is none other than Muḥammad himself. Christian and Muslim historians could agree that history had taken an altogether new turn with the Prophet, and that the momentous events required some kind of explanation. How is it that seventh-century Arabs, strangers to urbane and leisured Muslim historians of ninth- and tenth-century Iraq almost as much as they were to parochial monk-historians writing in Syriac, had produced this man, through whose vision, leadership and legacy, Muslim armies had routed Christians at nearly every turn? In both sets of eyes he was an agent of God's will. They disagreed only in what God had in mind. Christians saw Muḥammad as a pseudo-prophet, a trickster, magician or lunatic, and typically explained his armies' startling successes much as they explained plague and pestilence: it was a punishment God inflicted upon them for their own sinning (which, in so many of the histories that were written by monks, bishops and other men of the Church, usually meant rebelling against Church authority). Muslims naturally saw in the conquest armies the hand of God, too, but His hand was providential. In His infinite mercy, God had restored monotheism to Arabia; Muḥammad's followers, inspired as they were by their direct acquaintance with God's final prophet, responded to God's injunction to 'fight in the way of God'. To Christians (and some Jews), the conquests were proof that Muḥammad's claim to prophecy was a lie, for, as one very early Christian put it, 'Do prophets come with a sword?' (the answer was: no). To Muslims, the conquests were proof that Muḥammad's claims were true, for God had sent Muḥammad to make his religion prevail (Qurʾān 9:33 and 61:9), and this was exactly what God had had them do.[6]

In general, then, God's will was the ultimate cause of all events, the tools He preferred were the actions of élite individuals, and the standard to which He held his creatures had been made clear in His law. With God standing at the centre of history, the task that fell to Muslim historians was therefore not so much to *explain* human actions as it was to *exemplify* known truths and to teach lessons by describing them. This is why some modern scholars have hesitated to call *taʾrīkh* history proper (by which is meant the probative history of the classical tradition), suggesting instead that it is a 'peculiarly Islamic *genre* of miscellaneous information about humanity and the world, arranged with a passion for chronology which gives it simply the appearance of history in the Western sense'. There is some truth to this, but we must guard against judging Islamic historical writing by classical standards, particularly since these had been eclipsed by Christian styles of

[6] For some examples of how Christians responded to Islam, see Hoyland, *Seeing Islam*, esp. pp. 523ff., and Wolf, *Conquerors,* p. 30; for some comments on miracles and the conquests, C.F. Robinson, 'Prophecy and holy men in early Islam' in J. Howard-Johnston and P.A. Hayward, eds., *The Cult of Saints in Late Antiquity and the Early Middle Ages* (Oxford, 1999), pp. 243ff.

historiography during Late Antiquity. It may be that a classicizing tradition had survived into the early seventh century in Theophylact of Simocatta's history, but this does not mean that Thucydides (d. early fifth century, B.C.), the standard-bearer for secular and probative history, remained an option for Muslims of the eighth and ninth century A.D.: we stand closer in time (and in some respects in cultural distance) to al-Ṭabarī than al-Ṭabarī stood to Thucydides. By the eighth and ninth centuries, monotheism had come to determine not only the way most Christian lawyers and cleric-historians viewed the future, but the way they explained the past.[7]

There is no shortage of examples. The Byzantine historian Malalas, writing in Greek in the middle of the sixth century A.D. – that is, in the Late Antique world that earliest Muslims would come to know and in which they developed their culture of learning – begins with God's creation of the world, matter-of-factly informing his reader that Adam was six feet tall and lived precisely 930 years. His narrative is filled with signs of God's wrath (earthquakes, plagues, hailstorms, fires, locusts) and of His pleasure, too, the latter often in the form of spectacular miracles. A devastating earthquake in the northern Syrian city of Antioch kills 250,000 people, but some survive under the rubble for 20 or 30 days; buried women give birth and infants suckle at the breast of their dead mothers. The stories are fantastic to us, but not to Malalas: these were either Biblical truths or divine miracles, and the past was significant because it taught lessons about right belief. Besides, who was he to judge God's decision about the course of human affairs? It is to this strain of historical writing and thinking, which Byzantinists have conventionally (and often derisively) called chronicles, that early Muslims were heirs. Even those writing contemporary history – that category of history favoured by Thucydides, and which Byzantinists more generously regard as history proper – were credulous about the fantastic. 'Wondrous events' (*ʿajāʾib*) would become a prominent theme in the historiography of the Mamluk period, but already in the eleventh century a Baghdadi diarist dryly reports a story that Malalas himself might have recorded: a wild beast attacks a family, killing the mother; when local townspeople come across her partially devoured body, they find that 'the baby girl was still alive, nursing at her dead mother's breast, through God's power – exalted is He above all! – and the milk was being drawn freely from her breast'. When people got together to tell stories, the more fantastic the story, the better.[8]

[7] The quotation on *taʾrīkh* is from M. Brett, 'The way of the nomad', *BSOAS* 58 (1995), p. 252; on the classicizing historians, R.C. Blockley, *The Fragmentary Classicising Historians of the Later Roman Empire* (Liverpool, 1981); and on Theophylact, M. Whitby, *The Emperor Maurice and his Historian: Theophylact Simocatta on Persian and Balkan Warfare* (Oxford, 1988).

[8] For Byzantine historiography in general, see F. Winkelmann and W. Brandes, *Quellen zur Geschichte des frühen Byzanz: 4.-9. Jahrhundert* (Amsterdam, 1990) (for Malalas, pp. 190ff.); for Malalas in particular, E. Jeffreys et al., eds., *Studies in John Malalas* (Sydney, 1990); and for miracles in another Byzantine historian (Procopius), A. Cameron, 'History as text: coping with Procopius', in Holdsworth and Wiseman, *Inheritance of Historiography*, pp. 56ff.; on the diarist, G. Makdisi, 'Autograph diary of an eleventh-century historian of Baghdad – I', *BSOAS* 18 (1956), pp. 246 (Arabic)/258 (translation, which I reproduce); for a history of popular life under the Mamluks, which is based in part upon narratives of the 'wondrous' in the Mamluk chronographic tradition, B. Langner, *Untersuchungen zur historischen Volkskunde Ägyptens nach mamlukischen Quellen* (Berlin, 1983).

That seventh- and eighth-century Christian historiography was moving away from secular history may appear to go some way towards explaining the God-centredness of early Muslim historians, who shared their monotheistic perspective. Yet it cannot go very far: even had Christians been moving *towards* a classical model, one can hardly imagine that eighth- or ninth-century Muslim historians would closely follow models of history adapted to specifically Christian concerns. As we saw earlier, Muslims accommodated and appropriated a huge amount of non-Islamic learning, but it made no sense to import models for history. Their own historical experience provided the model. The historical divide between church and state in Christianity, which came to be mirrored in a Christian historiographical divide between secular and ecclesiastical historiography, did not obtain in Islam. Early Christians built the foundations of their religious tradition within a polity that was either indifferent or hostile to their faith, and they accommodated themselves accordingly. One could believe in Christ and his mission while remaining subject to a Roman governor who did not, and it took some creative thinking to integrate the history of that indifferent or hostile state into the providential history that God was supposed to guarantee: perhaps it precluded political pluralism long enough for the state to become Christian in the fourth century. But whereas Jesus was crucified at the hands of Roman authorities, Muḥammad died peacefully at the head of a Muslim polity, which two years earlier had subjugated the pagans of Mecca, and immediately upon his death, caliphs began to rule and conquer much of the civilized world in his name. Having replaced Byzantine and Sasanian rule in the Near East with the caliphate, the Muslims were free to hold a unitary model of religion and politics – and thus history.

Authority over all creatures and all things thus belonged to God, and those whom He had chosen to represent Him on earth (prophets, caliphs or imams) exercised His authority by proxy. That they might choose, in turn, to delegate even further, and that, in practice, the result would be offices and institutions ranging from what we would call the sacred (prayer leaders) to the profane (tax collectors), made no difference at all: the exercise of all authority was considered legitimate only in religious terms, and the state, by definition, was theocratic. Muslim lawyers were determined to ensure the privacy of individuals and families, and there certainly were theoretical and effective limits to the power that the theocratic state could wield. Even so, there was little of what we would now call 'civil society' – groups or organizations that could mediate between the individual and the state – and what we understand to be the secular realm of society simply did not exist as such. Muslims might fight civil wars and revolutions about who should lead the theocratic state, but they never doubted that it should remain theocratic.[9]

The consequences of this unitary model for the historiographic tradition were far reaching. The closest Muslims came to ecclesiastical history is the prosopographies of jurists, and even this is not terribly close (the *ṭabaqāt* works of jurists come rather closer to the sixth- or seventh-century *Book of the Popes*, which

[9] For history and the church, I draw on A. Momigliano, 'The disadvantages of monotheism for a universal state', *Classical Philology* 81 (1986), pp. 291f.

recorded the succession of popes all the way back to St Peter). Rather than recording how the Church had persevered within a hostile state, Islamic chronography generally concerned itself with the polity (the caliphate) that God had established to execute His will in a post-Prophetic age. Although the result may often appear to be political history of the most dull variety (war after war, political intrigue after political intrigue), it is thoroughly religious in inspiration and conception. Waging war and levying taxes were acts no less religious than leading the pilgrimage caravan to Mecca or leading the community in prayer (their authors were, after all, men of religious learning). Succession struggles, dramas in the caliphs' court, civil war – these, too, were matters of fundamental religious significance. Who was to lead the theocracy? How did he come to lead it? What were his qualifications? In chronography organized by caliphal reigns (*taʾrīkh al-khulafāʾ*), this concern with stewardship became the very organizing principle of narrative, but even in annalistic history, where it did not, much the same ground is covered. In sum, if there is a single goal that animates all of Islamic chronography, it is charting and learning from God's final experiment in organizing mankind along theocratic lines. Some have reasonably spoken of early Islamic history as 'salvation history'.[10]

God, society and historiographic forms: universal and local history

The historians' coverage of Prophetic and post-Prophetic history was therefore religious in character, because they took the polity (rather than 'society') as the object of their study. This polity had been set into motion by a providential God who also determined its course, from beginning (Creation) to end (the Eschaton), an event which is conventionally described in military terms, of battles between Muslims and non-Muslims, and God's ultimate victory over the anti-Christ. Historians being historians, they generally eschewed detailed discussion of the future, which was left to prophets to foresee. The rule is tested by the occasional exception, such as the monumental *al-Bidāya wa'l-nihāya* ('The Beginning and the End') of Ibn Kathīr (d. 1373), which begins with Creation and concludes with predictions of the cataclysmic End. Because this is an exception, we shall start at the Beginning. Since, during the course of the ninth century, Muslim historians disengaged this history from *sīra*, making it either a separate genre itself (the so-called *qiṣaṣ al-anbiyāʾ*, 'Stories of the prophets') or a sub-section of universal history, this means working with universal histories.

i. Universal history

Here we find exactly what we might have expected of monotheist historians, especially those with such a spectacularly successful story to tell of state building

[10] Cf. Hodgson, 'Two pre-modern Muslim historians'; the most forceful statement on Islamic 'salvation history' is J. Wansbrough, *The Sectarian Milieu* (London, 1978).

in Arabia and lightning-fast conquest outside of it, followed by imperial rule from the Atlantic Ocean to the Indus valley – the whole sequence unfolding under God's direction. What historians did was to make the history of the pre-Islamic world conform to the Islamic model of politics and history, and to treat Islamic history, for the most part, as the history of the caliphate.[11]

Although the earliest works that tackled what we would now recognize as universal history – the history of the world, from Creation on – do not survive, the idea seems to be about as old as the tradition itself. There is no clear Muslim analogue to Eusebius (d. 340), the founder of universal history writing in the Christian tradition, although, very broadly speaking, one can say that Muslim historians conformed to something of a Eusebian model. Just as Eusebius' scheme was apologetically determined (the project was in part to endow Christianity with an antique pedigree), so, too, was Islamic universal chronography, which located Muḥammad and his polity in a succession of monotheist events. Figures as early as Wahb b. Munabbih (d. 728) are said to have assembled material on Biblical history, especially the history of the prophets, and this would remain the mainstay of universal history. None other than Ibn Isḥāq himself seems to have taken a similar interest. As far as we can tell, his reconstruction of Prophetic history (the *mabᶜath* and *maghāzī* sections) was sandwiched on one side by a pre-Islamic section that began with Creation and, on the other, by a history of the caliphs; according to the terminology of the classical tradition, the former would be a *kitāb al-mubtadaᵓ* (a book on the Beginning), and the latter a *taᵓrīkh al-khulafāᵓ* (a history of the caliphs). From the perspective of the later tradition, the vision seems almost recklessly ambitious, but it accords well with the undifferentiated world of early Islamic learning, then still naïve of the specialisms that developed in the later eighth and early ninth centuries. In fact, if this four-part reconstruction of Ibn Isḥāq's work is accurate, the book's handling by Ibn Hishām exemplifies the reshaping of the historiographic tradition itself. In the hands of specialists to come, *sīra-maghāzī*, shorn of *mubtadaᵓ* and *taᵓrīkh* material, came to mean Prophetic history proper. Meanwhile, post-Prophetic history came to be handled primarily in either annalistic or caliphal history, and pre-Prophetic history became either a specialism in its own right in *qiṣaṣ al-anbiyāᵓ* works ('Tales of the prophets'), of which several survive, or was integrated into the pre-Prophetic sections of universal history. This, it must be said, is the tradition's main trajectory, because some later *sīra*s, such as those written by al-Kalāᶜī (d. 1237), Mughulṭāᵓī (d. 1361) and al-Diyārbakrī (d. *ca.* 1555), would blur some of the lines between *sīra* and chronography by carrying their biographies on into caliphal history. In what follows, I shall leave aside independent *qiṣaṣ al-anbiyāᵓ* works, as I have left aside caliphal and annalist history as it is recorded in these relatively late *sīra*s.[12]

[11] On universal histories, see Rosenthal, *History*, pp. 133ff.; Radtke, *Weltgeschichte*, pp. 9ff.; Springberg-Hinsen, *Universalgeschichten*; and Chabbi, 'La répresentation du passé', p. 28.

[12] On the shape of Ibn Isḥāq's work, see the works cited in chapter 2, note 25; on Ibn Isḥāq's *Kitāb al-mubtadaᵓ*, G.D. Newby, *The Making of the Last Prophet: A Reconstruction of the Earliest Biography of Muhammad* (Columbia, S.C., 1989), on which see Conrad, 'Recovering lost texts'; on *qiṣaṣ al-anbiyāᵓ* works, R. Tottoli, *I profeti biblici nella tradizione islamica* (Brescia, 1999); Mughulṭāᵓī's

As far as the classical tradition is concerned, we therefore have to do with universal history as recorded in annalistic or caliphal history. The earliest surviving example was written by Aḥmad b. Abī Yaᶜqūb al-Yaᶜqūbī (d. *ca.* 900), who was an enigmatic figure, even by historians' standards. He appears to have been brought up somewhere in Armenia, traveled widely and was employed as a bureaucrat in the court of the Ṭāhirids, a quasi-independent dynasty that ruled Iran during much of the ninth century. Three works of al-Yaᶜqūbī's survive: an important geography, an unimportant short essay, and the two-volume universal history (*Taʾrīkh*), which apparently began with Creation and ends in 259/872. We can only infer that it began with Creation, since the two surviving (and related) manuscripts pick up the story at a point at which Adam and Eve have already appeared on the scene.

Al-Yaᶜqūbī was something of a misfit. One of the few Shiᶜites to write a universal history that survives, he bucked the historiographic trends of the day by omitting *isnād*s, prefacing his work instead with a brief bibliography of his principal sources. He is distinctive, too, in what appears to be his *direct* reliance on Christian and Jewish informants for the rich Old and New Testament material that he includes. Most historians worked through intermediate Arabic translations; to judge from the linguistic evidence of the *History* itself, much of al-Yaᶜqūbī's material seems to come straight from Syriac. He occasionally synchronizes events with non-Islamic months, which is also unusual. Whether he commanded Syriac is an open question, and it may be that he was working with a Syriac-reading informant, perhaps even by dictation. In any event, the wide-ranging interests manifested in the *History* and *Geography* have been said to reflect the broad cultural tastes of the belletrists, rather than the more narrow concerns of the scripturally minded religious, and there is much to recommend this reading of the *History*'s intended audience. These interests are especially prominent in the pre-Islamic section of the work, which occupies a good third of the total; here he ranges as far east as India and China. What is more, he as much as courts controversy amongst the conservative-minded by prefacing most of the caliphal entries with a partial or complete horoscope of the caliph in question, astrology being as popular in ninth- and tenth-century courts as it was scorned by most monotheist authorities, be they *ᶜulamāʾ* or rabbis. A standard work of reference does not include al-Yaᶜqūbī amongst the historians, apparently postponing his appearance to a later volume that will be devoted to belles-lettres.[13]

most important *sīra*, the *Zahr al-bāsim fī sīrat Abī al-Qāsim*, remains unedited, but its epitome, *al-Ishāra ilā sīrat al-Muṣṭafā wa-taʾrīkh man baᶜdahā min al-khulafāʾ* is available (Damascus and Beirut, 1996); al-Diyārbakrī's *Taʾrīkh al-khamīs fī aḥwāl anfas nafīs* was published in Cairo, 1283 H.; at least two of these *qiṣaṣ* works have been translated into English: Ibn Kathir's as *Stories of the Prophets*, trans. R.A. Azami (Riyadh, 1999) and al-Kisāʾī's as *Tales of the Prophets of al-Kisāʾī*, trans. W. Thackston (Boston, 1978).

[13] On al-Yaᶜqūbī in general, see Duri, *Rise of Historical Writing*, pp. 64ff.; Petersen, *ᶜAlī and Muᶜāwiya*, pp. 169ff.; Donner, *Narratives of Islamic Origins*, p. 134; Khalidi, *Arabic Historical Thought*, pp. 120f. and 131f., Springberg-Hinsen, *Universalgeschichten*, pp. 29ff.; on his handling of pre-Islamic monotheism, R.Y. Ebied and L.R. Wickam, 'Al-Yaᶜqūbī's account of the Israelite prophets and kings,' *JNES* 29 (1970), pp. 80–98; on his Shiᶜism, Y. Marquet, 'Le šiᶜisme au IXᵉ siècle à travers l'histoire de Yaᶜqūbī', *Arabica* 19 (1972), pp. 1–45 and 101–138; for some later

Al-Yaᶜqūbī thus had relatively wide interests, and being a Shīᶜite of one variety or another (the work closes before events that would have made his perspective clearer), he probably felt less constrained by the conventions that had begun to prevail amongst Sunni historians. Similar things can be said about al-Masᶜūdī, whose *Murūj al-dhahab* is the work of a remarkably broad and catholic vision. Drawing upon a wide variety of sources, it marshals historical, geographic and ethnographic information on peoples from the west (Frankish kings), north (Slavs) and east (Indian kings, Chinese emperors). All of this said, there is no confusing al-Yaᶜqūbī's or al-Masᶜūdī's work with what would now be called a multi-cultural textbook of world history. The latter may have been a humanist of sorts, and this a good century before an Islamic humanism enjoyed its brief efflorescence. But he is a thoroughly monotheist one. Here, as elsewhere, history begins with God's work of Creation, and the underlying historical vision is both God-centred and teleological: history has a purpose, and the purpose of pre-Islamic history is to provide a sort of *praeparatio evangelica* for the events of the early seventh century and what followed: the prophecy of Muḥammad and the caliphs, all ruling in his succession. So it is not merely that al-Yaᶜqūbī's (or al-Masᶜūdī's) cultural interests (e.g., the invention of chess) reflect those of the Abbasid court. It is that the entire framework of pre-Islamic history – organized by a succession of polities, led by prophets or kings, and all transient – is made to presage the appearance of the Islamic polity under the leadership of Muḥammad and then of the Abbasid caliphate itself. Universal history in the hands of al-Ṭabarī is similarly teleological: some 14,000 years are covered in the *ca.* 8,000 pages of his *History of Prophets and Kings*, and history marches single file, the Islamic polity following the Persian, and the Persian following the Israelite – the great *translatio imperii* (succession of empires) that also interested historians of the Christian west. A similar shaping conditions character and event. Prophets familiar to us from the Biblical tradition, such as Moses and Abraham, are recast in terms made familiar to Muslims by Muḥammad's experience, while the pre-Islamic prophets in Arabia, who are entirely unfamiliar to anyone unread in the Qurᵓān, are also made to follow the monotheist pattern. None of this should be taken to suggest that al-Yaᶜqūbī's or al-Ṭabarī's pre-Islamic sections are homogeneous or one-dimensional: the two historians preserve a wide variety of material, especially al-Ṭabarī, to whom we owe much of our understanding of administrative and political history of the late Sasanian empire. This *is* universal history, at least much more so than what passes for universal history in contemporaneous Byzantine historiography, which can hardly compare in either ambition or execution. But it is universal history of a selective and very purposeful sort.[14]

polemics against astrologers, Y.J. Michot, 'Ibn Taymiyya on astrology: annotated translation of three fatwas', *Journal of Islamic Studies* 11 (2000), pp. 147–208; the standard work is *GAS*.

[14] For the Mosaic reading of Muḥammad's representation in the *sīra*, see Rubin, *Eye of the Beholder*, esp. pp. 190ff.; on al-Masᶜūdī's interests, Sboul, *Al-Masᶜūdī and his World*; and the articles in S.M. Ahmad, and A. Rahman, eds., *Al-Masᶜūdī Millenary Commemoration Volume* (Calcutta, 1960); the page count of al-Ṭabarī's history is from the Leiden edition; for a translation of some of al-Ṭabarī's pre-Islamic material, which includes a hugely valuable commentary, T. Nöldeke, *Geschichte der Perser und Araber zur Zeit der Sasaniden* (Leiden, 1879).

Prophetic and post-Prophetic history is no less selective, purposeful or Islamic. The literary patterning that characterizes pre-Islamic coverage also characterizes Prophetic history, with the result that it is made both relentlessly chronological and deeply mythical. The construction of Muḥammad in al-Ṭabarī (here based on Ibn Isḥāq) is complex, and scholars have argued both about its ingredients and how and when they were combined. Suffice it to say here, because of the heterogeneity of materials and outlooks in the *sīra*, we can be fairly sure that the biographers did not efface the historical figure: the historical Muḥammad may be elusive, but he *is* in there. This said, our historians certainly made Muḥammad conform to the monotheistic traditions that Muslims were themselves claiming – so much so, in fact, that his representation in the *sīra* presumes an understanding of early prophetic history, especially stories about Moses. Similar things can be said for seminal events of the early community (such as the Civil War of 656–661), whose narratives also echo the cycle of Promise, followed by Betrayal, and later political crises, such as another case of civil war, this between rival brothers to succeed Hārūn al-Rashīd (d. 809), where al-Amīn and al-Maʾmūn are in some respects patterned after Cain and Abel. Meanwhile, of events happening outside the caliphate's borders, we hear virtually nothing, and time itself is measured on the tradition's clock: either the succession of caliphs (al-Yaʿqūbī) or years of the Hijra (al-Ṭabarī). In both cases, life's rhythms are set not by the seasons or harvests, but by rituals and ritual politics of Islam, such as the pilgrimage to Mecca and Medina and the succession of caliphs.[15]

ii. Local history

To recapitulate: the way power was effected in society goes some way towards explaining our historians' focus on social élites, particularly the state and its court, and the model of history that they followed. The scope and range of tenth-century universal chronography mirror the absolutist claims and political history of the caliphate itself; at the level of narrative, pre-Islamic history is recast in Islamic terms, and Islamic history is patterned upon monotheist history. What happened outside the caliphate might have been of some interest to the curious, but information was necessarily scarce, and besides, why should it have a sure place in the historiographic vision if God had not yet made it part of His order by sending successful armies to conquer it?

The connection between politics and culture on the one hand, and historiographic form and narrative on the other, can be discerned elsewhere. If the universal

[15] For a reading of the First Civil War narratives, see R.S. Humphreys, 'Qurʾanic myth and narrative structure in early Islamic historiography', in F.M. Clover and R.S. Humphreys, eds., *Tradition and Innovation in Late Antiquity* (Madison, 1989), pp. 271–290; for al-Amīn and al-Maʾmūn, El-Hibri, *Reinterpreting Islamic Historiography*, pp. 172ff.; on Cain and Abel more generally, W. Bork-Qaysieh, *Die Geschichte von Kain und Abel (Hābil wa-Qābil) in der sunnitische-islamischen Überlieferung* (Berlin, 1993).

chronicle is emblematic of ninth- and tenth-century Abbasid absolutism, local chronography and non-Prophetic biography are emblematic of the late- and post-Abbasid world of the tenth to the thirteenth centuries, in which the unified state was replaced by a commonwealth of regional polities. These polities varied in any number of ways, some relying on slave soldiers for military support, others on nomads, some dynasties being Arab, some Turkic, others Persian; their ties to Baghdad were tighter or looser, depending largely on distance and ambition. For all their differences, they still shared the common culture of Islamic learning that had emerged during the first three centuries of Islam. They also shared a difficult problem. In an age when the caliph had lost nearly all his religious authority and political influence, how were provincial states to relate to the institution of the caliphate? The caliphs' religious authority had been in decline from the middle of the ninth century, and by the early tenth century it was only the exceptional caliph who made anything more than a symbolic contribution to the religious life of the community he was supposed to lead. A crucial moment in the collapse of Abbasid power was the Buyid occupation of Baghdad in 945, which set a constitutional crisis into motion. The caliphs had nearly always delegated their authority to subordinates in the provinces, but now, for the first time, the provincials had taken control of the caliphate itself. What role now remained for the caliph and those (such as provincial governors) whom he had appointed? What about those who had usurped his power by defeating one of these governors, and who now paid allegiance to him? How were Muslims to conduct themselves in this new world? The historians had a part in answering these questions. Universal history would continue to be written, but now, in a politically fragmented and culturally competitive world of provincial states, its horizons grew narrower. Universal historians writing in Iraq, such Ibn al-Jawzī, would present far less breadth in their pre-Islamic sections than had al-Yaᶜqūbī and al-Ṭabarī, and their Islamic history would focus upon Iraq, just as universal historians working in Damascus, such as Ibn Kathīr, would increasingly focus upon Damascus. Meanwhile, local chronography, biography and prosopography would serve to anchor dynasties and institutions within the cultural and legal commonwealth of late Abbasid rule.[16]

Local histories usually focused on cities. Islamic cities in our period may not have generated the particularism and independence enjoyed by many European cities in the high middle ages, not to mention their forms of local organization and government, but they did produce deep pride and (occasionally) fierce loyalties. The tradition's coverage varies across the Islamic world, the larger cities naturally attracting more attention than smaller towns. This is not simply because, as large cities, they generated more wealth and political power, although this certainly mattered. It was also because, as cities of wealth and power, they generated learning, especially traditionist learning. So Baghdad, Cairo and Damascus, which in

[16] On Ibn al-Jawzī's pre-Islamic interests in his *al-Muntaẓam fī taʾrīkh al-mulūk wa'l-umam* (Beirut, 1992 edition), see volume i, p. 39 (of the introduction); and Springberg-Hinsen, *Universalgeschichten*, pp. 57ff.

different periods all possessed both political and traditionist significance, were particularly well served: they enjoyed a full share of prosopographic and chronographic coverage, some of it sustained over several centuries. Much of it, especially in the case of the latter two, survives. Meanwhile, lesser cities, which enjoyed *either* political *or* traditionist significance, fared less well; in these cases, the historiographic coverage is frequently too thin to work with. Those cities and regions that possessed special religious significance by virtue of history and ritual were exceptions to this general rule: possessing little or no sustained political significance, they still came to possess a rich local tradition, particularly in prosopography. The three great examples of this final pattern are Jerusalem and the two Hijazi cities of Mecca and Medina.[17]

Both prosopographical and chronographic local history took shape almost as early as everything else took historiographic shape. Concern for the local contribution to traditionist learning may be signalled already in Ibn Sa^{c}d's *Ṭabaqāt* and Muslim b. Ḥajjāj's *Ṭabaqāt*, where traditionists are classified by generation *and* locality, but the first independent works that survive belong to a later period, the earliest examples being the *History of Wāsiṭ* by Baḥshal al-Wāsiṭī (d. 902) and the *History of al-Raqqa* by al-Qushayrī (d. 945). Both assemble capsule biographies of the learned men of their town. As far as non-prosopographical genres are concerned, a number of late eighth- and ninth-century compilers are credited with titles suggesting that local interests took written form. Some of these appear to have been little more than annotated lists: such is probably the case for a number of works credited by Ibn al-Nadīm to al-Haytham b. ^{c}Adī (d. 822) on the governors, judges and commanders of Kufa, Basra and Khurāsān. It is presumably this kind of material that gave rise to some examples of tenth-century local chronography, such as a work on the judges and governors of Egypt by al-Kindī (d. 961). On the other hand, at least one tenth-century local chronography, the *History of Mosul* by al-Azdī (d. 944), was written by someone who was very familiar with the chronographic tradition that produced universal history, including al-Ṭabarī himself. In fact, al-Azdī clearly reflects the exclusivity of historiographic genres in this period: he wrote a chronographic history of his town, the middle third of which survives, and a prosopography of its learned men, which is lost. Al-Azdī's chronography is annalistic; others are caliphal, such as Ibn al-Azraq's *History of Mayyāfāriqīn*.[18]

[17] For a brief discussion of Damascus from local sources, see Humphreys, *Islamic History*, pp. 238ff.; on the coverage of Medina, Ḥ. al-Jāsir, 'Muʾallafāt fī taʾrīkh al-Madīna', *al-^{c}Arab* 4 (1969), pp. 97–100, 262–267; and 4–5 (1970), pp. 327–335, 385–389; on Jerusalem, A. Elad, 'The history and topography of Jerusalem during the early Islamic period: the historical value of *faḍāʾil al-Quds* literature: a reconsideration', *JSAI* 14 (1991), pp. 41–83, and D.P. Little, 'Mujīr al-Dīn al-^{c}Ulaymī's vision of Jerusalem in the ninth-fifteenth century', *JAOS* 115 (1995), pp. 237–247.

[18] For a discussion of al-Haytham's *Namenlisten*, see Leder, *Korpus*, pp. 197ff.; *GAS*, p. 272; Baḥshal's *Taʾrīkh Wāsiṭ* was published in Baghdad, 1967, al-Qushayrī's *Taʾrīkh al-Raqqa* in Hama, 1959 and Damascus, 1998, and Ibn al-Azraq's *Taʾrīkh Mayyāfāriqīn* (partially) in Cairo, 1959; on the early sections of the latter, C.F. Robinson, 'Ibn al-Azraq, his *Taʾrīkh Mayyāfāriqīn*, and early Islam', *JRAS* (3rd ser.) 6 (1996), pp. 7–27; on later sections, C. Hillenbrand, *A Muslim Principality in Crusader Times: The Early Artuqid State* (Leiden, 1990); for a work that reconstructs early lists of judges in Damascus, G. Conrad, *Die Quḍāt Dimašq und der maḏhab Auzā^{c}ī* (Beirut, 1994).

In what sense are these local histories? A typical example is the *Taʾrīkh Jurjān*, or, perhaps more properly (certainly more revealingly), the *Kitāb maʿrifat ʿulamāʾ ahl Jurjān* ('Book of Information on the *ʿulamāʾ* from amongst the people of Jurjān'), which was written by al-Sahmī (d. 1035). In the introduction, al-Sahmī states that local history writing derives from local pride, especially because Companions of the Prophet had come and settled in Jurjān (a city and region in north-east Iran). He also provides a pseudo-etymology for the name itself: Jurjān, the reader is told, derives from a certain Jurdān, a descendant of Noah. Anchoring one's city in the mythical past is typical enough of local history. Having established the town's pedigree, al-Sahmī then moves quickly on to what made the city Islamic, crediting its conquest to the conquering caliph *par excellence*, ʿUmar b. al-Khaṭṭāb, signatory of a conquest treaty that survived in al-Sahmī's day. This, too, is typical, because post-conquest arrangements as stipulated in these treaties (authentic or otherwise) were held to be decisive in later disputes that arose between locals (Muslim and non-Muslim) on the one hand, and between local élites and imperial officials on other. Hereupon follow brief sections on those Companions who settled in the city, on those Followers who came next, on Umayyad administration, and on the early city's layout (*khiṭaṭ*). These introductory matters having come to a close, the work now catalogues, generation by generation, the traditionists of Jurjān.[19]

What is the point in this catalogue? In part, the point was to assert the orthodoxy of provincial learning, by anchoring the provincial learning undertaken by non-Arab converts to Islam in the heartland of Arabia. As Abū Isḥāq al-Shīrāzī puts it in his eleventh-century history of jurists, 'when the "ʿAbd Allāhs" died [a number of key jurists, all named ʿAbd Allāh], learning (*fiqh*) in all the provinces passed to converted Muslims (*mawālī*)'. By positing the continuous transmission of authoritative teaching from master to pupil over several generations, a local prosopography of the *ṭabaqāt* variety functions to link one of a multiplicity of branches (usually the local tradition of jurists) to a single trunk (Prophetic *sunna* as it was explicated in Medina, Basra, Kufa and Baghdad – the centres of eighth- and ninth-century learning, which produced the legal schools' eponyms). The empire may have fragmented and the caliph's authority shattered, but the *ʿulamāʾ* were agents of preservation, 'the heirs of the Prophet' (as a *ḥadīth* put it), the uninterrupted continuity of their *ṭabaqāt* echoing the unbroken *isnād*s of the *ḥadīth* they transmitted. Commanding a common set of skills, and reading a more or less common reservoir of texts, the *ʿulamāʾ* thus fashioned for themselves a common history.[20]

A local *ṭabaqāt* book makes more claims, all of which, in one way or another, champion provincial *ʿulamāʾ* vis-à-vis their competitors: that the local tradition of learning was substantial enough to generate its own, dedicated history (some cities could produce *ṭabaqāt*s, others could not); that its historical experience, expressed in the form of capsule biographies that only make the rarest allusion to the world

[19] Al-Sahmī's *Taʾrīkh Jurjān* was published in Hyderabad, 1950.
[20] Abū Isḥāq al-Shīrāzī, *Ṭabaqāt al-fuqahāʾ*, p. 58.

of politics, was distinguishable – and, in some sense, distinct from – the political vicissitudes of imperial or local rule; that this local tradition discharges the relevant religious responsibilities for and on behalf of the Muslim community. In short, local prosopography asserts the collective identity and status of the *ʿulamāʾ*, and since these *ʿulamāʾ* were almost invariably men from landowning and mercantile families, this assertion had political valence. If local chronography as patronized by a local dynasty could be said to legitimize that dynasty's claim to rule (either through delegation, loyalty or conquest), local prosopography can be said to chart how these local élites outfitted their economic capital with the symbolic capital of prestige knowledge.[21]

[21] For the view that the *madrasas* were about social prestige, rather than the transmission of knowledge, see M. Chamberlain, *Knowledge and Social Practice in Medieval Damascus, 1190–1350* (Cambridge, 1994).

CHAPTER 8

Historians and the truth

In the preceding chapter we saw that Muslim historians gave God an important role in their understanding of the world and its history. That this is so does not mean that they were indifferent to the problems inherent in describing the past, and it certainly does not make them bad historians. If organizing narrative into some kind of chronological scheme was what made an author an historian, having a real sense of the relative weight to accord to various kinds of evidence is one of the things that made him a good one (at least to us). By this standard, there is no shortage of very fine ones. Since Muslim historians are sometimes the subject of intemperate censure or uncritical acclaim, I devote this chapter to charting a path somewhere between these two extremes.

Documents and attitudes

We can begin by noting that our historians made claims to be writing in a critical spirit. One early chronographer (al-Yaᶜqūbī) says quite plainly that he writes in part because his predecessors disagreed about the *ḥadīth* and *akhbār* that they were transmitting. Much later, Ibn Ḥajar al-ᶜAsqalānī takes one of his predecessors to task for having integrated strings of entire pages from another historian's work without properly understanding the text, at times even falling into gross error. Ibn al-Qalānisī, who stands between al-Yaᶜqūbī and Ibn Ḥajar, explains that 'I have completed the narrative of events set forth in this chronicle, and I have arranged them in order and taken precautions against error and rashness of judgment and careless slips in the materials, which I have transcribed from the mouths of trustworthy persons, and have transmitted after exerting myself to make the fullest investigations so as to verify them.' Now all these fine words are programmatic, and although it is certainly true, to paraphrase one historian of France, that historians are about as trustworthy guides to their work as politicians are to their policies, there can be no question that something of a critical spirit underlies a great deal of Islamic historiography, especially in the later period.[1]

For many historians were alert to contradictory evidence, to fabrication, exaggeration and bias, and to the impossibility of some kinds of historical knowledge. 'As far as I can tell'; 'according to what I have been told'; 'this report is sounder than that one'; 'so-and-so claims, but …'; 'such is what is related, but only God knows' – these and many, many other similar phrases are nearly ubiquitous in the tradition, especially in chronography. Al-Ṣafadī (d. 1363) rejected a conquest-era treaty as forged because its date ran afoul of what he knew about conquest chronology (the treaty was dated before the city in question had fallen to the Muslims). For all but Israelite history, Ibn Ḥazm (d. 1063) quite sensibly sets the limit on historical knowledge at the conquests of Alexander the Great (since corroboration was impossible), and makes historical knowledge contingent upon written transmission. Ibn Kathīr (d. 1373), a Syrian historian writing in the heyday of Mamluk historiography, was aware that the Isrāʾīliyyāt – extra-Qurʾānic stories about the Hebrew prophets – were of dubious value, and he reassures his reader that he will relate only those that are in accord with the truth of the Qurʾān and the *sunna* (since the truth of the Qurʾān and *sunna* was incontrovertible). The same diarist, who tells of wild beasts, dead mothers and suckling babies, knows very well that reports can be exaggerated, and this is why he adduces the testimony of newly arrived visitors to corroborate rumours of an earthquake. Here, as elsewhere, eyewitness testimony could trump news that had travelled by word of mouth. On the basis of his own experience there, Abū Shāma (d. 1267) corrects Ibn al-Athīr on his understanding of the topography of Mecca; much as one might go about it nowadays, the same historian debunks the fabricated genealogy of the first Fatimid caliph, ʿUbayd Allāh (d. 934), by referring to books of Alid genealogy.[2]

In fact, for every historian who suppresses a fact or point of view, one can usually find another who provides it; and for every historian with a taste for the miraculous and the legendary, one can usually find another with a nose for documentary materials (or another who embraces both). It is not even too much to say that an archival ethos – the desire to record and preserve copies of important documents – underpins a great deal of historical writing. This feature of the tradition seems about as old as the tradition itself. We have already seen that the 'Constitution of Medina' found a place in the *sīra* of Ibn Isḥāq, and a variety of treaties, letters and speeches found their way into the conquest tradition of the late eighth and ninth centuries. Now many of these are clearly inauthentic, since they

[1] Al-Yaʿqūbī, *Taʾrīkh*, ii, p. 3; for Ibn Ḥajar, his *Inbāʾ al-ghumr*, i, p. 3; for Ibn al-Qalānisī, his *Dhayl Taʾrīkh Dimashq* (Beirut, 1908), p. 283, but I draw upon a slightly modified translation by H.A.R. Gibb, *The Damascus Chronicle of the Crusades* (London, 1932; reprinted, 1967), p. 10; the French historian is Theodore Zeldin in R.J. Evans, *In Defense of History* (New York and London, 1997); for a discussion of a particularly misleading introduction, B. Hamad, 'History and biography', *Arabica* 45 (1998), pp. 215–232.

[2] For al-Ṣafadī, see *al-Wāfī bi'l-wafayāt*, i, pp. 44f.; for Ibn Ḥazm, the *Rasāʾil Ibn Ḥazm*, iv, p. 79; for Ibn Kathīr, his *Bidāya,* i, p. 6; for the diarist, Makdisi, 'Autograph diary, I', pp. 244/256; for Abū Shāma, his *Kitāb al-Rawḍatayn*, i^2, pp. 349f. and 510.

manifest a number of anachronisms: the historiographic vision of men living in what had become a relatively well ordered and bureaucratic empire (the ninth century) imposed elaborate and formulaic diplomatics upon a seventh-century world that was naïve of anything more than a very modest documentary culture. Thanks to the secretaries and bureaucrats who contributed so much to the tradition, particularly from the eleventh century, the flow of authentic documentary material into historical sources would grow altogether stronger as history unfolded: even those who kept themselves at some distance from the ruling court frequently cite official documents *in extenso*, the most spectacular example from this period being the documents drawn up by Hārūn al-Rashīd for his (ill-fated) succession. According to the principal accounts, when the documents were first raised up to be hung for storage in the Kaᶜba in 186/802 (one account has them put in 'cylinders of silver'), they fell upon the ground; and this, it is said, presaged the breakdown of the succession arrangements – the civil war that would erupt between Hārūn's two sons soon after his death in 809.[3]

So official correspondence (both originals and archived copies), dispatches, and documents of various sorts (diplomas of investiture, promissory notes, contracts, deeds, petitions, commendations) are frequently quoted by historian-bureaucrats and historian-*qāḍī*s, whose office gave them free access to material of this kind. Assessing the authenticity of this material is difficult, but not impossible. On the one hand, the presence of documentary material in historical narrative can often be explained in literary terms, since it can lend authority to the well-placed writer, and change the texture of what might otherwise be monotonous indirect speech. This said, we slight our historians if we interpret their documentary material *exclusively* in terms of rhetoric. When one tenth-century *qāḍī*-historian quotes extensively from property deeds written in the early eighth, he is certainly showing off his access to an archive of documents to which he, as *qāḍī*, enjoyed special access, but he is also highlighting the propertied background of one of his city's most prominent families – that is, adducing evidence to explain their prominent role in city politics. For his biography of Saladin, ᶜImād al-Dīn al-Iṣfahānī (d. 1201) drew on his diary and a variety of memos, documents and private and semi-private correspondence (in the wake of one battle in 1179, he spent the night recording the names of the prisoners taken). For a trained bureaucrat like ᶜImād al-Dīn, recording and documenting were intrinsic to writing itself. Ibn al-ᶜAdīm (d. 1262) quotes at some length from a decree announcing the remission of taxes in year 407/1016, which was in his possession, 'headed', we are

[3] For the succession documents, I draw on al-Ṭabarī, *Taʾrīkh*, iii, pp. 651ff., which is translated by M. Fishbein as *The ᶜAbbāsid State in Equilibrium* (Albany, 1989; al-Ṭabarī translation, vol. xxx), pp. 179ff.; and al-Azdī al-Mawṣilī, *Taʾrīkh al-Mawṣil*, p. 302; for a discussion of all the principal accounts, see R. Kimber, 'Hārūn al-Rashīd's Meccan settlement of AH 186/AD 802', *Occasional Papers of the School of Abbasid Studies*, 1 (1986), pp. 55–79; for documents and archives in general, Cahen, *Introduction*, pp. 51ff. and Humphreys, *Islamic History*, pp. 40ff.; for some background, R.G. Khouri, ed., *Urkunden und Urkundenformulare im klassischen Altertum und in den orientalischen Kulturen* (Heidelberg, 1999).

reassured, 'by the signature sign (*ᶜalāma*) of al-Ḥākim'. That it was a piece of propaganda issued by the (Ismāᶜīlī Shīᶜite) al-Ḥākim, caliph of the Fatimid state (ruled in Egypt, 969–1071) – the 'Prophetic dynasty' in the language of the decree – did not stop this (Sunni) historian from sharing it with his readers. In a world where official announcements were not only read out in the mosques, but pasted on mosque and market walls and along city streets, this is what we might expect. On some occasions we can even compare a copy of the original document with its reproduction in a history; such is the case, for example, for one historian of the Fatimids. Treaties between Muslims and Byzantines, and Muslims and Crusaders, have been culled from the ninth-, tenth- and eleventh-century tradition, and no fewer than eleven treaties written on behalf of two Mamluk Sultans (al-Ẓāhir Baybars, rg. 1260–1277; and Qalāwūn, rg. 1280–1290) have also been isolated in the later tradition, six of them coming from Ibn ᶜAbd al-Ẓāhir's royal biography of the latter. They all shed a bright and direct light on the Mamluks' policies towards, and diplomatic relations with, Armenian, Byzantine and Western Christians.[4]

That so much documentary material was copied into the historiographic tradition is immensely important, since it makes available to modern historians precisely the detailed and official documentation that they are so regularly trained to crave, but which, in their original forms, are in extremely small supply. That the *originals* were produced in massive numbers is beyond question: a wide range of government bureaus, both military and civil, in addition to private and semi-private institutions such as mosques, *madrasa*s and libraries, all generated mountains of documents. Precisely when institutions were created to house archived documents is difficult to say. As far as the state is concerned, the tradition itself generally credits the caliph ᶜUmar (rg. 634–644) with putting in place archival practices, but ᶜUmar is credited with altogether too many administrative initiatives, and one might rather think that they belong to a later period: copying official correspondence, according to some sources, was instituted by Ziyād b. Abīhi, governor in the East (Iraq and greater Iran) during the reign of Muᶜāwiya b. Abī Sufyān (661–680). They were certainly in place by the early Abbasid period, when the imperial bureaucracy grew rapidly in size and complexity. In any case, aside from a handful of exceptions (notably documents from St. Catherine's Monastery in the Sinai, and Mamluk

[4] On documents and rhetoric, see Meisami, *Persian Historiography,* pp. 290f.; the local historian and *qāḍī* is al-Azdī al-Mawṣilī, *Taʾrīkh al-Mawṣil,* p. 214; Richards, 'ᶜImād al-Dīn al-Iṣfahānī', esp. pp. 138ff.; also M.S. Khan, 'The use of letters and documents in the contemporary history of Miskawaih', *IQ* 14 (1970), pp. 41–49; for Ibn al-ᶜAdīm, his *Zubdat al-ḥalab min taʾrīkh Ḥalab* (Damascus, 1968), i, p. 214; and, for the Fatimid historian, M. Brett, 'Fatimid historiography: a case study – the quarrel with the Zirids, 1048–58', in Morgan, ed., *Medieval Historical Writing*, pp. 47ff.; for the official posters, Abū Shāma, *Kitāb al-Rawḍatayn*, i^2, p. 513 (the work is filled with excerpted documents); for how one historian got his access to official documents, al-Balawī, *Sīrat Aḥmad b. Ṭūlūn*, pp. 100f.; also Rosenthal, *History*, pp. 118ff.; for Muslim-Byzantine treaties, A. Kaplony, *Konstantinopel und Damaskus: Gesandtschaften und Verträge zwischen Kaisern und Kalifen 639–750* (Berlin, 1996); for the Crusader treaties, M.A. Köhler, *Allianzen und Verträge zwischen fränkischen und islamischen Herrschern im Vorderen Orient* (Berlin, 1991); for the Mamluk treaties, P.M. Holt, *Early Mamluk Diplomacy (1260–1290): Treaties of Baybars and Qalāwūn with Christian Rulers* (Leiden, 1995).

Jerusalem and Cairo), precious little survives from before the Ottoman period, and what has survived has generally been discovered piecemeal, rather than intact.[5]

Why is this so? The answer is in part environmental, in part economic, and in part even cultural. We have already seen that the medium of which the documents came to be made – wood fibres pressed into leaves – was fragile; although paper may have been cheaper and handier than parchment and papyrus, which is why it replaced them fairly early on, in hot and humid climates it is not nearly as durable. (It was not always so cheap as to make recycling unattractive, however; scholars and bureaucrats alike often reused sheets of paper by scraping away used layers.) Paper also burns well, and in places such as Syria and Egypt, where fuel was frequently in short supply, we can understand why great loads of paperwork could be fed into ovens for cooking or into fires for heating, as we know they were. Official documents very frequently also fell victim to the disruption and violence that accompanied dynastic change: new dynasties might abandon old capitals for new ones, and newly hired bureaucrats might destroy or abandon their predecessors' work. One reads, for example, that Hārūn al-Rashīd's son, al-Amīn, burned (or ordered burned, or tore up) the succession documents that set out how he was to rule alongside his brother al-Maʾmūn. Finally, cultural attitudes may have been at work, too, since the archives (such as they were) of private or semi-private institutions among the Christian communities of the Near East (such as St. Catherine's) seem to have fared better than those of contemporaneous Muslim institutions. From this perspective, it might be said that one of the functions of historiography was to archive in literary form records that were otherwise considered expendable.

In the preceding I have spoken about our historians' critical spirit in great generalities, and there was naturally some change over time. The biographer who took 'precautions against error and rashness of judgment' is from the twelfth century, and many contemporary historians of this and later periods seem to have drawn on their own experience in the field to write with a clear-headedness all too lacking in many of the bookish historians of the ninth and tenth centuries, who usually wrote about events of the seventh and eighth centuries. Traditionist backgrounds may have made for decent *isnād*s, but, spectacular exceptions aside, it gave these historians precious little insight into how battles were won or lost and how politics actually worked. As far as detail and texture are concerned, nothing written during the first three or four centuries of Islam can rival Ibn Shaddād's gripping accounts of the siege of Acre in 1191 or the conquest of Ṣahyūn. He was there and watched as the Muslim army broke into the bailey of the Crusaders'

[5] For Ziyād, see al-Yaʿqūbī, *Taʾrīkh*, ii, p. 279 (*waḍaʿa al-nusakh li'l-kutub*); for the thin evidence for early archiving, M.M. Bravmann, 'The state archives in the early Islamic period', *Arabica* 15 (1968), pp. 87–89, reprinted in his *The Spiritual Background of Early Islam* (Leiden, 1972); for an overview of the St. Catherine's material, H.R. Roemer, 'The Sinai documents and the history of the Islamic world: state of the art – future tasks', in W. al-Qāḍī, ed., *Studia Arabica et Islamica: Festschrift for Iḥsān ʿAbbās on his Sixtieth Birthday* (Beirut, 1981), pp. 381–391 (samples from one period can be found in S.M. Stern, *Fāṭimid Decrees: Original Documents from the Fāṭimid Chancery* [London, 1964]); also D.P. Little, 'Documents as a source for Mamluk history', *MSR* 1 (1997), pp. 1–13.

stronghold, abandoned only moments before: 'I was watching our men seize the cooking pots in which food had just been prepared, and eat while battling against the castle'. With this kind of material now being written (and it is not coincidental that military manuals only become commonplace in this period), we can actually write real military history. Not only do battles come into clearer focus, but politicians do, too. Ibn al-Furāt (d. 1405) for instance, writes incisively of al-Malik al-Muᶜaẓẓam, the Ayyubid ruler of Egypt (rg. 1218–1227). Great things had been expected of him, but he was fickle, undiplomatic and impolitic; account after account is adduced, all of which provide ample reason why his Mamluk retainers would eventually assassinate him, an event for which Ibn al-Furāt provides no fewer than three versions. For all that his end was poignant, it was entirely deserved, since he had failed to offer the rewards and patronage that the political system required, and, abandoned by those whom he had abandoned, he was slaughtered and left unburied for three days, 'swollen on the bank of the [Nile] river without anyone daring to help him'. Earlier historians often thought the same of their subjects, but rarely did they make their views so clear.[6]

Abū al-Fidāᵓ (d. 1331), to take another example, was from a princely family of the Syrian city of Hama, and after years of political jockeying, secured the governorship of his home town in 1310; within two years, he began to rule autonomously, even receiving the title of 'sulṭān' from the caliph. He was a witness to many of the events he narrates, and being an historian and man of politics himself, was a keen observer of men, their ambitions, glory, incompetence and greed. Thus we read that the Mongols defeated a Mamluk army on 23 December 1299 because '… the [Muslim] force was very deficient through bad management and much corruption …'; the defeat of 1305 is explained in similar ways: 'Qashtamur [a Mamluk commander sent by the governor of Aleppo] was weak witted, a poor organizer and fuddled with wine, so he failed to control his troops, did not get intelligence of the army, and underrated them …' Abū al-Fidāᵓ makes ample room for the mundane factors that a military historian might nowadays adduce in explaining defeat. Once again, there is no doubt that these same factors were frequently at play in earlier battles, but, limited as we are to narratives penned by lawyers and traditionists, we would hardly know so from the texts themselves.[7]

[6] I draw the translation of Bahāᵓ al-Dīn Ibn Shaddād's *al-Nawādir al-sulṭāniyya* from Richards, *The Rare and Excellent History of Saladin*, p. 85 (for the original, *Sīrat Ṣalāh al-Dīn*, p. 91: *la-qad kuntu ushāshid al-nās wa-hum yaᵓkhudhūn al-qudūr…*); for photographs and plans of Ṣahyūn, R.C. Smail, *Crusading Warfare (1097–1193)* (Cambridge, 1956); for writing military history in this period, M. Shatzmiller, 'The Crusades and Islamic warfare – a re-evaluation', *DI* 69 (1992), pp. 247–288; for al-Muᶜaẓẓam, Ibn al-Furāt, *Taᵓrīkh al-duwal wa'l-mulūk*, ed. and trans. by U. and M.C. Lyons as *Ayyubids, Mamlukes and Crusaders* (Cambridge, 1971), i, pp. 39ff./ii, pp. 32ff.

[7] For Abū al-Fidāᵓ and his battle scene, see P.M. Holt, tr., *The Memoirs of a Syrian Prince: Abu'l-Fidāᵓ, Sultan of Ḥamāh (672–732/1273–1331)* (Wiesbaden, 1983), pp. 35 and 44f. (the translation is his) and D.P. Little, *An Introduction to Mamlūk Historiography* (Wiesbaden, 1970), pp. 142ff.

Classical conventions and modern expectations

For all their insights, Abū al-Fidā᾽ and Ibn al-Furāt differ from the military and political historians who now practise. This is because they remained loyal to the God-centred view of the world that I described earlier, subject to the frequently extreme limitations of their evidence, and committed to the ethical and didactic function of history writing. In other words, although pre-modern Muslim historians may have frequently exercised sound judgment, striven hard to secure the best sources, and often aspired to accurate representations of the past, they remained pre-modern monotheists. Constrained by a tradition that was naïve of the lofty ideals and standards that had not yet been set, they wrote according to conventions organized principally for the purposes of *illustration* rather than *explanation.* I have made this claim already; here I should like to make it clearer by briefly discussing three prominent features of the tradition: literary patterning, miracles and dreams.

We saw that ingredients of pre- and early Islamic history, such as the succession of Arabian prophets and the career of Muḥammad himself, owe something to mythic patterns already discernible in the Hebrew Bible, and that, just as *sīra* could be modelled upon early monotheistic narrative, so, too, could later chronography be modelled upon this narrative or upon *sīra* itself: al-Amīn and al-Ma᾽mun, brothers and rivals to succeed their father Hārūn al-Rashīd, are made to bear some resemblance in the chronography of the tenth century to Cain and Abel of the Hebrew Bible. Similarly, a Mamluk–Mongol battle could be directly patterned after one of the Prophet's battles as described in the *Sīra*, when God sent soldier-angels to fight alongside him against the godless Meccans. The right flank of the army under the leadership of Sayf al-Dīn Qabjaq (a Mamluk commander) falters and breaks before the Mongols, but God, here almost literally *deus ex machina*, comes to the rescue by sending 'His help' to the centre and left. The Mongols are predictably routed. Now this is obviously an attractive theme (God helps His favoured to defeat His enemies) – and not just to Muslim historians: the Israelites had been helped out of Egypt by an angel, and Christian historians, too, were wont to enrol angels and saints in Christian armies (in the *Chronicle* of Alfonso III, God goes so far as to redirect Muslim arrows heading for a shrine of the Virgin). The theme thus holds out the promise for all manner of allusion and development, particularly when we consider the prominent role of warfare in politics and historical narrative. In this case, where a Muslim army battles a non-Muslim army, the scene being narrated in the historian's third person, the debt of the chronographer (Abū al-Fidā᾽) to the biographer (Ibn Isḥāq) is almost blindingly obvious, if not necessarily direct, because by Abū al-Fidā᾽'s time, helping angels had become stereotypical in warfare narrative, and in some sense even mythic. In other cases, things are less obvious, but no less effective. Usāma b. Munqidh (d. 1188) recounts in his memoirs how he found himself precariously perched on a mountain side, struggling to keep both himself and his mount from tumbling down its steep slopes. Suddenly a man appeared, who miraculously saved him: he 'came down to me from the mountain and held me by the hand, my other hand holding the pack horse, until he got me to the summit. No, by Allah, I did not know who the man was and never saw him again … He was none other than an angel whom Allah, moved by his compassion toward me, sent to my aid'. Here Usāma assembles the account of his 'experience' with pieces that form part of the very structure of our stereotype – Muslim armies fought armies, (righteous) men fought their fear, and God could offer his succour to whomever He wished. Literary patterning was a potent device, which, provided the theme in question was suitably mythic, could imprint itself across the historiographical forms.[8]

By now it should come as no surprise that God (or one of his proxies) might appear as an agent in the historical process. God could, if He desired, interrupt His silent directing of human affairs in any number of ways, and amongst these, miracles were about as useful to pre-modern historians as they are distressing to their modern readers. Miraculous things *could* happen (they are numerous in the Qurʾān, where they are called 'signs', and later, in connection with holy men and saints, where they are called *karāmāt*, 'tokens of nobility'). And they happened to serve God's purpose, which on the written page was to edify and inspire. A single, complex example can suffice.[9]

A twelfth-century Shīʿite history recounts the travels of the severed head of al-Ḥusayn b. ʿAlī, Muḥammad's grandson martyred at Karbalāʾ (in southern Iraq), which found its way to a monastery near Antioch (in northern Syria). According to this version of the story (there are others), the head, though hidden inside a bag, still projected a radiant column of light into the night sky, and its discovery by a monk attending a call of nature occasioned the near instantaneous conversion to Islam of the monastery's 700 monks. The monastery was accordingly refitted as a mosque. The nice story struck several chords because the miracle was compound, its result providential and the characters multi-valent. For severed heads are supposed to decay (so much so that they were frequently perfumed) and are not supposed to cast beams of light towards heaven. This one not only cast such a beam, but triggered a mass conversion (the providential result) by 'illuminating' to Christian holy men the truth of Islam in general, and the truth of Ḥusayn's holiness in particular. In the context of this Shīʿite history, it thus forms part of a larger argument for the Shīʿite cause, in which Ḥusayn's failed rebellion and martyrdom represent a crucial moment. Because sympathy for the slain Ḥusayn extended to many non-Shīʿites, it would have had broader appeal as well, especially since it makes the result of Ḥusayn's death (his severed head) the agent of conversion to Islam, and implied no political activism on the part of his followers. Here it is

[8] The Israelites are aided by angels in Exodus 14:19 and 23:20; on the Christian parallel, N. Baynes, 'The supernatural defenders of Constantinople', *Byzantine Studies and Other Essays* (London, 1955), pp. 248–260; for God redirecting arrows, Wolf, *Conquerors*, p. 168; the *Kitāb al-Iʿtibār* of Usāma b. Munqidh has been translated several times; I draw on P.K. Hitti's *An Arab-Syrian Gentleman and Warrior in the Period of the Crusades* (New York, 1929; reprinted Princeton, 1987), p. 123.

[9] A useful summary of miracles in the Qurʾān can be found in P. Antes, *Prophetenwunder in der Ašʿarīya bis al-Ġazālī (Algazel)* (Freiburg im Breisgau, 1970), pp. 21ff.; see also *EI*², '*Muʿdjiza*' (Wensinck) and *karāma* (Gardet).

significant that those converting – those 'seeing' – were not merely Christians, but Christians of deep piety and religious authority. As such, they echo the priests and holy men of the early Islamic tradition, who are frequently given by historians to witness and reveal Islamic truths: a common *sīra* account has a monk named Baḥīrā recognize the 'signs of prophethood' on the child Muḥammad, and a less common anecdote has a priest prophesy that ᶜUmar would one day ascend to the caliphate. Finally, the legend also furnishes an appealing (if apocryphal) explanation for one mosque's origins, a common enough problem, since many mosques occupied abandoned and confiscated churches. In this last feature, the refitting of monastery into mosque functions as a metaphor for religious claims: Christianity (represented metonymically by churches) was made obsolete by Islam (represented by mosques).[10]

This multi-layered legend is a spectacular case, but God need not operate in such spectacular fashion. He might quietly reveal His will in dreams, and these, too, were extremely useful to Muslim historians. A fairly prosaic example is the dream reported by Tughril Beg (d. 1063), sultan of the great Saljuk dynasty that ruled much of Iran and Iraq from the middle of the eleventh century to the coming of the Mongols in the middle of the thirteenth. The description of the dream itself is included in the account of Tughril Beg's death.

> When I was in Khurāsān, I had a dream that I was carried up to Heaven. I was in a mist, unable to see a thing, but I could smell something sweet. Then I was addressed: 'You are close to the Creator. Make a request, so that it can be granted to you.' I said to myself, 'I shall request a long life.' The voice said: 'You have seventy years.' I then said: 'O Lord, it is not enough for me.' The reply, again, was 'You have seventy years.' 'O Lord, it is not enough for me,' I repeated. And again, the words: 'You have seventy years.'

The reader is then informed that Tughril Beg died at the precise age of 70.

Much as popular Freudianism holds that we are most truthful to ourselves in our dreams, medieval Muslims held that dreams revealed truths, especially future truths – that is, prophecies. Accordingly, they developed an elaborate science of dream interpretation (oneiromancy) in order to squeeze as much meaning as possible from these dreams. Tughril Beg's dream includes none of the metaphoric language that this science was equipped to translate, and its meaning is fairly straightforward: however great and extensive his power in this world, the Sultan was at the mercy of God, who, having ordained his lifetime, naturally possessed precise knowledge of its length. Other dreams are cast in considerably more metaphoric language, and reveal truths of much greater significance than an individual's life span. Ibn al-Dawādārī (d. 1336), for example, describes the vision dreamt by Chingiz Khān (Genghis Khan), which foretold the Mongols' defeat by the Mamluks in the battle of ᶜAyn Jālūt (3 September 1260): the great Mongol leader, standing on the eastern borders of China, witnesses the sun set in the west.

[10] For Ḥusayn's head, see Ibn al-ᶜImrānī, *al-Inbāʾ fī taʾrīkh al-khulafāʾ*, pp. 53ff.; cf., for another version, the (Persian) *Tārīkh-i Sīstān* (Tehran, 1994), pp. 52f.; and Meisami, *Persian Historiography*, p. 112; for Baḥīrā, Hoyland, *Seeing Islam*, pp. 476ff.

In another version, the defeat is symbolized by dregs in a drinking vessel. Two short chapters in Ibn al-Jawzī's biography of ᶜUmar (rg. 634–644) are devoted to the dreams the caliph had and to some of those in which he himself appeared.

In prophesying the future, these dreams are typical, and so, too, in form (particularly in Tughril Beg's thrice-repeated request) and orthodoxy. Having visions while awake generally made one a holy man – that is, a miracle maker – or a prophet, which, in a world that the *ᶜulamāᵓ* insisted was post-Prophetic, meant being a heretic. By contrast, hearing God while asleep simply made one human. If there is a wrinkle in the account of Tughril Beg's dream, it is only that the number 70, much like the number 700 that appeared in the conversion legend, usually functions as a topos (pl. topoi; see below), a cliché-like motif that customarily has figurative, rather than literal, meaning. By '700 monks' the intended reader would have understood 'a great number', and we should, too. Here Tughril Beg – or, more precisely, his narrator – took it to denote a precise number: 70 years of life was not enough for him. Of course, whether Tughril Beg ever dreamt this dream is unknowable. One presumes that Ibn al-Athīr, following his informant, al-Kundurī, thought so, but since Tughril Beg related it privately to al-Kundurī, there is no question of corroborating it; even if we did possess other purported revelations, one could not preclude literary borrowing. That is as far as one can take the question of veracity, and this is why it is more important to recognize that dreams were an extremely useful literary device for historians, particularly those working within a tradition that otherwise eschewed precisely the private, reflective – at times, even confessional – mode of self-narration that dreams expressed. It was in this way that fears, aspirations and motivations could be imputed to historical actors, and even how institutions could be legitimized.[11]

Dreams were just one of many narrative devices that served our historians. Because the function of history was principally to exemplify truths and teach lessons, it should come as no surprise that real licence was taken in historical narration. In addition to the features I have outlined above, there is a long catalogue of devices, practices and conventions, which were all as useful to medieval historians as they are deeply problematic for modern ones determined to recover what they trust is an original 'kernel' of truth. Accounts might be given anachronistic details and moralizing endings that appealed to their readers. They may also contain 'topoi', images or passages that occur so frequently that they can only be counted as narrative motifs upon which inventive historians might draw in order to fill out and spice up what might otherwise be fairly lean and prosaic accounts. Conquest army after army has its champion 'cross over' before battle to meet his adversary, shout 'God is great!', and ride elephants into battle; no matter how well

[11] For Tughril Beg's dream, see Ibn al-Athīr, *al-Kāmil*, x, p. 26; for Chingiz Khān's, Haarmann, 'Arabic in speech, Turkish in lineage', p. 111; for ᶜUmar's, Ibn al-Jawzī, *Sīrat ᶜUmar b. al-Khaṭṭāb* (Cairo, n.d.), pp. 161ff.; on dreams and dream interpretation, G.E. von Grunebaum and R. Caillois, eds., *Le rêve et les sociétés humaines* (Paris, 1967); Malti-Douglas, 'Dreams', pp. 142ff.; and L. Kinberg, 'The legitimization of the *madhāhib* through dreams', *Arabica* 32 (1985), pp. 47–79; for 'dreams of sovereignty', Mottahedeh, *Loyalty and Leadership*, pp. 69ff.

trained, real armies do not act so formulaically. Dialogue was invented as a matter of course, and conventionally recorded in a register of language so lofty as to be unutterable by human tongue: colloquial dialects – that is, the languages that people actually used in the everyday speech – only appear with any frequency in the chronography of the Mamluk period, when the *ᶜajāʾib*, 'wondrous miracles', also seem to grow in prominence. Letters and speeches were drafted by (usually) well-meaning historians to be placed in the mouths of caliphs and governors. Numbers were often used stereotypically, four, seven and eleven and their multiples being particular favourites; they were also routinely inflated, with the result that soldiers frequently appear in the hundreds of thousands. What are we to make of an account that has five Khārijites assassinate a governor protected by 1,500 armed guards? The more closely modern historians examine our sources, the more distortions of 'reality' they uncover, and although this is especially true of the early historical tradition, when the events were both remoter in time and fuller in significance, contemporary history often follows the same conventions. As one modern historian has put it, 'accuracy as to "fact" was much less important than validity as to life-vision'.[12]

A great deal has been written about these and related problems; here it is enough to say that about none of these 'departures' from historical reality should we get too exercised. For whatever position was granted to God's role in human history, it is in the nature of pre-modern historiography that the transformation of event witnessed or remembered into story recorded and transmitted was perilous: the absence of God (or one of His works, such as miracles) can scarcely guarantee the reliability of a given historical report. No reasonable historian doubts that the Battle of Hastings (14 October 1066) or Battle of Ṣiffīn (mid-657) took place, but describing these in any detail, even more so explaining them, turns on so many imponderables that no reasonable historian would claim to possess the full 'truth' of what happened. And the limitations apply, *a fortiori*, to less public events: it is hard to think that we shall ever know if Eleanor of Aquitaine (d. 1204) or ᶜĀʾisha bt. Abī Bakr (d. 678), the Prophet's second wife, committed the adultery their critics charged they committed, what with '... some possible innocent activity giving rise to whispered rumours which would soon congeal into hard certainty, itself prompting fictional embellishment until any truth remained only as a distinct echo ...' 'Historical truth in the Middle Ages', the same historian of Eleanor has said, 'was a perishable commodity.' Or, as a biographer of Crazy Horse put it, 'fact withers in the heat of myth'.[13]

[12] For some conquest topoi and forgeries, see Noth/Conrad, *Early Arabic Historical Tradition*, pp. 109ff.; E. Manzano-Moreno, 'Oriental «topoi» in Andalusian historical sources', *Arabica* 39 (1992), pp. 42–58; the Khārijite account is in al-Yaᶜqūbī, *Taʾrīkh*, ii, p. 383; the modern historian is Hodgson in his 'Two pre-modern Muslim historians'.

[13] The quotation and material on Eleanor come from D.D.R. Owen, *Eleanor of Aquitaine: Queen and Legend* (Oxford and Cambridge, Mass., 1993), pp. 103 and 160; the most recent examination of the *ḥadīth al-ifk*, which recounts ᶜĀʾisha's alleged adultery, is in Schoeler, *Charakter und Authentie*; the biographer is L. McMurtry, *Crazy Horse* (New York, 1999), p. 5.

So the problem is not just that history was God-centred, nor simply that historians had to rely upon informants with poor memories or axes to grind. It is in the nature of representation and history writing that these 'departures' from historical reality take place. Even now, when we hold that history is a discrete discipline, one founded upon rules of evidence and rhetoric, and aspiring towards an objective accounting of events passed, no matter how good the sources and thorough the research, historical narrative is *always* informed, to a greater or lesser extent, by the historian's subjective vision and imagination. Bad historians can be careless or heedless; they may ask the wrong questions or follow red herrings; driven by animus or blind adulation, they can distort, invent, suppress and even lie. Good historians do relatively few of these things, and the result is history that more faithfully describes and more reasonably explains things. (I leave aside the view that historians should advocate for political causes, even when this advocacy comes at the expense of professional standards of evidence and argument.) Try as they might to 'record' or 'to let the sources speak for themselves', good historians must still make choices and judgments about their topic, about what is important and what is not, and these invariably reflect the individual and social circumstances in which they find themselves.

Some critics go so far as saying that the historian's project is necessarily a project of creating as much as preserving, that in the very acts of recording and representing the past in intelligible, meaningful and useful forms, Israelite historians, Classical historians, Christian historians and Muslim historians were compelled to draw upon imaginative resources. That those who did so deliberately were held in disrepute by those who did not is in this regard unimportant; then, as now, writing arrant falsehoods – *lying* – was generally held to be beyond the pale. So too, at least for the moment, is it unimportant to calibrate the scale with which one is to weigh the possibility of historical reconstruction: suffice it to say, the later the period, the more probable the reconstruction usually becomes. What matters is that imposing narrative form upon disparate materials drawn from memory, oral and written reports and documents, is itself a creative act, and the techniques the historian uses to tell his story, such as characterizing, handling time, introducing and concluding, are akin – some would say *identical* – to those used by fiction writers to tell theirs. Where does one draw the line between non-fictional historical narrative which relies upon storytelling techniques that are usually associated with imaginative literature, and historical fiction, in which characters and stories are grounded in past events, particularly if the two projects share a common purpose – to edify, entertain or illustrate what their authors hold to be truths? As a practising historian, I am inclined to think that a line should be drawn, whereas a literary critic – that is, someone who has no stake (professional or otherwise) in drawing it – may not, or may draw it differently. But it is surely to the credit of literary critics that one is now aware that the lines are drawn at least in part in the act of reading and in the formation of 'interpretive communities', who impose readings upon texts. In sum, it seems to me incontrovertible that the past is unalterably gone, and that the success with which it is conjured up depends as much on some kind of collusion between the writer and reader as it does on the quality of sources upon which the writer originally worked.[14]

Some historians are reluctant to recognize that these lines are drawn by readers as well as by writers, insisting that history is different in essential ways from imaginative literature, and holding to a definition of history-as-science. These historians are usually the same who pronounce on what history should or should not be, or how it should or should not be conducted: 'History is past politics and politics is present history'; 'Study problems, not periods'; 'Study first the histories, not the history'. Prescriptions such as these can be useful enough, but they often say more about those prescribing them than they do any historical truths. They might be taken with a grain of salt. In any case, those prescribing and proscribing are now in a declining minority, and the more reasonable, when pressed, propose that history is a science only in the weakest sense of the word, a craft that differs from fiction writing in some of its aspirations and conventions, but shares a great deal with other forms of narrative. Medieval Muslim historians, who were in many cases less dogmatic than the eighteenth- and nineteenth-century Europeans who invented modern 'scientific' historiography, would have agreed.[15]

[14] For a programmatic treatment, see H. White, 'The historical text as literary artifact', in R.H. Canary and H. Kozicki, eds., *The Writing of History: Literary Form and Historical Reconstruction* (Madison, 1978), pp. 41–62; also D. Harlan, 'Intellectual history and the return of literature', *AHR* 94 (1989), pp. 581–609, and J. Demos, 'In search of reasons for historians to read novels', *AHR* 103 (1998), pp. 1526–1529; on falsehoods, C. Behan McCullagh, 'Bias in historical description, interpretation and explanation', *History and Theory* 39 (2000), pp. 39–66; cf. Leder, ed., *Story-telling in the Framework of Non-fictional Arabic Literature*; a useful and exceptionally clear overview of the issues can be found in R. Chartier, 'Texts, printing, readings', in L. Hunt, ed., *The New Cultural History* (Berkeley and Los Angeles, 1989), pp. 154–175.

[15] For history as a weak craft, see Evans, *In Defense of History*, p. 62.

PART III

How historians worked

CHAPTER 9

Vocations and professions

We have seen how traditionism and traditionalism conditioned how Muslim historians understood and described the past, how their work fared relative to other disciplines, and how, starting in Ayyubid and Mamluk Egypt and Syria, the traditionalist stranglehold on historiography was broken. It was in this period that historians broke new ground and began to manifest some signs of their belated professionalization: not only self-confidence and assertiveness vis-à-vis the traditionalist establishment, but petty jealousies and rivalries, too. Here we shall move from the texts to the historians who wrote them. For in addition to ideas, time, energy, writing tools and access to historical resources – the people, books, archives, and material evidence that form the basis of research – writing history requires financial resources of one kind or another. What was the social background of our historians, and how did they support themselves in a culture without university history departments? Answers to these questions can shed some light on the shape of the historiographic tradition, and on its conservatism and dynamism. We can begin by recalling how comparable historians outside of the Islamic tradition operated.

In the Christian east and west of our period, historians were drawn from élite families in general, and from the clergy, the legal profession, the court or other kinds of state service (such as it was) in particular. It was typically as clerics or lawyers or administrators, rather than as historians, that they were paid and otherwise supported. The Syriac source that tells us so much about rural history in the second half of the eighth century was written by a monk who lived in a relatively modest, northern Syrian monastery. He seems to have travelled little (his chronicle is extraordinarily parochial), and his monastery would have provided for all of his modest needs. Very different examples are provided by two other historians of Syriac Christianity, Dionysius of Tell-Mahre (d. 845), who came from a privileged family in Northern Mesopotamia, and Michael the Syrian (d. 1199), who also came from a background of privilege. Both were men of the church, indeed much more than that: both served in their day as the church's Patriarch, its supreme head. No doubt they lived far more glamorous lives than our anonymous monk; but they, too, were provided for by the wealth of the church, based as it was upon rents, treasures and tithes. For all that they wrote invaluable histories according to long-held conventions of Syriac historiography, neither was a professional historian. Byzantine historians in this period were also frequently drawn from the church, in addition to the bureaucracy; we even have the occasional Emperor, writing during his enforced retirement (Kantakouzenos, rg. 1346–1354). What we do not have, once again, is a professional class of historians. Similar things can be said of other Christian traditions of the pre-modern Near East, such as the Armenian.[1]

This pattern, according to which historians were drawn principally from families of wealth, and then maintained by the wealth of the Church, holds for a great deal of pre-modern historiography, even if history writing in Syriac tailed off considerably after the thirteenth century. There was a time not so long ago when wealthy 'gentlemen scholars' worked at their leisure, drawing on resources of their own (the first professorship of history at Yale was founded as recently as 1865). But 'independent scholars' are now notable (and deliberately noted) exceptions, and those historians who live off the profits of their (necessarily) popularizing histories can be unfairly derided as mere 'amateurs' by the professionals. The church having lost its privileged position to secular institutions as the focus of élite patronage, modern historians now generally rely upon universities, research centres and libraries, which are typically either dependent upon the state, or on some combination of state support and the generosity of benefactors, to provide their salaries, their tools and their access. As a result of the professionalization of history in secular institutions, particularly those held accountable to rising standards of diversity, historiography is now much less the preserve of wealth and privilege, and, with a membership that is more heterogeneous in class, ethnicity, race and gender than it used to be, it is altogether more given to controversy about its functions and principles. It is true that professional historians have always tended to be a contentious lot, but long-standing ideals (of truth and objectivity), along with the function of the historian in public life, are now open to rancorous criticism. That a consensus has broken down amongst historians nowadays is not unrelated to the increasing heterogeneity of its membership.[2]

Pre-modern Muslim historians resembled their Syriac, Byzantine and Armenian analogues of the ninth and twelfth centuries far more than either they or their Christian analogues might have cared to recognize. As a group they were far more homogeneous and more privileged than their present-day counterparts, a fact that has some bearing on the conservatism of their tradition. And when there are breaks in this relative conservatism, these can frequently be associated with changing patterns in their background, employment and training.

[1] The best survey of Syriac historiography (which discusses the three Syriac historians mentioned here) is S.P. Brock, 'Syriac historical writing: a survey of the main sources', *Journal of the Iraqi Academy* 5 (1979–80), pp. 1–30 (English section), which is reprinted in his *Studies in Syriac Christianity: History, Literature and Theology* (Hampshire, 1992); for the anonymous monk, Witakowski, *The Syriac Chronicle of Pseudo-Dionysius of Tel-Maḥrē*, and now Harrak's edition of the *Zuqnin Chronicle*, introduction; for (the real) Dionysius, R. Abramowski, *Dionysius von Tellmahre: jakobitischer Patriarch von 818–845* (Leipzig, 1940).

[2] For one discussion of the controversies, see J. Scott, 'History in crisis? The others' side of the story', *AHR* 94 (1989), pp. 681–692.

Families, wealth, conservatism

To begin with, Muslim historians were likely to have been drawn from families that belonged to the ruling or non-ruling élite, families of wealth and status. More likely than not, they typically came from families that had already showed some signs of learning. This gave them an enormous edge over non-élites in their initial steps of training and education.

Now the reach and character of educational systems are always historically conditioned: they vary from culture to culture, and from period to period. The last 100 years or so has marked something of a change, as education in the developing and developed world has become increasingly uniform and universal, especially through the introduction of compulsory primary education. Pre-modern societies did have institutions for primary education (in the Islamic Middle East they were usually called *kuttāb*s), but only modern nation states have the power to compel their citizens to send their young children to school. Still, education has always been as much about inculcating social attitudes and practices as about transferring particular bodies of knowledge or skills. In the case of modern states, the system is designed to universalize such cultural values as nationalism, capitalism and liberalism, and also to accelerate economic development. Education in classical Islam was also about social formation (if not *only* about social formation), and the élite being interested in neither nationalism nor economic development, it served principally as a vehicle for that élite's reproduction – that is, passing down skills, practices and ideas by which it could distinguish itself from non-élites. The major consequence of this is that higher education, by its very design, was on the whole closed to non-élites.[3]

Estimating rates of literacy is all but impossible for the pre-modern period, with guesses for early nineteenth-century Morocco ranging from 1 per cent to 30 per cent of the urban population; it is probably safe to assume that well under 1 per cent of the population reached advanced stages of education. One imagines that the rate of attrition for those climbing the educational ladder was as high as the percentage of males who stepped on its first rung was low. For only those whose already very clever minds had been honed by years of intensive training could move from the ranks of the taught to the teachers, be this in mosques, markets, and private houses, or in the institutions of learning that emerged during the tenth and eleventh centuries. Moreover, it was wealthy families that could get along without the labour of their children, that had the resources to purchase the services of tutors and schools for these non-productive children and then send them off for study tours, many of which could last years. It was at the feet of (relatively) leisured and learned fathers that sons (and, to a lesser extent, daughters) secured a privileged spot, and in those cases when fathers enjoyed good access, historians not infrequently cited them as sources. One even hears of the occasional

[3] For some sense of *kuttāb* life, see Lecomte, 'Le livre des règles de conduite des maîtres d'école par Ibn Saḥnūn'.

impostor-son, who tried to capitalize on the scholarly reputation of a now-dead 'father'. Privilege and learning, to put it bluntly, were closely related.[4]

Examples of the pattern are plentiful. We have seen that Ibn al-Athīr was the author of the standard annalistic history of his time (the thirteenth century) and of a local history of the ruling dynasty of his town (the Atabegs of Mosul). He came from a landed family that had had enough resources to endow a Sufi monastery, and that had already dabbled in the kind of learning in which he, and two brothers, would distinguish themselves (he is one of those historians who cite their fathers as a source). Like many other Ibāḍī historians from North Africa, al-Darjīnī (d. late thirteenth century) hailed from a family of learning and wealth: his great-grandfather had been a merchant, his grandfather a jurist, and his father a traditionist. The paternal grandfather, uncle and father of Ibn Ḥajar al-^{c}Asqalānī had all been men of learning, while his mother had come from a wealthy family of merchants. Family connections enabled him to survive the early death of both of his parents, and also provided him with the means necessary for the requisite course of study. At the age of 25, he married into even more wealth, and would leave his newlywed for a three-year study tour a year later; it was only after completing this tour in 1400 that he settled down to a career as administrator, librarian, judge and teacher. Study tours could be much more extensive (and expensive) than Ibn Ḥajar's. Al-Ṭabarī, who had left home by twelve and finally settled in Baghdad at about 30, funded his studies from the income of rents sent from properties in his home town of Āmul, a city in northern Iran, just south of the Caspian Sea. One of a series of historians of Mecca, Muḥammad b. Aḥmad b. ^{c}Alī al-Fāsī, was born there in 1373, and four years later he travelled with his mother to Medina, where he spent no fewer than nine years studying under the direction of a local learned woman (to have done so after puberty might have presented a certain awkwardness). He then spent the next twenty years or so in study and travel, including trips to Egypt, Syria, Palestine and the Yemen. By the age of 31 or 32, he had already secured his family's prize: appointment as the *qāḍī* (chief judge) of Mecca.[5]

So families invested heavily in the education of their sons, and the investment usually paid off. Just as there were dynasties of rulers in medieval Islam, so, too, were there dynasties of learned men, who sprang, generation after generation, from families of wealth (usually landed), each passing its advantages onto the next. Dynasties such as these were often very long lived, 200- or 300-year-old trees

[4] Figures from the Moroccan census of 1931 (following Eickelman, 'The art of memory', p. 497), suggest that the percentage of those in higher education was about 0.2 per cent; for one impostor-son, see Bulliet, *Patricians of Nishapur*, p. 50, note 7.

[5] For Ibn al-Athīr, see Richards, 'Ibn al-Athīr'; on Ibn al-Athīr's brothers, I. Ahmad, 'Ibn al-Athir al-muḥaddith – life and works', *IS* 23 (1984), pp. 33–43; Ibn al-Athīr cites his father in Abū Shāma, *Kitāb al-Rawḍatayn*, i^{2}, on pp. 352 and 525; on al-Darjīnī and other Ibāḍī historians, T. Lewicki, 'Les historiens, biographes et traditionnistes ibādites-wahbites de l'Afrique du Nord du viiie au xvie siècle', *Folia Orientalia* 3 (1961), pp. 1–134; on Ibn Ḥajar, A.A. Rahmani, 'The life and works of Ibn Ḥajar al-^{c}Asqalānī', *IC* 45 (1971), pp. 203–212, and 275–293; 46 (1972), pp. 75–81, 171–178, 265–272 and 353–362; 47 (1973), pp. 57–74; and the beautifully concise overview of Rosenthal's in *EI*^{2}, 'Ibn Ḥadjar', which deserves special mention; on al-Ṭabarī's education, Gilliot, 'La formation intellectuelle de Tabari', and Robinson, 'al-Ṭabarī'; on Muḥammad b. Aḥmad, the Patna/Bankipore *Catalogue of the Arabic and Persian Manuscripts*, xv, pp. 168f.; *GAL* ii, 172.

whose roots could sink as deep as the conquest period of the mid-seventh century, and which could weather the tumultuous changes of the political order. Dynasties might fall, taking with them their armies and courtiers, but the religious institutions almost always survived, and there was nearly always a steady demand for men of learning. The family of al-Muᶜāfā b. ᶜImrān (d. 801) had first settled in Mosul in the wake of the conquests of the middle of the seventh century; within two or three generations, these conquering tribesmen had transformed themselves into landowners, men of politics and scholars, too. The Ṣaṣrā family, also of northern Mesopotamia, first appear in the middle of the tenth century, and they flourished as teachers and jurists until the end of the fourteenth. The Jamāᶜa family from Syria first appear in the thirteenth century, and they petered out only in the sixteenth.[6]

If the basis of these families' wealth was typically the land, the core of their learning was usually traditionism, a form of knowledge that not only enabled these families to survive a generation or two of mediocre minds, but to tighten or loosen their ties with the state. Depending on the circumstances, a learned and well-connected son could always accept appointment into the state's judiciary: the Jamāᶜa family as much as monopolised the Shāfiᶜī judgeship for almost a century. Appointments such as these could bring steady salaries, high status, and in the case of the *qāḍī*, access to real power, since judges often oversaw certain fiscal affairs, in addition to the judiciary proper. One of the recurring patterns of Abbasid political history is a rapid turnover amongst the provincial governors, usually career politicians who moved from one appointment to the next, which was counterweighted by the very slow turnover of local judges, who were typically drawn from local families, whose interests they almost invariably represented. Such was presumably the case for our historian of Mecca, who took up the judgeship of the city; it almost certainly was the case for the Mosuli chronographer and prosopographer, Yazīd b. Muḥammad (d. 945), an Azdī judge in a city long dominated by Azdīs. There, in Mosul, we have that familiar pattern of administration (governors come and go, but judges hold long terms of office). Of al-Azdī's own family, we know very little, but to judge from what survives of his chronography, it seems that his tribe had supplied the town with judges for about as long as the town had had judges. Of course accepting such posts as the judgeship carried some risk as well. The official who appointed was often the same official who could dismiss (one Ḥanafī was fired for failing to deliver the correct judgment on the licitness of wine), and this is why a learned and landed son could always decline such invitations, relying instead on rents, endowments, or the fees he received by teaching.[7]

[6] On the family of al-Muᶜāfā b. ᶜImrān, see Robinson, 'al-Muᶜāfā b. ᶜImrān and the beginnings of the *ṭabaqāt* literature', pp. 114–120; on the Ṣaṣrā family, W.M. Brinner, 'The Banū Ṣaṣrā: a study in the transmission of a scholarly tradition', *Arabica* 7 (1960), pp. 167–195; for the Jamāᶜa, K. Salibi, 'The Banū Jamāᶜa: a dynasty of Shāfiᶜite jurists in the Mamluk period', *SI* 9 (1958), pp. 97–109.

[7] For al-Azdī al-Mawṣilī, see C.F. Robinson, 'A local historian's debt to al-Ṭabarī: the case of al-Azdī's *Taʾrīkh al-Mawṣil*', in Kennedy, ed., *Al-Ṭabarī*; and for the Mosul example, idem, *Empire and Elites after the Muslim Conquest* (Cambridge, 2000), pp. 161f.; for the Ḥanafī example, al-Maqrīzī, *Kitāb al-Muqaffā al-kabīr*, ii, p. 71; on declining state service, the classic discussion is A.J. Wensinck, 'The refused dignity', in T.W. Arnold and R.A. Nicholson. eds., *A Volume of Oriental Studies Presented to Edward G. Browne* (Cambridge, 1922), pp. 491–499; cf. W. Madelung, 'A treatise of the

The extent to which families specialized within the traditionist core is hard to know, although we might expect that the strengths of the father were not infrequently passed down to the son. Certainly sons very frequently appear as transmitters of their father's material, perhaps especially in the early period: Aḥmad b. Ḥanbal's son Ṣāliḥ not only transmitted a great deal of *ḥadīth* and *akhbār* from his father, but also assembled biographical material about Aḥmad. Much later on, with the establishment of the *madrasa*s, many sons were appointed to succeed their fathers. The precocious al-Suyūṭī (d. 1505) assumed his father's *madrasa* chair in Cairo at the age of eighteen. Now in his particular case, it may actually be that his scholarly qualifications recommended him for the job. We also know of cases of less benign nepotism, however, and some endowment deeds went so far as to stipulate that a given professorship remain, if possible, in the family of the founder. One of the biographers of Saladin, ᶜImād al-Dīn al-Iṣfahānī, seems to have entered the *madrasa* at the age of fifteen, and he secured his first real job only at the age of 32. He, too, benefited from family connections, which had a part in landing him his position at the right hand of Saladin, when he was about 50 years of age.[8]

Being marginal to traditionism, non-Prophetic biography and chronography were only infrequently cultivated as a family specialty. Ibn ᶜAbd al-Ẓāhir (d. 1292) wrote a biography of Baybars, and so, too, did his nephew, Shāfiᶜ b. ᶜAlī (d. 1330), who comments on his uncle's work. Another notable case (there is a small handful of others) is the historian Sibṭ Ibn al-Jawzī (d. 1256), who was the grandson of the historian Ibn al-Jawzī (d. 1201). Sibṭ Ibn al-Jawzī spent some of his childhood living in his grandfather's house, and, naturally enough, he drew on his grandfather's history for his own. We should not make too much of these examples, however, and there may be nothing accidental about the fact that the most spectacular dynasty of chronographers was the Ṣābiʾ family, pagan natives of the northern Syrian city of Harran who rose to prominence in Baghdad in the tenth century, serving as the caliphs' courtiers and physicians even well into the twelfth. Several members of this family took an interest in history, and four are especially noteworthy.[9]

The first of these was Thābit b. Sinān (d. 976), who served as the physician to the caliph al-Rāḍī (rg. 934–940), and wrote a now-lost history that began with the

Sharīf al-Murtaḍā on the legality of working for the government (*masʾala fī ʾl-ᶜamal maᶜa ʾl-sulṭān*)', *BSOAS* 43 (1980), pp. 18–31.

[8] On the career of al-Suyūṭī, see E.M. Sartain, *Jalāl al-Dīn al-Suyūṭī: Biography and Background* (Cambridge, 1975), and M.J. Saleh, 'Al-Suyūṭī and his work: their place in Islamic scholarship from Mamluk times to the present', *MSR* 5 (2000), pp. 73–89; for *madrasa* foundation documents that stipulate the family of post-holders, J. Berkey, *The Transmission of Knowledge in Medieval Cairo* (Princeton, 1992), p. 104, and J. Gilbert, 'Institutionalization of Muslim scholarship and professionalization of the *ᶜulamāʾ* in medieval Damascus', *SI* 52 (1980), p. 120; on ᶜImād al-Dīn, see Richards, 'ᶜImād al-Dīn al-Iṣfahānī'.

[9] Ibn ᶜAbd al-Ẓāhir's biography is the *Taʾrīkh al-mālik al-Ẓāhir* (Wiesbaden, 1983), and Shāfiᶜ b. ᶜAlī's *Ḥusn al-manāqib al-sariyya* (Riyadh, 1976), on which see P.M. Holt, 'Some observations on Shāfiᶜ b. ᶜAlī's biography of Baybars', *JSS* 29 (1984), pp. 123–130.

reign of the caliph al-Muqtadir (rg. 908–932), where al-Ṭabarī's great chronicle had come to an end, and concluded in *ca.* 975; it was used by a number of historians, such as Ibn Miskawayh and Abū al-Fidāʾ (d. 1331). Thābit's nephew, Ibrāhīm b. Hilāl (d. 994), served in the court of the Buyids, the Daylamite dynasty that had occupied Baghdad and taken *de facto* control of the caliphate in 945; he was thus a contemporary of Ibn al-Nadīm's, in whose *Fihrist* he is mentioned. We are told that one of the Buyid emirs, having put Ibrāhīm under house arrest, proceeded to commission a history of the dynasty, and directed him to send successive instalments to be corrected and returned. Ibrāhīm's grandson, Hilāl b. al-Muḥassin (d. 1055), wrote a history of viziers, this in addition to an imperial history that continued Thābit b. Sinān's; both survive only in fragments. After four generations of service to the caliphs, Hilāl seems to have been the first member of the family to convert to Islam, a fact that says something about the cosmopolitan character of the caliphate (as does the case of Ibn Miskawayh, another chronographer of this period). Finally, Hilāl's son, who came to be called Ghars al-Niʿma (d. 1088), wrote a continuation of his father's history that survives only in quotations in later books, particularly the *Mirʾāt al-zamān* by Sibṭ Ibn al-Jawzī; it began in 1056, and appears to have been the definitive account of his day.[10]

In earlier chapters we saw that one of these Ṣābiʾ histories influenced al-ʿUtbī in his *al-Kitāb al-Yamīnī*. Baghdad would continue to produce historians, but none would equal this Ṣābiʾ tradition; the capital's time had come and gone. In the course of his biographical notice on Ghars al-Niʿma, Ibn al-Jawzī, drawing as he often does upon a work of Ibn ʿAqīl (d. 1119) in an autograph copy (*naqaltu min khaṭṭ*), tells us how Ibn ʿAqīl attended a meeting, during which it was asked 'Has there remained in Baghdad a historian (*muʾarrikh*) after the death of Ibn al-Ṣābiʾ?' The answer given was no, and far from a matter of despair, this was to the city's benefit, for 'when the city was filled with the best people and great worthies (*al-akhyār wa-ahl al-manāqib*), God sent to it people to tell [of its glories]; but when they disappeared, and [only] those harmful and of vile action remained, He eliminated all historians (*aʿdama al-muʾarrikh*). This was to hide the shame'. Individual historians can appear in virtually any society that attaches some value to the past, but robust historiographical traditions rely on some measure of prosperity.[11]

[10] On the Ṣābiʾ historians I draw on the particularly fine entry in *EI*^{2}, 'Ṣābiʾ' (de Blois); on Ibrāhīm, see W. Madelung, 'Abū Isḥāq al-Ṣābī on the Alids of Ṭabaristān and Gilān', *JNES* 26 (1967), pp. 17–57; and Ghars al-Niʿma, C.E. Bosworth, 'Ghars al-Niʿma b. Hilāl al-Ṣābiʾ's *Kitāb al-Hafawāt al-nādira* and Buyid history', in A. Jones, ed., *Arabicus Felix ... Essays in Honour of Professor A.F.L. Beeston's Eightieth Birthday* (Reading, 1991), pp. 129–141; M.S. Khan, 'A manuscript of an epitome of al-Ṣābī's *Kitāb al-Tāǧī*', *Arabica* 12 (1965), pp. 27–44; Yāqūt, *Irshād*, ii, pp. 397f., and al-Ṣafadī, *al-Wāfī bi'l-wafayāt*, x, pp. 463f. (on Thābit b. Qurra).

[11] My knowledge of this anecdote comes from G. Makdisi, *Ibn ʿAqil: Religion and Culture in Classical Islam* (Edinburgh, 1997), p. 195, but the accompanying note is incorrect; I draw the translation from Ibn al-Jawzī, *al-Muntaẓam*, xvi, pp. 275f.

Career patterns

The Ṣābiʾ family was exceptionally productive of chronographers, and in composing successive instalments of something like a family history of the caliphate, they almost amount to what might be called a 'diachronic syndicate'. As courtiers to Buyid rulers who commissioned dynastic histories, the Ṣābiʾ family also illustrates the affinity between chronography and ruling courts, which we first came upon in chapter 6. It seems that chronography, which for most of our period never managed to secure a place within the traditionalist establishment, responded to the patronage of states with perhaps only slightly less regularity than these states, which were always struggling to outfit their military power with legitimizing authority, hired chronographers to tutor their children and tell their stories (especially now in the form of dynastic histories or biographies). Odd exceptions aside, such as the Saljuks, nearly all states offered at least some patronage to historians, and even minor rulers regularly insisted on surrounding themselves with courtiers, sycophants and learned men, including historians. One late twelfth- and early thirteenth-century ruler of the Syrian town of Hama employed something like 200 men of learning at his court, and one late eleventh-century ruler in northern Iraq is said to have possessed 500 concubines and 500 eunuchs, in addition to a number of poets and scholars who sought out his court, where food was prepared by chefs trained in Egypt. It may be that the weaker the claim to legitimacy, the more the historians were pressed into service. Why do we possess such a cluster of biographies of Saladin, Baybars (rg. 1260–1277) and Qalāwūn (rg. 1279–1290), especially when the biographical coverage is so spotty otherwise? At least for those writing contemporary history, the answer must be that each ruler saw in historiography the opportunity to (mis)represent his path to power: the 'uncouth' Baybars, for example, is made over into the 'true heir' of the crusading Saladin. Meanwhile, if relatively weak states could always entice the occasional learned man (and exceptional non-Muslim family) into service, strong social élites preserved their status in part by producing conservative traditionists (it seems that traditionist prosopography was nearly always robust) who generally supplemented their landed or commercial wealth through teaching in houses, shops and mosques.[12]

In general, then, wealth and learning tended to appear together, and this goes some way towards explaining the conservatism of the tradition. It almost goes without saying that there are exceptions to this pattern, the self-made historian who came from neither wealth nor learning: the obstacles were not insurmountable. The system was probably less open than the very meritocratic Chinese model, which relied on a fairly rigid regime of examinations to determine entry into the

[12] I borrow the phrase 'diachronic syndicate' from R.A. Markus, in Croke, 'The origins of the Christian world chronicle', p. 116; the ruler of Hama was al-Manṣūr Muḥammad (d. 1220), on whom see Holt's translation of Abū al-Fidāʾ, *Memoirs of a Syrian Prince*, p. 1; the ruler of Northern Mesopotamia was the Marwānid, Naṣr b. Aḥmad (d. 1061), on whom see Ibn al-Athīr, *al-Kāmil*, x, p.17; for the biographies of Qalāwūn and Baybars, I rely on Holt, 'Three biographies', and L. Northrup, *From Slave to Sultan: The Career of al-Manṣūr Qalāwūn and the Consolidation of Mamluk Rule in Egypt and Syria (678–689 A.H./1279–1290 A.D.)* (Stuttgart, 1998), pp. 23ff.

bureaucracy, but more open than the highest ranks of the contemporaneous Christian world. In fact, it was more often than not through education (both academic and vocational) that individuals could make vertiginous climbs up the social ladder. Still, the odds were stacked against non-élites, and the success stories were noted: 'a commoner becoming a teacher … was therefore a rare enough phenomenon to call for special, almost astonished, mention', as one historian of eleventh-century Iran has put it.[13]

More important than these exceptions is a variation on the pattern, which took place in Mamluk Egypt during the thirteenth to sixteenth centuries, when the system of military recruitment made for the constant circulation of non-Arab and non-Muslim slave soldiers into the state, and the conventions of succession made it very difficult for sons to follow their fathers into political careers. What resulted was a succession of *arriviste* rulers hungry for the status that learning could confer, and a steady supply of ambitious sons, who, discouraged from military service, threw their energy into learning. In this context, historians were frequently outsiders and frequently produced within a single generation. Baybars al-Manṣūrī (d. 1325), author of a large (and still largely unpublished) universal history, arrived in Egypt at the age of fourteen, and was more or less promptly entered into a school to learn the Qurʾān. According to one biographical notice, he spent his nights in prayer and Qurʾānic recitation, and his days in *ḥadīth* recitation and research; we also know that he held high positions in the military and bureaucracy. The father of Ibn Taghrī Birdī, an Egyptian historian of the fifteenth century, had been one of the Greek slave-soldiers brought into Egypt under the patronage of Sultan al-Ẓāhir Barqūq (rg. 1382–1389), rising in rank and eventually serving as governor of Damascus no fewer than three times. Al-ʿAynī (d. 1451) found favour with one Mamluk Sultan by lecturing on history and translating works into Turkish. The Mamluk period even produced several examples of 'statesmen-historians', authors who recorded the history they had themselves made. We have already met two examples, Abū al-Fidāʾ and Baybars al-Manṣūrī. Another is Ibn al-Dawādārī (d. 1335), son of a provincial governor and attendant to the Sultan, with whom he gained experience in Mamluk politics; he would find employment as a functionary himself. His universal history is important not only as a record of his day, but as an archive of now-lost sources and example of the Mamluk 'literarized' historical narrative. 'Statesmen-historians' were certainly not unique to the Mamluk period – the trend starts already amongst the Ayyubids – but they are part of the Mamluk embrace of learning.[14]

---

[13] The commoner in question is Abū Sahl Muḥammad al-Ḥafṣī, on whom Bulliet, *Patricians of Nishapur*, p. 57.

[14] For a recent overview of the Mamluk system, see A. Levanoni, *A Turning Point in Mamluk History: The Third Reign of al-Nāṣir Muḥammad Ibn Qalāwūn, 1310–1341* (Leiden, 1995), pp. 5ff.; on Baybars al-Manṣūrī, see al-Maqrīzī, *Kitāb al-Muqaffā al-kabīr*, ii, pp. 531ff.; Little, *Introduction*, pp. 4f.; and the introduction to the new (partial) edition, *Zubdat al-fikra fī taʾrīkh al-hijra* (Beirut, 1998); on Ibn Taghrī Birdī's career, A. Darrāğ, 'La vie d'Abūl-Maḥāsin Ibn Taġrī Birdī'; for al-ʿAynī, B. Flemming, 'Literary activities in Mamluk halls and barracks', in M. Rosen-Ayalon, ed., *Studies in Memory of Gaston Wiet* (Jerusalem, 1977), p. 252 (citing Schimmel); on Ibn al-Dawādārī, Haarmann, *Quellenstudien*, pp. 61ff.; Little, *Introduction*, pp. 10ff.; for the rhetoric, see chapter 5, note 26.

Amidst the broad continuity of medieval Islamic learning and historiography, there was thus some real change. Historians would continue to be drawn from the ranks of the traditionists, but others served the state. And while élite families would continue to supply scholarship with historians, it is one of the striking features of twelfth- and thirteenth-century learning that historians began to draw their salaries from institutions of learning, chiefly the *madrasa*s, which were founded and endowed by members (or aspiring members) of the ruling élite. By the end of the twelfth century, there were something like 30 of these in Baghdad, and by the end of the thirteenth, they had spread and taken root in Syria and Egypt; according to one count, at least 74 *madrasa*s were founded in Cairo between 1250 and 1389. The institutionalization of learning in the form of the *madrasa*, in addition to the teaching mosque and Sufi convent, thus reinforced what had been temperamental patronage offered by rulers to chronographers, and introduced them into the fiercely competitive culture and politics of the time. With *madrasa*s being thrown up by wealthy patrons and academic appointments being bought and sold, teaching and writing now functioned as much as signposts of status as they did signposts of learning. The result was a new brand of professional academic, who, by following a more or less clear career track of well-paid, high-status positions, provided teaching and reading for a hungry market of students and readers. *Madrasa* deeds of endowment stipulate monthly salaries for professors that generally range from 100 to 300 dirhams per month, but they could go as high as 500. Teaching appointments were an important enough part of the culture of learning that they are recorded as part of the historical record itself.[15]

Signs of the new pattern are discernible already in the career of the Baghdadi traditionist Ibn al-Jawzī. The leading Ḥanbalī of his time, he enjoyed the patronage of the vizier, taught throngs of students (his grandson puts the number of those attending his sessions in the tens of thousands), delivered widely influential sermons, and at one point looked after no fewer than five *madrasa*s. According to his own reckoning (again, as transmitted by his grandson), he wrote 2,000 volumes, while another estimate puts the number at 1,000. How much of Ibn al-Jawzī's activity was *copying* rather than composing is difficult to say, because in addition to being a renowned traditionist, he was a renowned scribe. The Chester Beatty Library in Dublin possesses an attractive manuscript of the *Adab al-kātib* by Ibn Qutayba (d. 889), a manual for secretaries, which he copied in 1148. (Another of Ibn Qutayba's books, a collection of anecdotal biographies, seems to have been the model for one of Ibn al-Jawzī's works.) In any event, his output was so prodigious that it was greeted with incredulity by many, including the prosopographer Ibn Khallikān (d. 1282), whose words record one of the stories told about his prolixity:

[15] On the spread of *madrasa*s and their professors' salaries, see D. Sourdel, 'Réflexions sur la diffusion de la madrasa en Orient du xie au xiiie siècle', *REI* 44 (1976), pp. 165–184; J. Gilbert, 'Institutionalization', pp. 105–134; Berkey, *The Transmission of Knowledge in Medieval Cairo*; and U. Haarmann, 'Mamluk endowment deeds as a source for the history of education in late medieval Egypt', *al-Abhath* 28 (1980), p. 36; for some contrary views on the nature of the *madrasa*, see Chamberlain, *Knowledge and Social Practice in Medieval Damascus*, pp. 69ff.; on teaching appointments in history, Ibn Ḥajar, *Inbāʾ al-ghumr*, passim.

> We shall close this list by merely stating that his works are too numerous to be counted. The quantity of sheets which he wrote with his own hand was very great, but people exaggerate when they say that on summing up the number of quires [*kurrāsa*, which was usually five folded sheets] written by him and taking into account the length of his life, if the former be divided by the latter, it will give nine *kurrāsa*s a-day; but this is a result so extraordinary that it can hardly be admitted by any reasonable man. It is related also that the parings of the reed-pens with which he wrote the Traditions were gathered up and formed a large heap; these, in pursuance to his last orders, were employed to heat the water for washing his corpse [a standard Ḥanafī Muslim practice], and there was even more than enough for the purpose.

Whatever the exact number, Ibn al-Jawzī's works include his huge *Muntaẓam*, which is among the first works to combine systematically chronography and prosopography. It is true that many chronographers writing annalistic history had followed the practice of concluding annual entries with necrologies of those worthies who had died during the course of the year; but Ibn al-Jawzī's change is much more than incremental. He not only makes the practice consistent for the length of his work, but throws traditional chronography out of balance: the obituaries ('those worthies who died', *man tuwuffiya min al-akābir*) now frequently outweigh the 'events' (*ḥawādith*). It is tempting to think that the appearance of this hybrid form at the very time in which *madrasa*s were employing traditionist-historians in prominent positions is not entirely accidental, and, further, that the emergence of chronographic-prosopographic hybrids, a form that was especially cultivated in Mamluk Syria, relates to the rapprochement between traditionism and historiography that took place in this period. 'History as recorded by these Syrian historians is not only a record of events, but a register of Muslim religious learning, as well as a selective anthology of the cultural and literary heritage of the time.'[16]

Bahāᵓ al-Dīn Ibn Shaddād (d. 1235) was less prolific than Ibn al-Jawzī, but his career path was similarly conditioned by the opportunities put in place by new institutions. He spent four years teaching in the Niẓāmiyya *madrasa* in Baghdad before returning to his native town of Mosul, where he took up a teaching post in a *madrasa* founded by a local official; he then went into the employ of Saladin, who made him chief judge of the army, thus placing him in the midst of his *jihād* (holy war) against the Crusaders. Little surprise, perhaps, that it was for Saladin that he wrote a number of works, including a legal work on the *jihād*, along with a biography that portrayed Saladin as the holy warrior *par excellence*. After his patron's death, he moved to Aleppo, where he founded a *madrasa* of his own. There is, finally, the great polymath-historian Jalāl al-Dīn al-Suyūṭī, who, in addition to holding two *madrasa* teaching posts, held administrative posts in two Sufi institutions – posts that offered steady salaries, stipends and students. The combination of extraordinary productivity and prolixity (he began the first of his

[16] For a biography of Ibn al-Jawzī, see Sibṭ Ibn al-Jawzī, *Mirᵓāt al-zamān*, viii² pp. 481ff.; cf. Ibn Khallikān, *Wafayāt al-aᶜyān*, iii, p. 141, but I cite the attractively loose translation by M. de Slane, *Ibn Khallikan's Biographical Dictionary* (Britain and Ireland, 1842–1871; reprinted, Beirut, 1970), ii, p. 97; see also ᶜA.Ḥ. ᶜAlwajī, *Muᵓallafāt Ibn al-Jawzī* (Baghdad, 1965); the quotation is from Guo, 'Mamluk historiographic studies', p. 38.

approximately 550 titles at the age of fourteen, leaving something like 83 works unfinished because he had lost interest), breadth (he wrote on virtually every topic that could matter to a traditionist) and shameless self-promotion (he had no scruples about misrepresenting his training and exaggerating his abilities), made al-Suyūṭī very controversial. In all of this he represents Mamluk-era learning at its best and worst.[17]

[17] The standard work on al-Suyūṭī is Sartain, *Jalāl al-Dīn al-Suyūṭī: Biography and Background*.

CHAPTER 10

Writing history

At least in part, successful religious traditions are successful because they adapt and transform the cultural ingredients available to them. Early Christianity was born in the Graeco-Roman world, which means that early Christians drew upon a culture of learning that they shared with contemporary pagans and Jews, including language (Greek, Latin, Hebrew) and the technology of learning (ink written upon scrolls made of papyrus or parchment). As they grew in number and confidence, Christians began to generate a culture of learning that was distinctively Christian, and the emblem of this change was the codex – the double-sided, folded bundle of leaves that is the direct forefather of our modern book.

If the codex became emblematic for Christians, learning through audition and orality – that is, reading out loud, memorizing massive amounts, hearing and reading texts back to their authors, publishing through lecturing – became emblematic for traditionalist Muslims. Knowledge did not lie inertly in written texts, to be acquired by students working on their own in quiet studies; it came alive on the tongues of teachers and students, reciting, reading aloud and questioning each other. There was no room in classical Islam for Open Universities or correspondence courses, two institutions of learning in which books (and now computers) dissolve the age-old marriage of teacher to student, because knowledge was held to reside in teachers and their own, carefully informed readings. For pre-modern Muslims to acquire this knowledge properly, they had to know these teachers personally. To understand Islamic historiography, then, we have to know something about the culture of Islamic learning, especially how it handled listening, reading and writing. In what follows I outline this culture and then turn to how Muslim historians worked within it.[1]

[1] On the codex, see C.H. Roberts and T.C. Skeat, *The Birth of the Codex* (London, 1983); cf. A.J. Blanchard, *Les débuts du codex* (Turnhout, 1989) and R. Lane Fox, 'Literacy and power in early Christianity', in Bowman and Woolf, eds., *Literacy and Power,* pp. 141f.; for the miscellany, A. Petrucci, *Writers and Readers in Medieval Italy: Studies in the History of Written Culture*, ed. C.M. Radding (New Haven, 1995), chapter 1.

Reading and writing

It is hard to see behind the mountains of books that Muslim scholars wrote during the classical period, but there is some reason to think that behind them lay not merely some indifference to writing's potentialities, but some real wariness about the practice of writing itself. Thus we frequently read of the aged scholar who burns his books, fearing that the (written) mistakes they contain will lead others astray. According to one story, the notebooks (*dafātir*) of Abū ᶜAmr b. al-ᶜAlāᵓ (d. 770) were piled up to the ceiling of his house, but he took an ascetic turn and torched them all. There were cultural reasons why some may have distrusted writing. Some considered paperwork as a low-status, administrative task fit only for lower status, non-Arab protégés, holding fast to pre-Islamic customs (or at least their view of them), which championed orality. The caliph Sulaymān b. ᶜAbd al-Malik (rg. 715-717) is given to remark: 'I am amazed by these non-Arabs (*ᶜajam*): for a thousand years they ruled, not needing us in their governing for a single moment. We've ruled a century, and not for a single moment have we been able to get by without them!' Meanwhile, others may have been discomforted by the state's patronage of paper (early types, e.g., Barmakī and Ṭāhirī, were named after administrators and governors, respectively) and the universalisation of knowledge amongst the literate that it promised. This last factor – the threat that writing can pose to those whose status turns on their special oral and aural skills – is familiar to historians of early Christianity and Judaism, and was presumably decisive. For opposition to writing was particularly associated with the early traditionists, just as it was with Rabbis committed to the oral law, and there is good reason to posit some continuity between the two.[2]

In the long run, the traditionists' opposition to writing down *ḥadīth* would be overcome. But this does not mean that orality and aurality would disappear altogether from the world of learning. A robust culture of memorization makes this clear enough. Children of seven or eight typically learned (and still learn) the Qurᵓān by heart, and when they did not, pushy parents would complain to their teacher, as we know they did in tenth-century North Africa. The father of ᶜAbd al-Laṭīf al-Baghdādī (d. 1231) used his connections to stuff his precocious son with memorized learning from very early on. Ibn Ḥajar al-ᶜAsqalānī (d. 1449) was nine when he first demonstrated that he knew the entire text of the Qurᵓān, and he seems to have been considered a bit late (al-Ṭabarī knew it by the time he was seven). At this very young age, the point was certainly not to understand what God meant in the Qurᵓān, since the student was still far too young and under-educated for this. Nor was it merely to benefit from his reciting, although this was a meritorious act of piety in its own right. The primary function of memorizing the

[2] Resistance to writing down traditions was noted already by Guillaume, *Traditions of Islam*, pp. 16ff., but the problem was discussed fully only by Cook, 'The opponents of the writing of tradition in early Islam', pp. 437–530 (where the Jewish antecedent is argued); on Abū ᶜAmr b. al-ᶜAlāᵓ, Yāqūt, *Irshād*, vi[4], pp. 217f.; for Sulaymān's words, al-Zubayr b. Bakkār, *Akhbār al-muwaffaqiyyāt*, p. 190.

text at this tender age was propaedeutic: because of its rhymes and rhythm, memorizing the Qurʾān made for a very good start towards mastering other kinds of texts, particularly *ḥadīth* (an exercise that itself began quite early, perhaps around the age of eight). And the technique worked. ʿAbd al-Laṭīf al-Baghdādī reports that he could memorize a quire a day, which, assuming a standard size, would amount to some ten pages of work (or more, since quires might consist of more pages). We read of *muḥaddith* after *muḥaddith* who memorized tens of thousands of reports with astounding accuracy, a particularly common story being the travelling *muḥaddith* who transmits thousands of reports from memory, returns home to consult his notes, and makes only a handful of very minor corrections. It may be hard to believe now, but some early *ḥadīth* transmitters are even said to have been illiterate. Since pre-moderns from a variety of cultures were endowed with comparable skills, accounts such as these may say as much about our now-slavish reliance upon visual signals and written records as they do about medieval Muslims' ability to memorize.[3]

If the cult of memorization was a notable feature of Islamic learning, it did not flourish at the expense of writing, nor does it qualify as the distinctive feature of this culture. Writing came to be as crucial to Islamic learning as it is to any other high cultural tradition, its instruments fetishized nearly as much as laptop computers and mobile phones amongst businessmen today. One reads that saffron was the perfume of comely maidens, but ink was the perfume of men, and that the learned man's ink is as precious as the martyr's blood. (Of course books could be abused, too, and readers were occasionally warned against using them as 'as cushions, fans, props to lean on or lie upon, or fly swatters'; sturdy bindings and covers were invented.) Some books commanded very high prices: one Mamluk biographer is said to have left behind no fewer than eighteen cases of especially valuable books; his widow knew the value of each of them, and would sell them off as a pension. Only a savvy scholar, one imagines, would have compiled such a library, and only a reclusive scholar, one imagines, could equate perfume with ink, ascribing his idea to the (apparently illiterate) Prophet. But broader cultural values were at work. The late seventh- (or early eighth-) century translation of the tax registers from Greek and Persian into Arabic is said to have been ordered by an Umayyad caliph when he learned that one of his (non-Muslim) scribes had urinated in an inkpot. The idea that administrative change this fundamental could be triggered in this way is preposterous, and certainly the causes and circumstances of the change were altogether more complex. But the anecdote enjoyed verisimilitude because it reflected cultural attitudes that knotted together language, writing and religion, and that occasionally endowed Arabic script with almost iconic status. The story thus parallels Christian accounts of outrage when a Jew reportedly

[3] For the pushy parents, see Muḥammad b. Saḥnūn, *Kitāb Ādāb al-muʿallimīn*, p. 92; for ʿAbd al-Laṭīf, Ibn Abī Uṣaybiʿa, *ʿUyūn al-anbāʾ*, pp. 683f. and, in general, Makdisi, *Rise of Colleges*, pp. 84ff.; for al-Ṭabarī's age, Gilliot, 'Formation intellectuelle de Tabari', p. 205; for some age data, R. Bulliet, 'The age structure of medieval Islamic education', *SI* 57 (1983), pp. 105–117; for book burning, Cook, 'The opponents of the writing of tradition in early Islam', pp. 79f. (with more bibliography).

urinated on an icon of Christ (or the Virgin) in sixth-century Antioch, which is said to have triggered the expulsion of the Jews from the city. The emergence of classical Arabic – that is, the codification of its grammar and the marriage of one particular script with Qurʾānic language – is intimately tied to the emergence of the Islamic religious tradition.[4]

What makes Islamic learning distinctive is thus not simply that it values orality or writing so highly, but that it valued *both*: Muslims engineered an interplay between orality and literacy, between the spoken and the written word, and this interplay lies at the heart of the science of *ḥadīth*. This being the queen of the Islamic sciences, it also underpins other branches of knowledge. This is particularly the case for history, since many historians were first and foremost jurists, and it was from *ḥadīth* transmission, rather than history writing, that they would have derived their academic skills and social prestige. I write this book of history at my computer or on lined paper, in the privacy of my office or study, and in the quiet of the library: the words go straight from my head onto the page or screen. By contrast, much of what is attributed to early Muslim 'authors' never actually issued from their pens: as we have already seen, it consisted of lecture and dictation notes taken by students, compiled (and approved) during the lifetime of the 'author', or assembled (without approval) after it had ended. Such, for example, is almost certainly the case for the material attributed to seventh- and many eighth-century scholars such ʿĀṣim b. ʿUmar b. Qatāda (d. 737), who was directed by the caliph to lecture on the Prophet's life in the mosque of Damascus. We saw earlier that notions of authorship hardened considerably during the eighth and ninth centuries, and from this period on, texts were increasingly 'authorized' by their authors, which is another way of saying that composition and transmission were disentangled. Textuality was increasingly valued, and, of course, the availability of written sources (including a variety of documents) grew as well. Despite all of this change, the authority of the written text never entirely eclipsed that of the person who construed it. Reading (frequently out loud), reciting, dictating and writing remained interwoven.

We can see this in the conventions that traditionist-historians used. They might be working exclusively from written materials, but authors as renowned as al-Ṭabarī conventionally cited their sources in terminology generated by *ḥadīth* transmitters for the purpose of *ḥadīth* transmission. 'He told me', as used by al-Ṭabarī and many, many others for non-contemporaneous history, often means precisely what we mean when we cite long-dead authors as if they were alive: 'As Tocqueville says in his *Democracy in America* ...' *Ḥadīth* conventions being more deeply ingrained amongst medieval Muslims than they were amongst nineteenth-century Frenchmen, Arabic book learning was more thoroughly penetrated by oral

[4] For book abuse, see F. Rosenthal, *The Technique and Approach of Muslim Scholarship* (Rome, 1947), p. 11; the Mamluk biographer is Shāfiʿ b. ʿAlī, and the story can be found in al-Ṣafadī, *Nakt al-himyān fī nukat al-ʿumyān*, p. 164; on the icon, Agapius of Manbij, *Kitāb al-ʿUnwān*, ed. and trans. by A.A. Vasiliev in *Patrologia Orientalis* 8 (1912) pp. 439f.; on the interdependence of memory and literacy in the west, M. Carruthers, *The Book of Memory* (Cambridge, 1990).

conventions. We have already seen one result: the line between teaching and composing would always remain blurry. Away from his own material while travelling, Ibn al-Athīr relied on the notes his students had taken from his lectures to compile his *Usd al-ghāba fī maʿrifat al-ṣaḥāba*, his prosopography of the Prophet's contemporaries. Even though historiography would eventually emancipate itself from *ḥadīth* learning, many historians would continue to represent (or, as it happened, misrepresent) their methods in terms of *ḥadīth* transmission. In one of the fullest theoretical statements about historiography, al-Ījī wrote in the fourteenth century that its principles are 'the oral transmission from authorities through listening (to their lecturing) and a written tradition of assured continuity. The process of transmission has its particular ways and methods which have been adequately explained by the leading *ḥadīth* scholars'.[5]

Of course notes can be assembled to form a book only when students understand and accurately transcribe their teachers' lectures; and it must be said that in this respect, medieval Muslims were far better students than today's. This is not merely because Muslim students possessed such carefully honed memories. It is also because the conventions of learning differed so greatly from today's. Nowadays diplomas certify that a given student has satisfied (the anonymous agents of) an *institution* that he possesses sufficient knowledge (both general and particular) in a chosen field, his command of the material often coming as much from his own reading and study as it does from lectures or discussion with his teachers. Close relations can and do develop between students and their teachers (something which is most clearly expressed in the German word for 'thesis supervisor', *Doktorvater*), but they need not. In classical Islam, students were generally supposed to follow the principle that a book learnt properly was a book learnt orally from its author or from someone who had already been taught *that particular book*, the process often including the student's reading of the book *back* to his teacher ('to read back' often means nothing other than 'to study under someone'). In so doing, these students collected not diplomas, but *ijāza*s ('permission certificates'), which authorized them to transmit and/or teach the books that they had been authoritatively taught, and to use their copies of the books as the basis for further copies. The historian/philosopher Ibn Miskawayh came to know the *History* of al-Ṭabarī not by buying or borrowing it, but through the instruction of Abū Bakr Aḥmad b. Kāmil, whose death in year 350/968 he records: 'He was a student of Abū Jaʿfar [al-Ṭabarī],' Ibn Miskawayh writes, 'and had "heard" [that is, transmitted] a great deal from him; but I have "heard" from him of Abū Jaʿfar's work only this work [i.e., the *History*], some of it by reading it [back to him] and some of it by [having been granted an] *ijāza*.' (In fact, Aḥmad b. Kāmil was one of al-Ṭabarī's most important transmitters, and a biographer of his, too.) Even in the days of the *madrasa*, a scholar's biography of any length will always enumerate his teachers and students, but only very rarely mention an institution of learning. Expectations being that one's understanding of a book came only in these forms, scholars were taken to task for having

[5] For Ibn al-Athīr, the introduction to his *Usd al-ghāba*; for al-Ījī, Rosenthal, *History*, p. 205.

claimed that they had studied a book under the direction of its author, or someone qualified to teach it by virtue of an *ijāza*, when they had actually only read it on their own. Far from indicating maturity or initiative on the part of a student, independent study marked recklessness – even arrogance. In a culture where studying a book meant learning it from its author or authorized teacher, 'life-long learning' was more than just a slogan: studying in this way took money, time and energy, because there were always more books and more scholars to study under.[6]

This, in any case, was the way the scholars envisioned the system to work, and it remained the ideal. In the middle of the fourteenth century al-Dhahabī (d. 1348) was still compiling a list of scholars who had lived 80 years after the death of their teachers (or their 'auditions'): then, as earlier and later, long-lived scholars were valued because they minimized the number of links required to transmit a given text (the more links, the more opportunities for mistakes to slip in). Even so, with so many books in so many fields, even amongst the *ḥadīth* transmitters it was frequently conceded that the terminology of learning no longer reflected its actual practice. In the first volume of Ibn al-ᶜAdīm's prosopography of Aleppo, the *Bughyat al-ṭalab fī taʾrīkh Ḥalab*, a wide variety of citing strategies are used: we have full *isnād*s leading back to authorities, books cited with and without *ijāza*s, even untitled books. But already in the ninth century, the critics of one of the biographers of Abū Ḥanīfa, Aḥmad b. al-Ṣalt (d. 902), accused him of misrepresenting his knowledge: he claimed to know books by audition from their authors, but he had actually bought them from book dealers. Much later, Ibn Ḥajar al-ᶜAsqalānī would remark that teachers were now giving *ijāza*s to students whom they had never met.

There were other abuses too, some grosser than others: single *ijāza*s were granted for the entirety of a scholar's work, and were also occasionally granted to young children or even infants. But debasing the currency of *ijāza*s made securing authentic ones all the more desirable, and *ijāza*s would remain the preferred mode of textual transmission. To 'hand a book over' (from a scholar to a student) (*munāwala*) and to 'find a book' (in a recognized scholar's hand) (*wijāda*) came to be accepted forms of transmission, but the culture of audition, straining as it did against the rising tide of books, was never completely inundated. Students and scholars would continue to travel to learn from teachers (sometimes even noting their failure to secure an *ijāza*), attention to the integrity of transmitters always outweighed the attention paid to scribal accuracy, and teachers would continue to compose not only by writing, but by lecturing. H. Ritter (d. 1971), a German Orientalist who lived in Istanbul for many years, recounts knowing a Turkish

6 For material on *ijāza*s in this and the next paragraph, I draw on Ṣ. al-Dīn al-Munajjid, 'Ijāzāt al-samāᶜ fī al-makhṭūṭāt al-qadīma', *Majallat Maᶜhad al-Makhṭūṭāt al-ᶜArabiyya, Revue de l'institut des manuscrits arabes* (Cairo), 1 (1955), pp. 232–251; G. Vajda, *La transmission du savoir en Islam* (London, 1983) (which includes several detailed articles on the *ijāza*); H. Ritter, 'Autographs in Turkish libraries', *Oriens* 6 (1953), pp. 63–90; Pedersen, *The Arabic Book*, chapter 3; and Leder, al-Sawwās and al-Ṣāgharjī, *Muᶜjam al-samāᶜāt al-Dimašqiyya*; for Ibn Miskawayh, his *Tajārib al-umam*, ii, p. 184; one *madrasa* that does get occasionally mentioned is the Niẓāmiyya: thus Ibn Qāḍī Shuhba, *Kitāb Ṭabaqāt al-Shāfiᶜiyya*, i, p. 292.

scholar, Hoja Ismail, who possessed an unparalleled knowledge of Arabic manuscripts, and who seems to have regarded reading anything printed (rather than written in a scribe's hand) as something of a bore. For all his deep knowledge, Hoja Ismail did not take credit for writing a single book: he dictated them, and they would go into circulation under colleagues' names. Another Orientalist, S. Goitein (d. 1985), tells of his acquaintance with an immensely learned Jew from Yemen, who, living in a world of memorizing, reciting and lecturing, had the awkward handwriting of a child: 'I am not a business clerk' was his response to Goitein's surprise. In at least some respects, these very late Ottomans might have been living a thousand years earlier.[7]

Innovation and imitation

A work of history characteristically begins with an idea that is jotted down in a notebook, and that grows at variable rates into an article or a book as material is added and subtracted, arguments sharpened, rough drafts sculpted and polished into final typescripts, and typescripts transformed by publishers into what are called page proofs, which, once checked by the author and (perhaps) an editor, are sent off to be mechanically printed and bound. Provided that one allows for the intertwining of lecturing, learning, composing and reading – of audition and textuality – that is characteristic of Muslim learning, and one replaces the mechanical or electronic machinery of printing with the human copyist, the process can also be said to describe the conventions followed by many Muslim historians working from the ninth century and beyond – that is, the classical period of the historiographic tradition, when paper was in free supply, and notions of authorship had crystallized. Now it must be emphasized that the preceding applies to those historians who took it upon themselves to write a work from scratch. Many in the traditionalist culture of medieval Islam did not, choosing instead to epitomize, continue, update, or otherwise improve pre-existing works. Their goals and practices differed accordingly. In sum, although historiography was certainly subject to forces of conservatism, it could also be subject to powerful forces for innovation. As a second-class discipline that attracted many first-class minds, historiography was in many respects more creative than hard-core traditionism.

[7] Al-Dhahabī's work is *Asmāʾ man ʿāsha thamānīn sana baʿda shaykhihi aw baʿda samāʿihi* (Beirut, 1997); for a *ḥadīth* transmitter acknowledging written transmission based on collation (rather than audition), see Ibn al-Ṣalāḥ in J. Robson, 'The transmission of Muslim's Ṣaḥīḥ', *JRAS* (1949), p. 47; for Aḥmad b. al-Ṣalt, Dickinson, 'Aḥmad b. al-Ṣalt', p. 410; for Ibn Ḥajar and Hoja Ismail, Ritter, 'Autographs', pp. 63f.; for the learned Jew, S.D. Goitein, *A Mediterranean Society: The Jewish Community of the Arab World as Portrayed by the Documents of the Cairo Geniza* (Los Angeles, 1967–1993), ii, p. 179; for a translation of a modern *ijāza,* the introduction to Ibn al-Naqīb's *The Reliance of the Traveller*, trans. N.H.M. Keller (Evanston, 1991): 'The writer of these words ... says: Brother Noah Ha Mim ... has heard from me all the chapters of this book ... he understands the texts of this volume and is qualified ...; this took place in sessions, the first of which was in the month of Rajab ...'

The historian's method was determined in part by the subject matter, in part by his ambition, and in part by his purpose. The later the historian, the more models and material he had to choose from, and if he saw his task as one of making increasingly obscure material more widely accessible, he might choose a classic upon which to base an epitome (*ikhtiṣār; mukhtaṣar*), a continuation (*dhayl*; *ṣila*) or a recasting (*tahdhīb*). The result could be an ongoing enterprise of several generations, all subsequent works in greater or lesser degrees derivative from the first, but all offering something fresh, either in the form of new material or organization, or a more judicious choice of material. Perhaps the most spectacular example begins with the *al-Kamāl fī maᶜrifat al-rijāl* ('The Comprehensive Work on the Knowledge of Men') by Taqī al-Dīn al-Maqdisī (d. 1203), a prosopography of all the transmitters who appear in the six canonical *ḥadīth* collections of the ninth and early tenth century. Al-Mizzī (d. 1341) then compiled a *tahdhīb* of al-Maqdisī's work, which he naturally called the *Tahdhīb al-Kamāl* ('The Refinement of the Comprehensive Work'). Now this is a substantial and cumbersome work (it has recently been edited in 35 volumes), so Ibn Ḥajar al-ᶜAsqalānī (d. 1449) thought it appropriate to undertake a *tahdhīb* of his own, which appeared already in chapter 3: the 'Refinement of the Refinement'. This, in turn, was itself the subject of an abridgment (a *taqrīb*). The filiation of this last work, expressed in genealogical language, would thus be the *taqrīb* of the *tahdhīb* of the *tahdhīb* of al-Maqdisī's *Kamāl*. Ibn Ḥajar was as deeply imbued with the traditionalist ethos as any, and in his *tahdhīb* the traditionalist's reverence for the past manifests itself both in form and in subject matter (the transmitters of the most widely respected *ḥadīth* connections). Another one of his works, the *Rafᶜ al-iṣr ᶜan quḍāt Miṣr*, stands closer to the beginning of another multi-generational chain of works. It began with a poem by Muḥammad b. Dāniyāl (d. 1310), which mentioned all the judges of Egypt to his day. Ibn Ḥajar took an updated version of this poem and transformed it into a prosopography, to which al-Sakhāwī added a *dhayl*, a work that was itself subject to a *mukhtaṣar*.[8]

Many chronographers also chose to begin where standard works had broken off or petered out, a project that usually took them into recent or contemporaneous history – and thus the rich vein of oral history and testimony that was available to the hard-working and well-placed historian-secretary or historian-judge. We have already seen how the Ṣābiʾ historians took up where al-Ṭabarī had left off (others did too), and the same pattern was at work outside of Iraq. Thus Ibn Muyassar (d. 1278) continued a work first started by al-Musabbiḥī (d. 1029). Al-Yūnīnī wrote a continuation of the *Mirʾāt al-zamān* by Sibṭ Ibn al-Jawzī (d. 1256), a work itself inspired by the *Muntaẓam* of Sibṭ Ibn al-Jawzī's grandfather, drawing on the oral testimony of Syrian notables, Egyptian learned men, and low-ranking Mamluks. The oldest extant copy, which was written out according to the dictation of the

[8] On al-Mizzī and his successors, see Auchterlonie, *Arabic Biographical Dictionaries*, pp. 13f., and *EI*[2], 'al-Mizzī' (Juynboll); for a description of Ibn Ḥajar's work, the Patna/Bankipore *Catalogue of the Arabic and Persian Manuscripts*, xii, pp. 149f.

historian al-Birzālī (d. 1339), seems to represent al-Yūnīnī's first draft, and between this, and another, later draft, he changed his mind about a matter as fundamental as how to arrange his biographies. Writing up year 394/1003 in his history, Ibn al-Dawādārī (d. 1335) states that 'here is the end of what is in the hand of the *shaykh* Abū al-Qāsim ᶜAlī b. Muḥammad b. Yaḥyā al-Sumaysāṭī [d. early eleventh century], may God have mercy on him. I copied from it [on matters] concerning Syria; what comes after this is [nothing more than] appended rough notes' (*fa-mudhayyal ᶜalayhi min al-musawwadāt*). Al-Sumaysāṭī's book, here clearly still a work in progress, does not survive.[9]

It was not just prosopography and chronography that generated epitomes and recastings. Of all the Prophetic biographies, the classic (Ibn Hishām's) was itself an expurgated version of Ibn Isḥāq's *Sīra*, which (assuming for the moment that there was an 'original') seems to have covered a great deal of pre-Islamic and post-Prophetic material that was omitted by Ibn Hishām. This epitome in turn inspired several subsequent epitomes, one of which was written by Ibn ᶜAbd al-Barr (d. 1071). Here we can see how innovation expressed itself within the constraints of an imitating project. On the one hand, Ibn ᶜAbd al-Barr makes plain that he abridges from the works of two of the greatest early *sīra* authorities, Mūsā b. ᶜUqba and Ibn Isḥāq (in the recension of Ibn Hishām), and readily volunteers that in narrative structure (*al-nasaq kulluhu*) he follows the latter. This is a work of abridgment, and one naturally abridges authoritative works. On the other hand, he does not limit himself to Mūsā and Ibn Isḥāq: 'At times I mention something which is not from the two [books]', he tells us. What is more, he breaks from their precedent by omitting Muḥammad's birth, childhood and pre-Prophetic experience, having treated these in a previous book, a prosopography of the Prophet's Companions. And Ibn ᶜAbd al-Barr's work would serve, in its own turn, as the basis for the *Sīra* composed by a contemporary, Ibn Ḥazm (d. 1064). Al-Shīrāzī (d. 1083) based his *Ṭabaqāt al-fuqahāʾ* on the work of his teacher Abū Ṭayyib al-Ṭabarī, which he tried to outstrip.[10]

So epitomizing could mean innovating – within bounds. The interplay between imitation and innovation can also be seen in the act of commenting. Notes taken by a teacher in the margin of the classic he was studying or teaching might eventually be published (sometimes by a student) as a commentary on the classic; this kind of composition should be distinguished from the more 'accidental' migration of commentary or corrections into texts, which can occur when a scribe mistakes an earlier scribe's marginal notes for the author's work. Material that al-Ṣafadī would later integrate into his *al-Tibr al-masbūk* began as marginal notes to his own copy of Ibn Taghrī Birdī's *Ḥawādith al-duhūr*. The *Maᶜālim al-īmān fī maᶜrifat ahl al-Qayrawān* is a prosopography of the scholars of the North African city of

[9] On al-Yūnīnī, see Guo, *Early Mamluk Syrian Historiography*; on Ibn al-Dawādārī, his *Kanz al-durar wa-jāmiᶜ al-ghurar* (Cairo, 1961), vi, p. 272; on continuations in general, see C. Farah, *The Dhayl in Medieval Arabic Historiography* (New Haven, 1967).

[10] See Ibn ᶜAbd al-Barr, *al-Durar fī ikhtiṣār al-maghāzī wa'l-siyar* (Cairo, 1966), p. 29; and Jarrar, *Prophetenbiographie*, pp. 138ff.

Qayrawān, which was first founded in the early ninth century. The three-volume book consists in the work of two Qayrawānī scholars, al-Dabbāgh (d. 1296), and Ibn Nājī al-Tanūkhī (d. 1435), the latter having taken up, commented upon, and integrated his comments into the former's work. A commentary, written, as it often was, in the margins of a classic, naturally added to its bulk, and this could set the train back in motion towards an epitome. To move momentarily from history to law: one eleventh-century Andalusian jurist wrote a commentary on the *Muwaṭṭaʾ* of Mālik b. Anas (d. 795), for which he then wrote an epitome; he then proceeded to epitomize this epitome.[11]

Writing history: practices and conventions

These, then, were some of the practices, possibilities and constraints that governed historical writing. How did our historians actually do their work?

We may first ask when they researched and wrote. We have already seen that historical writing was usually carried out by those who were employed to do something else: scholars tended to teach (usually the law) and secretaries were employed to draft documents, letters and speeches. For those so employed, writing history was generally left for spare moments, especially at night. For those of independent means, who could accordingly devote as much time as they wanted to their scholarship, things were naturally different. We read that Ibn al-Athīr, who seems to have lived most of his life as a private scholar, wrote much of his great chronography at a country home, perhaps looking out upon the ruins of an Abbasid palace; if so, it must have been a salutary reminder of the transience of life and the fickleness of fortune. Research and writing, then, as now, tended to be a solitary affair, the occasional exception being noted. There is some reason to think that Baybars al-Manṣūrī employed a Christian to undertake some of his research. A very different exception is illustrated by Usāma b. Munqidh (d. 1188), who seems to have dictated his memoirs to a copyist, moving from story to story as his memory prompted him. Had he begun earlier in his life, he presumably would have composed his work in more conventional ways, since he had been steeped in Arabic letters, and was a first-class poet in his own right. As it was, he was 90 when he sat down to tell his stories, and by his own description in no shape to write it all down himself.[12]

Research itself often began with notes, and these typically taken on slips and/or in notebooks. One imagines that Ibn al-Dawādārī, who was working with a draft of al-Sumaysāṭī's book, would have supplemented al-Sumaysāṭī's text with material from his own notebooks. Slips (*juzāzāt*; *ruqayʿāt*) seem to have been especially

[11] For al-Dabbāgh and Ibn Nājī al-Tanūkhī, see the *Maʿālim al-īmān fī maʿrifat ahl al-Qayrawān* (Cairo, 1968); the Andalusian jurist is Sulaymān b. Khalaf (d. 1100), on whom see Yāqūt, *Irshād*, vi[4], pp. 251ff.

[12] For Ibn al-Athīr, see Richards, 'Ibn al-Athīr', p. 78; for Baybars and his Christian research assistant, the editor's introduction to the partial edition of his *Zubdat al-fikra*, pp. xxi f.; for Usāma and his declining health, see the *Arab-Syrian Gentleman*, especially pp. 190ff.

useful for prosopographers, much of whose work consisted in reorganizing, reclassifying, editing or supplementing biographical material they inherited from existing research, be it their own or their predecessors'. We know that Ibn Ḥajar al-ᶜAsqalānī used them, and so too al-Sakhāwī, from whose amazing and quite idiosyncratic corpus one scholar has quite reasonably inferred the presence of an elaborate card index of traditions and traditionists. One of al-Sakhāwī's works lists examples of traditions according to the circumstance of their transmission or transmitters, e.g., 'a tradition received at the Kaᶜba', 'a tradition transmitted by a chain of Muḥammads', and 'a tradition transmitted by an informant while paring his nails on a Thursday' (Prophetic *ḥadīth* encourage nail paring, but some authorities opposed it on the day of prayer, Friday); the author documents no fewer than 101 such categories. Cards and slips were thus immensely useful, but they were also dead ends. By contrast, the notebook (usually *kitāb*, less frequently *daftar*) was a potential book in and of itself. We have already seen that the earliest Prophetic biography may have emerged from private and semi-private notebooks, which were intended for teaching or study and recorded by teachers or their students, and which then slipped into circulation in a number of recensions. As notions of authorship sharpened, so too did the distinction between private notebooks and published works, but the notebook would often remain the building block of historical narrative. Trained primarily as a *ḥadīth* specialist, al-Yūnīnī still found time from a young age to keep notebooks, many of which would later emerge as authored books. Al-Ṭabarī seems to have been at least 60 years old when he finally finished a draft of at least parts of his monumental *Taʾrīkh*, which he made public in lectures during 906 or 907; some of its *isnād*s suggest that he had been collecting historical material already as a teenager, attending lectures that gave him access to the work of late eighth-century chronography and *sīra*. These were presumably recorded in notebooks. A historian of the following generation felt comfortable enough to refer to 'my notebook' (*kitābī*) in a history of his own.[13]

If notebooks typically contained lecture notes (al-Ṭabarī, for example, would compare the notes he took from the lectures of one of his teachers to the books this teacher had himself used), they might also contain material gathered in a number of ways, which, once topically or chronologically arranged, could be progressively revised into a finished work. When limited to contemporary events, the chronologically arranged notebook is what we would normally call a diary, and we are fortunate to have one eleventh-century example, which was written by a Ḥanbalī of Baghdad. The text, in the form that we have it, was clearly not intended for publication, and it seems to be the kernel of what would have become a larger and

[13] On Ibn Ḥajar and his slips, see Rahmani, 'Life and works', 46 (1972), p. 361; Kohlberg, *Medieval Muslim Scholar*, p. 86, and Rosenthal, *Technique and Approach*, p. 7; for al-Sakhāwī, A.J. Arberry, *Sakhawiana: A Study Based on the Chester Beatty MS. Arab. 773* (London, 1951), pp. 32ff.; for a discussion of the relevant *ḥadīth* about nail paring, M.J. Kister, '"Pare your nails": a study of an early tradition', in his *Society and Religion from Jāhiliyya to Islam* (Aldershot, 1990); on al-Yūnīnī, Guo, *Early Mamluk Syrian Historiography*, p. 10; for 'my notebook', Robinson, *Empire and Elites*, p. 132, note 39.

more finished work (in fact, other versions are cited by later authorities, who call it a 'history' [*taʾrīkh*]). Taking as his organizing principle the first day of each (lunar) month, Ibn al-Bannāʾ records events and personalities of personal interest. He seems to have had a special enthusiasm for dream interpretation – an interest common enough amongst medieval Muslims – but he also includes details of quotidian Baghdad life: the comings and goings of notable men, controversies, deaths, the occasional riot; there are fears of the plague, and the narrator, noticing some boils on his skin, foregoes his usual trip to the mosque. The whole very much reads as the still-private document that it was. The official diary written by al-Qāḍī al-Fāḍil (d. 1200) seems to have been a very different kind of text, but it, too, was clearly organized by daily entries; in fact, Ḥājjī Khalīfa calls it a 'history arranged according to days' (*taʾrīkh al-Qāḍī al-Fāḍil murattab ʿalā al-ayyām*). Ibn al-Qalānisī (d. 1160), who was writing in Damascus, frequently prefaces his reports with the phrase 'And news from x arrived, that …' This is a common updating formula.[14]

Written as it was by an eleventh-century historian, Ibn al-Bannāʾ's diary is an extraordinary find. It is also noteworthy as an example of contemporary history, in which the historian, through direct observation, listening to news and a variety of oral reports, sourced himself. Books that drew upon a remoter past relied not only upon slips and notebooks, but earlier works of history. Now in some cases, such as the chronographer al-Yaʿqūbī (a quite early example) and the Prophetic biographers Ibn Sayyid al-Nās and Mughulṭāʾī, historians do us the favour of including a bibliography of many of the most often used sources. Al-Kalāʿī (d. 1237), like some of the other late biographers of the Prophet, discusses his sources in some detail, even giving us a sense of his method. He knows of al-Wāqidī's *Maghāzī*, but it is no longer available to him; no matter: since it accords with Ibn Isḥāq, he can dispense with al-Wāqidī 'by virtue of Ibn Isḥāq's linguistic elegance in presentation, the beauty of his expression …' In the introduction to this prosopography, Ibn Ḥajar patiently lists the sources he consulted, pointing out that he frequently used autograph copies. In some cases, particularly large prosopographies where space could be at a premium, a variety of *sigla* could be used to mark important sources: 'whenever I use the expression "our *shaykh*"', writes al-Sakhāwī, 'I mean Ibn Ḥajar, our teacher'. Other abbreviations were used, too.[15]

[14] For the diary, see Makdisi, 'Autograph diary, I'; for composing from notebooks, Bellamy, 'Sources', p. 18; for al-Qāḍī al-Fāḍil, Ḥājjī Khalīfa, *Kashf al-ẓunūn*, ii, p. 139; cf. the use of official diaries in the 'historiographical office' in T'ang China in Twitchett, *The Writing of Official History under the T'ang*, pp. 13 and 35ff.; for Ibn al-Qalānisī, his *Dhayl Taʾrīkh Dimashq*, p. 282.

[15] On scholarly conventions in general, see Rosenthal, *Technique and Approach*; for al-Ṣafadī, Popper, 'Sakhāwī's criticism of Ibn Taghrī Birdī', p. 372; on al-Yaʿqūbī's bibliography, F. Rosenthal, 'On medieval authorial bibliographies: al-Yaʿqūbī and Ibn Ḥajar', in M. Mir, ed., *Literary Heritage of Classical Islam: Arabic and Islamic Studies in Honor of James A. Bellamy* (Princeton, 1993), pp. 255–274; for Mughulṭāʾī, his *al-Ishāra ilā sīrat al-Muṣṭafā*, pp. 465ff. (on the sources of the potted history that follows the *sīra* section); for al-Kalāʿī, *al-Iktifāʾ*, p. 7; for Ibn Ḥajar, his *Inbāʾ al-ghumr*, i, pp. 2f.; for al-Sakhāwī's '*shaykhunā*', his *al-Ḍawʾ al-lāmiʿ li-ahl al-qarn al-tāsiʿ*, i, p. 5; for other abbreviations, Endress, 'Handschriftenkunde', p. 285.

Precisely how earlier works were cited varied from one historian to the next and from one period to the next. Modern historians, particularly those interested in uncovering the sources that lie behind historical narrative, conventionally heap praise upon those medieval historians whose practices most closely approximate their own. Thus we are particularly fond of those historians who quote *verbatim*, who clearly identify both the author and his work, and who clearly signal where the quotation begins and where it ends. Ibn al-Furāt (d. 1405), to take one of many possible examples, frequently cites (Muḥammad b. ᶜAlī) Ibn Shaddād (d. 1285) and his *al-Aᶜlāq al-khaṭīra fī dhikr al-Shām wa'l-Jazīra* according to this method. Those who draw liberally on earlier sources without any attribution are harder to work with. These include Ibn al-Athīr, who volunteers his reliance on al-Ṭabarī, but otherwise speaks only of 'well-known histories and famous books'. This is not very helpful. Working in the northern Iraqi city of Mosul, which was out of the Iraqi academic mainstream, Ibn al-Athīr also tried to disarm his critics by explaining away his omissions on the grounds that 'what is in the far east and west must by nature remain inaccessible to he who is in Mosul'; one should take such passages with a grain of salt. Those historians who cite early sources through later intermediaries *without noting these intermediary sources*, are misleading to us moderns, since they give the false impression of scholarly rigour and the survival of early material. The practice was also distressing to some pre-modern scholars: al-Suyūṭī tells us in an autobiographical notice that he found precisely this at work in one of his teacher's books. As we have already seen, these 'secondary' sources might be supplemented as appropriate by materials the historian had managed to secure: everything from pieces of correspondence (especially in chronography) to book titles (especially in prosopography).[16]

And where does the *isnād* figure in all of this? It might be thought that this would be a boon to modern historians. For while historians of Greek and Syriac typically have to work with works of history that obstinately refuse to name their sources, ours attach what is advertised as an exact transmission history to *each individual account*. In practice, however, historians of Greek and Syriac historiography often have an easier time of it. It may be the rare Syriac history that explicitly names its sources (an example is the early eleventh-century Elijah of Nisibis), but one frequently finds that their works have a relatively straightforward architecture: successive sections, each consisting principally of one source, are 'layered' chronologically, with a minimum of seepage between the layers or redactional interference on the part of the compiler-author. An example is the eighth-century 'Zuqnin Chronicle', which was compiled by the anonymous monk from northern Syria; it can be said to consist of six principal layers (or thereabouts). And because stratifying these sources is a relatively straightforward project, we can even isolate and recover otherwise lost sources: the history written

[16] For Ibn al-Athīr's comments, see his *al-Kāmil,* i, pp. 2f.; on Mamluk practices of source citation (especially Ibn al-Dawādārī), Haarmann, *Quellenstudien,* pp. 192ff.; on relatively late sources' use of early sources without noting intermediaries, Landau-Tasseron, 'On the reconstruction of lost sources'; for al-Suyūṭī, his autobiography in his *Ḥusn al-muḥāḍara*, p. 154.

by Dionysius of Tell Mahre has not survived, but by working through two later sources, we have a very good sense of what it must have been like. Now careful *isnād* analysis can occasionally tell us what individuals thought, but the circulation of *akhbār* was so widespread, and the passage of a given *khabar* so tortuous, that reconstructing sources in any detail is usually impossible.[17]

Finishing histories

Because the passage from a work's conception to its successful completion – that is, from the historian's mind to a first draft (usually called a *musawwada* or *muswadda*) to the copyist's final copy or fair copy (*mubayyaḍa* or *mubyaḍḍa*) – could be a difficult one, some works were finished, some left partially finished, and some abandoned completely. Life being uncertain, delays were not uncommon, and several projects were often juggled at the same time.

Then, as now, historians worked at their own pace and schedule, the rhythm of their work being determined by time, energy and incentives: Ibn ᶜAbd al-Ẓāhir (d. 1292) read out instalments of his royal biography to its subject (the Sultan), who would reward him with costly robes. Some historians worked quickly: al-Qasṭallānī (d. 1517) completed the draft of his life of the Prophet on the 2nd of Shawwāl 898 (25 July 1493), and by the 15th of Shaᶜbān (30 May 1494) the fair (final) copy had been completed. Some got a start, then bogged down. In the course of his work, Ibn al-Athīr found himself paralyzed by a combination of indolence and self-doubt, and left a draft of his chronography (*al-Kāmil*) untouched for some twenty years; it was only through the help of colleagues (and the pressure of a sovereign) that he returned to the task. Although he may have spent as many as ten years making revisions and updating the work, it is not at all clear if he ever considered the work finished. Others worked slowly and tinkered: al-Ṣafadī is said to have read the entirety of his contemporary prosopography out loud in Damascus in 1356–7, but he would continue to work on it until his death in 1363. (In fact, authors of much shorter works have found it difficult to stop tinkering: Walt Whitman seems to have produced no fewer than nine editions of his *Leaves of Grass* over a nearly 40-year period.) Ibn Taghrī Birdī had written a detailed account of a Rhodes campaign, but lost it, so he had to rewrite it in a condensed form. In the case of the *Khiṭaṭ* of al-Maqrīzī (d. 1442), we are fortunate to have an early draft of the work, to which one can compare the finished product; written on used paper, it is very much a work in progress, scraps of additional material having been inserted in several spots.[18]

[17] For Dionysius' history as reconstructed from two later sources and translated, A. Palmer, *The Seventh Century in the West-Syrian Chronicles* (Liverpool, 1993), pp. 85–221.

[18] For Ibn ᶜAbd al-Ẓāhir, see Holt, 'Three biographies', p. 20; for al-Ṣafadī, Little, 'al-Ṣafadī', p. 198; for al-Qasṭallānī, the Patna/Bankipore *Catalogue of the Arabic and Persian Manuscripts*, xv, p. 83; for Ibn al-Athīr, Richards, 'Ibn al-Athīr', p. 79; for Ibn Taghrī Birdī, Popper, 'Sakhāwī's criticism', p. 375; for al-Maqrīzī's draft, the edition by A.F. Sayyid, *Musawwadat kitāb al-mawāᶜiẓ wa'l-iᶜtibār* (London, 1995) and his 'Early methods of book composition'.

In some cases, gaps were left in drafts for good reason. Much like 'advancers' in today's newspapers, obituaries of contemporary figures could be written up in advance, the death dates being added when they became available. The *Ṭabaqāt* of Ibn Saᶜd (d. 845), as we have already seen, came to a close after its author's demise: a student seems to have added his death date, and the work also includes figures who died a full twenty years after Ibn Saᶜd's death. Ibn al-Qalānisī, who spent several years polishing his history of Damascus, tells us that he left blank spaces so that in revising his draft he could insert corrections he had been unable to make earlier. Ibn Ḥajar al-ᶜAsqalānī seems to have finished a draft of his prosopography of eighth-century figures in 830/1426, but he continued to make additions until 837/1433, adding a few supplementary notices after that, too. Ibn Khaldūn (d. 1406) filled out the sections of his *Muqaddima* concerning the East after he had travelled there. One ninth-century historian from Fez somewhat apologetically explains that he cannot provide the name of the official who led the pilgrimage in year 226/840–841 because he was in Egypt; in this case, one imagines that his travels prevented him taking appropriate notes.[19]

Barring a catastrophe of one kind or another – one work was lost because its Cordovan author passed it on to his servant, who then promptly fell into the Guadalquiver River – once an historian decided that his work was indeed finished, he was faced with the challenge of publication – in the idiom of commercial publishing, the work's reproduction, distribution and marketing. Multiple reproduction was relatively straightforward: authors could copy out their own work (autograph copies of historical works only begin to appear in some numbers from the thirteenth century), employ professional scribes, scholars with time on their hands (Yaḥyā b. ᶜAdī claimed to have copied 100 leaves a day) or eager students. Writing was certainly tiring work: one member of the Ṣābiᵓ family of courtiers and historians would rest or nap after making rough drafts, since his handwriting would become so poor with fatigue. The work of copying out one manuscript of Ibn ᶜAsākir's huge history of Damascus (recently edited in some 80 volumes) had to be divided up amongst ten scribes. In some cases, distribution served as a form of promotion: books could be given to colleagues (al-Samᶜānī [d. 1167] sent a book of his to Ibn ᶜAsākir [d. 1176], who reciprocated with some lines of poetry), or donated to libraries. One such gift, presented by Ibn Khaldūn to a North African library, still survives.[20]

In giving away copies of their newly published works, authors no doubt hoped for positive reviews, but we also know that they tried to *guarantee* good reviews by

[19] For Ibn al-Qalānisī, see his *Dhayl Taᵓrīkh Dimashq*, p. 283; for Ibn Ḥajar, see the Patna/Bankipore *Catalogue of the Arabic and Persian Manuscripts*, xii, p. 11; for Ibn Khaldūn, W.J. Fischel, *Ibn Khaldūn in Egypt* (Berkeley and Los Angeles, 1967), p. 4; on dating matters in Ibn Saᶜd, chapter 4; the scholar from Fez is Yaᶜqūb b. Sufyān al-Fasawī in his *Kitāb al-Maᶜrifa wa'l-taᵓrīkh*, i, p. 207.

[20] For Yaḥyā, see Ibn al-Nadīm, *Fihrist*, p. 322 (Dodge, *Fihrist*, p. 631); for the tired Ṣābiᵓ historian, F. Rosenthal, *Four Essays on Art and Literature in Islam* (Leiden, 1971), p. 30; for Ibn ᶜAsākir's ten scribes, Rosenthal, *Technique and Approach*, p. 2; for al-Samᶜānī and Ibn ᶜAsākir, Gilbert, 'Institutionalization', p. 110; for Ibn Khaldūn's gift, E. Lévi-Provençal, 'Note sur l'exemplaire du *Kitâb al-ᶜIbar* offert par Ibn Ḫaldûn à la bibliothèque d'al-Ḳarawîyîn à Fès', *JA* 103 (1923), pp. 161–168.

having a 'blurb' (*taqrīẓ*) written by trusted mentors or ambitious students, which was then inserted into copies of the work in question. Not unlike the hyperbolic copy that is printed on back covers of books nowadays, these were typically written in an ornate style appropriate to the occasion. One such 'blurb' was written by Ibn Ḥajar:

> I have read this book, which attests that its author is an arbiter who does not accept bribes, and which is unique, although it has its fellows [that is, works of comparable quality] in [other] works of his. I have contemplated its chapters and found joy coming to me from each ... When all this instructive information shone forth from it, the sharp edge of my tongue was too dull to describe (praise) it ...

Another 'blurb' was written by none other than Ibn Khaldūn himself:

> I have read this book, a meadow for frequent visitors, a pleasure park for people to traverse, a cure for ignorant doubters ... It is an ocean with billowing waves, pure pruning bringing out the essence, pride for the scholarly community for obvious reasons, a shady garden of manifold information of renewed youthful vigor, and the equivalent of perfection for human thought and linguistic science with its gate wide open.[21]

Authors might arrange to have their book favourably reviewed, but this did not stop bad press, particularly amongst professional academics. Perhaps this explains why Ibn Ḥajar, upon completing one of his many, many compositions, threw himself a party, which seems to have amounted to nothing less than what we would call a book launch. Particularly in this period, Muslim historians were no strangers to self-promotion.[22]

Nor were they strangers to controversy. Sibṭ Ibn al-Jawzī's *Mirʾāt al-zamān* seems to have been roundly criticized in its time, and al-Suyūṭī, one reads, took offence at al-Qasṭallānī's unacknowledged use of his own work in his Prophetic biography; he went so far as to make his views public, leading al-Qasṭallānī to travel to Cairo to offer his apologies in person. There was nothing new in professional jealousies (al-Khaṭīb al-Baghdādī had been accused of everything from plagiarism and homosexuality to drunkenness), but al-Qasṭallānī was working inside what had become a hothouse of Syrian and Egyptian historiography, where jealousies and rivalries were commonplace (al-Sakhāwī and al-Suyūṭī were frequently at each other's throats), where the standards of history writing were now clear, and the associated anxieties and insecurities nearly palpable. Ibn Kathīr (d. 1373) recounts a dream in which he is taken to task by a *ḥadīth* specialist for having failed to cite a well-known authority in one of his compositions. Nearly all historians could empathize with that.[23]

[21] For the 'blurb', see F. Rosenthal, '"Blurbs" (*Taqrīẓ*) from fourteenth-century Egypt', *Oriens* 27–8 (1981), pp. 177–196 (the translations, which are very slightly modified, are his, on pp. 190ff.); also al-Suyūṭī, *Ḥusn al-muḥāḍara,* p. 154 (for mention of two *taqrīẓ*es).

[22] The launch (of his *Fatḥ al-bārī*) can be found in al-Maqrīzī, *Kitāb al-sulūk* (Cairo, 1973), iv, p. 1108.

[23] For Sibṭ Ibn al-Jawzī, see Guo, *Early Mamluk Syrian Historiography*, p. 17; for al-Suyūṭī and al-Qasṭallānī, Ḥājjī Khalīfa, *Kashf al-ẓunūn*, vi, pp. 245ff.; for Ibn Ḥajar, F. Malti-Douglas, 'Controversy and its effects in the biographical tradition of al-Khaṭīb al-Baghdādī', *SI* 46 (1977), pp. 115–30; for Ibn Kathīr, H. Laoust, 'Ibn Kaṯīr historien', *Arabica* 2 (1955), p. 59.

Conclusion

This has been a small book about a very large subject. In words that should now be familiar to the reader, it is in some sense a *mukhtaṣar* – a concentrate of information intended only to suggest the contours of a much larger and deeper reservoir of learning.

And so it must be. Only a small fraction of an immensely productive literary tradition has been edited and understood, and much of this is early chronography, to which the tradition itself attached less value than it did to other historiographic forms. Considering how few and fragmentary the manuscripts are for the great chronographies written by al-Ṭabarī, Ibn Miskawayh, the Ṣābiʾ historians, and al-Musabbiḥī, one might reasonably conclude that the tradition focused its attention and resources elsewhere – especially in Prophetic biography and traditionist prosopography. Considering how much time and effort modern historians have spent identifying, piecing together, editing, translating and commenting upon al-Ṭabarī, Ibn Miskawayh, the Ṣābi' historians and al-Musabbiḥī, one might also conclude that European scholars had time and money to spare (both of which are absurd), or that their interests differed markedly from those of pre-modern Muslim historians and readers (which is the case). This small book has tried to accommodate these differing perspectives, but I leave it to others to profit fully from the rapid pace of publishing in the Middle East, which makes available a wider spectrum of historiography. Much of this is being put online in the form of searchable electronic texts, which promise to change how scholars read and research.[1]

Why al-Ṭabarī mattered so much more to nineteenth-century Europeans than he did to nineteenth-century Ottomans is an important question, but it is the topic of another book. This one may usefully end by restating the development and function of Islamic historiography.

We have seen that historiography and historians stood on the margins of an academic establishment designed by and for lawyers. Rather than generate truths, it could only reflect or exemplify truths already made manifest by God, either directly (through revelation), or indirectly, through the jurist's study of the law. Its

[1] One of these is http://www.alwaraq.com, which boasts that it makes available over 1,000,000 pages of Arabic texts online.

function was accordingly restricted to instructing, moralizing, entertaining and archiving, and its range was initially constrained by traditionalist scruples, particularly taboos against contemporary history. The traditionist admitted history into the Islamic sciences, but he hardly celebrated it, and this remained true even after the twelfth and thirteenth centuries, when a more self-confident historiographic tradition emerged, one animated by interests and governed by conventions that were increasingly independent of the traditionists' concerns. For nearly all of our period, authors were historians only as part-timers, and such social status as they enjoyed derived from other activities that they may have pursued, academic or otherwise. On the other hand, already well before the twelfth and thirteenth centuries, an enormous amount of historiography had been written, and Muslims were well on their way to generating a tradition that outstrips in size and quality anything written by contemporaneous Jews or Christians. The impulse was two-fold. The spectacular success of empire building during the seventh and eighth centuries created a market of readers hungry for historical narrative, especially several forms of chronography, which offered lessons and models to rulers, their courts and urban elites; and this market survived the breakup of the empire during the tenth and eleventh centuries, when many successor states rationalized their experience of political power by patronizing local historiography. Second, although dyed-in-the-wool traditionists might not have advertised their interest in historiography, many were enthusiastic about those historiographic forms that reinforced traditionist institutions (especially the schools of law) and attitudes (especially reverence for the Prophet Muḥammad, whose model they claimed to transmit). In practice, this meant that they wrote a great many prosopographies of jurists and a great many biographies of the Prophet.

So historiography occupied an ambivalent position in the republic of letters, and the fact that it was never fully institutionalized may explain its relative dynamism. We did see that pre-modern Muslim historians shared something of the conservatism of other pre-modern historians: the 'classics' were revered and imitated, and genres, once established, were very durable. Historical narrative had grown alongside other forms of narrative, including *ḥadīth*, and the emerging discipline of *ḥadīth* influenced historiography considerably. But whereas there was no room for authorship in the transmission of the Prophet's words and deeds (at least theoretically), there certainly was room for it in the transmission and production of historical narrative. And although it may have taken some time for the two to be disentangled, historians would begin to 'innovate incrementally', blurring genres, experimenting with language, and shifting their attention to new periods and interests. I pointed out earlier that historiography was a second-class profession that attracted a great many first-class minds.

The shape of the tradition can also be described in terms of states and élites. Islamic historiography was generated by a combination of relatively strong social élites and relatively weak states. The former produced educated sons equipped with all the tools necessary to write history, men who might turn to it on their own, since representations of the past could function to exemplify truths and provide models for fellow believers, and set standards to which contemporary rulers might be unfavourably compared. For their part, states had a stake in learning in general and historiography in particular. Nearly all patronized representations of the past that legitimized their exercise of power (strong and weak states alike sought to translate the power to coerce into the ability to persuade), and large-scale learning (such as sophisticated historiography) depended on urban networks of knowledge – reading, teaching, writing – that states cultivated and defended. It is this – the mutual attraction of historians and ambitious states – that explains the shape of the chronology of historians standing at the beginning of this book. In starting in Iraq and ending in Egypt, the chronology traces the path of the caliphate itself, from early Abbasid Kufa and Basra, to Ayyubid and Mamluk Cairo.

Suggestions for further reading

Readers may find useful the following lists, which are intended to be representative rather than exhaustive, and emphasize recent publications at the expense of some older material. For an especially thorough list of titles on the early period, see A.A. Duri, *The Rise of Historical Writing Among the Arabs*, ed. and trans. by L.I. Conrad (Princeton, 1983), pp. 12f., note 1. For the Mamluk period, readers should consult the online Mamluk Bibliography, which can be found at: http://www.lib.uchicago.edu/e/su/mideast/MamBib.html

I Surveys, studies, bibliographies, collections and the relevant reference works

I.i Reference works

P. Auchterlonie, *Arabic Biographical Dictionaries: A Summary Guide and Bibliography* (Durham, 1987).

C. Brockelmann, *Geschichte der arabischen Litteratur* (Weimar, Leipzig and Leiden, 1898–1949).

Encyclopaedia Iranica (London, 1985–).

The Encyclopaedia of Islam (Leiden, 1913–1936; Supplement, 1938; New Edition, 1954–).

ᶜU. Kaḥḥāla, *Muᶜjam al-muʾallifīn* (Damascus, 1957–1961; multiple Beirut reprints).

J.S. Meisami and P. Starkey, eds., *Encyclopedia of Arabic Literature* (London and New York, 1998).

M.B. Norton, gen. ed., *The American Historical Association's Guide to Historical Literature* (3rd ed.) (New York, 1995).

F. Sezgin, *Geschichte des arabischen Schrifttums*, vol. 1 (Leiden, 1967).

D.R. Woolf, ed., *A Global Encyclopedia of Historical Writing* (New York, 1988).

I.ii Monographs, surveys, collected works

J. Ashtiany et al., eds., *ᶜAbbasid Belles-Lettres* (Cambridge History of Arabic Literature; Cambridge, 1990).

A.F.L. Beeston et al., eds., *Arabic Literature to the End of the Umayyad Period* (Cambridge History of Arabic Literature; Cambridge, 1983).

C. Cahen, *Introduction à l'histoire du monde musulman médiéval: VIIe-XVe siècle (méthodologie et éléments de bibliographie)* (Paris, 1983), a revision of J. Sauvaget and C. Cahen, *Introduction à l'histoire de l'Orient musulman* (Paris, 1961), the latter translated as *Introduction to the History of the Muslim East: A Bibliographical Guide* (Berkeley, 1965).

M. Cooperson and S.M. Toorawa, eds., *Arabic Literary Culture, 500–925* (The Dictionary of Literary Biography; Detroit, 1978–; forthcoming).

D.M. Dunlop, *Arab Civilization to A.D. 1500* (London and Beirut, 1971).

C. Farah, *The Dhayl in Medieval Arabic Historiography* (New Haven, 1967).

U. Haarmann, ed., *Geschichte der arabischen Welt* (Munich, 1987).

R.S. Humphreys, *Islamic History: A Framework for Inquiry* (Princeton, rev. ed., 1991).

T. Khalidi, *Arabic Historical Thought in the Classical Period* (Cambridge, 1994).

B. Lewis and P.M. Holt, eds., *Historians of the Middle East* (London, 1962).

D.O. Morgan, ed., *Medieval Historical Writing in the Christian and Islamic Worlds* (London, 1982).

T. Nagel, *Die islamische Welt bis 1500* (Munich, 1998).

S. Muṣṭafā, *al-Taʾrīkh al-ʿarabī waʾl-muʾarrikhūn* (Beirut, 1978–1979).

B. Radtke, *Weltgeschichte und Weltbeschreibung im mittelalterlichen Islam* (Beirut and Stuttgart, 1992).

D.F. Reynolds, ed., *Interpreting the Self: Autobiography in the Arabic Literary Tradition* (Berkeley and Los Angeles, 2001).

F. Rosenthal, *A History of Muslim Historiography* (Leiden, 2nd rev. ed., 1968).

M.J.L. Young et al., eds., *Religion, Learning and Science in the ʿAbbasid Period* (Cambridge History of Arabic Literature; Cambridge, 1990).

I.iii Articles

M. Abiad, 'Origine et développement des dictionnaires biographiques arabes', *BEO* 31 (1979), pp. 7–15.

L. Ammann, 'Kommentiertes Literaturverzeichnis zu Zeitvorstellungen und geschichtlichen Denken in der islamischen Welt', *WI* 37 (1997), pp. 28–87.

H. Busse, 'Arabische Historiographie und Geographie', in H. Gätje, ed., *Grundriß der Arabischen Philologie, Band II: Literaturwissenschaft* (Wiesbaden, 1987), pp. 264–297.

C. Cahen, 'Notes sur l'historiographie dans la communauté musulmane médiévale', *REI* 44 (1976), pp. 81–88.

A. Cheddadi, 'Historiographie musulmane', in A. Burguière, ed., *Dictionnaire des sciences historiques* (Paris, 1986), pp. 482–484.

H.A.R. Gibb, 'Taʾrīkh', *EI*, Supplement (Leiden, 1938), pp. 233–245; reprinted in his *Studies on the Civilization of Islam*, ed. S.J. Shaw and W.R. Polk (Princeton, 1962), pp. 108–137.

S. Günther, '*Maqâtil* literature in medieval Islam', *JAL* 25 (1994), pp. 192–212.

I. Hafsi, 'Recherches sur le genre *«Ṭabaqāt»* dans la littérature arabe, I, II, III', *Arabica* 23 (1976), pp. 227–265; 24 (1977), pp. 1–41 and 150–186.

R.S. Humpreys, 'Historiography – Islamic' in J. Strayer, ed., *Dictionary of the Middle Ages* (New York, 1985), vi, pp. 249–255.

R.S. Humphreys, 'Taʾrīkh: II. Historical writing', *EI²*, x, pp. 271–280.

T. Khalidi, 'Islamic biographical dictionaries: a preliminary assessment', *MW* 63 (1973), pp. 53–65.

B. Lewis, 'Perceptions musulmanes de l'histoire et de l'historiographie', in R. Curiel and R. Gyselen, eds., *Itinéraires d'Orient: hommages à Claude Cahen* (*Res Orientales*, vi) (Bures-sur-Yvette, 1994), pp. 77–81.

B. Lewis, 'Reflections on Islamic historiography', *Middle Eastern Lectures* 2 (1997), pp. 69–80.
G. Makdisi, 'The diary in Islamic historiography: some notes', *History and Theory* 25 (1986), pp. 173–185.
G. Makdisi, '*Ṭabaqāt*-biography: law and orthodoxy in classical Islam', *IS* 32 (1993), pp. 371–396.
D.O. Morgan, 'The evolution of two Asian historiographical traditions', in M. Bentley, ed., *Companion to Historiography* (London, 1997), pp. 11–22 (on the Islamic and Chinese).
W. al-Qāḍī, 'Biographical dictionaries: inner structure and cultural significance', in G.N. Atiyeh, ed., *The Book in the Islamic World: The Written Word and Communication in the Middle East* (Albany, 1995), pp. 93–122.
B. Radtke, 'Towards a typology of Abbasid universal chronicles', *Occasional Papers of the School of Abbasid Studies* 3 (1991), pp. 1–18.
B. Radtke, 'Das Wirklichkeitsverständnis islamischer Universalshistoriker', *DI* 62 (1985), pp. 59–70.
G. Richter, *Das Geschichtsbild der arabischen Historiker des Mittelalters* (Tübingen, 1933; *IC* 33 [1959]; translated into English as 'Medieval Arabic historiography', *IS* 23 (1984), pp. 225–247.
J. de Somogyi, 'The development of Arabic historiography', *JSS* 3 (1958), pp. 373–387.
B. Spuler, 'Islamische und abendländische Geschichtsschreibung', *Saeculum* 6 (1955), pp. 125–137.

II The Tradition until about 1500

II.1 From the beginnings to about 950

II.1.i Monographs and collections

N. Abbott, *Studies in Arabic Literary Papyri I: Historical Texts* (Chicago, 1957).
G. Conrad, *Abū'l-Ḥusain al-Rāzī (-347/958) und seine Schriften: Untersuchungen zur frühen damaszener Geschichtsschreibung* (Stuttgart, 1991).
L.I. Conrad, ed., *History and Historiography in Early Islamic Times: Studies and Perspectives* (Princeton, forthcoming).
M. Cooperson, *Classical Arabic Biography: The Heirs of the Prophets in the Age of al-Maʾmūn* (Cambridge, 2000).
F.M. Donner, *Narratives of Islamic Origins: The Beginnings of Islamic Historical Writing* (Princeton, 1998).
A.A. Duri, *The Rise of Historical Writing Among the Arabs*, ed. and trans. by L.I. Conrad (Princeton, 1983).
T. El-Hibri, *Reinterpreting Islamic Historiography: Hārūn al-Rashīd and the Narrative of the ʿAbbāsid Caliphate* (Cambridge, 1999).
S. Günther, *Quellenuntersuchungen zu den 'Maqātil aṭ-Ṭālibiyyīn' des Abū'l-Farağ al-Iṣfahānī (gest. 356/967)* (Hildescheim, 1991).
Ibn Warraq, ed., *The Quest for the Historical Muhammad* (Amherst, New York, 2000).
H. Kennedy, ed., *Al-Ṭabarī: A Muslim Historian and his Work* (Princeton, forthcoming).
J. Lassner, *Islamic Revolution and Historical Memory* (New Haven, 1986).
S. Leder, *Das Korpus al-Haiṯam ibn ʿAdī (st. 207/822): Herkunft, Überlieferung, Gestalt früher Texte der aḫbār Literatur* (Frankfurt am Main, 1991).

H. Motzki, ed., *The Biography of Muḥammad: The Issue of the Sources* (Leiden, 2000).

A. Noth, *Quellenkritische Studien zu Themen, Formen und Tendenzen frühislamischer Geschichtsüberlieferung* (Bonn, 1973); revised edition (in collaboration with L.I. Conrad), translated by M. Bonner as *The Early Arabic Historical Tradition* (Princeton, 1994).

E.L. Petersen, *ᶜAlī and Muᶜāwiya in Early Arabic Tradition: Studies on the Genesis and Growth of Islamic Historical Writing until the End of the Ninth Century* (Copenhagen, 1964; 2nd ed. Odense, 1974).

F. Rosenthal, *General Introduction, and From the Creation to the Flood* (al-Ṭabarī translation, vol. i; Albany, 1989).

U. Rubin, *Between Bible and Qurʾān: The Children of Israel and the Islamic Self-image* (Princeton, 1999).

U. Rubin, *The Eye of the Beholder: The Life of Muḥammad as Viewed by the Early Muslims: A Textual Analysis* (Princeton, 1995).

U. Rubin, ed., *The Life of Muḥammad* (Aldershot, 1998).

G. Schoeler, *Charakter und Authentie der muslimischen Überlieferung über das Leben Mohammeds* (Berlin, 1996).

M. Schöller, *Exegetisches Denken und Prophetenbiographie: Eine quellenkritische Analyse der Sīra-Überlieferung zu Muḥammads Konflikt mit den Juden* (Wiesbaden, 1998).

U. Sezgin, *Abū Miḫnaf: Ein Beitrag zur Historiographie des umaiyadischen Zeit* (Leiden, 1971).

II.1.ii Articles

J. Chabbi, 'La représentation du passé aux premiers âges de l'historiographie califale', in R. Curiel and R. Gyselen, eds., *Itinéraires d'Orient: hommages à Claude Cahen* (*Res Orientales*, vi) (Bures-sur-Yvette, 1994), pp. 21–47.

L.I. Conrad, 'Abraha and Muḥammad: some observations apropos of chronology and literary *topoi* in the early Arabic historical tradition', *BSOAS* 50 (1987), pp. 225–240; reprinted in Ibn Warraq, ed., *The Quest for the Historical Muhammad* (Amherst, New York, 2000), pp. 368–391.

L.I. Conrad, 'The conquest of Arwād: a source-critical study in the historiography of the early medieval Near East', in A. Cameron and L.I. Conrad, eds., *The Byzantine and Early Islamic Near East I: Problems in the Literary Source Material* (Princeton, 1992), pp. 317–401.

L.I. Conrad, 'Recovering lost texts: some methodological issues', *JAOS* 113 (1993), pp. 258–263; reprinted in Ibn Warraq, ed., *The Quest for the Historical Muhammad* (Amherst, New York, 2000), pp. 476–485.

L.I. Conrad, 'Theophanes and the Arabic historical tradition: some indications of intercultural transmission', *Byzantinische Forschungen*, 15 (1990), pp. 1–44.

C. Gilliot, 'La formation intellectuelle de Tabari (224/5–310/839–923)', *JA* 276 (1988), pp. 201–244.

S. Günther, 'New results in the theory of source-criticism in medieval Arabic literature', *al-Abhath* 42 (1994), pp. 4–15.

M. Hinds, '*Maghāzī* and *sīra* in early Islamic scholarship', in T. Fahd, ed., *La vie du prophète Mahomet* (Paris, 1983), pp. 57–66; reprinted in his *Studies in Early Islamic History*, ed. J. Bacharach et al. (Princeton, 1996), pp. 188–198.

M. Hinds, 'Sayf b. ʿUmar's sources on Arabia', in A.M. Abdalla et al., eds., *Sources for the History of Arabia* (Riyadh, 1979), part ii, pp. 3–16; reprinted in his *Studies in Early Islamic History*, ed. J. Bacharach et al. (Princeton, 1996), pp. 143–159.

M.G.S. Hodgson, 'Two pre-modern Muslim historians: pitfalls and opportunities in presenting them to moderns', in J. Neff, ed., *Towards World Community* (The Hague, 1968), pp. 53–68.

R.S. Humphreys, 'Qurʾanic myth and narrative structure in early Islamic historiography', in F.M. Clover and R.S. Humphreys, eds., *Tradition and Innovation in Late Antiquity* (Madison, 1989), pp. 271–290.

G.H.A. Juynboll, 'Some thoughts on early Muslim historiography', *Bibliotheca Orientalis* 49 (1992), cols. 685–691.

E. Landau-Tasseron, 'On the reconstruction of lost sources', in L.I. Conrad, ed., *History and Historiography in Early Islamic Times: Studies and Perspectives* (Princeton, forthcoming).

E. Landau-Tasseron, 'Processes of redaction: the case of the Tamīmite delegation to the Prophet Muḥammad', *BSOAS* 49 (1986), pp. 253–270.

E. Landau-Tasseron, 'Sayf ibn ʿUmar in medieval and modern scholarship', *DI* 67 (1990), pp. 1–26.

M. Lecker, 'Biographical notes on Ibn Shihāb al-Zuhrī', *JSS* 41 (1996), pp. 21–63.

M. Lecker, 'The death of the Prophet Muḥammad's father: did Wāqidī invent some of the evidence?', *ZDMG* 145 (1995), pp. 9–27.

M. Lecker, 'Wāqidī's account on the status of the Jews in Medina: a study of a combined report', *JNES* 54 (1995), pp. 15–32.

S. Leder, 'Authorship and transmission in unauthored literature: the *akhbār* attributed to al-Haytham ibn ʿAdī', *Oriens* 31 (1988), pp. 67–81.

S. Leder, 'Features of the novel in early historiography – the downfall of Xālid al-Qasrī', *Oriens* 32 (1990), pp. 72–96.

F.E. Peters, 'The quest for the historical Muhammad', *IJMES* 23 (1991), pp. 291–315; reprinted in Ibn Warraq, ed., *The Quest for the Historical Muhammad* (Amherst, New York, 2000), pp. 444–475.

C.F. Robinson, 'al-Muʿāfā b. ʿImrān and the beginnings of the *ṭabaqāt* literature', *JAOS* 116 (1996), pp. 114–120.

C.F. Robinson, 'The study of Islamic historiography: a progress report', *JRAS* (3rd ser.) 7 (1997), pp. 199–227.

G. Rotter, 'Abū Zurʿa al-Dimašqī (st. 281/894) und das Problem der frühen arabischen Geschichtsschreibung in Syrien', *Die Welt des Orients* 6 (1971), pp. 80–104.

G. Rotter, 'Formen der frühen arabischen Geschichtsschreibung', in G. Rotter, ed., *Deutsche Orientalistik am Beispiel Tübingens* (Basel, 1974), pp. 63–71.

G. Rotter, 'Zur Überlieferung einiger historischer Werke Madāʾinīs in Ṭabarīs *Annalen*', *Oriens* 23–24 (1974), pp. 103–133.

R. Sellheim, 'Prophet, Chalif und Geschichte: die Muhammed-Biographie des Ibn Isḥāq', *Oriens* 18–19 (1967), pp. 33–91.

II.2 From 950 to about 1500

II.2.i Monographs and collections

M. Arkoun, *L'humanisme arabe au ive/xe siècle: Miskawayh, philosophe et historien* (Paris, 2nd rev. ed., 1982).

A.S. Atiya, *The Crusades: Historiography and Bibliography* (Bloomington, 1962).
A. Al-Azmeh, *Ibn Khaldūn in Modern Scholarship: A Study in Orientalism* (London, 1981).
M. Brett, *Ibn Khaldun and the Medieval Maghreb* (Aldershot, 1999).
A. Cheddadi, *Peuples et nations du monde: la conception de l'histoire, les Arabes du Machrek et leurs contemporains, les Arabes du Maghreb et les Berbères* (Paris, 1986).
W.J. Fischel, *Ibn Khaldūn in Egypt* (Berkeley and Los Angeles, 1967).
G. Graf, *Die Epitome der Universalchronik Ibn ad-Dawādārīs im Verhältnis zur Langfassung: eine quellenkritische Studie zur Geschichte der ägyptischen Mamluken* (Berlin, 1990).
L. Guo, *Early Mamluk Syrian Historiography: Al-Yūnīnī's Dhayl Mirʾāt al-Zamān* (Leiden, 1998).
U. Haarmann, *Quellenstudien zur frühen Mamlukenzeit* (Freiburg im Breisgau, 1969).
M. Jarrar, *Die Prophetenbiographie im islamischen Spanien* (Frankfurt am Main, 1989).
H. Kennedy, ed., *The Historiography of Islamic Egypt, c. 950–1800* (Leiden, 2000).
T. Khalidi, *Islamic Historiography: The Histories of Masʿūdī* (Albany, 1975).
D.P. Little, *History and Historiography of the Mamluks* (London, 1986).
D.P. Little, *An Introduction to Mamlūk Historiography* (Wiesbaden, 1970).
M. Mahdi, *Ibn Khaldûn's Philosophy of History* (London, 1957).
J.S. Meisami, *Persian Historiography to the End of the Twelfth Century* (Edinburgh, 1999).
D. Morray, *An Ayyubid Notable and his World: Ibn al-ʿAdīm and Aleppo as Portrayed in his Biographical Dictionary of People Associated with the City* (Leiden, 1994).
L. Richter-Bernburg, *Der syrische Blitz: Saladins Sekretär zwischen Selbstdarstellung und Geschichtsschreibung* (Beirut, 1998).
E. Sartain, *Jalāl al-Dīn al-Suyūṭī: Biography and Background* (Cambridge, 1975).
B. Schäfer, *Beiträge zur mamlukischen Historiographie nach dem Tode al-Malik an-Nâṣirs* (Freiburg im Breisgau, 1971).
M. Shatzmiller, *L'historiographie mérinide: Ibn Khaldūn et ses contemporains* (Leiden, 1982).
A. Shboul, *Al-Masʿūdī and his World* (London, 1979).
O. Weintritt, *Formen spätmittelalterlicher islamischer Geschichtsdarstellung: Untersuchungen zu an-Nuwairī al-Iskandarānīs Kitāb al-Ilmām und verwandten zeitgenössischen Texten* (Beirut, 1992).

II.2.ii Articles

M. Brett, 'Fatimid historiography: a case study – the quarrel with the Zirids, 1048–58', in D.O. Morgan, ed., *Medieval Historical Writing in the Christian and Islamic Worlds* (London, 1982), pp. 47–59.
A. Darrāğ, 'La vie d'Abū'l-Maḥāsin Ibn Taġrī Birdī et son oeuvre', *Annales Islamologiques* 11 (1972), pp. 163–181.
H.E. Fähndrich, 'The *Wafayāt al-aʿyān* of Ibn Khallikān: a new approach', *JAOS* 93 (1973), pp. 432–445.
J.C. Garcin, 'Histoire et hagiographie de l'Égypte musulmane à la fin de l'époque mamelouke et au début de l'époque ottomane', in *Hommages à la mémoire de Serge Sauneron*, ii (Cairo, 1979), pp. 287–316.
J.C. Garcin, 'Al-Maqrīzī, un historien encyclopédique du monde afro-oriental' in C.-A. Julien, ed., *Les Africains* ix (Paris, 1977), pp. 197–223.
L. Guo, 'Mamluk historiographic studies: the state of the art', *MSR* 1 (1997), pp. 15–43.

U. Haarmann, 'Auflösung und Bewahrung der klassischen Formen arabischer Geschichtsschreibung in der Zeit der Mamluken', *ZDMG* 121 (1971), pp. 46–60.

A. Hartmann, 'al-Malik al-Manṣūr (gest. 617/1220), ein ayyūbidischer Regent und Geschichtsschreiber', *ZDMG* 136 (1986), pp. 570–606.

P.M. Holt, 'The presentation of Qalāwūn by Shāfiᶜ b. ᶜAlī', in C.E. Bosworth et al., eds., *The Islamic World from Classical to Modern Times: Essays in Honor of Bernard Lewis* (Princeton, 1989), pp. 141–150.

P.M. Holt, 'Some observations on Shāfiᶜ b. ᶜAlī's biography of Baybars', *JSS* 29 (1984), pp. 123–130.

P.M. Holt, 'Three biographies of al-Ẓāhir Baybars', in D.O. Morgan, ed., *Medieval Historical Writing in the Christian and Islamic Worlds* (London, 1982), pp. 19–29.

H. Laoust, 'Ibn Kaṯīr historien', *Arabica* 2 (1955), pp. 42–88.

D.P. Little, 'Historiography of the Ayyūbid and Mamlūk epochs', in C.F. Petry, ed., *The Cambridge History of Egypt, Volume I: Islamic Egypt, 640–1517* (Cambridge, 1998), pp. 412–444.

D.P. Little, 'Al-Ṣafadī as biographer of his contemporaries', in D.P. Little, ed., *Essays in Islamic Civilization Presented to Niyazi Berkes* (Leiden, 1976), pp. 190–210.

L. Pouzet, 'Remarques sur l'autobiographie dans le monde arabo-musulman au moyen âge', in U. Vermeulen and D. de Smet, eds., *Philosophy and Arts in the Islamic World* (Louvain, 1998), pp. 97–106.

D.S. Richards, 'A consideration of two sources for the life of Saladin', *JSS* 25 (1980), pp. 46–65.

D.S. Richards, 'Ibn al-Athīr and the later parts of the *Kāmil*: a study of aims and methods', in D.O. Morgan, ed., *Medieval Historical Writing in the Christian and Islamic Worlds* (London, 1982), pp. 76–108.

D.S. Richards, 'ᶜImād al-Dīn al-Iṣfahānī: administrator, littérateur and historian', in M. Shatzmiller, ed., *Crusaders and Muslims in Twelfth-Century Syria* (Leiden, 1993), pp. 133–146.

L. Richter-Bernburg, 'Observations on ᶜImād al-Dīn al-Iṣfahānī's al-Fatḥ al-qussī fī al-fatḥ al-qudsī', in W. al-Qāḍī, ed., *Studia Arabica et Islamica: Festschrift for Iḥsān ᶜAbbās* (Beirut, 1981), pp. 373–379.

J. Sublet, 'L'historiographie mamelouke en question', *Arabica* 22 (1975), pp. 71–77.

III Some translations

The following is a small selection of the available translations, which vary in quality. There are many more. For a fairly comprehensive list of English translations to 1977, see M. Anderson, *Arabic Materials in English Translation* (Boston, 1980), pp. 113–131; for a bibliography that lists the great number of Andalusian and North African histories that have been translated into Spanish, see H. Kennedy, *Muslim Spain and Portugal* (London, 1996), pp. 316ff.; and for a list that draws on a broader base of historiographical, administrative, geographic and legal works in both Arabic and Persian, see T. Nagel, *Die islamische Welt bis 1500* (Munich, 1998), pp. 235–247.

III.i Collections

H.F. Amedroz and D.S. Margoliouth, *The Eclipse of the Abbasid Caliphate: Original Chronicles of the Fourth Islamic Century* (Oxford, 1921).

A.J. Arberry, *Aspects of Islamic Civilization as Depicted in the Original Texts* (London, 1964).

C. Barbier de Meynard, *Recueil des historiens des croisades. Historiens orientaux* (Paris, 1886).

M. Bergé, *Les Arabes: histoire et civilisation des Arabes et du monde musulman, des origines à la chute du royaume de Grenade, racontées par les témoins* (Paris, 1978).

F. Gabrieli, *Arab Historians of the Crusades*, tr. (from the Italian) by E.J. Costello (Berkeley and Los Angeles, 1969).

B. Lewis, *Islam from the Prophet Muhammad to the Capture of Constantinople* (London, 1976).

D.F. Reynolds, ed., *Interpreting the Self: Autobiography in the Arabic Literary Tradition* (Berkeley and Los Angeles, 2001), pp. 105–240.

J. Sauvaget, *Historiens arabes: pages choisies, traduites et présentées* (Paris, 1988).

J. Sublet, *Les trois vies du sultan Baïbars* (Paris, 1992).

III.ii From the beginning to about 950

al-Balādhurī, *The Origins of the Islamic State* (*Futūḥ al-buldān*), English tr. P.K. Hitti and F.C. Murgotten (New York, 1916–1924; reprinted Beirut, 1966 and New York, 1969); German tr. O. Rescher, *El-Balâḏorî's kitâb futûḥ al-buldân (Buch der Eroberung der Länder)* (Stuttgart, 1923).

Ibn ʿAbd al-Ḥakam, *Conquête de l'Afrique du Nord et de l'Espagne* (selections from the *Futūḥ Miṣr*), tr. A. Gateau, 2nd ed. (Algiers, 1948).

Ibn Isḥāq/Ibn Hishām, *The Life of Muhammad* (*al-Sīra al-nabawiyya*), tr. A. Guillaume (London, 1955; reprinted Karachi, 1978).

Ibn Saʿd, *The Women of Madina* (selections from the *Kitāb al-Ṭabaqāt al-kubrā*), tr. A. Bewley (London, 1995); *Ibn Saʿd's Kitab al-Tabakat*, tr. S. Moinul Haq (Karachi, 1967–) (apparently only 1 volume published so far).

al-Jahshiyārī, *Das Buch der Wezire und Staatssekretäre* (*Kitāb al-Wuzarāʾ wa'l-kuttāb*), partial tr. by J. Latz (Walldorf-Hessen, 1958).

al-Ṣūlī (Abū Bakr), *Histoire de la dynastie abbaside de 322 à 333/933 à 944* (*Akhbâr al-Râḍî billâh wa-l-Muttaqî billâh*) (extracted from *al-Awrāq*), tr. M. Canard (Algiers, 1950).

al-Ṭabarī, *The History of al-Ṭabarī* (*Taʾrīkh al-rusul wa'l-mulūk*), various translators, general ed. E. Yar-Shater (Albany, 1985–1999); *Geschichte der Perser und Araber zur Zeit der Sasaniden* (partial translation and commentary of the pre-Islamic section), T. Nöldeke (Leiden, 1879).

al-Wāqidī, *Muhammed in Medina* (selections from the *Kitāb al-Maghāzī*), tr. J. Wellhausen (Berlin, 1882).

III.iii From about 950 to 1500

ʿAbd al-Laṭīf al-Baghdādī, *Relations de l'Égypte par Abd al-Latif* (*Kitāb al-Ifāda wa'l-iʿtibār*), tr. S. de Sacy (Paris, 1810); English tr. K.H. Zand et al., *The Eastern Key* (London, 1965).

Abū al-Fidāʾ, *The Memoirs of a Syrian Prince: Abu'l-Fidāʾ, Sultan of Ḥamāh (672–732/1273–1331)* (selections from *al-Mukhtaṣar fī akhbār al-bashar*), tr. P.M. Holt (Wiesbaden, 1983).

Bahāʾ al-Dīn, Ibn Shaddād, *The Rare and Excellent History of Saladin* (*al-Nawādir al-sulṭāniyya wa'l-maḥāsin al-Yūsufiyya*), tr. D.S. Richards (Aldershot, 2001).

al-Dhahabī, *Les dynasties de l'Islam* (years 447–656/1055–1258) selections from the *Kitāb Duwal al-Islām*), tr. A. Nègre (Damascus, 1979).

Ibn ʿAbd al-Ẓāhir, *Baybars I of Egypt* (*al-Rawḍ al-zāhir*), tr. S.F. Sadeque (Dacca, 1956).

Ibn al-Athīr, *The History of the Seljuk Turks* (selections from *al-Kāmil*), tr. D.S. Richards (London, 2002).

Ibn al-Furāt, *Ayyubids, Mamlukes and Crusaders* (selections from the *Taʾrīkh al-duwal waʾl-mulūk*), ed. and tr. U. and M.C. Lyons (Cambridge, 1971).

Ibn Kathīr, *The Life of the Prophet Muḥammad* (extracted from his *al-Bidāya wa'l-nihāya*), tr. T. Le Gassick (London, 1998–2000).

Ibn Khaldūn, *The Muqaddimah: An Introduction to History* (*al-Muqaddima*), tr. F. Rosenthal (London, 1958; 2nd, corrected ed., Princeton, 1967; abridged ed., Princeton, 1969).

Ibn Khallikān, *Ibn Khallikan's Biographical Dictionary* (*Wafayāt al-aʿyān*), tr. M. de Slane (Britain and Ireland, 1842–1871; reprinted, Beirut, 1970).

Ibn al-Qalānisī, *The Damascus Chronicle of the Crusades* (selections from the *Dhayl Taʾrīkh Dimashq*), tr. H.A.R. Gibb (London, 1932; reprinted, 1967).

Ibn Ṣaṣrā, *A Chronicle of Damascus, 1389–1397* (*al-Durra al-muḍīʾa fī al-dawla al-ẓāhiriyya*), ed. and tr. W.M. Brinner (Berkeley, 1963).

Ibn Suqāʿī, *Tālī Kitāb Wafayāt al-aʿyān: un fonctionnaire chrétien dans l'administration mamelouke,* ed. and tr. J. Sublet (Damascus, 1974).

Ibn Taghrī Birdī, *Les biographies du Manhal al-ṣāfī*, tr. G. Wiet (Cairo, 1932).

Ibn Taghrī Birdī, *History of Egypt, 1382–1469 A.D.* (*al-Nujūm al-zāhira fī mulūk Miṣr wa'l-Qāhira*), tr. W. Popper (Berkeley, 1954–1963; reprinted, New York, 1976).

Ibn al-Ṭiqṭaqā, *Al-Fakhri; On the Systems of Government and the Moslem Dynasties, Composed by Muhammad son of ʿAli son of Tabataba* (*al-Fakhrī*), tr. C.E.J. Whitting (London, 1947); French tr. E. Amar, *Histoire des dynasties musulmanes depuis la mort de Mahomet jusqu'à la chute du khalifat abbâsîde de Baghdâd* (Paris, 1910).

ʿImād al-Dīn (al-Kātib) al-Iṣfahānī, *Conquête de la Syrie et de la Palestine par Saladin* (*al-Fatḥ al-qussī fī al-fatḥ al-qudsī*), tr. H. Massé (Paris, 1972).

al-Jazarī, *La chronique de Damas d'al-Jazarī (années 689–698 H)* (selections from *Ḥawādith al-zamān*), tr. J. Sauvaget (Paris, 1949).

al-Maqdisī, *Le livre de la création et de l'histoire* (*Kitāb al-Badʾ wa'l-taʾrīkh*), tr. C. Huart (Paris, 1899–1919).

al-Maqrīzī, *Livre des admonitions et de l'observation pour l'histoire des quartiers et des monuments ou: description historique et topographique de l'Égypte* (*al-Mawāʿiẓ wa'l-iʿtibār fī dhikr al-khiṭaṭ wa'l-āthār*), tr. P. Casanova (Cairo, 1906, 1920).

al-Maqrīzī, *Al-Maqrīzī's 'Book of contention and strife concerning the relations between the Banū Umayya and the Banū Hāshim'* (*Kitāb al-nizāʿ wa'l-takhāṣum fīmā bayn Banī Umayya wa-Banī Hāshim*), tr. C.E. Bosworth (Manchester, 1980).

al-Maqrīzī, *Histoire des sultans mamlouks de l'Égypte* (*Kitāb al-Sulūk li-maʿrifat duwal al-mulūk*), partially tr. E. Quatremère (Paris, 1837–1845); *Histoire d'Égypte de Makrizi*, tr. E. Blochet (Paris, 1908); English. tr. R. Broadhurst, *A History of the Ayyūbid Sultans of Egypt* (Boston, 1980).

al-Masʿūdī, *Le livre de l'avertissement et de la revision* (*Kitāb al-tanbīh wa'l-ishrāf*), tr. B. Carra de Vaux (Paris, 1896).

al-Masʿūdī, *Les prairies d'or* (*Murūj al-dhahab wa-maʿādin al-jawhar*), tr. C. Barbier de Meynard and J.-B. Pavet de Courteille, rev. by C. Pellat (Paris, 1966–1997); selections from the Abbasid period tr. P. Lunde and C. Stone as *Meadows of Gold: the Abbasids* (London and New York, 1989).

Mufaḍḍal b. Abī al-Faḍāʾil, *Histoire des sultans mamlouks* (*al-Nahj al-sadīd wa'l-durr al-farīd fīmā baʿda Taʾrīkh Ibn al-ʿAmīd*), ed. and tr. E. Blochet (Paris, 1920–1928).

al-Qāḍī ʿIyāḍ, *Muhammad Messenger of Allah: ash-Shifa of Qadi ʿIyad* (*al-Shifāʾ*), tr. A.A. Bewley (Granada, 1991).

al-Suyūṭī, *History of the Caliphs* (*Taʾrīkh al-khulafāʾ*), tr. H.S. Jarrett (Calcutta, 1881; reprinted Amsterdam, 1970).

Usāma b. Munqidh, *An Arab-Syrian Gentleman and Warrior in the Period of the Crusades* (*Kitāb al-Iʿtibār*), tr. P.K. Hitti (New York, 1929; reprinted Princeton, 1987)

Bibliography

Primary Sources

N.B. When multiple editions are given for Arabic works, the first is cited in the text.

ᶜAbbās, I., *Shadharāt min kutub mafqūda fī al-taʾrīkh* (Beirut, 1988).
ᶜAbd Allāh b. Muḥammad b. ᶜAbd al-Wahhāb, *Mukhtaṣar sīrat rasūl Allāh* (Cairo, 1379 H).
ᶜAbd al-Laṭīf al-Baghdādī, *Kitāb al-Ifāda wa'l-iᶜtibār* (Damascus, 1983).
ᶜAbd al-Malik b. Ḥabīb, *Taʾrīkh* (Madrid, 1990).
ᶜAbd al-Razzāq al-Muqarram, *Maqtal al-Ḥusayn* (Qum, *ca.* 1990).
ᶜAbd al-Razzāq al-Ṣanᶜānī, *al-Muṣannaf* (Beirut, 1972).
Abraham Ibn Daud, *The Book of Traditions (Sefer ha-qabbalah)*, ed. and trans. G.D. Cohen (Philadelphia, 1967).
Abū al-Fatḥ, *Kitāb al-Taʾrīkh (Annales Samaritani)* (Gotha, 1865).
Abū al-Fidāʾ, *The Memoirs of a Syrian Prince: Abu'l-Fidāʾ, Sultan of Ḥamāh (672–732/ 1273–1331)*, trans. P.M. Holt (Wiesbaden, 1983).
Abū Isḥāq al-Shīrāzī, *Ṭabaqāt al-fuqahāʾ* (Beirut, 1970).
Abū Shāma, *Kitāb al-Rawḍatayn fī akhbār al-dawlatayn*, i[1] (Cairo, 1956); i[2] (Cairo, 1962).
Agapius of Manbij, *Kitāb al-ᶜUnwān*, ed. and trans. A.A. Vasiliev in *Patrologia Orientalis* 8 (1912).
Aḥmad b. Ibrāhīm al-ᶜAsqalānī, *Shifāʾ al-qulūb fī manāqib banī Ayyūb* (Baghdad, 1978).
Akhbār majmūᶜa, ed. and trans. as *Ajbar Machmuâ* (Madrid, 1867).
al-ᶜĀmirī, *Bahjat al-maḥāfil wa-bughyat al-amāthil* (Medina, 1969).
al-Azdī al-Baṣrī, *Futūḥ al-Shām* (Calcutta, 1854).
al-Azdī al-Mawṣilī, *Taʾrīkh al-Mawṣil* (Cairo, 1967).
Babur, *The Baburnama: Memoirs of Babur, Prince and Emperor*, trans. W.M. Thackston (Washington, D.C., 1996).
Bahāʾ al-Dīn Ibn Shaddād, *Sīrat Ṣalāḥ al-Dīn (al-Nawādir al-sulṭāniyya wa'l-maḥāsin al-Yūsufiyya)* (Cairo, 1962); trans. D.S. Richards as *The Rare and Excellent History of Saladin* (Aldershot, 2001).
Baḥshal al-Wāsiṭī, *Taʾrīkh Wāsiṭ* (Baghdad, 1967).
al-Balādhurī, *Ansāb al-ashrāf*, ivb (Jerusalem, 1938); v (Jerusalem, 1936); vib (Jerusalem, 1993).
——, *Futūḥ al-buldān* (Leiden, 1866).
al-Balawī, *Sīrat Aḥmad b. Ṭūlūn* (Cairo, 1939).
Baybars al-Manṣūrī, *Zubdat al-fikra fī taʾrīkh al-hijra* (Beirut, 1998).

Bede, *Bede's Ecclesiastical History of the English People*, ed. and trans. B. Colgrave and R.A.B. Mynors (Oxford, 1991, reprint).

al-Bukhārī, *al-Ṣaḥīḥ* (Leiden, 1862–1908).

——, *al-Taʾrīkh al-kabīr*, 2nd ed. (Hyderabad, 1958).

al-Dabbāgh and Ibn Nājī al-Tanūkhī, *Maʿālim al-īmān fī maʿrifat ahl al-Qayrawān* (Cairo, 1968).

al-Dhahabī, *Asmāʾ man ʿāsha thamānīn sana baʿda shaykhihi aw baʿda samāʿihi* (Beirut, 1997).

——, '*al-Sīra*' (Beirut, 1981).

al-Dīnawarī, *al-Akhbār al-ṭiwāl* (Leiden, 1888).

al-Diyārbakrī, *Taʾrīkh al-khamīs fī aḥwāl anfas nafīs* (Cairo, 1283 H).

al-Fasawī, *Kitāb al-Maʿrifa wa'l-taʾrīkh* (Beirut, 1981; Medina, 1410 H.).

Ḥājjī Khalīfa, *Kashf al-ẓunūn* (Leipzig, 1835–1858).

al-Ḥakīm al-Tirmidhī, *Kitāb Khatm al-awliyāʾ* (Beirut, 1965).

Ḥanbal b. Isḥāq, *Dhikr miḥnat al-imām Aḥmad b. Ḥanbal* (Cairo, 1977).

Ibn ʿAbd al-Barr, *al-Durar fī ikhtiṣār al-maghāzī wa'l-siyar* (Cairo, 1966).

Ibn ʿAbd al-Munʿim al-Ḥimyarī, *al-Rawḍ al-miʿṭār fī khabar al-aqṭār* (Beirut, 1975).

Ibn ʿAbd al-Salām al-Sulamī, *Bidāyat al-saʾūl fī tafḍīl al-rasūl* (Beirut and Damascus, 1983).

Ibn ʿAbd al-Ẓāhir, *Taʾrīkh al-mālik al-Ẓāhir* (Wiesbaden, 1983).

Ibn Abī Shayba, *al-Muṣannaf* (Beirut, 1989).

Ibn Abī Uṣaybiʿa, *ʿUyūn al-anbāʾ fī ṭabaqāt al-aṭibbāʾ* (Beirut, 1965).

Ibn Abī Yaʿlā, *Ṭabaqāt al-Ḥanābila* (Cairo, 1952).

Ibn al-ʿAdīm, *Bughyat al-ṭalab fī taʾrīkh Ḥalab* (Damascus, 1988).

——, *Zubdat al-ḥalab min taʾrīkh Ḥalab* (Damascus, 1968).

Ibn ʿAsākir, *Taʾrīkh madīnat Dimashq* (Beirut, 1998).

Ibn Aʿtham al-Kūfī, *Kitāb al-Futūḥ* (Hyderabad, 1968–1975).

Ibn al-Athīr, *al-Kāmil fī al-taʾrīkh* (Beirut, 1965).

——, *al-Taʾrīkh al-bāhir fī al-dawla al-atābakiyya* (Cairo, 1963; Baghdad, 1963).

——, *Usd al-ghāba* (Būlāq, 1871).

Ibn al-Azraq al-Fāriqī, *Taʾrīkh Mayyāfāriqīn* (Cairo, 1959).

Ibn al-Dawādārī, *Kanz al-durar wa-jāmiʿ al-ghurar* (Cairo, 1961).

Ibn al-Farrāʾ, *Kitāb Rusul al-mulūk* (Beirut, 1972).

Ibn al-Furāt, *Ayyubids, Mamlukes and Crusaders*, ed. and trans. U. and M.C. Lyons (Cambridge, 1971).

Ibn Ḥajar al-ʿAsqalānī, *al-Durar al-kāmina fī aʿyān al-miʾa al-thāmina* (Cairo, 1349 H).

——, *Inbāʾ al-ghumr bi-abnāʾ al-ʿumr* (Hyderabad, 1967–1976).

——, *al-Jawāhir wa'l-durar fī tarjamat shaykh al-Islām Ibn Ḥajar* (Cairo, 1986).

——, *al-Muʿjam al-mufahras* (Beirut, 1998).

——, *Tahdhīb al-tahdhīb* (Hyderabad, 1327 H).

Ibn Ḥazm, *Kitāb al-Akhlāq wa'l-siyar,* ed. and trans. N. Tomiche as *Épître morale* (Beirut, 1961).

——, *Rasāʾil Ibn Ḥazm al-Andalusī* (Beirut, 1987).

Ibn Hishām, *al-Sīra al-nabawiyya*, al-Saqqā, et al., eds. (Cairo, numerous reprints); trans. A. Guillaume as *The Life of Muhammad* (London, 1955; reprinted Karachi, 1978).

Ibn al-ʿImrānī, *al-Inbāʾ fī taʾrīkh al-khulafāʾ* (Leiden, 1973).

Ibn al-Jawzī, *al-Muntaẓam fī taʾrīkh al-mulūk wa'l-umam* (Beirut, 1992).

——, *Sīrat ʿUmar b. al-Khaṭṭāb* (Cairo, n.d.).

Ibn Kathīr, *al-Bidāya wa'l-nihāya* (Beirut reprint of Cairo, 1932–1977).
——, *al-Fuṣūl fī sīrat al-rasūl* (Beirut, 1993).
——, '*al-Sīra*' (Cairo, 1966); trans. T. Le Gassick as *The Life of the Prophet Muḥammad* (London, 1998–2000).
——, *Stories of the Prophets*, trans. R.A. Azami (Riyadh, 1999).
Ibn Khaldūn, *Muqaddima*, trans. by F. Rosenthal as *The Muqaddimah* (New York, 1958; 2nd corrected ed., Princeton, 1967; abridged ed., Princeton, 1969).
Ibn Khallikān, *Wafayāt al-aᶜyān* (Beirut, 1968–1972); trans. M. de Slane as *Ibn Khallikan's Biographical Dictionary* (Britain and Ireland, 1842–1871; reprinted, Beirut, 1970).
Ibn Māja, *Taʾrīkh al-khulafāʾ* (Beirut, 1979).
Ibn Miskawayh, *Tajārib al-umam* (London, 1921; Tehran, 1987–); partially trans. H.F. Amedroz and D.S. Margoliouth as *The Eclipse of the Abbasid Caliphate: Original Chronicles of the Fourth Islamic Century* (Oxford, 1921).
Ibn al-Nadīm, *al-Fihrist* (Tehran, 1971; several reprints, Beirut); trans. B. Dodge as *The Fihrist of al-Nadīm* (New York, 1970).
Ibn al-Naqīb, *The Reliance of the Traveller*, trans. N.H.M. Keller (Evanston, 1991).
Ibn Qāḍī Shuhba, *Kitāb Ṭabaqāt al-Shāfiᶜiyya* (Hyderabad, 1978; Cairo, 1998).
Ibn al-Qalānisī, *Dhayl Taʾrīkh Dimashq* (Beirut, 1908); selections trans. H.A.R. Gibb as *The Damascus Chronicle of the Crusades* (London, 1932; reprinted, 1967).
Ibn Qutayba, *Kitāb al-Maᶜārif* (Cairo, 4th printing, 1981).
Ibn Rajab, *Dhayl ᶜalā ṭabaqāt al-Ḥanābila* (Cairo, 1953).
Ibn Saᶜd, *Kitāb al-Ṭabaqāt al-kubrā* (Leiden, 1904–1940; Beirut, 1957–1968).
Ibn al-Sāᶜī, *Mukhtaṣar akhbār al-khulafāʾ* (Cairo, 1309 H).
Ibn Ṣaṣrā, *A Chronicle of Damascus, 1389–1397*, ed. and trans. W.M. Brinner (Berkeley, 1963).
Ibn al-Ṭiqṭaqā, *al-Fakhrī* (Cairo, 1923).
Ibn Wāṣil, *Mufarrij al-kurūb fī akhbār banī Ayyūb* (Cairo, 1953).
al-Iṣfahānī, *Kitāb al-Aghānī* (Cairo, 1927–1974).
al-Jāḥiẓ, *Risāla fī al-Nābita* in *Rasāʾil al-Jāḥiẓ* (Cairo, 1965), ii, pp. 7–23; trans. C. Pellat as 'La «Nâbita» de Djâhiz: (un document important pour l'histoire politico-religieuse de l'Islâm),' *Annales de l'Institut des Études Orientales* (Algiers) 10 (1952), pp. 302–325.
al-Jahshiyārī, *Kitāb al-Wuzarāʾ wa'l-kuttāb* (Cairo, 1938); and other fragments as *Nuṣūṣ ḍāʾiᶜa min kitāb al-wuzarāʾ wa'l-kuttāb* (Beirut, 1964).
al-Kalāᶜī, *al-Iktifāʾ* (Beirut, 1997).
Khalīfa b. Khayyāṭ, *Ṭabaqāt* (Damascus, 1966).
——, *Taʾrīkh* (Beirut, 2nd ed. of Baghdad, 1967; Damascus, 1967; Beirut, 1995).
al-Khaṭīb al-Baghdādī, *Taʾrīkh Baghdād* (Cairo, 1931).
al-Khwārizmī, *Mafātīḥ al-ᶜulūm* (Leiden, 1895).
al-Kindī, *Kitāb al-Wulāh wa-Kitāb al-Quḍāh* (London, 1912).
al-Kisāʾī, *Tales of the Prophets of al-Kisāʾī*, trans. W.M. Thackston (Boston, 1978).
Kitāb al-ᶜUyūn wa'l-ḥadāʾiq fī akhbār al-ḥaqāʾiq, part of ii (ed. as *Fragmenta Historicorum Arabicorum*) (Leiden, 1869); iv[1] (Damascus, 1972); iv[2] (Damascus, 1973).
al-Laḥjī, *The* Sīra *of Imām Aḥmad b. Yaḥyā al-Nāṣir li-Dīn Allāh* (Exeter, 1990).
Lyall, C.J., ed., *The Mufaḍḍalīyāt: An Anthology of Ancient Arabian Odes* (Oxford, 1921–1924).
al-Maqrīzī, *Kitāb al-Khiṭaṭ* (Būlāq, 1270 H).
——, *Kitāb al-Muqaffā al-kabīr* (Beirut, 1991).
——, *Kitāb al-Sulūk li-maᶜrifat duwal al-mulūk*, ii (Cairo, 1958); iv (1973).
——, *Musawwadat kitāb al-mawāᶜiẓ wa'l-iᶜtibār* (London, 1995).

al-Masᶜūdī, *Kitāb al-Tanbīh wa'l-ishrāf* (Leiden, 1893).
——, *Murūj al-dhahab wa-maᶜādin al-jawhar* (Beirut, 1962–1979); trans. C. Barbier de Meynard and J.-B. Pavet de Courteille as *Les prairies d'or* (Paris, 1966–1997).
al-Mizzī, *Tahdhīb al-kamāl* (Beirut, 1992).
al-Muᵓayyad fī al-Dīn al-Shīrāzī, *Sīra* (Cairo, 1949).
Mughulṭāᵓī, *al-Ishāra ilā sīrat al-Muṣṭafā wa-taᵓrīkh man baᶜdahu min al-khulafāᵓ* (Damascus and Beirut, 1996).
Muḥammad b. ᶜAbd al-Wahhāb, *Mukhtaṣar sīrat rasūl Allāh* (Beirut, 1995).
Muḥammad b. Saḥnūn, *Kitāb Ādāb al-muᶜallimīn* (Algiers, 1973).
Muḥibb al-Dīn al-Ṭabarī, *Khulāṣat al-siyar fī aḥwāl sayyid al-bashar* (Delhi, 1343 H).
al-Musabbiḥī, *al-Juzᵓ al-arbaᶜūn min akhbār Miṣr* (Cairo, 1978).
Muslim b. al-Ḥajjāj, *Kitāb al-Ṭabaqāt* (Riyadh, 1991).
Nubdha min kitāb al-taᵓrīkh (Moscow, 1960).
ps.-Wāqidī, *Futūḥ al-Shām* (Calcutta, 1854).
——, *Taᵓrīkh futūḥ al-Jazīra wa'l-Khābūr wa-Diyār Bakr wa'l-ᶜIrāq* (Damascus, 1996).
al-Qāḍī ᶜIyāḍ, *al-Ghunya: fihrist shuyūkh al-Qāḍī ᶜIyāḍ* (Beirut, 1982).
——, *al-Shifāᵓ* (Cairo, 1977); trans. A. A. Bewley as *Muhammad Messenger of Allah: ash-Shifa of Qadi ᶜIyad* (Granada, 1991).
al-Qalqashandī, *Ṣubḥ al-aᶜshā* (Cairo, 1964).
al-Qifṭī, *Akhbār al-ḥukamāᵓ* (Cairo, 1326 H).
al-Qushayrī, *Taᵓrīkh al-Raqqa* (Hama, 1959; Damascus, 1998).
al-Ṣābiᵓ, Hilāl, *Tuḥfat al-umarāᵓ fī taᵓrīkh al-wuzarāᵓ* (London, 1904).
al-Ṣafadī, *Aᶜyān al-ᶜaṣr wa-aᶜwān al-naṣr* (Frankfurt, 1990).
——, *Nakt al-himyān fī nukat al-ᶜumyān* (Cairo, 1911).
——, *al-Wāfī bi'l-wafayāt* (Leipzig, Istanbul and Beirut, 1931–).
al-Sahmī, *Taᵓrīkh Jurjān* (Hyderabad, 1950).
al-Sakhāwī, *al-Dawᵓ al-lāmiᶜ li-ahl al-qarn al-tāsiᶜ* (Cairo, 1355 H).
Ṣāliḥ b. Aḥmad b. Ḥanbal, *'Sīra'* (Alexandria, 1981; Riyadh, 1995).
Sayf b. ᶜUmar, *Kitāb al-ridda wa'l-futūḥ and Kitāb al-jamal wa-masīr ᶜĀᵓisha wa-ᶜAlī: A Facsimile Edition of the Fragments Preserved in the University Library of Imam Muhammad Ibn Saᶜud Islamic University in Riyadh* (Leiden, 1995).
al-Ṣaymarī, *Akhbār Abī Ḥanīfa wa-aṣḥābihi* (Hyderabad, 1974; reprinted Beirut, 1976).
Sebeos (attributed), *The Armenian History Attributed to Sebeos*, trans. by R.W. Thomson with commentary by J. Howard-Johnston (Liverpool, 1999).
Shāfiᶜ b. ᶜAlī, *Ḥusn al-manāqib al-sariyya* (Riyadh, 1976).
Sibṭ Ibn al-Jawzī, *Mirᵓāt al-zamān fī taᵓrīkh al-aᶜyān*, viii² (Hyderabad, 1952).
al-Suhaylī, *al-Rawḍ al-unuf fī sharḥ al-sīra al-nabawiyya* (Cairo, 1967).
al-Ṣūlī, *Akhbār al-Rāḍī lillāh wa'l-Muttaqī lillāh* (Beirut, 1935); trans. M. Canard as *Histoire de la dynastie abbaside de 322 à 333/933 à 944* (Algiers, 1950).
——, *Ashᶜār awlād al-khulafāᵓ* (London, 1936).
——, *al-Awrāq* (St. Petersburg, 1998).
al-Suyūṭī, *Ḥusn al-muḥāḍara fī akhbār Miṣr wa'l-Qāhira* (Cairo, 1863).
——, *al-Shamārīkh fī ᶜilm al-taᵓrīkh* (Leiden, 1894).
al-Ṭabarī, *Das konstantinopler Fragment des Kitāb Iḫtilāf al-fuqahāᵓ des Abū Ğaᶜfar Muḥammad b. Ğarīr aṭ-Ṭabarī* (Leiden, 1933).
——, *Taᵓrīkh al-rusul wa'l-mulūk* (Leiden, 1879–1901; Cairo, 1960–1969); trans. as *The History of al-Ṭabarī* by F. Rosenthal, *General Introduction, and From the Creation to the Flood* (Albany, 1989; al-Ṭabarī translation, vol. i); T. Nöldeke as *Geschichte der Perser und Araber zur Zeit der Sasaniden* (Leiden, 1879); M.V. McDonald as *The*

Foundation of the Community (Albany, 1987; al-Ṭabarī translation, vol. vii); E. Rowson as *The Marwānid Restoration* (Albany, 1989; al-Ṭabarī translation, vol. xxii); M. Hinds as *The Zenith of the Marwānid House* (Albany, 1990; al-Ṭabarī translation, vol. xxiii); D.S. Powers as *The Empire in Transition* (Albany, 1989; al-Ṭabarī translation, vol. xxiv); M. Fishbein as *The ᶜAbbāsid State in Equilibrium* (Albany, 1989; al-Ṭabarī translation, vol. xxx).

al-Tanūkhī, *Nishwār al-muḥāḍara* (Beirut, 1973); trans. D.S. Margoliouth as *The Table-talk of a Mesopotamian Judge* (London, 1922).

Taʾrīkh al-khulafāʾ (Moscow, 1967).

Tārīkh-i Sīstān (Tehran, 1994).

al-Thaᶜālibī, *The Book of Curious and Entertaining Information*, trans. C.E. Bosworth (Edinburgh, 1968).

Thaᶜlab, *Majālis* (Cairo, 1960).

al-ᶜUlaymī, *Mukhtaṣar ṭabaqāt al-Ḥanābila* (Damascus, 1921; Beirut, 1983).

ᶜUmar b. Shabba, *Taʾrīkh al-madīna al-munawwara* (Beirut, 1990).

Usāma b. Munqidh, *An Arab-Syrian Gentleman and Warrior in the Period of the Crusades*, trans. P.K. Hitti (New York, 1929; reprinted Princeton, 1987).

al-Wāqidī, *Kitāb al-Maghāzī* (London, 1966; reprinted Beirut).

al-Yaᶜqūbī, *Taʾrīkh* (Leiden, 1883).

Yāqūt, *Irshād al-arīb ilā maᶜrifat al-adīb* (London and Leiden, 1907–1913; Beirut, 1993).

al-Zubayr b. Bakkār, *Akhbār al-muwaffaqiyyāt* (Baghdad, 1972).

Zuqnin Chronicle (third and fourth part), trans. A. Harrak as *The Zuqnin Chronicle, Parts III and IV, AD 488–755* (Toronto, 1999).

Secondary Sources

Abbott, N., *Studies in Arabic Literary Papyri I: Historical Texts* (Chicago, 1957).

Abiad, M., 'Origine et développement des dictionnaires biographiques arabes', *BEO* 31 (1979), pp. 7–15.

Abramowski, R., *Dionysius von Tellmahre: jakobitischer Patriarch von 818–845* (Leipzig, 1940).

Afinogenov, D.E., 'Some observations on genres of Byzantine historiography', *Byzantium* 62 (1992), pp. 13–31.

Ahlwardt, W., *Verzeichnis der arabischen Handschriften* (Berlin, 1887–1899).

Ahmad, I., 'Ibn al-Athir al-muḥaddith – life and works', *IS* 23 (1984), pp. 33–43.

Ahmad, S.M., and A. Rahman, eds., *Al-Masᶜūdī Millenary Commemoration Volume* (Calcutta, 1960).

Alter, R., *The Pleasures of Reading in an Ideological Age* (New York, 1996).

ᶜAlwajī, ᶜA.Ḥ., *Muʾallafāt Ibn al-Jawzī* (Baghdad, 1965).

Antes, P., *Prophetenwunder in der Ašᶜarīya bis al-Ġazālī (Algazel)* (Freiburg im Breisgau, 1970).

Arberry, A.J., *A Handlist of the Arabic Manuscripts* (Dublin, 1955–1964).

——, *Sakhawiana: A Study Based on the Chester Beatty MS. Arab. 773* (London, 1951).

——, *A Twelfth-Century Reading List* (London, 1951).

Arjomand, S.A., 'The law, agency, and policy in medieval Islamic society: development of the institutions of learning from the tenth to the fifteenth century', *Comparative Studies in Society and History* 41 (1991), pp. 263–293.

Arkoun, M., *L'humanisme arabe au ive/xe siècle: Miskawayh, philosophe et historien* (Paris, 2nd rev. ed., 1982).
——, *Rethinking Islam*, ed. and trans. by R.D. Lee (Boulder, 1994).
Ashtiany, J., et al., eds., *ᶜAbbasid Belles-Lettres* (Cambridge History of Arabic Literature; Cambridge, 1990).
Ashtiany Bray, J., '*Isnād*s and models of heroes: Abū Zubayd al-Ṭāᵓī, Tanūkhī's sundered lovers and Abū 'l-ᶜAnbas al-Ṣaymarī', *Arabic and Middle Eastern Literatures* 1 (1998), pp. 7–30.
Athamina, K., 'al-Qasas: its emergence, religious origin and its socio-political impact on early Muslim society', *SI* 76 (1992), pp. 53–74.
Auchterlonie, P., *Arabic Biographical Dictionaries: A Summary Guide and Bibliography* (Durham, 1987).
Auden, W.H., *Lectures on Shakespeare*, ed. A.C. Kirsch (Princeton, 2001).
Avila, M.L., *La sociedad hispanomusulmana al final del califato: aproximación a un estudio demográfico* (Madrid, 1985).
Al-Azmeh, A., *Ibn Khaldūn in Modern Scholarship: A Study in Orientalism* (London, 1981).
——, 'Muslim genealogies of knowledge', *History of Religion* 31 (1992), pp. 403–411.
Baynes, N., 'The supernatural defenders of Constantinople', in his *Byzantine Studies and Other Essays* (London, 1955), pp. 248–260.
Beeston, A.F.L., *Epigraphic South Arabian Calendars and Dating* (London, 1956).
——, 'Parallelism in Arabic prose', *JAL* 5 (1974), pp. 134–146.
——, *Samples of Arabic Prose in its Historical Development* (Oxford, 1977).
Beeston, A.F.L., et al., eds., *Arabic Literature to the End of the Umayyad Period* (Cambridge History of Arabic Literature; Cambridge, 1983).
Behan McCullagh, C., 'Bias in historical description, interpretation and explanation', *History and Theory* 39 (2000), pp. 39–66.
Bellamy, J., 'Sources of Ibn Abī 'l-Dunyā's *Kitāb Maqtal amīr al-muᵓminīn ᶜAlī*', *JAOS* 104 (1984), pp. 3–19.
Berkey, J., *The Transmission of Knowledge in Medieval Cairo* (Princeton, 1992).
Berlin, I., *The Proper Study of Mankind: An Anthology of Essays* (London, 1997).
Blanchard, A.J., ed., *Les débuts du codex* (Turnhout, 1989).
Blockley, R.C., *The Fragmentary Classicising Historians of the Later Roman Empire* (Liverpool, 1981).
Bloom, J., *Paper Before Print: The History and Impact of Paper in the Islamic World* (New Haven, 2001).
Bork-Qaysieh, W., *Die Geschichte von Kain und Abel (Hābil wa-Qābil) in der sunnitische-islamischen Überlieferung* (Berlin, 1993).
Bosworth, C.E., 'Ghars al-Niᶜma b. Hilāl al-Ṣābiᵓ's *Kitāb al-Hafawāt al-nādira* and Buyid history', in A. Jones, ed., *Arabicus Felix … Essays in Honour of Professor A.F.L. Beeston's Eightieth Birthday* (Reading, 1991), pp. 129–141.
——, 'The terminology of the history of the Arabs in the Jāhiliyya according to Khwārizmī's "Keys of the sciences"', in S. Morag, ed., *Studies in Judaism and Islam Presented to Shelomo Dov Goitein on the Occasion of his Eightieth Birthday* (English volume) (Jerusalem, 1981), pp. 27–43; reprinted in C.E. Bosworth, *Medieval Arabic Culture and Administration* (London, 1982).
Bowersock, G.W., 'Momigliano's quest for the person', *History and Theory* 30 (1991), pp. 27–36.
Bowman, A.K., and G. Woolf, eds., *Literacy and Power in the Ancient World* (Cambridge, 1994).

Braudy, L., *Narrative Form in History and Fiction: Hume, Fielding, and Gibbon* (Princeton, 1970).
Bravmann, M.M., 'The state archives in the early Islamic period', *Arabica* 15 (1968), pp. 87–89; reprinted in his *The Spiritual Background of Early Islam* (Leiden, 1972).
Brett, M., 'Fatimid historiography: a case study – the quarrel with the Zirids, 1048–58', in D.O. Morgan, ed., *Medieval Historical Writing in the Christian and Islamic Worlds* (London, 1982), pp. 47–59.
——, *Ibn Khaldun and the Medieval Maghrib* (Aldershot, 1999).
——, 'The way of the nomad', *BSOAS* 58 (1995), pp. 251–269.
Brettler, M.Z., *The Creation of History in Ancient Israel* (London and New York, 1995).
Brinner, W.M., 'The Banū Ṣaṣrā: a study in the transmission of a scholarly tradition', *Arabica* 7 (1960), pp. 167–195.
Brock, S.P., 'Syriac historical writing: a survey of the main sources', *Journal of the Iraqi Academy* 5 (1979–80), pp. 1–30 (English section); reprinted in his *Studies in Syriac Christianity: History, Literature and Theology* (Hampshire, 1992).
——, 'Two letters of the Patriarch Timothy from the late eighth century on translations from Greek', *Arabic Sciences and Philosophy* 9 (1999), pp. 233–246.
Brockelmann, C., *Geschichte der arabischen Litteratur* (Weimar, Leipzig and Leiden, 1898–1949).
Brockopp, J.E., 'Early Islamic jurisprudence in Egypt: two scholars and their *mukhtaṣar*s', *IJMES* 30 (1998), pp. 167–182.
Brown, D., *Rethinking Tradition in Modern Islamic Thought* (Cambridge, 1996).
Brown, G.H., *Bede the Venerable* (Boston, 1987).
Brown, P., comments in the '*SO* debate: the world of late antiquity revisited', *Symbolae Osloenses* 72 (1997), pp. 5–30, 70–90.
Brown, R.E., *The Birth of the Messiah: A Commentary on the Infancy Narratives in the Gospels of Matthew and Luke* (New York, 1993, updated ed.).
Bulliet, R., 'The age structure of medieval Islamic education', *SI* 57 (1983), pp. 105–117.
——, *The Patricians of Nishapur* (Cambridge, Mass., 1972).
——, 'A quantitative approach to medieval Muslim biographical dictionaries', *JESHO* 13 (1970), pp. 195–211.
Busse, H., 'Arabische Historiographie und Geographie', in H. Gätje, ed., *Grundriß der Arabischen Philologie, Band II: Literaturwissenschaft* (Wiesbaden, 1987), pp. 264–297.
Cahen, C., '[c]Abdallatif al-Baghdadi, portraitiste et historien de son temps: extraits inédits de ses mémoires', *BEO* 23 (1970), pp. 101–128.
——, 'Fiscalité, propriété, antagonismes sociaux en Haute-Mésopotamie au temps des premiers [c]Abbāsides d'après Denys de Tell-Mahré', *Arabica* 1 (1954), pp. 136–152.
——, *Introduction à l'histoire du monde musulman médiéval: VIIe-XVe siècle (méthodologie et éléments de bibliographie)* (Paris, 1983), a revision of J. Sauvaget and C. Cahen, *Introduction à l'histoire de l'Orient musulman* (Paris, 1961), which is translated as *Introduction to the History of the Muslim East: A Bibliographical Guide* (Berkeley, 1965).
Calder, N., 'Friday prayer and the juristic theory of government: Sarakhsī, Shīrāzī, Māwardī', *BSOAS* 49 (1986), pp. 35–47.
——, 'Law', in S.H. Nasr and O. Leaman, eds., *History of Islamic Philosophy* (London, 1996), pp. 979–998.
——, *Studies in Early Muslim Jurisprudence* (Oxford, 1993).
Cameron, A., 'History as text: coping with Procopius', in C. Holdsworth and T.P. Wiseman, eds., *The Inheritance of Historiography 350–900* (Exeter, 1986), pp. 53–66.

Canary, R.H., and H. Kozicki, eds., *The Writing of History: Literary Form and Historical Understanding* (Madison, 1979).
Carruthers, M., *The Book of Memory* (Cambridge, 1990).
Carter, M.G., 'Language control as people control in medieval Islam: the aims of the grammarians in their cultural context', *al-Abhath* 31 (1983), pp. 65–84.
Caskel, W., *Das Schicksal in der altarabischen Poesie: Beiträge zur arabischen Literatur und zur allgemeinen Religionsgeschichte* (Leipzig, 1926).
The Catalogue of the Arabic and Persian Manuscripts in the Oriental Public Library at (Bankipore) Patna (Patna, 1908–1940).
Chabbi, J., 'La représentation du passé aux premiers âges de l'historiographie califale', in R. Curiel and R. Gyselen, eds., *Itinéraires d'Orient: hommages à Claude Cahen* (*Res Orientales*, vi) (Bures-sur-Yvette, 1994), pp. 21–47.
Chamberlain, M., *Knowledge and Social Practice in Medieval Damascus, 1190–1350* (Cambridge, 1994).
Chartier, R., 'Texts, printing, readings', in L. Hunt, ed., *The New Cultural History* (Berkeley and Los Angeles, 1989), pp. 154–175.
Chaumont, E., '*Kitâb al-Luma*ᶜ *fî uṣûl al-fiqh* d'Abû Isḥâq al-Šîrâzî (m. 476–1083), Introduction, édition critique et index', *Mélanges de l'Université Saint-Joseph* 53 (1993–1994), pp. 9–241.
Cheddadi, A., *Peuples et nations du monde: la conception de l'histoire, les Arabes du Machrek et leurs contemporains, les Arabes du Maghreb et les Berbères* (Paris, 1986).
Chejne, A., 'The boon-companion in early ᶜAbbāsid times', *JAOS* 85 (1965), pp. 327–335.
Clanchy, M.T., *From Memory to Written Record: England 1066–1307* (Oxford, 2nd ed., 1993).
Cohen, H., 'The economic background and the secular occupations of Muslim jurisprudents and traditionists in the classical period of Islam', *JESHO* 13 (1970), pp. 16–61.
Conrad, G., *Abū'l-Ḥusain al-Rāzī (-347/958) und seine Schriften: Untersuchungen zur frühen damaszener Geschichtsschreibung* (Stuttgart, 1991).
——, *Die Quḍāt Dimašq und der maḏhab Auzāᶜī* (Beirut, 1994).
Conrad, L.I., 'Al-Azdī's history of the Arab conquests in Bilad al-Sham: some historiographical observations', in M. A. Bakhit, ed., *Proceedings of the Second Symposium on the History of Bilād al-Shām during the Early Islamic Period up to 40 A.H./640 A.D.* vol. 1 (Amman, 1987), pp. 28–62.
——, 'The conquest of Arwād: a source-critical study in the historiography of the early medieval Near East', in A. Cameron and L.I. Conrad, eds., *The Byzantine and Early Islamic Near East I: Problems in the Literary Source Material* (Princeton, 1992), pp. 317–401.
——, 'Recovering lost texts: some methodological issues', *JAOS* 113 (1993), pp. 258–263; reprinted in Ibn Warraq, ed., *The Quest for the Historical Muhammad* (Amherst, N.Y., 2000), pp. 476–485.
Cook, M., 'ᶜAnan and Islam: the origins of Karaite scripturalism', *JSAI* 9 (1987), pp. 161–182.
——, *Commanding Right and Forbidding Wrong in Islamic Thought* (Cambridge, 2000).
——, 'An early Islamic apocalyptic chronicle', *JNES* 52 (1993), pp. 25–29.
——, 'The Heraclian dynasty in Muslim eschatology', *al-Qanṭara* 13 (1992), pp. 3–23.
——, 'The historians of pre-Wahhābī Najd', *SI* 76 (1992), pp. 163–176.
——, 'The opponents of the writing of tradition in early Islam', *Arabica* 44 (1997), pp. 437–530.

Cooperson, M., *Classical Arabic Biography: The Heirs of the Prophets in the Age of al-Maʾmūn* (Cambridge, 2000).

——, 'The purported autobiography of Ḥunayn ibn Isḥāq', *Edebiyât* n.s. 7 (1997), pp. 235–249.

Cox. P., *Biography in Late Antiquity: A Quest for the Holy Man* (Berkeley and Los Angeles, 1983).

Croke, B., 'City chronicles in Late Antiquity', in G. Clarke, et al., eds., *Reading the Past in Late Antiquity* (Sydney, 1990), pp. 165–203; reprinted in his *Christian Chronicles and Byzantine History, 5th-6th Centuries* (London, 1992).

——, 'The origins of the Christian world chronicle', in B. Croke and A.M. Emmett, eds., *History and Historians in Late Antiquity* (Sydney, 1983), pp. 116–131; reprinted in his *Christian Chronicles and Byzantine History, 5th–6th Centuries* (London, 1992).

Crone, P., *Meccan Trade and the Rise of Islam* (Princeton, 1987).

——, *Pre-industrial Societies* (Oxford and Cambridge, Mass., 1989).

——, review of Samarrai's edition of Sayf b. ᶜUmar, *Kitāb al-Ridda wa'l-futūḥ, JRAS* (3rd ser.) 6 (1996), pp. 237–240.

——, *Slaves on Horses: The Evolution of the Islamic Polity* (Cambridge, 1980).

Crone, P., and M. Cook, *Hagarism: The Making of the Islamic World* (Cambridge, 1977).

Crone, P., and M. Hinds, *God's Caliph: Religious Authority in the First Centuries of Islam* (Cambridge, 1987).

Crone, P., and F. Zimmermann, *The Epistle of Sālim b. Dhakwān* (Oxford, 2001).

Crossan, J.D., *Jesus: A Revolutionary Biography* (San Francisco, 1994).

Daiber, H., *Wāṣil ibn ᶜAṭāʾ als Prediger und Theologe* (Leiden, 1988).

Dale, S., 'Steppe humanism: the autobiographical writings of Zahir al-Din Muhammad Babur, 1483–1530'), *IJMES* 22 (1990), pp. 37–58.

Daniel, E., 'Manuscripts and editions of Balᶜamī's Tarjamah-i tārīkh-i Ṭabarī', *JRAS* (3rd ser.) 2 (1990), pp. 282–321.

——, 'The Samanid "translations" of al-Ṭabarī', in H. Kennedy, ed., *Al-Ṭabarī: A Muslim Historian and his Work* (Princeton, forthcoming).

Darrāǧ, A., 'La vie d'Abū'l-Maḥāsin Ibn Taġrī Birdī et son oeuvre', *Annales Islamologiques* 11 (1972), pp. 163–181.

Davies, J.K., 'The reliability of the oral tradition', in L. Foxhall and J.K. Davies, eds., *The Trojan War: Its Historicity and Context* (Bristol, 1984), pp. 87–110.

de la Grange, H.-L., *Gustav Mahler: Vienna, Triumph and Disillusion (1904–1911)* (Oxford, 2000).

Demos, J., 'In search of reasons for historians to read novels', *AHR* 103 (1998), pp. 1526–1529.

Déroche, F., 'Les manuscrits arabes datés du iiie/ixe siècle', *REI* 55–57 (1987–9), pp. 343–379.

Déroche, F., and F. Richard, eds., *Scribes et manuscrits du Moyen-Orient* (Paris, 1997).

de Slane, M., *Catalogue des manuscrits arabes* (Paris, 1883).

Deverdun, G., 'Un registre d'inventaire et de prêt de la bibliothèque de la mosquée ᶜAli ben Youssef à Marrakech daté de 1111 H./1700 J.-C.', *Hespéris* 31 (1944), pp. 55–60.

Dickinson, E., 'Aḥmad b. al-Ṣalt and his biography of Abū Ḥanīfa', *JAOS* 116 (1996), pp. 406–417.

Donner, F.M., *The Early Islamic Conquests* (Princeton, 1981).

——, 'The formation of the Islamic state', *JAOS* 56 (1986), pp. 283–296.

——, *Narratives of Islamic Origins: The Beginnings of Islamic Historical Writing* (Princeton, 1998).

Duri, A.A., *The Rise of Historical Writing Among the Arabs*, ed. and trans. by L.I. Conr (Princeton, 1983).

Ebied, R.Y., and L.R. Wickam, 'Al-Yaᶜqūbī's account of the Israelite prophets and king *JNES* 29 (1970), pp. 80–98.

Eche, Y., *Les bibliothèques arabes* (Damascus, 1967).

Eickelman, D.F., 'The art of memory: Islamic education and its social reproductior *Comparative Studies in Society and History* 20 (1978), pp. 485–516.

Elad, A., 'The history and topography of Jerusalem during the early Islamic period: the hi torical value of *faḍāʾil al-Quds* literature: a reconsideration', *JSAI* 14 (1991), pp. 41–8.

——, 'The Southern Golan in the early Muslim period: the significance of two newl discovered milestones of ᶜAbd al-Malik', *DI* 76 (1999), pp. 33–88.

El-Hibri, T., *Reinterpreting Islamic Historiography: Hārūn al-Rashīd and the Narrative of the ᶜAbbāsid Caliphate* (Cambridge, 1999).

Ellis, A.G., *Catalogue of the Arabic Books in the British Museum* (London, 1894).

The Encyclopaedia of Islam (Leiden, 1913–1934; Supplement 1938).

The Encyclopaedia of Islam, New Edition (Leiden, 1954–).

Endress, G., 'Handschriftenkunde', in W. Fischer, ed., *Grundriß der Arabischen Philologie, Band I: Sprachwissenschaft* (Wiesbaden, 1982), pp. 271–315.

Evans, J.A.S., *Herodotus, Explorer of the Past: Three Essays* (Princeton, 1981).

Evans, R.J., *In Defense of History* (New York and London, 1997).

Fadiman, J., *When We Began There Were Witchmen: An Oral History from Mount Kenya* (Berkeley, 1993).

Fähndrich, H.E., 'The *Wafayāt al-aᶜyān* of Ibn Khallikān: a new approach', *JAOS* 93 (1973), pp. 432–445.

Farah, C., *The Dhayl in Medieval Arabic Historiography* (New Haven, 1967).

Finley, M.I., 'Myth, memory and history', in his *The Use and Abuse of History* (London, 1990 reprint), pp. 11–33.

Fischel, W.J., *Ibn Khaldūn in Egypt* (Berkeley and Los Angeles, 1967).

Fischer, W., 'Die Prosa des Abū Miḫnaf', in R. Gramlich, ed., *Islamwissenschaftliche Abhandlungen* (Festschrift for F. Meier) (Wiesbaden, 1974), pp. 96–105.

Flemming, B., 'Literary activities in Mamluk halls and barracks', in M. Rosen-Ayalon, ed., *Studies in Memory of Gaston Wiet* (Jerusalem, 1977), pp. 249–260.

Fornara, C.W., *The Nature of History in Ancient Greece and Rome* (Berkeley and Los Angeles, 1988).

Fowden, G., *Empire to Commonwealth: Consequences of Monotheism in Late Antiquity* (Princeton, 1993).

Freedman, P., and G.M. Spiegel, 'Medievalisms old and new: the rediscovery of alterity in North American medieval studies', *AHR* 103 (1998), pp. 677–704.

Fück, J., 'Die Rolle des Traditionalismus im Islam', *ZDMG* 93 (1939), pp. 1–32; in M. Swartz, ed. and trans., *Studies on Islam* (New York and Oxford, 1981), pp. 99–122.

Geertz, C., *Islam Observed: Religious Development in Morocco and Indonesia* (Chicago, 1968).

Gibb, H.A.R., 'Taʾrīkh', *EI,* Supplement (Leiden, 1938), pp. 233–245; reprinted in his *Studies on the Civilization of Islam*, ed. S.J. Shaw and W.R. Polk (Princeton, 1962), pp. 108–137

Gilbert, J., 'Institutionalization of Muslim scholarship and professionalization of the *ᶜulamāʾ* in medieval Damascus', *SI* 52 (1980), pp. 105–134.

Gilliot, C., 'La formation intellectuelle de Tabari (224/5–310/839–923)', *JA* 276 (1988), pp. 201–244.

Gohlman, W., *The Life of Ibn Sina* (New York, 1974).
Goitein, S.D., *A Mediterranean Society: The Jewish Communities of the Arab World as Portrayed by the Documents of the Cairo Geniza* (Berkeley and Los Angeles, 1967–1993).
Goldziher, I., *Muslim Studies*, trans. by C.R. Barber and S.M. Stern (Chicago, 1966).
Goody, J., *The Domestication of the Savage Mind* (Cambridge, 1977).
——, *The Logic of Writing and the Organization of Society* (Cambridge, 1986).
Grabar, O., 'The painting of the six kings at Quṣayr ᶜAmrah', *Ars Orientalis* 1 (1954), pp. 185–187.
Grafton, A., *The Footnote: A Curious History* (Cambridge, Mass., 1997, rev. ed.).
Graham, W., 'Traditionalism in Islam: an essay in interpretation', *Journal of Interdisciplinary History* 23 (1993), pp. 495–522.
Grandin, N., and M. Gaborieau, eds., *Madrasa: la transmission du savoir dans le monde musulman* (Paris, 1997).
Green, W.S., 'What's in a name? – the problematic of "rabbinic biography"', in W.S. Green, ed., *Approaches to Ancient Judaism: Theory and Practice* I (Missoula, 1978), pp. 77–96.
Guest, A., 'A list of writers, books and other authorities mentioned by El Maqrīzī in his Khiṭaṭ', *JRAS* (1902), pp. 103–125.
Guillaume, A., *The Traditions of Islam* (Oxford, 1924; reprinted Beirut, 1966).
Günther, S., '*Maqâtil* literature in medieval Islam', *JAL* 25 (1994), pp. 192–212.
——, 'New results in the theory of source-criticism in medieval Arabic literature', *al-Abhath* 42 (1994), pp. 4–15.
——, *Quellenuntersuchungen zu den 'Maqātil aṭ-Ṭālibiyyīn' des Abū'l-Farağ al-Iṣfahānī (gest. 356/967)* (Hildescheim, 1991).
Guo, L., *Early Mamluk Syrian Historiography: Al-Yūnīnī's Dhayl Mirʾāt al-Zamān* (Leiden, 1998).
——, 'Mamluk historiographic studies: the state of the art', *MSR* 1 (1997), pp. 15–43.
Gutas, D., *Greek Thought, Arabic Culture* (London, 1998).
Haarmann, U., 'Arabic in speech, Turkish in lineage: Mamluks and their sons in the intellectual life of fourteenth-century Egypt and Syria', *JSS* 33 (1988), pp. 81–114.
——, 'Auflösung und Bewahrung der klassischen Formen arabischer Geschichtsschreibung in der Zeit der Mamluken', *ZDMG* 121 (1971), pp. 46–60.
——, 'The library of a fourteenth century Jerusalem scholar', *DI* 61 (1984), pp. 327–333.
——, 'Mamluk endowment deeds as a source for the history of education in late medieval Egypt', *al-Abhath* 28 (1980), pp. 31–47.
——, *Quellenstudien zur frühen Mamlukenzeit* (Freiburg im Breisgau, 1969).
Hafsi, I., 'Recherches sur le genre «*Ṭabaqāt*» dans la littérature arabe, I, II, III', *Arabica* 23 (1976), pp. 227–265; 24 (1977), pp. 1–41 and 150–186.
Hallaq, W., *Authority, Continuity and Change in Islamic Law* (Cambridge, 2001).
——, *A History of Islamic Legal Theories* (Cambridge, 1997).
Halm, H., 'Die Anfänge der madrasa', *ZDMG* Supp. 3 (1977), pp. 438–448.
——, *The Fatimids and their Traditions of Learning* (London, 1997).
Hamad, B., 'History and biography', *Arabica* 45 (1998), pp. 215–232.
Harlan, D., 'Intellectual history and the return of literature', *AHR* 94 (1989), pp. 581–609.
Harries, J., 'Sozomen and Eusebius: the lawyer as church historian in the fifth century', in C. Holdsworth and T.P. Wiseman, eds., *The Inheritance of Historiography 350–900* (Exeter, 1986), pp. 45–52.

Heath, P., *The Thirsty Sword: Sīrat ᶜAntar and the Arabic Popular Epic* (Salt Lake City, 1996).

Henige, D., *The Chronology of Oral Tradition* (Oxford, 1974).

Hezser, C., *The Social Structure of the Rabbinic Movement in Roman Palestine* (Tübingen, 1997).

Hillenbrand, C., 'Jihad propaganda in Syria from the time of the First Crusade until the death of Zengi: the evidence of monumental inscriptions', in K. Athamina and R. Heacock, eds., *The Frankish Wars and their Influence on Palestine* (Bir Zeit, 1994), pp. 60–69.

——, *A Muslim Principality in Crusader Times: The Early Artuqid State* (Leiden, 1990).

Hinds, M., '*Maghāzī* and *sīra* in early Islamic scholarship', in T. Fahd, ed., *La vie du prophète Mahomet* (Paris, 1983), pp. 57–66; reprinted in his *Studies in Early Islamic History*, ed. J. Bacharach et al. (Princeton, 1996), pp. 188–198.

——, 'Sayf b. ᶜUmar's sources on Arabia', in A.M. Abdalla et al., eds., *Sources for the History of Arabia* (Riyadh, 1979), part ii, pp. 3–16; reprinted in his *Studies in Early Islamic History*, ed. J. Bacharach et al. (Princeton, 1996), pp. 143–159.

Hodgson, M.G.S., 'Two pre-modern Muslim historians: pitfalls and opportunities in presenting them to moderns', in J. Neff, ed., *Towards World Community* (The Hague, 1968), pp. 53–68.

Hoenerbach, W., *Waṯīma's Kitāb ar-Ridda aus Ibn Ḥağar's Iṣāba* (Wiesbaden, 1951).

Holdsworth, C., and T.P. Wiseman, eds., *The Inheritance of Historiography, 350–900* (Exeter, 1986).

Holt, P.M., *Early Mamluk Diplomacy (1260–1290): Treaties of Baybars and Qalāwūn with Christian Rulers* (Leiden, 1995).

——, 'The presentation of Qalāwūn by Shāfiᶜ b. ᶜAlī', in C.E. Bosworth et al., eds., *The Islamic World from Classical to Modern Times: Essays in Honor of Bernard Lewis* (Princeton, 1989), pp. 141–150.

——, 'Some observations on Shāfiᶜ b. ᶜAlī's biography of Baybars', *JSS* 29 (1984), pp. 123–130.

——, 'Three biographies of al-Ẓāhir Baybars', in D.O. Morgan, ed., *Medieval Historical Writing in the Christian and Islamic Worlds* (London, 1982), pp. 19–29.

Horowitz, J., 'The earliest biographies of the Prophet and their authors', *IC* 1 (1927), pp. 535–559; and 2 (1928), pp. 22–50, 164–182 and 495–526.

Hoyland, R., *Seeing Islam as Others Saw It: A Survey and Evaluation of Christian, Jewish and Zoroastrian Writings on Early Islam* (Princeton, 1997).

Humphreys, R.S., *Islamic History: A Framework for Inquiry* (Princeton, rev. ed., 1991).

——, 'Modern Arab historians and the challenge of the Islamic past', *Middle Eastern Lectures* 1 (1995), pp. 119–131.

——, 'Qurᵓanic myth and narrative structure in early Islamic historiography', in F.M. Clover and R.S. Humphreys, eds., *Tradition and Innovation in Late Antiquity* (Madison, 1989), pp. 271–290.

Hurvitz, N., 'Biographies and mild asceticism: a study of Islamic moral imagination', *SI* 85 (1997), pp. 41–65.

Ibn an-Nadim und die mittelalterliche arabische Literatur (Wiesbaden, 1996).

Ibn Warraq, ed., *The Quest for the Historical Muhammad* (Amherst, New York, 2000).

Jarrar, M., *Die Prophetenbiographie im islamischen Spanien* (Frankfurt am Main, 1989).

al-Jāsir, Ḥ., 'Muᵓallafāt fī taᵓrīkh al-Madīna', *al-ᶜArab* 4 (1969), pp. 97–100, 262–267; and 4–5 (1970), pp. 327–335, 385–389.

Jeffreys, E., et al., eds., *Studies in John Malalas* (Sydney, 1990).

Jenkins, K., 'A post-modern reply to Perez Zagorin', *History and Theory* 39 (2000), pp. 181–200.

Johansen, B., *Contingency in a Sacred Law: Legal and Ethical Norms in Muslim Fiqh* (Leiden, 1999).

Jones, A., *Early Arabic Poetry, Volume I: Marāthī and Ṣuᶜlūk Poems* (Reading, 1992).

Joyce, P., 'History and post-modernism I', *Past and Present* 133 (1991), pp. 204–209.

Juynboll, G.H.A., 'Muslim's introduction to his *Ṣaḥīḥ* translated and annotated with an excursus on the chronology of *fitna* and *bidᶜa*', *JSAI* 5 (1984), pp. 263–311.

——, *Muslim Tradition: Studies in Chronology, Provenance and Authorship of Early Ḥadīth* (Cambridge, 1983).

——, 'The origins of Arabic prose', in G.H.A. Juynboll, ed., *Studies on the First Century of Islamic Society* (Carbondale and Edwardsville, 1982), pp. 161–175, 254–259.

Kaplony, A., *Konstantinopel und Damaskus: Gesandtschaften und Verträge zwischen Kaisern und Kalifen 639–750* (Berlin, 1996).

Kennedy, H., *The Armies of the Caliphs: Military and Society in the Early Islamic State* (London, 2001).

——, 'From oral tradition to written record in Arabic genealogy', *Arabica* 44 (1997), pp. 531–544.

Khalidi, T., *Arabic Historical Thought in the Classical Period* (Cambridge, 1994).

Khan, M.S., 'A manuscript of an epitome of al-Ṣābī's *Kitāb al-Tāǧī*', *Arabica* 12 (1965), pp. 27–44.

——, 'The use of letters and documents in the contemporary history of Miskawaih', *IQ* 14 (1970), pp. 41–49.

Khazanov, A., 'Muhammad and Jenghiz Khan compared: the religious factor in world empire building', *Comparative Studies in History and Society* 35 (1993), pp. 461–479.

Khouri, R.G., *Wahb b. Munabbih: der Heidelberger Papyrus PSR Heid Arab 23* (Wiesbaden, 1972).

——, ed., *Urkunden und Urkundenformulare im klassischen Altertum und in den orientalischen Kulturen* (Heidelberg, 1999).

Kilpatrick, H., 'Autobiography and classical Arabic literature', *JAL* 22 (1991), pp. 1–20.

Kimber, R., 'Hārūn al-Rashīd's Meccan settlement of AH 186/AD 802', *Occasional Papers of the School of Abbasid Studies* 1 (1986), pp. 55–79.

Kinberg, L., 'The legitimization of the *madhāhib* through dreams', *Arabica* 32 (1985), pp. 47–79.

Kister, M.J., '*Lā taqraʾū l-qurʾāna ᶜalā l-muṣḥafiyyīn wa-lā taḥmilū l-ᶜilma ᶜani l-ṣaḥafiyyīn*: some notes on the transmission of *ḥadīth*', *JSAI* 22 (1998), pp. 127–162.

——, '"Pare your nails": a study of an early tradition', *Journal of the Ancient Near Eastern Society* 11 (1979), pp. 63–70, reprinted in his *Society and Religion from Jāhiliyya to Islam* (Aldershot, 1990).

——, 'Sīra', in L.I. Conrad, ed., *History and Historiography in Early Islamic Times: Studies and Perspectives* (Princeton, forthcoming).

Köhler, B., 'Die Frauen in al-Wāqidī's *Kitāb al-maġāzī*', *ZDMG* 147 (1997), pp. 303–353.

Köhler, M.A., *Allianzen und Verträge zwischen fränkischen und islamischen Herrschern im Vorderen Orient* (Berlin, 1991).

Kohlberg, E., *A Medieval Muslim Scholar at Work: Ibn Ṭāwūs and his Library* (Leiden, 1992).

Kraemer, J., *Humanism in the Renaissance of Islam: The Cultural Revival during the Buyid Age* (Leiden, 2nd rev. ed., 1993).

Lambton, A.K.S., 'Persian local histories: the tradition behind them and the assumptions of their authors', in *Yād-Nāma in memoria di Alessandro Bausani* (Rome, 1991), i, pp. 227–238.

Landau-Tasseron, E., 'From tribal society to centralized polity: an interpretation of events and anecdotes of the formative period of Islam', *JSAI* 24 (2000), pp. 180–216.

——, 'On the reconstruction of lost sources', in L.I. Conrad, ed., *History and Historiography in Early Islamic Times: Studies and Perspectives* (Princeton, forthcoming).

——, 'Processes of redaction: the case of the Tamīmite delegation to the Prophet Muḥammad', *BSOAS* 49 (1986), pp. 253–270.

——, 'Sayf ibn ᶜUmar in medieval and modern scholarship', *DI* 67 (1990), pp. 1–26.

Lane Fox, R., 'Literacy and power in early Christianity', in A.K. Bowman and G. Woolf, eds., *Literacy and Power in the Ancient World* (Cambridge, 1994), pp. 126–148.

Langner, B., *Untersuchungen zur historischen Volkskunde Ägyptens nach mamlukischen Quellen* (Berlin, 1983).

Laoust, H., 'Ibn Kaṯīr historien', *Arabica* 2 (1955), pp. 42–88.

Laroui, A., *Islam et histoire: essai d'épistémologie* (Paris, 1999).

Lassner, J., *Islamic Revolution and Historical Memory* (New Haven, 1986).

——, *The Topography of Baghdad in the Early Middle Ages: Texts and Studies* (Detroit, 1970).

Lecker, M., 'Biographical notes on Ibn Shihāb al-Zuhrī', *JSS* 41 (1996), pp. 21–63.

——, 'The death of the Prophet Muḥammad's father: did Wāqidī invent some of the evidence?', *ZDMG* 145 (1995), pp. 9–27.

——, *Muslims, Jews and Pagans: Studies on Early Islamic Medina* (Leiden, 1995).

——, 'Wāqidī's account on the status of the Jews in Medina: a study of a combined report', *JNES* 54 (1995), pp. 15–32.

Lecomte, G., 'Le livre des règles de conduite des maîtres d'école par Ibn Saḥnūn', *REI* 21 (1953), pp. 77–105.

Leder, S., 'Authorship and transmission in unauthored literature: the *akhbār* attributed to al-Haytham ibn ᶜAdī', *Oriens*, 31 (1988), pp. 67–81.

——, 'Features of the novel in early historiography – the downfall of Xālid al-Qasrī', *Oriens* 32 (1990), pp. 72–96.

——, 'Grenzen der Rekonstruktion alten Schrifttums nach den Angaben im *Fihrist*' in *Ibn an-Nadim und die mittelalterliche arabische Literatur* (Wiesbaden, 1996), pp. 21–31.

——, *Das Korpus al-Haiṯam ibn 'Adī (st. 207/822): Herkunft, Überlieferung, Gestalt früher Texte der aḫbār Literatur* (Frankfurt am Main, 1991).

——, ed., *Story-telling in the Framework of Non-fictional Arabic Literature* (Wiesbaden, 1998).

Leder, S., and H. Kilpatrick, 'Classical Arabic prose literature: a researchers' sketch map', *JAL* 23 (1992), pp. 2–26.

Leder, S., Y.M. al-Sawwās and M. al-Ṣāgharjī, *Muᶜjam al-samāᶜāt al-Dimašqiyya* (Damascus, 1996).

Lev, Y., *State and Society in Fatimid Egypt* (Leiden, 1991).

Levanoni, A., *A Turning Point in Mamluk History: The Third Reign of al-Nāṣir Muḥammad Ibn Qalāwūn, 1310–1341* (Leiden, 1995).

Levi Della Vida, G., 'La traduzione araba delle storie di Orosio', *al-Andalus* 19 (1954), pp. 257–293.

Lévi-Provençal, E., 'Note sur l'exemplaire du *Kitâb al-ᶜIbar* offert par Ibn Ḫaldûn à la bibliothèque d'al-Ḳarawîyîn à Fès,' *JA* 103 (1923), pp. 161–168.

Lewicki, T., 'Les historiens, biographes et traditionnistes ibādites-wahbites de l'Afrique du Nord du viiie au xvie siècle', *Folia Orientalia* 3 (1961), pp. 1–134.

Lewis, B., and P.M. Holt, eds., *Historians of the Middle East* (London, 1962).

Librande, L.T., 'The scholars of Hadith and the retentive memory', *Cahiers d'onomastique arabe* 1988–1992 (1993), pp. 39–48.

Little, D.P., 'Al-Ṣafadī as biographer of his contemporaries', in D.P. Little, ed., *Essays in Islamic Civilization Presented to Niyazi Berkes* (Leiden, 1976), pp. 190–210.

——, 'Documents as a source for Mamluk history', *MSR* 1 (1997), pp. 1–13.

——, *An Introduction to Mamlūk Historiography* (Wiesbaden, 1970).

——, 'Mujīr al-Dīn al-ᶜUlaymī's vision of Jerusalem in the ninth-fifteenth century', *JAOS* 115 (1995), pp. 237–247.

Lowenthal, D., *The Past is a Foreign Country* (Cambridge, 1985).

Lowry, J.E., 'Time, form and self: the autobiography of Abū Shāma', *Edebiyât* n.s. 7 (1997), pp. 313–325.

Luther, K.A., 'Islamic rhetoric and the Persian historians, 1100–1300 A.D.', in J.A. Bellamy, ed., *Studies in Near Eastern Culture and History in Memory of Ernest T. Abdel-Massih* (Ann Arbor, 1990), pp. 90–98.

Lyons, M.C., *The Arabian Epic: Heroic and Oral Story-telling: Volume 1: Introduction* (Cambridge, 1995).

Lyons, M.C., and D. Jackson, *Saladin: The Politics of the Holy War* (Cambridge, 1982).

Madelung, W., 'Abū Isḥāq al-Ṣābī on the Alids of Ṭabaristān and Gilān', *JNES* 26 (1967), pp. 17–57.

——'A treatise of the Sharīf al-Murtaḍā on the legality of working for the government (*masʾala fī ʾl-ᶜamal maᶜa ʾl-sulṭān*)', *BSOAS* 43 (1980), pp 18–31.

Madelung, W., and P. Walker, *The Advent of the Fatimids: A Contemporary Shiᶜi Witness* (London, 2000).

Mahdi, M., *Ibn Khaldûn's Philosophy of History* (London, 1957).

Makdisi, G., 'Autograph diary of an eleventh-century historian of Baghdad – I', *BSOAS* 18 (1956), pp. 9–31, 239–260.

——, 'The diary in Islamic historiography: some notes', *History and Theory* 25 (1986), pp. 173–185.

——, *Ibn ᶜAqil: Religion and Culture in Classical Islam* (Edinburgh, 1997).

——, *Ibn ᶜAqīl et la résurgence de l'Islam traditionaliste au xie siècle* (Damascus, 1963).

——, *The Rise of Colleges: Institutions of Learning in Islam and the West* (Edinburgh, 1981).

——, *The Rise of Humanism in Classical Islam and the Christian West* (Edinburgh, 1990).

——, '*Ṭabaqāt*-biography: law and orthodoxy in classical Islam', *IS* 32 (1993), pp. 371–396.

Malti-Douglas, F., 'Controversy and its effects in the biographical tradition of al-Khaṭīb al-Baghdādī', *SI* 46 (1977), pp. 115–130.

——, 'Dreams, the blind, and the semiotics of the biographical notice', *SI* 51 (1980), pp. 137–162.

——, 'Texts and tortures: the reign of al-Muᶜtaḍid and the construction of historical meaning', *Arabica* 46 (1999), pp. 313–336.

Mango, C., 'The tradition of Byzantine chronography', *Harvard Ukrainian Studies* 12–13 (1988–89), pp. 360–372.

Manzano-Moreno, E., 'Oriental «topoi» in Andalusian historical sources', *Arabica* 39 (1992), pp. 42–58.

Maraqten, M., 'Writing materials in pre-Islamic Arabia', *JSS* 43 (1998), pp. 287–310.

Marincola, J., *Authority and Tradition in Ancient Historiography* (Cambridge, 1997).
Marquet, Y., 'Le šiᶜisme au IXᵉ siècle à travers l'histoire de Yaᶜqūbī', *Arabica* 19 (1972), pp. 1–45, 101–138.
Massa, M.S., *Charles Augustus Briggs and the Crisis of Historical Criticism* (Minneapolis, 1990).
McMurtry, L., *Crazy Horse* (New York, 1999).
Meisami, J.S., 'Dynastic kingship and the ideal of kingship in Bayhaqi's *Tarikh-i Masᶜudi*', *Edebiyât* n.s. 3 (1989), pp. 57–77.
——, *Persian Historiography to the End of the Twelfth Century* (Edinburgh, 1999).
Melchert, C., 'Bukhārī and early hadith criticism', *JAOS* 121 (2001), pp. 7–19.
——, *The Formation of the Sunni Schools of Law, 9th–10th Centuries C.E.* (Leiden, 1997).
——, 'How Ḥanafism came to originate in Kufa and traditionalism in Medina', *Islamic Law and Society* 6 (1999), pp. 318–347.
Meyer, E., *Der historische Gehalt der Aiyām al-ᶜArab* (Wiesbaden, 1970).
Mez, A., *The Renaissance of Islam,* trans. S.K. Bakhsh and D.S. Margoliouth (Patna, 1937).
Michot, Y.J., 'Ibn Taymiyya on astrology: annotated translation of three fatwas', *Journal of Islamic Studies* 11 (2000), pp. 147–208.
Mojaddedi, J., 'Legitimizing Sufism in al-Qushayri's *Risala*', *SI* 90 (2000), pp. 37–50.
Momigliano, A., *The Classical Foundations of Modern Historiography* (Berkeley and Los Angeles, 1990).
——, *The Development of Greek Biography: Four Lectures* (Cambridge, Mass., 1971).
——, 'The disadvantages of monotheism for a universal state', *Classical Philology* 81 (1986), pp. 285–297.
——, 'The place of Herodotus in the history of historiography', in his *Studies in Historiography* (New York and Evanston, 1966), pp. 127–142.
Morray, D.W., *An Ayyubid Notable and his World: Ibn al-ᶜAdīm and Aleppo as Portrayed in his Biographical Dictionary of People Associated with the City* (Leiden, 1994).
——, *The Genius of Usāma ibn Munqidh* (Durham, 1987).
Mottahedeh, R.P., *Loyalty and Leadership in an Early Islamic Society* (Princeton, 1980).
——, 'The Shuᶜûbîyah controversy and the social history of early Islamic Iran', *IJMES* 7 (1976), pp. 161–182.
——, 'Some attitudes towards monarchy and absolutism in the early Islamic world of the eleventh and twelfth centuries AD', *Israel Oriental Studies* 10 (1980), pp. 86–91.
Motzki, H., *Die Anfänge der islamischen Jurisprudenz: ihre Entwicklung in Mekka bis zur Mitte des 2./8 Jahrhunderts* (Stuttgart, 1991).
——, *The Biography of Muḥammad: The Issue of the Sources* (Leiden, 2000).
——, 'The *Muṣannaf* of ᶜAbd al-Razzāq al-Ṣanᶜānī as a source of authentic *aḥādīth* of the first century A.H.', *JNES* 50 (1991), pp. 1–21.
——, *The Origins of Islamic Jurisprudence: Meccan Fiqh before the Classical Schools* (Leiden, 2001).
Mourad, S., 'On early Islamic historiography: Abū Ismāᶜīl al-Azdī and his *Futūḥ al-Shām*', *JAOS* 120 (2000), pp. 577–593.
al-Munajjid, Ṣ. al-Dīn, 'Ijāzāt al-samāᶜ fī al-makhṭūṭāt al-qadīma', *Majallat Maᶜhad al-Makhṭūṭāt al-ᶜArabiyya, Revue de l'institut des manuscrits arabes* (Cairo), 1 (1955), pp. 232–251.
Muranyi, M., *Beiträge zur Geschichte der Ḥadīṯ- und Rechtsgelehrsamkeit der Mālikiyya in Nordafrika bis zum 5. Jh. d.H.* (Wiesbaden, 1997).

——, 'Zur Entwicklung der *ᶜilm al-riǧāl*-Literatur im 3. Jahrhundert d.H.', *ZDMG* 142 (1992), pp. 57–71.

——, 'Ibn Isḥāq's *Kitāb al-maġāzī* in der *riwāya* von Yūnus b. Bukair', *JSAI* 14 (1991), pp. 214–275.

——, *Die Rechtsbücher des Qairawāners Saḥnūn b. Saᶜīd: Entstehungsgeschichte und Werküberlieferung* (Stuttgart, 1999).

Murray, O., 'Herodotus and oral history' in H. Sancisi-Weerdenburg and A. Kuhrt, eds., *Achaemenid History II: The Greek Sources* (Leiden, 1987), pp. 93–115.

Muth, F.-C., *Die Annalen von aṭ-Ṭabarī im Spiegel der europäischen Bearbeitungen* (Frankfurt am Main, 1983).

Neusner, J., 'Judaic uses of history in Talmudic times', in A. Rapoport-Albert, ed., *Essays in Jewish Historiography* (Middletown, CT, 1988) (=*History and Theory*, Beiheft 27), pp. 12–39.

Newby, G.D., *The Making of the Last Prophet: A Reconstruction of the Earliest Biography of Muhammad* (Columbia, S.C., 1989).

Northrup, L., *From Slave to Sultan: The Career of al-Manṣūr Qalāwūn and the Consolidation of Mamluk Rule in Egypt and Syria (678–689 A.H./1279–1290 A.D.)* (Stuttgart, 1998).

Noth, A., *Quellenkritische Studien zu Themen, Formen und Tendenzen frühislamischer Geschichtsüberlieferung* (Bonn, 1973); revised edition (in collaboration with L.I. Conrad) translated by M. Bonner as *The Early Arabic Historical Tradition* (Princeton, 1994).

Novick, P., *That Noble Dream: The 'Objectivity Question' and the American Historical Profession* (Cambridge, 1988).

Oleson, J.P. et al., 'Preliminary report of the al-Humayma Excavation Project, 1995, 1996, 1998', *Annual of the Department of Antiquities of Jordan* 43 (1999), pp. 411–450.

Olson, D., *The World on Paper: The Conceptual and Cognitive Implications of Writing and Reading* (Cambridge, 1994).

Ouyang, W., *Literary Criticism in Medieval Arabic-Islamic Culture: The Making of a Tradition* (Edinburgh, 1997).

Owen, D.D.R., *Eleanor of Aquitaine: Queen and Legend* (Oxford and Cambridge, Mass., 1993).

Palmer, A., *The Seventh Century in the West-Syrian Chronicles* (Liverpool, 1993).

Paret, R., 'Die legendäre futūḥ-Literatur', in *La poesia epica e la sua formazione* (Rome, 1970), pp. 735–749.

Patterson, L., *Negotiating the Past: The Historical Understanding of Medieval Literature* (Madison, 1987).

Pedersen, J., *The Arabic Book*, trans. G. French (Princeton, 1984).

Pellat, C., 'Les encyclopédies dans le monde arabe', *Cahiers d'histoire mondiale* 9 (1966), pp. 631–658.

——, *Le milieu basrien et la formation de Ǧāḥiẓ* (Paris, 1953).

——, 'La «Nâbita» de Djâhiz: (un document important pour l'histoire politico-religieuse de l'Islâm)', *Annales de l'Institut des Études Orientales* (Algiers) 10 (1952).

——, 'The origin and development of historiography in Muslim Spain', in P.M. Holt and B. Lewis, eds., *Historians of the Middle East* (London, 1962), pp. 118–125.

——, 'Was al-Masᶜūdī an historian or an *adīb*?', *Journal of the Pakistan Historical Society* 9 (1961), pp. 231–234.

Peskes, E., *Muḥammad b. ᶜAbd al-Wahhāb im Widerstreit: Untersuchungen zur Rekonstruktion der Frühgeschichte der Wahhābiyya* (Beirut, 1993).

Peters, F.E., 'The quest for the historical Muhammad', *IJMES* 23 (1991), pp. 291–315; reprinted in Ibn Warraq, ed., *The Quest for the Historical Muhammad* (Amherst, N.Y., 2000), pp. 444–475.

Petersen, E.L., *ᶜAlī and Muᶜāwiya in Early Arabic Tradition: Studies on the Genesis and Growth of Islamic Historical Writing until the End of the Ninth Century* (Copenhagen, 1964; 2nd ed. Odense, 1974).

Petrucci, A., *Writers and Readers in Medieval Italy: Studies in the History of Written Culture*, ed. C.M. Radding (New Haven, 1995).

Petry, C., *The Civilian Elite of Cairo in the Later Middle Ages* (Princeton, 1981).

Pingree, D., 'Historical horoscopes', *JAOS* 82 (1962), pp. 487–502.

Pinto, O., 'The libraries of the Arabs during the time of the Abbasides', *IC* 3 (1929), pp. 210–248.

Popovic, A., *La révolte des esclaves en Iraq au IIIᵉ, IXᵉ siècle* (Paris, 1976); translated by L. King as *The Revolt of African Slaves in Iraq in the 3rd/9th Century* (Princeton, 1999).

Popper, W., 'Sakhāwī's criticism of Ibn Taghrī Birdī', *Studi Orientalistici in onore di Giorgio Levi Della Vida* (Rome, 1956), pp. 371–389.

Pouzet, L., 'Remarques sur l'autobiographie dans le monde arabo-musulman au moyen âge', in U. Vermeulen and D. de Smet, eds., *Philosophy and Arts in the Islamic World* (Louvain, 1998) (Orientalia Lovaniensia Analecta 87), pp. 97–106.

Provan, I., 'The end of (Israel's) history?', (review article) *JSS* 42 (1997), pp. 283–300.

Pulleyblank, E.G., 'The historiographical tradition', in R. Dawson, ed., *The Legacy of China* (Oxford, 1964), pp. 143–164.

Pulleyblank, E.G., and W.G. Beasley, eds., *Historians of China and Japan* (Oxford, 1961).

al-Qāḍī, W., 'Biographical dictionaries: inner structure and cultural significance', in G.N. Atiyeh, ed., *The Book in the Islamic World: The Written Word and Communication in the Middle East* (Albany, 1995), pp. 93–122.

Radtke, B., *al-Ḥakīm at-Tirmiḏī: ein islamischer Theosoph des 3./9. Jahrhunderts* (Freiburg, 1980).

——, 'Towards a typology of Abbasid universal chronicles', *Occasional Papers of the School of Abbasid Studies* 3 (1991), pp. 1–18.

——, *Weltgeschichte und Weltbeschreibung im mittelalterlichen Islam* (Beirut and Stuttgart, 1992).

Radtke, B. and J. O'Kane, *The Concept of Sainthood in Early Islamic Mysticism* (Richmond, 1996).

Rahmani, A.A., 'The life and works of Ibn Ḥajar al-ᶜAsqalānī', *IC* 45 (1971), pp. 203–212, and 275–293; 46 (1972), pp. 75–81, 171–178, 265–272, 353–362; and 47 (1973), pp. 57–74.

Rathbone, J., *The Last English King* (London, 1997).

Reynolds, D.F., ed., *Interpreting the Self: Autobiography in the Arabic Literary Tradition* (Berkeley and Los Angeles, 2001).

Richards, D.S., 'A consideration of two sources for the life of Saladin', *JSS* 25 (1980), pp. 46–65.

——, 'Ibn al-Athīr and the later parts of the *Kāmil*: a study of aims and methods', in D.O. Morgan, ed., *Medieval Historical Writing in the Christian and Islamic Worlds* (London, 1982), pp. 76–108.

——, 'ᶜImād al-Dīn al-Iṣfahānī: administrator, littérateur and historian', in M. Shatzmiller, ed., *Crusaders and Muslims in Twelfth-Century Syria* (Leiden, 1993), pp. 133–146.

Richter-Bernburg, L., *Der syrische Blitz: Saladins Sekretär zwischen Selbstdarstellung und Geschichtsschreibung* (Beirut, 1998).
Ritter, H., 'Autographs in Turkish libraries', *Oriens* 6 (1953), pp. 63–90.
Roberts, C.H., and T.C. Skeat, *The Birth of the Codex* (London, 1983).
Robinson, C.F., *Empire and Elites after the Muslim Conquest: The Transformation of Northern Mesopotamia* (Cambridge, 2000).
——, 'Ibn al-Azraq, his *Taʾrīkh Mayyāfāriqīn*, and early Islam', *JRAS* (3rd ser.) 6 (1996), pp. 7–27.
——, 'A local historian's debt to al-Ṭabarī: the case of al-Azdī's *Taʾrīkh al-Mawṣil*', in H. Kennedy, ed., *Al-Ṭabarī: A Muslim Historian and his Work* (Princeton, forthcoming).
——, 'al-Muᶜāfā b. ᶜImrān and the beginnings of the *ṭabaqāt* literature', *JAOS* 116 (1996), pp. 114–120.
——, 'Prophecy and holy men in early Islam', in J. Howard-Johnston and P.A. Hayward, eds., *The Cult of Saints in Late Antiquity and the Early Middle Ages* (Oxford, 1999), pp. 241–262.
——, 'The study of Islamic historiography: a progress report', *JRAS* (3rd ser.) 7 (1997), pp. 199–227.
——, 'al-Ṭabarī', in M. Cooperson and S.M. Toorawa, eds., *Arabic Literary Culture, 500–925* (The Dictionary of Literary Biography; Detroit, 1978–; forthcoming).
Robinson Waldman, M., '"The otherwise unnoteworthy year 711": a reply to Hayden White', *Critical Inquiry* 7 (1981), pp. 784–792.
Robson, J., 'The transmission of Muslim's Ṣaḥīḥ', *JRAS* (1949), pp. 46–60.
Roded, R., *Women in Islamic Biographical Collections: From Ibn Saᶜd to Who's Who* (Boulder, 1994).
Roemer, H.R., 'The Sinai documents and the history of the Islamic world: state of the art – future tasks', in W. al-Qāḍī, ed., *Studia Arabica et Islamica: Festschrift for Iḥsān ᶜAbbās on his Sixtieth Birthday* (Beirut, 1981), pp. 381–391.
Rogerson, J., *Old Testament Criticism in the Nineteenth Century: England and Germany* (London, 1984).
Rosenthal, F., 'Die arabische Autobiographie', *Studia Arabica* 1 (1937), pp. 1–40.
——, '"Blurbs" (*Taqrīẓ*) from fourteenth-century Egypt', *Oriens* 27–8 (1981), pp. 177–196.
——, *The Classical Heritage in Islam* (Berkeley and Los Angeles, 1975).
——, *Four Essays on Art and Literature in Islam* (Leiden, 1971).
——, *Humour in Early Islam* (Leiden, 1956).
——, *A History of Muslim Historiography* (Leiden, 2nd rev. ed., 1968).
——, '"Of making many books there is no end": the classical Muslim view', in G.N. Atiyeh, ed., *The Book in the Islamic World: The Written Word and Communication in the Middle East* (Albany, 1995), pp. 33–55.
——, 'On medieval authorial bibliographies: al-Yaᶜqūbī and Ibn Ḥajar', in M. Mir, ed., *Literary Heritage of Classical Islam: Arabic and Islamic Studies in Honor of James A. Bellamy* (Princeton, 1993), pp. 255–274.
——, *The Technique and Approach of Muslim Scholarship* (Rome, 1947).
Rotter, G., 'Abū Zurᶜa al-Dimašqī (st. 281/894) und das Problem der frühen arabischen Geschichtsschreibung in Syrien', *Die Welt des Orients* 6 (1971), pp. 80–104.
——, 'Zur überlieferung einiger historischer Werke Madāʾinīs in Ṭabarīs *Annalen*', *Oriens* 23–24 (1974), pp. 103–133.
Rowson, E.K., 'History as prose panegyric: al-ᶜUtbī and the beginnings of euphuistic historiography', unpublished typescript.

Rubin, U., *Between Bible and Qur'ān: The Children of Israel and the Islamic Self-image* (Princeton, 1999).
——, *The Eye of the Beholder: The Life of Muḥammad as Viewed by the Early Muslims: A Textual Analysis* (Princeton, 1995).
——, ed., *The Life of Muḥammad* (Aldershot, 1998).
Saenger, P., *Space between Words: The Origins of Silent Reading* (Stanford, 1997).
Saleh, M.J., 'Al-Suyūṭī and his work: their place in Islamic scholarship from Mamluk times to the present', *MSR* 5 (2000), pp. 73–89.
Salibi, K., 'The Banū Jamāᶜa: a dynasty of Shāfiᶜite jurists in the Mamluk period', *SI* 9 (1958), pp. 97–109.
Sanjian, A., *Colophons of Armenian Manuscripts, 1301–1480: A Source for Middle Eastern History* (Cambridge, Mass., 1969).
Sartain, E.M., *Jalāl al-Dīn al-Suyūṭī: Biography and Background* (Cambridge, 1975).
Sauvaire, H., 'Description de Damas', *JA* 7 (1896), pp. 185–285.
Sayyid, A.F., 'Early methods of book composition: al-Maqrīzī's draft of the *Kitāb al-Khiṭaṭ*', in Y. Dutton, ed., *The Codicology of Islamic Manuscripts* (London, 1995), pp. 93–101.
Sbath, P., *Choix de livres qui se trouvaient dans les bibliothèques d'Alep* (Cairo, 1946) (*Mémoires de l'Institut d'Égypte* 49).
Schacht, J., 'On Mūsā b. ᶜUqba's «*Kitāb al-maghāzī*»', *Acta Orientalia* 21 (1953), pp. 288–300.
——, 'A revaluation of Islamic traditions', *JRAS* (1949), pp. 143–154; reprinted in Ibn Warraq, ed., *The Quest for the Historical Muhammad* (Amherst, N.Y., 2000), pp. 358–367.
——, 'The schools of law and later developments of jurisprudence', in M. Khadduri and H.J. Liebesny, eds., *Law in the Middle East I: Origin and Development of Islamic Law* (Washington D.C., 1955), pp. 57–84.
Schoeler, G., *Charakter und Authentie der muslimischen Überlieferung über das Leben Mohammeds* (Berlin, 1996).
——, 'Mūsā b. ᶜUqba's *Maghāzī*', in H. Motzki, ed., *The Biography of Muḥammad: The Issue of the Sources* (Leiden, 2000), pp. 67–97.
——, 'Schreiben und Veröffentlichen: Zu Verwendung und Funktion der Schrift in den ersten islamischen Jahrhunderten', *DI* 69 (1992), pp. 1–43; partially translated as 'Writing and publishing: on the use and function of writing in the first centuries of Islam', *Arabica* 44 (1997), pp. 423–435.
Schöller, M., *Exegetisches Denken und Prophetenbiographie: Eine quellenkritische Analyse der Sīra-Überlieferung zu Muḥammads Konflikt mit den Juden* (Wiesbaden, 1998).
Schützinger, H., 'Abū Yaᶜlā al-Mauṣilī: Leben und Lehrerverzeichnis (*Kitāb al-Muᶜǧam*)', *ZDMG* 131 (1981), pp. 281–296.
Scott, J., 'History in crisis? The others' side of the story', *AHR* 94 (1989), pp. 681–692.
Sellheim, R., 'Muhammad's erstes Offenbarungserlebnis: zum Problem mündlicher und schriftlicher Überlieferung in 1./7. und 2./8. Jahrhundert', *JSAI* 10 (1987), pp. 1–16.
——, 'Prophet, Chalif und Geschichte: die Muhammed-Biographie des Ibn Isḥāq', *Oriens* 18–19 (1967), pp. 33–91.
Serjeant, R.B., 'The "Constitution of Medina"', *IQ* 8 (1964), pp. 3–16.
Şeşen, R., 'Esquisse d'une histoire du développement des colophons dans les manuscrits musulmans', in F. Déroche and F. Richard, eds., *Scribes et manuscrits du Moyen-Orient* (Paris, 1997), pp. 189–221.
Sezgin, F., *Geschichte des arabischen Schrifttums*, vol. 1 (Leiden, 1967).

Sezgin, U., *Abū Miḫnaf: Ein Beitrag zur Historiographie des umaiyadischen Zeit* (Leiden, 1971).
Sharon, M., ed., *Corpus Inscriptionum Arabicorum Palestiniae*, vol. 1 (Leiden, 1997).
Shatzmiller, M., 'The Crusades and Islamic warfare – a re-evaluation', *DI* 69 (1992), pp. 247–288.
——, *L'historiographie mérinide: Ibn Khaldūn et ses contemporains* (Leiden, 1982).
Shboul, A., *Al-Masᶜūdī and his World* (London, 1979).
Shoshan, B., *Popular Culture in Medieval Cairo* (Cambridge, 1993).
Shryock, A., *Nationalism and the Genealogical Imagination: Oral History and Textual Authority in Jordan* (Berkeley and Los Angeles, 1997).
——, 'Popular genealogical nationalism: history writing and identity among the Balqa tribes of Jordan', *Comparative Studies in Society and History* 37 (1995), pp. 325–357.
Sibai, M.M., *Mosque Libraries: An Historical Study* (London and New York, 1987).
Siddiqui, M.Z., *Hadith Literature* (Cambridge, 1993).
Smail, R.C., *Crusading Warfare (1097–1193)* (Cambridge, 1956).
Sourdel, D., 'Réflexions sur la diffusion de la madrasa en Orient du xie au xiiie siècle', *REI* 44 (1976), pp. 165–184.
Spear, T., 'Oral traditions: whose history?', *History in Africa* 8 (1981), pp. 165–181.
Speight, M., 'Narrative structures in the *ḥadīth*', *JNES* 59 (2000), pp. 265–271.
Spiegel, G., *The Past as Text: The Theory and Practice of Medieval Historiography* (Baltimore, 1997).
Spies, O., *Beiträge zur arabischen Literaturgeschichte* (Leipzig, 1932).
Springberg-Hinsen, M., *Die Zeit vor dem Islam in arabischen Universalgeschichten des 9. bis 12. Jahrhunderts* (Würzburg, 1989).
Stern, S.M., 'Abū ᶜĪsā ibn al-Munajjim's chronography' in S. Stern, et al., eds., *Islamic Philosophy and the Classical Tradition* (Oxford, 1972), pp. 437–466.
——, *Fāṭimid Decrees: Original Documents from the Fāṭimid Chancery* (London, 1964).
Stetkevych, S.P., 'The ᶜAbbāsid poet interprets history: three qaṣīdahs by Abū Tammām', *JAL* 10 (1979), pp. 49–64.
——, *Abū Tammām and the Poetics of the ᶜAbbasid Age* (Leiden, 1991).
——, *The Mute Immortals Speak: Pre-Islamic Poetry and the Poetics of Ritual* (Ithaca and London, 1993).
Sublet, J., *Les trois vies du sultan Baïbars* (Paris, 1992).
Subtelny, M.E., and A.B. Khalidov, 'The curriculum of Islamic higher learning in Timurid Iran in the light of the Sunni revival under Shāh-Rukh', *JAOS* 115 (1995), pp. 210–236.
Tottoli, R., *I profeti biblici nella tradizione islamica* (Brescia, 1999).
Twitchett, D., *The Writing of Official History under the T'ang* (Cambridge, 1992).
Vajda, G., *La transmission du savoir en Islam* (London, 1983).
van Ess, J., 'Das *Kitāb al-irǧāʾ* des Ḥasan b. Muḥammad b. al-Ḥanafiyya', *Arabica* 21 (1974), pp. 20–52.
Van Seters, J., *In Search of History: Historiography in the Ancient World and the Origins of Biblical History* (New Haven, 1983).
Van Voorst, R.E., *Jesus Outside the New Testament: An Introduction to the Ancient Evidence* (Grand Rapids, 2000).
von Grunebaum, G.E., and R. Caillois, eds., *Le rêve et les sociétés humaines* (Paris, 1967).
Veyne, P., *Writing History* (Middletown, 1984).
Walzer, M., *Exodus and Revolution* (New York, 1985).
Wansbrough, J., *Quranic Studies: Sources and Methods of Scriptural Interpretation* (London, 1977).

——, *The Sectarian Milieu* (London, 1978).

Wasserstein, D., 'Ibn Ḥazm on names meet for the caliphs', *Cahiers d'onomastique arabe*, 1988–1992 (1993), pp. 61–88.

Weiss, B., 'Knowledge of the past: the theory of *tawâtur* according to Ghazâlî', *SI* 61 (1985), pp. 81–105.

Wensinck, A.J., 'The refused dignity', in T.W. Arnold and R.A. Nicholson, eds., *A Volume of Oriental Studies Presented to Edward G. Browne* (Cambridge, 1922), pp. 491–499.

Werkmeister, W., *Quellenuntersuchungen zum Kitāb al-ᶜIqd al-farīd des Andalusiers Ibn ᶜAbdrabbih (246/860–328/940)* (Berlin, 1983).

Whitby, M., *The Emperor Maurice and his Historian: Theophylact Simocatta on Persian and Balkan Warfare* (Oxford, 1988).

——, 'Greek historical writing after Procopius: variety and vitality', in A. Cameron and L. Conrad, eds., *The Byzantine and Early Islamic Near East I: Problems of the Literary Source Material* (Princeton, 1992), pp. 25–80.

White, H., 'The historical text as literary artifact', in R.H. Canary and H. Kozicki, eds., *The Writing of History: Literary Form and Historical Understanding* (Madison, 1978), pp. 41–62.

Wickens, G.M., 'Notional significance in conventional Arabic "Book" titles: some unregarded potentialities', in C.E. Bosworth, et al., eds., *The Islamic World from Classical to Modern Times: Essays in Honor of Bernard Lewis* (Princeton, 1989), pp. 369–388.

Wieber, R., *Das Schachspiel in der arabischen Literatur von den Anfängen bis zur zweiten Hälfte des 16. Jahrhunderts* (Walldorf-Hessen, 1972).

Wiet, G., 'Les classiques du scribe égyptien au XVᵉ siècle', *SI* 18 (1963), pp. 41–80.

Winkelmann, F., and W. Brandes, *Quellen zur Geschichte des frühen Byzanz: 4.-9. Jahrhundert* (Amsterdam, 1990).

Wiseman, T.P., 'Practice and theory in Roman historiography', *Historia* 66 (1981), pp. 375–393.

Witakowski, W., *The Syriac Chronicle of Pseudo-Dionysius of Tel-Maḥrē: A Study in the History of Historiography* (Uppsala, 1987).

Wolf, K.B., *Conquerors and Chroniclers of Early Medieval Spain* (Liverpool, 1999; 2nd ed.).

Yerushalmi, Y.H., *Zakhor: Jewish History and Jewish Memory* (Seattle and London, 1982).

Young, M.J.L., et al., eds., *Religion, Learning and Science in the ᶜAbbasid Period* (Cambridge History of Arabic Literature; Cambridge, 1990).

Zagorin, P., 'History, the referent, and narrative: reflections on post-modernism now', *History and Theory* 38 (1999), pp. 1–24.

——, 'Rejoinder to a post-modernist', *History and Theory* 39 (2000), pp. 201–209.

Zambaur, E. von, *Manuel de généalogie et de chronologie pour l'histoire de l'Islam* (Hannover, 1927).

Index